THE LOVE LIVES OF THE ARTISTS

Daniel Bullen

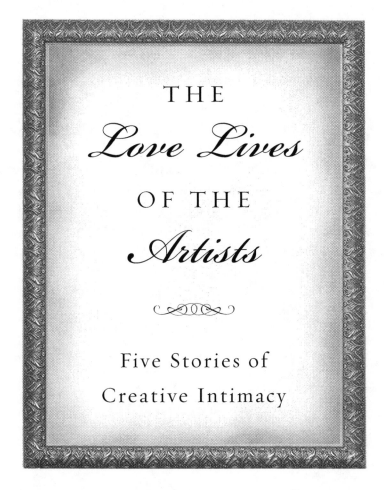

THE

Love Lives

OF THE

Artists

Five Stories of
Creative Intimacy

COUNTERPOINT

BERKELEY

Library of Congress Cataloging-in-Publication Data is available.

ISBN: 978-1-61902-100-6

Cover design by Ann Weinstock
Interior design by David Bullen

Printed in the United States of America

COUNTERPOINT
2560 Ninth Street, Suite 318
Berkeley, CA 94710
www.counterpointpress.com

To Meaghan, with love and admiration

Contents

I know now your eyes are wide open. Certain things you will never believe any more, certain gestures you will never repeat, certain sorrows, misgivings, you will never again experience. A kind of white, criminal fervor in your tenderness and cruelty. Neither remorse nor vengeance; neither sorrow nor guilt. A living it out, with nothing to save you from the abyss but a high hope, a faith, a joy that you tasted, that you can repeat when you will.

HENRY MILLER TO ANAÏS NIN, 1932

Introduction

What do we wish to know of any worthy person so much, as how he has sped in the history of [love]? RALPH WALDO EMERSON

So far all that has given colour to existence still lacks a history: where could you find a history of love, of avarice, of envy, of conscience, of piety, of cruelty? ... Has anyone done research on the different ways of dividing up the day or of the consequences of a regular schedule of work, festivals, and the rest? ... Has anyone collected people's experiences of living together ... Has anyone depicted the dialectic of marriage and friendship? FRIEDRICH NIETZSCHE

We are just now reaching the point where we can observe objectively and without judgment the relationship of one individual to a second one. Our attempts to live such a relationship are without a model. Yet, there already exist within our time frame some things intended to help our faint-hearted beginner's steps. RAINER MARIA RILKE

The old ideals are dead as nails—nothing there. It seems to me there remains only this perfect union with a woman—sort of ultimate marriage— and there isn't anything else. D. H. LAWRENCE

I.

For almost two hundred years, now, it has been customary to talk about marriage as an institution in crisis. Not only has divorce become commonplace, but domestic arrangements and sexual practices that used to be scandalous no longer raise more than an eyebrow in casual conversation. In the ocean of sex-drenched advertising, entertainment, and fashion, pornography, perversion, and the most sordid aspects of love have seeped into everyday culture—so much so that parents today worry not that their children's generation won't respect the institution of marriage, but that their children's friends and classmates might already be so saturated—so medicated, disaffected, and overwhelmed—that they won't even feel anything when they make their early experiments in sex. The hope that marriage might still have any sanctity has been so widely abandoned that our modern decline is measured against its decay.

And yet—in spite of these pervasive lamentations, hasn't something been gained in our modern freedoms? We are free now because our ancestors wanted the freedom to make their attachments where they found them, to break them when they chafed, and then to make new attachments—haven't we just fulfilled what they wanted for themselves? If we have lost some cosmic or traditional belonging, we have also gained that freedom—surely we can discern some progress, from the old traditions to this new freedom, which seems to fulfill an ancient promise.

There are benefits by which we can measure our freedom: we can express, fulfill, create ourselves in unprecedented ways. To our new modern eyes, the soul has become a work yet to be made—and as modern individuals, we extend the soul's promise into our relationships. We have come to believe that each soul's fulfillment will be unique—so, too, then, should every relationship be a work of art, an original collaboration in each partner's fulfillment. In this view, marriage has just been one more conventional form that has to be reinvented every generation, if modern people should ever perfect their freedom and individuality in a new or higher way. If parents and grandparents have complained about modern changes, young people have known since the beginning of the twentieth century at least that their ancestors' marriages would never be sufficient to their new freedoms.

We are modern, we know too much: we know that love is a fleeting ripeness of the soul—we know that desire is a constant struggle of the self against the self, of the spirit against the body. We know that we need to see things for ourselves if we're ever going to trust them: we think that if we arrive at marriages like our grandparents' generation made— marriages we think of as noble lifeworks, grounded in shared faith—it will only be after we've found and tried faith of our own in a variety of experiences first.

So why shouldn't a man take a wife, and also see other women on the side, as he seeks himself and his fulfillment? And why should a woman's satisfactions be limited to the one man she has married, when there are sides of herself that will still always need to be expressed? Why shouldn't partners allow each other this freedom, when each of them knows that the other's possibilities exceed them? These are questions we each have to answer in our own fashion, but regardless of how we each solve them, our liberty itself persists in asking them, so even if we come to one solution today, the question will only be framed anew tomorrow, every time someone resonates with the promises we believe we carry, in our hearts and in our loins, in our selves.

Most people, confronting these questions, recognize almost instinctively that erotic freedom is really an invitation to chaos and drama, fights, fits, and ultimately loneliness and misery. If they begrudge their peace and stability, they nevertheless keep to one spouse, as much as they can, and keep infidelity in reserve for desperate situations or rare opportunities. They keep to one spouse and they moralize, they relegate infidelity to the desperate people who can't get enough affection, the children who aren't mature enough yet to handle the commitment. This is how traditional marriage persists: as a bias against the restless or immature people who can't settle down with one spouse.

Nevertheless, we cannot escape the suspicion that individuality might be inhibited by marriage, and we wonder whether people in open relationships might not really be braver than the rest—as if freedom were ultimately a matter of courage, of irreverence and honesty, of rebelliousness. Ever since *The Scarlet Letter* and *Madame Bovary* were published in the 1850s—and then *Anna Karenina* in the 1870s—modern people have been drawn to adulterers: we look for the promised freedoms in their brave stories, and we shudder to see the consequences of knowledge gained outside marriage.

So soon as the early 1900s, though, it was not enough to read novels about erotic freedom and adultery. Restrictive conventions were dissolving, and even before the convulsive world wars, there was an air of permanent revolution in European culture, so that bohemians and artists were beginning to experiment with new forms of love and relationship in addition to methods of representation. Berlin, New York, Zurich, and Montparnasse were beginning to be known as places where artists were drawing new lines for marriage. By the time Freud exploded the virtue of bourgeois restraints—by the time the Great War turned love and sex into the final refuge where people could hide from the horrors of modern industrial culture, affairs and unconventional marriage arrangements were already signs of artistic genuineness. When *Lady Chatterley's Lover* was published in 1928, infidelity had become the ultimate sign of vitality, even the fulfillment of individuality: it was man's—and equally woman's—salvation against machine-deadness and decadence both.

There were plenty of Picassos and Hemingways who made themselves

famous for marrying and remarrying and remarrying—and there were
plenty of other artists in other scandalous arrangements—but D. H. Law-
rence saw the love relationship itself as a new medium, and bohemians
and artists, following in his line, have made art as much from their own
relationships as from the stories or poems or paintings they inherited
with their culture. After all the dislocations and disorientations that
came with industrialism, love itself was the last art form, and its master-
piece had yet to be made.

If people were going to seek the strong forces that moved them, and
claim the new machine forces, productive and destructive alike—if people
were going to claim and incorporate everything men had invented and
changed in a hundred years—if people were going to balance the internal
self against all that newly released power, they would have to create a
new kind of solidarity between partners. Marital fidelity was an obstacle,
now, for if lovers were going to be true to themselves, and to each other,
each individual had to reconcile himself not only to the reality of desire,
but also to the reality of his partner's desire: now desire itself was just a
powerful raw material in the hands of people who felt brave enough to
work with it. Now it was clear what power two lovers could harness, to
make their love a unique work of art: the enterprising partners had only
to find some way to balance love with each partner's fulfillment.

II.

My interest in this subject has not been academic: I wrote this book when
I was looking for the language with which to reconcile marriage and desire
in my own life. In my reading I was drawn to the biographies, letters, and
journals of artists who were infamous for their affairs: I found that their
lives touched my questions about my own obligations—to myself and to
my lover at the time. I read as many stories as I could find, about artists
who took lovers in addition to their lifelong marriages—about artists
who gave each other that freedom. I wanted to know why people like
Diego and Frida and Sartre and Beauvoir and Henry Miller and Anaïs
Nin took lovers, I wanted to know why they tolerated each other's lovers,
and I wanted to know whether their careers as artists justified—or
even required—their unconventional arrangements. I wanted to know
whether their creativity had really extended so far as to make a new defi-
nition of marriage, a new category of art, even of morality.

I chose to tell the stories of these five couples in particular because both partners were artists, and they both saw the question of open relationships as part of their creative projects. Unlike the artists who took models or assistants as partners, these people found artists of equal stature, and in the atmosphere of equality, they saw the question of love as an artistic opportunity: they would establish their relationships themselves as faces of their creativity. When I read the biographies, though, I was consistently disappointed with the lack of details from the artists' actual love lives. The conventional wisdom about artists and love was reduced to two narrow archetypes: the enfant terrible—who was too childish to resist the tempting variety of lovers—and the culture hero, who bravely transcended the limitations of marriage to preserve his freedom as well as his partner's affection. There were other archetypes as well, of course—the weeping woman, who suffered the eternal torment of her husband's affairs—and the pathological seductress, who turned each encounter into a poetry of freedom—but the general sense that pervaded the biographies was that artists were simply larger than life, and their love lives were flamboyant or bohemian aberrations—or else, perhaps, rare, brave artworks, unattainable by mere mortals. In either case, the artists seemed to be exempt from normal morality: their desires were not our desires, their decisions were not our decisions, and their love lives were separate and new, unprecedented in the same way that every modern thing must be free of precedent.

The artists themselves generally realized that their innovations in love would bolster their careers in art. They capitalized on the notoriety they gained from their unconventional love lives, and they claimed in their memoirs, journals, and letters that their creativity had justified, even required their affairs. Then, as the institution of marriage seemed to deteriorate throughout the twentieth century, people looked to their examples, and their defiant pronouncements about love and marriage were trumpeted from books and articles, biographies and portraits: marriage was a bourgeois sham. Self-reliance obligated the artist to erotic freedom. Creativity was a stronger bond than marriage, since it embraced all of marriage's failures and still remained honest and true. On the strength of brave statements like these, artists like Diego Rivera, Jean-Paul Sartre, and Simone de Beauvoir became pop culture fixtures, whose reputations rested as much on their infamous loves as on their art or philosophy.

Considering the transformation in marriage in the last hundred years,

I don't think we can underestimate the extent to which the married artists, who insisted on their freedom to have affairs—and who gave each other this same freedom—forged the future of marriage. Sartre and Beauvoir and Miller and Nin in particular paved the way for the sexual revolution of the 1960s, but Rilke and Lou Andreas-Salomé, Stieglitz and O'Keeffe, and Diego and Frida all played significant roles in tearing marriage out of the nineteenth century and turning it into a flexible bond that fostered each partner's self-fulfillment.

III.

If the artists themselves had seized the masks of the culture hero and the enfant terrible—if these archetypes allowed them the freedom to test themselves against their times—and to test their art against their relationships—these were only the public faces of the artists' love lives. If you read deeper into the artists' journals and letters, you can see that they often knew all too well that the relationships that seemed to prove their unconventional, artistic genuineness were really just playing upon carica-tures. If they hid in these caricatures themselves—and not infrequently, their letters and journals acknowledge that erotic heroism was just a pose—the public record itself often contradicted their bold or rebellious claims about their freedom, or their indifference to each other's affairs.

The myths were not ruffled by these contradictions. Biographers generally accepted the caricatures—or else they tried to skirt them, and they glazed over the love lives as if they could keep their own narratives from being entangled in the artists' conflicting accounts of their sexual experiences. Instead of tracing the artists' decisions and actions in love—instead of following their desires from inward creative urges out through artistic expression to their consequences in injury, regret, or fulfillment—instead of trying to grapple with the artists' lives in love, they stayed in safe territory, and described their social lives, or the development of their art. The artists' creative influences and their visions—their train-ing, their theories, their craft, their careers, their commissions and sales, and their artistic legacies were all described in detail, but their influences and visions and the lives they lived in love were narrated inconsistently at best, and affairs that were treated as scandalous in one biography were not infrequently omitted altogether from the next. The artists' decisions in love—their expectations and their tendencies, their accomplishments, their crises, and their resolutions—the decisions they made, their creativity in love went almost unexamined. Nowhere was love described as art's twin, a parallel expression of the soul.

This absence was surprising, because when I turned to the artists' own letters and journals, I found that they had almost all wrestled in earnest with the obligation to express their visions of personal uniqueness, which they felt compelled to establish at every opportunity. Their daemons had not chosen between love and art as the media for their expression: by their own accounts, their unique and creative individuality not only permitted but actively required that they be as unique in their marriages as they were in their art. As they developed as artists, their journals and letters, and even their artwork, were full of their thoughts about what kinds of lovers they needed, and their feelings for their spouses and various lovers. They speculated about what kind of person they thought might fulfill them; they prophesied the fulfillment they thought they might find in a like-minded artist; they wrote expansive letters to their friends, to say how happy they were when they found each other's art; they wrote delirious letters when they entered each other's love, and if they wrote in their journals, they frequently wrote candid letters to each other as well, to justify their affairs and reconciliations.

The thoughtfulness and deliberation that have characterized biographers' descriptions of the artists' lives in art were hardly evident in their descriptions of the artists' relationships, even though the same principles—of rebellious genuineness, of honesty and beauty, and also of emotional recklessness in the name of creativity—informed their marriages, their affairs, and their tolerance of each other's lovers. The uniqueness of vision that made them artists, though, was not examined in the narratives of their love lives. The artists were consistently stubborn and tenacious in protecting their individuality when overwhelming or absorbing experiences threatened to influence their work too strongly—but the biographers could not see this same trait in their love lives. They would have seen that artists who could be fierce in asserting and defending their creative freedom, could also be magnanimous in admitting other artists' influence, and that the same magnanimity was evident in how they let each other exercise the erotic freedoms they knew were essential to making art.

If the artists reveled in their public roles as sacred monsters and creative terrors, their letters and journals contain a deep equivocation about their affairs, and their partners', for they always paid a certain price for the performance they put on, of creative, irreverent love. From depressions to nervous breakdowns to dependence on drugs and alcohol to petty or retributive affairs, neither their freedom nor their endurance of each other's affairs came without a price, and if they were confident that these were necessary dues, they were not always comfortable as they paid: their letters and journals betray some despair, some terror when their affairs filled them with feelings that seemed to be bottomless, endless, chaotic, or just profoundly lonely.

Still, they were artists, and if they had opened themselves to experience—even as children—and if they had committed themselves to make their account of all the experiences life had to offer them, they generally accepted as fated those things they could neither contain nor control: they simply mastered them into art as best they could. They still had the artist's creative aloofness and remove: they looked at their own lives as if they were reading the novels they had already written by living—they divorced themselves from their sufferings and also from their blisses. But their lives were not measured by art alone—they were measured against their original commitments: to live their lives fully. Their art would be measured by their actual decisions, in love as much as in writing or painting.

Their art, of course, was only the most presentable manifestation of their self-assertions—but their decisions on the whole showed a calculated effort to protect their creative individuality: they rebelled against their families; they lived in poverty, or took demeaning jobs to support their art; they outraged bourgeois conventions; they flaunted dramatic costumes, but in love more than in any other sphere, they asserted the uniqueness of their experiences—they proclaimed the breadth of their visions and their commitment to living them out. They had already given up everything that would allow them to live the comfortable, insulated lives that the modern world, with all its machines and cities offered up to them. They had already turned against comfort in favor of experience itself, in favor of their own emotions, and the language for their expression. They had given up marriage and normal domestic routines—they gave up children; they cared nothing for their own health: what mattered was that they should express themselves. When they found other artists to love, they allowed each other their freedom: their jealousies and even their betrayals, they thought, would only measure their ability to harness experience with creativity. They were artists, and they would not humiliate themselves by making dishonest work. They would give desire its due, and if they suffered, they would take strength from human emotions, the last things left to them by the cities and the machines.

IV.

Having found, in the artists' own writing, that they remained artists even in love, my reading on art and love and the artists' love lives turned into full-blown research and then into writing, and I found myself trying to answer elemental questions about artists' open relationships: what had the artists' decisions in love done for them as artists, and what had their works of art done for them as lovers? What techniques had they developed that were common to love and to art? What roles had they played, and how had they found each role useful in their careers, whether as artists or as lovers? Had their creativity driven them to take lovers, and had it really helped them bear their jealousy when their partners took lovers who threatened to replace them?

This book does not exactly answer these questions: they were simply guides as I told the stories of how the artists experienced them themselves in their creative and amorous lives. To be honest, these were not even questions I wanted to answer, per se, so much as they simply guided my curiosity. "Answers" would have been beside the point, a stepping aside from the living question: any "answer," I found, would have had to be made in kind, as the meaning of a piece of art can only be another piece of art, and the meaning of a biography has to be another set of decisions, to be lived out as actions, and then perhaps described in a further biography.

So the present book reflects the circumstances under which it was written. I did not have the luxury of funding for exhaustive academic research: I didn't do any archival research—I found all my sources in bookstores and university libraries. I just told the stories—in the artists' words as much as possible—since I couldn't allow myself the novelist's interpretive liberties. But I didn't just tell the stories of individual relationships and the most prominent affairs: I told the stories of the artists' development as lovers, from birth through their major and minor relationships to death—with just as much space for the crises in love as for the brave beauties of shared inspiration and major creative periods.

What I found by keeping a sharp focus on the artists' love lives was that their brazen and sometimes contradictory commitments—to truth and to self-expression—had been instrumental in teaching them first the nature of their souls and then the twin crafts of their souls' expression in love and in art. Having followed their intuitions through their relationships—and having then worked to bear out the truth of what were really fairly commonplace experiences—of love and jealousy, rage and loss, redemption or new love—they had nonetheless put themselves in positions where they were free to strike their own balance between commitment and freedom. As individuals, their love lives followed the eternal, archetypal experiences of innocence lost, of wide experience, and ultimately, sometimes, of wisdom gained, but as modern people, they were marked by their times: they did not have any connection with nature, and if their lives were formed by new industrial technologies— new, more destructive weapons, and newly mechanized cities—their lives together were marked by modern freedoms as well: they were not limited by tradition or convention. They shared a world that had lost its God, and if they had come to see human nature as a war of the self against the self, now—even if the war could never be won, they knew that it could at least be conducted honestly and bravely through creativity. Their relationships turned them into collaborators, acting, directing, witnessing, and criticizing their responses to modern times. Whether or not they redeemed themselves against their modernity and fulfilled their new freedoms, they stayed together, they let their lives happen to them, even each other's decisions, and they gave birth to whatever works of art they felt they needed, to keep themselves alive as human beings.

Their experiences were not always pure liberation. All of the artists found that someone always paid a price for freedom and insight— whether it was their partners, who wanted more commitment or freedom than they would give, or the lovers who wanted more love or access than they were getting, or the artists themselves, who in moments of crisis were liable to feel that they were corrupting or diminishing themselves with their affairs. But regardless of the price, they always paid as much as they could, and they continued to insist on freedom for themselves and for each other.

Whether their stories do or do not unveil the brave new marriage, they do describe the faces of and uses for desire—for creative as much as for amorous freedom. In their open relationships, the artists describe the creative forces by which human beings can survive the confusing, dehumanizing conditions of modern times. In love as much as in their art, they describe the creative control by which deliberate acts and decisions can use even the experience of being overwhelmed—and the jealous experience of being all but replaced by another lover—to give form and artistic expression to the modern human soul, in its new situation of being perpetually threatened with being replaced by machines, or erased altogether by wars. By virtue of their very modernity, the artists found that even the term "human being" had been thrown into question: their relationships—with each other and, through each other, with their own hardest feelings, of rage, jealousy, and despair—were their attempts to define what human beings could be in industrial times.

V.

It seems important to add a final note that cultural conditions have changed drastically since the 1960s and '70s, when their works and their lives had their greatest impact on their cultures. The last of these artists died in the 1980s, but even by that time, their stories seemed dated in light of the self-revelations of subsequent artists—and they seem even more dated now, in the light of the digital technologies that made self-revelation both easy and commonplace.

But there is such a lag time between an artist's death and the publication of their letters and journals that I could not tell the stories of any more recent relationships. Gay artists especially begged for inclusion, but gay or lesbian couples did not begin to write about open relationships candidly long enough ago that their letters and journals have made it into print yet. Like all the more recent couples, their letters and journals and their lovers' letters and journals have still not been published—they have not been dead long enough that their stories could be told without prejudice or injury—and who would trust any living lover to discourse upon the nature of his relationship, its benefits and the injuries that had to be suffered? In another fifty years, when another generation's letters and journals become available, and the numerous biographies have been written on each artist, stories will be able to be told that cannot be told just yet. Until then, they will surely continue to gestate, to evolve where we can hardly perceive them, in the experiences that will always come before art: in our own lives.

THE
Love Lives
OF THE
Artists

Chapter One

The Great Triangulators

Lou Andreas-Salomé and Rainer Maria Rilke

⟨✦⟩

People who are not "faithful" do not necessarily desert one person for another, but are often simply driven *home to themselves* ... Their infidelity is hence no betrayal ... it need not be a gesture of abandonment for them to set free the person to whom they have clung; more likely it is a gesture of reverence, returning him to the world ...

A woman has no other choice than to be unfaithful or to be only half herself ... Let it not be taken for arrogance that she requires a new beginning again and again: is it not humility to burden herself with [starting new relationships from scratch]. Lou Andreas-Salomé

... all companionship can consist only in the strengthening of two neighboring solitudes, whereas everything that one is wont to call giving oneself is by nature harmful to companionship. Rainer Maria Rilke

I.

When Lou Andreas-Salomé met Rainer Maria Rilke, it was not immediately clear that they would be important figures in each other's lives. They became lovers within two weeks of meeting, and they remained lovers for more than three years, but Andreas-Salomé was married when they met, and even though she would never consummate her marriage, her husband had already refused to divorce her five years earlier, when she had fallen in love with a journalist. "He was simply fixated," she wrote of that time in her memoir, "on the idea that our relationship was a given, incontrovertibly real, in spite of all that had happened." For five years,

3

now, when she took lovers, she had to make sure that they would not threaten her marriage.

Fred Charles Andreas, Lou's husband, was an erudite professor of Persian language and culture—he was almost fifteen years older than his then-thirty-six-year-old wife, who was already well known as an author in her own right when he met her. Andreas was not threatened by Rilke, who was twenty-one, with no accomplishments, only sentimental verse and poetic ambition to recommend him. Andreas treated Rilke as a guest, not a rival, and Rilke was apparently content to be included in the Andreas household: there is no evidence that he was tormented by his new lover's marriage. There are, however, signs that he counted himself fortunate to be intimate with a writer who took an interest in him, some-one who could introduce him to editors and writers.

Rilke was not Andreas-Salomé's only lover at the time. In 1897, when she met Rilke, she was still carrying on an intermittent affair with Friedrich Pineles, a doctor eight years younger than herself: she would see Pineles—Zemek, as he was called—for holidays and travels until 1908, but Zemek too was a minor lover, not someone she wrote about. By 1895, when she met him, she had already written a novel about her passionate attachment with her teacher, Hendrik Gillot, at seventeen, and a memoir of her friendship with Friedrich Nietzsche at twenty-one. Between these two relationships—and then her marriage in 1887, and her affair with the journalist in 1892—she already had a lifetime's material for her novels.

Rilke himself might have been in love with the beautiful older woman, but at least in the beginning, she seems to have kept her head as she put him in his place among the men in her life. Lou Andreas-Salomé had always been a formidable presence—she drew men to her with her beautiful auburn hair, her poetic and stubborn temperament, and a deep grounding in religion and the philosophies of individual freedom. Long before she met Nietzsche in 1882, she had been determined to follow her own spiritual intuition—to define in her own terms the God she did and then did not believe in—and then to say how she would live in her God's absence. After meeting her for the first time, Nietzsche had written that she embodied the bravery with which he hoped to define a new morality, and he may or may not have proposed to her. "Never forget," he had told her, "that it would be a calamity if you did not carve a memorial to your full innermost mind in the time left to you." By the time she met Rilke in 1897, Andreas-Salomé had outlasted Nietzsche, who lost his mind and stopped writing in 1889—and her current lover, Zemek, was a young doctor who looked after her health and did not give her trouble about her marriage. After Nietzsche and Zemek, she could not have expected young Rilke to teach her anything—rather he was going to test her ability to mold a young artist. He was already shaping poetry out of his keen observations, but he was still subject to hysterical fears. Would Andreas-Salomé be able to save him from the madness that had claimed Nietzsche when art demanded too much from him? Rilke was young, he was just beginning: he had been engaged to a young noblewoman for two years, but he was trying to establish himself as a poet before he made any commitments to a woman. His poetry—his future poetry—had stood in the way of any real engagement.

After an initial passion, Andreas-Salomé and Rilke spent their first three years together as study partners. Rilke had written sentimental love letters at first—"I want to see no flower," he wrote, in a typical letter, "no sky, no sun—except in you. How much more beautiful and like a fairy tale is everything gazed at through your eyes . . . I want to see the world through you; for then I will see not the world but always and only you, you, you!"—but she ignored his poetry, even as she focused his reading.

They spent their first summer together outside of Munich, before Rilke followed her and her husband north to Berlin. There, as an instructor and surrogate mother, Andreas-Salomé oversaw his studies in Renaissance art, and she fostered his poetry—by holding it to the standard of lived experience. When his studies took him to Italy, she asked him to keep a journal, but when he showed it to her on returning, he added a long tortured passage when she was not impressed: "I hated you like something *too great*," he wrote. "*I* wanted this time to be the rich one, the giver, the host, the master, and You were supposed to come and be guided by my care and love and stroll about in my hospitality."

Andreas-Salomé's failure to see any genius in his writing only strengthened Rilke's desire to write something that would touch her, to form her as she had formed him. Continuing to see intimacy between them as a possibility, they turned their attention toward Russia, where the peasants were still just emerging from folk religion and feudalism into modernity, a cultural situation that seemed pregnant with spiritual experiences: they would be able to say for themselves what gods lived in the landscape and in the peasant religion. In two trips, in 1899—with Andreas—and then again in 1900, alone together, they traveled widely, savoring the premodern spiritual life of the peasants, as well as the modern art in the galleries.

These travels turned them from study partners to travel companions, but by the end of their second trip, Andreas-Salomé was losing her patience with Rilke's feverish need to turn everything into a poem—which came out in panicked outbursts when he could not harness it in verse. They parted company, and Rilke went to an artists' colony in Germany, where he used his experience with Andreas-Salomé as the foundation for a new partnership, with sculptor Clara Westhoff. By this time, Andreas-Salomé had already effectively cast Rilke out, but when he told her that he planned to marry, she wrote him a blistering "Last Appeal," which warned that if he tried to live a conventional life, he would be courting madness and suicide. She asked him to burn her letters to him, and he complied, effectively negating the time she had spent with him. She had already consigned her husband and her minor lovers to the same silence by refusing to write about them—now Rilke would join the ranks of men she had erased from her life.

For the next two years, Rilke did not correspond with Andreas-Salomé, who returned to Zemek almost immediately, but Rilke's marriage was ultimately no more conventional than Andreas-Salomé's unconsummated tie. Whereas Andreas-Salomé had insisted on the right to her affairs, Rilke broke up his household within a year and a half of his wedding: he moved to Paris to write a monograph on Rodin, leaving his wife to dispose of their things and to deposit their eight-month-old daughter with her parents, while she tried to support herself with commissions and students.

Rilke only resumed contact with Andreas-Salomé after a year in Paris had left him exhausted, depressed, and full of fears again. Freed from his wife, he asked Andreas-Salomé for guidance and encouragement as he always had, but now he could also send her his monograph on Rodin, which described artistic craftsmanship as a form of semidivine creativity—whose product was not only art but the world itself. With this book, Andreas-Salomé saw value in Rilke's writing for the first time. She kept her distance from him—she was still seeing Zemek—but she encouraged Rilke to conquer his fears by writing them down. This was the beginning of their relationship's fulfillment, as Rilke, who had always prostrated himself before Andreas-Salomé—"You alone know who I am," he told her, even now—elicited her admission that they were "allies in the difficult mysteries of living and dying, two people united in that sense of the eternal which binds human beings together. From this moment on you can count on me." It did not seem to matter that their physical relationship was effectively over—or that Andreas-Salomé was still seeing Zemek. It would still be another two years until they saw each other in person, but at least in their letters, the intimacy was finally established on firm footing, and they would be loyal to each other, in their way, in spite of every other tie. Never again would Andreas-Salomé suggest that she and Rilke destroy their correspondence.

They were not, however, in any way sexually loyal to each other—nor to their spouses—over the next twenty-five years. Nor was their relationship a consistent presence in their lives: they were separated by their constant travels, to Italy, Germany, and Switzerland, Paris, Russia, and Scandinavia—and there were several two- to three-year stretches when they hardly corresponded at all. They both remained married for the rest of their lives, and they both retained their freedom to have affairs—which Andreas-Salomé never discussed and Rilke would sketch in his letters. But in correspondence and visits, from 1903 until his death in 1926, Rilke turned to Andreas-Salomé whenever he needed insight into his feelings, and Andreas-Salomé's letters showed him the way toward the God they felt like they shared, the divinity who existed as a consequence of their devotion and creativity. In his poems, and also in a lifestyle reserved for writing, Rilke created this devotion as a fact in the world. By encouraging his writing, Andreas-Salomé could feel that she had a hand in creating him herself.

Centered, as it was, on Rilke's writing, their relationship was unique among their marriages and affairs: Rilke would not reveal himself in such depth to anyone else, and no one else gave Andreas-Salomé the power she had, to give him insight into his soul, to echo his worries back to him in the bravest terms, of artistic courage, creative transformation, and divine longing. Nor would anyone else give Andreas-Salomé the image of herself as a creator—as someone whose thoughts and whose presence alone could create life and direct it. Andreas-Salomé never really confessed herself to Rilke during his life, but three years before she died, he was the only lover she addressed directly in her memoirs:

> If I was your wife for years, it was because you were the first *truly real* person in my life, body and man indivisibly one, unquestionably a fact of life itself. I could have confessed to you word for word what you said in declaring your love: "You alone are real." Thus we were a couple even before we had become friends, and becoming friends wasn't so much a matter of choice as it was the fulfillment of that underlying marriage. We were not two halves seeking the other: we were a whole which confronted that inconceivable wholeness with a shiver of surprised recognition. We were thus siblings—but from a time before incest had become sacrilege.

II.

Lou von Salomé's faith, in an innocence so deep that even incest was sacred and free of guilt, had its origin in a puritanical expatriate community of German Pietists in St. Petersburg. Gustav von Salomé, her father, was a Baltic German soldier who had distinguished himself in battle and risen to the rank of general in Tsar Alexander II's service, and he and his wife, Louise Wilm—the daughter of a wealthy sugar producer originally from Hamburg, and a Danish mother—maintained a luxurious lifestyle in the largely international Russian court. They lodged in the magnificent General Staff Building across the street from the tsar's Petersburg Winter Palace, and they spent summers near the tsar's estate in Peterhof, on the Finnish coast.

The Pietist community within the tsar's court had very little contact with a Russian culture that was totally transformed when the tsar abolished serfdom in 1861. Sheltered inside the tsar's retinue, Gustav von Salomé was fifty-seven years old and secure in an administrative position when his thirty-eight-year-old wife gave birth to their sixth child and only daughter, in February of that year. Named after her mother, the child went by a Russian nickname, Lyolya, but she was raised in a German household, with a French governess and Russian nurse, and her parents told her stories of a Germany where everything was better, more rational, and more ordered than in Russia. One biographer notes that she did not meet Russians socially until after the age of sixteen.

There are hardly any records of Lyolya's actual childhood—only her memoirs, which she wrote in her sixties, but these are suspiciously consistent in promoting a philosophical view of childhood as a time of blissful unities: after some unspecified source of disillusionment, experience and aging would then return her to her original happy state. She stuck to this script in all of her writing—even in her journal entries, where biographers note that she drafted things out before she wrote final copy. Omissions, inconsistencies, and unrealistic claims have caused biographers to distrust this narrative, so they have had to reconstruct her life from letters and journal entries—and also from her fiction, where her psychology reveals itself indirectly, but seems, nonetheless, to dwell on certain relationships. Fortunately, biographers have filled in many of the gaps in Lou's record and we can describe her life in a way that accounts for her consistency as well as for what it omitted or suppressed.

According to Andreas-Salomé's memoir, she was very close to her father as a young girl: they were "bound by small, secret demonstrations of tenderness which . . . we would break off when Mushka [mother] entered the room, since she did not favor such open expressions of feeling." Her affections explicitly excluded her mother, though: once, when her mother was swimming, she called out, "Couldn't you drown just once?" Her mother objected that then she would be dead, but Andreas-Salomé recalled having "roared back as loudly as I could . . . 'So what?'" It is not clear where Lyolya von Salomé found grounds for feeling isolated among her parents and five brothers, but at fifty-two, she wrote in her diary that she had been "bitterly lonely among them all and given to absolute fantasy as her sole joy." As she said in her memoir, "My parents and their viewpoints were in a sense abandoned (almost betrayed) in favor of a more all-embracing absorption. I devoted myself to a higher power and shared in its authority, even its omnipotence." At first, she recalled, she believed in a grandfatherly God "who spoiled me mightily, who approved of everything I did, who enjoyed giving me gifts so much it seems his pockets were overflowing." In the evenings, she told her God stories, inventing dramas based on the people she saw around her, but she never identified what made her invented world preferable to the aristocratic world she lived in. "Perhaps," she wrote, portentously, "I knew too much: some sort of ancient knowledge must have impressed itself upon my basic temperament." Filled with this "ancient knowledge," she soon found God insufficient: her memoir described losing him when he failed to respond directly to her stories and questions.

Lyolya had just turned seventeen when her father died in 1878, and she was left in the care of her less permissive mother, who complained that a young girl will "rarely . . . have had everything so much her own way as she had." Without faith in God, Lyolya refused to be confirmed in her family's Orthodox Pietist church, but shortly after her father's death, she requested an interview with Hendrik Gillot, a charismatic and independent Dutch Pietist preacher, twenty-five years older than her: he was tutor to the tsar's children, and popular with the youth in St. Petersburg. In Lyolya's first meeting with Gillot, she saw him as a commanding spiritual guide to replace her father: "now all loneliness is at an end," she wrote in her diary, "this is what I've been looking for . . . a real person . . . he exists." Gillot agreed to take her as a student, and he schooled her thoroughly in philosophy and literature. He had been strongly influenced by Spinoza's rationalist philosophy, which saw God and nature as the same entity—and he shared the Romantic belief that this divinity could be experienced individually. Gillot's individualistic, anti-institutional stance made him popular with the Petersburg youth— particularly with the Narodniki, a youth movement based in nostalgia for the prefeudal peasants' folk customs: Lyolya was not the only youth who took his preaching as an invitation to personal spirituality.

Lyolya at first struggled against Gillot's strict teaching, but when he threatened to let her go, she "capitulated completely," as her mother put it, and soon Gillot had "stepped into God's place," as Lyolya described it in her memoir. One of Gillot's first acts was to change the Russian Lyolya to Lou, which he found easier to pronounce, but more importantly, he forced her to give up fiction for the strict study of philosophy, which she absorbed so thoroughly that when she met philosophers Paul Rée and Friedrich Nietzsche in 1882, she was, by some accounts, the most widely read of the three. She would never write philosophy, though, and she returned to fiction by 1884, and when she wrote about Gillot in her autobiographical novel *Ruth*, she described having to escape from her chaperone to meet with him, giving their meetings the sense of a clandestine affair—an atmosphere she intensified by taking her lessons on his lap. When her mother found out about her illicit lessons and called on Gillot to explain, he declared that he "*want[ed]* to be responsible for this child": he went so far as to propose abandoning his wife and two children to marry her. Later in life, Andreas-Salomé would write that "when he misjudged me . . . he ceased to be," but it was still Gillot she chose as the preacher who should confirm her when she needed a passport to leave the country.

Doctors recommended a healthier climate after Salomé's long nights, spent brooding into her books about religion and her father's death, had damaged her health: she complained of "sleeplessness, loss of appetite, bleeding lungs, an aching heart, and fits of deathly gloom," which her aunt Caro attributed to "excessive nervous irritation and mental strain," which "produces physical fatigue in its turn." Nevertheless, on doctors' orders, Salomé and her mother prepared to leave for Zurich, where universities allowed female students, and she would be able to audit classes in comparative religion. Having refused Gillot's proposal, Salomé nevertheless claimed him in her choice of the confirmation text he read—in Dutch, which made its erotic overtones unintelligible to her mother: "fear not, for I have chosen you; I have called you by name, you are mine." Her response, following the biblical text, was: "you bless me, for I do not leave you."

Before she left for Zurich in 1880, Lyolya wrote two poems that described her world-weariness: "Deathbed Request" portrays love as a feeling consummated only in death, and "To Pain" strikes a note of dark optimism in its hunger for experience:

> To live for centuries, to think
> Wrap me in your arms again,
> If you have no more joy to give,
> At least you still grant pain.*

Chaperoned by her mother, Salomé audited classes in Zurich for a year before showing further signs of illness—she fainted, coughed blood, and had a weak heart (all signs of depression, nervous strain, and

---

* Biographer Rudolph Binion notes that Andreas-Salomé later added a proviso, "on Freud's account . . . that the pain be merely mental."

overexcitement as much as of heart trouble, which never manifested)—and her doctors recommended that she and her mother move further south for a warmer climate.

III.

Moving to Rome, Salomé recovered completely: her symptoms would never reappear. She met feminist Malwida von Meysenbug, who ran a salon where young women met for lectures and intellectual conversation. Meysenbug was impressed by Salomé, and she encouraged her, "Yours is a great task: we shall yet speak much of it." When Meysenbug invited philosopher Paul Rée to lecture to the girls in March of 1882, Salomé claimed him instantly as her next instructor. Twelve years older than her, Rée had just published his second book—which argued for a practical, evolutionary origin of morality—but his concise arguments were strictly academic, and did not address the morality of his gambling habit, nor the disgust he felt for his own Jewishness. Neither did his philosophy prevent him from carrying a vial of poison should he ever want to kill himself.

Considering herself safe in Rée's refined and philosophical self-loathing, Salomé scandalized her mother and Roman society by walking alone with him late at night after the salon. She would say later that love between herself and Rée was at all times impossible, but Rée took what she said in her memoir was "a completely false tack, to my sorrow and rage, suggesting . . . that we get married." Outraged again by a man's marriage proposal, she wrote in her memoir that she struggled "to make him envision and understand what the 'self-contained' love life I had settled upon as a permanent condition meant in combination with my impulse toward a totally unconstrained freedom." Instead of marriage, Salomé idealized a chaste intellectual companionship: "a simple dream first convinced me of the feasibility of my plan . . . In it I saw a pleasant study filled with books and flowers, flanked by two bedrooms, and us walking back and forth between them, colleagues, working together in a joyful and earnest bond."

Full of enthusiasm for Salomé, Rée sang her praises to his friend Friedrich Nietzsche, whom he had known since 1873 in Basel. Five years older than Rée—seventeen years older than Salomé—Nietzsche was descended from preachers, and had become a professor of philosophy in Basel at the unprecedented age of twenty-four. The two philosophers shared an interest in morality, and in the early 1880s, Nietzsche had just begun to clarify the ideas that would ultimately banish God and put man in charge of overcoming his own contradictory nature: he said that he expected to set up "a new image and ideal of the free spirit." It was in this heady atmosphere, with all his joyful and iconoclastic work coming into view, that Nietzsche received Rée's praises of the "forceful, unbelievably clever being with the most girlish, even childlike qualities." From Genoa, he asked Rée to

> Greet the Russian girl for me, if that makes any sense: I am greedy for souls of that species. In fact, in view of what I mean to do these next ten years, I need them! Matrimony is quite another story. I could consent at most to a two-year marriage, and then only in view of what I mean to do these next ten years.

Nietzsche's friends the Overbecks said that after he met Salomé in Rome, and walked up the Monte Sacro with her, he returned "full of urgent desire for a new way of life." She was, Nietzsche said, "astoundingly well prepared for precisely *my* way of thinking and my thoughts."

Socially proper in spite of his iconoclastic philosophy, Nietzsche met Salomé's mother, and then left Rome for a week in the Italian lakes with Salomé and Rée in May of 1882. By the time they parted, Salomé's letters already described the threesome as a "Trinity," with a "winter plan" to live and study together for the winter of 1882–1883. This plan was not Salomé's alone: ever since 1879, when Nietzsche left the university in Basel because of his health, he had talked about living with Rée in what he called a "garden of Epicurus." Nietzsche's friend Ida Overbeck later wrote that

> Mentally passionate nonmarital relationship was an ideal always dear to him. Passion there was, but also the desire not to let himself be carried away by it. It reassured him that Rée should be the third in the party, and from Rée's serviceable, selfless nature he expected much.

Salomé and Nietzsche would meet again in Tautenberg that summer and then in Leipzig in the fall, but communication between them would never be straightforward. As early as their meeting in Rome, Nietzsche had feared that he might have proposed to Salomé when he wrote that he "should consider myself duty-bound to offer you my hand so as to protect you from what people might say" if they did in fact live and study together. Salomé had indeed construed his statement as a proposal, and she was preparing to refuse him until they clarified themselves in the landmark conversation where they agreed on the Trinity with Rée.

This plan did indeed cause their friends to worry: Meysenbug cautioned Salomé that

> Firmly as I am convinced of *your* neutrality, just as surely does the experience of a long lifetime tell me that it will not work without a heart's cruelly suffering in the noblest case, otherwise a friendship's being destroyed . . . Nature will not be mocked, and before you know it the fetters are there . . . I wish only to protect you from nearly unavoidable sorrow such as you have experienced once already [presumably with Gillot].

The Overbecks were supportive, but while Rée's mother offered the intellectuals her home in Stibbe as a base, Nietzsche's family was proud of its devout clerical lineage and could not be told. As Nietzsche wrote to Salomé, "Neither Mrs. Rée in Warmbrunn nor Miss von Meysenbug in Bayreuth nor my family need break their heads and hearts over things that *we, we, we* alone are and shall be up to, whereas they may strike others as dangerous fantasies." Her mother protested to Gillot, but Salomé defended herself against his reprimand: "I can't live according to some model . . . but I intend to shape my life for myself . . . Let's see whether the so-called 'insurmountable barriers' life puts in most people's way don't in fact turn out to be harmless chalk lines!"

Ultimately the ménage à trois was undermined more from within than without, for even in the beginning, Rée wrote to Salomé, "*You are the only person in the world whom I love*," and after their visit in the lakes, he confessed that he was

> not so wholly open and honest in my relationship to Nietzsche, especially since a certain little girl has bobbed up from abroad . . . I am and shall remain entirely *your* friend alone; I have no scruples about behaving a little crookedly, a little falsely, a little mendaciously and deceitfully toward anyone except you.

The person Rée deceived most was Salomé herself: he told her that Nietzsche really wanted her as a secretary and concubine, and he undermined her view of Nietzsche's character. Rée's stories caused an uproar when Salomé met Nietzsche's very proper sister that summer in Jena. As Elizabeth described it in a letter to a friend,

> Lou burst forth with a flood of invective against my brother: "he's a madman who doesn't know what he wants, he's a common egoist who wanted only to exploit her mental gifts ... Besides, were they to pursue any aims together, two weeks wouldn't go by before they were sleeping together, men all wanted only that, pooh to mental friendship! and she knew first-hand what she was talking about, she had been caught *twice* already in that kind of relationship." As I, now naturally beside myself, said that might well be the case with her Russians only she didn't know my pure-minded brother, she retorted full of scorn (word for word): "who first soiled our study plan with his low designs, who started up with mental friendship when he couldn't get me for something else, who first thought of concubinage—your brother!" ... [I was] utterly out of my element: never in my life had I heard such indecent talk ... when on top of it all *she* had proposed *their living together*!! What is one to think of such a girl?! ... When we were in Tautenberg ... she broke out again in a fury against Fritz ... "just don't go thinking that I care beans for your brother or am in love with him, I could sleep in the same room with him without getting worked up." Would you believe it possible! I too was altogether beside myself and shouted at her repeatedly: "stop this indecent talk!" "Pooh," she said, "with Rée I talk a lot more indecently."

Ultimately Nietzsche set Salomé straight:

> *Never* did I think that you should "read aloud and write" for me, but I very much wished that I might be your *teacher*. To tell the whole truth: I am now seeking people who could be my heirs; I carry something around with me absolutely not to be read in my books—and am seeking the finest, most fertile soil for it.

While Nietzsche and Salomé clarified their relationship, Rée's letters indulged a baby talk that biographer Rudolph Binion paraphrases thus: Rée wondered whether "Snailie [Salomé] was her Housie's [Rée's] tenant or proprietor and how even out in the big world Snailie might crawl back into her Housie now and again if only she would." Nietzsche himself was slow to catch on to Rée's duplicity, and it was only later that he complained to Rée that "From the moment Lou was in Stibbe you wrote me no more letters."

Rée's opposition to Nietzsche dovetailed with Elizabeth's attempts to protect her brother from Salomé. "I cannot deny it," Elizabeth wrote, "[she is] my brother's philosophy *personified*: that raging egoism which knocks down anything in its way and that utter want of morality." Relaying the scene with Salomé, Elizabeth poisoned Nietzsche against her, so that he called off their winter plan, but they reconciled during a five-week visit in Leipzig in August 1882. The visit was not enough: Elizabeth's poison, combined with Salomé's haughtiness—which was fed by Rée's rumors—caused a final break in the fall, when Nietzsche put together the whole picture and saw Rée's, Elizabeth's, and Salomé's parts: he broke with all of them. He would reconcile, later, only with his sister.

Seeing Rée's and Salomé's behavior clearly at last, Nietzsche wrote to his friend Ida Overbeck that Salomé

> is and remains for me a being of the first rank, about whom it is a pity forever. Given her energy of will and originality of mind, she was headed for something great; given her practical morality, though, she may well belong rather in a penitentiary or madhouse. I *miss* her, for all her bad qualities: we were disparate enough for something useful to have been always sure to come out of our talks; I have found no one so unprejudiced, so clever, so well prepared for my sort of problems.

In November, he described her as "Capable of enthusiasm for people without love for them, yet love for God: need for effusion; shrewd and fully self-controlled in respect of men's sensuality; heartless and incapable of loving; emotionally always sickly and close to madness." He would ultimately write to Meysenbug that "This sort of person who lacks reverence must be avoided."

In ten days in January 1883, Nietzsche wrote *Also Spoke Zarathustra*, which reads, in places, as a lecture to Salomé about the necessity of self-creation and self-overcoming—of living in good faith with her divided constitution. His *Genealogy of Morals*, published in 1887, said "No, proposition by proposition, conclusion by conclusion," to Rée's theories about conscience, and Nietzsche described a morality that originated not in nature but in the two types of power: of masters' and slaves'. After 1883,

Nietzsche wrote steadily for the next five years—reading Salomé and
Rée's literary output without writing to either of them—but eventually
his headaches became so violent as to blind and then paralyze him, pre-
venting any further writing after 1889.

IV.

After the split with Nietzsche, Salomé and Rée moved to Berlin in late
1882: there they started a salon of their own, receiving intellectuals and
students in a drawing room flanked by two bedrooms. Salomé would
later describe her time with Rée as "a relationship which may never exist
again in such intimacy and reticence," although she does note that Rée
"was known . . . as my 'maid of honor.'" Quoting one of Nietzsche's apho-
risms from the period, Salomé proposed that "A woman may well enough
form a friendship with a man, but to sustain it she needs the help of a
little physical antipathy . . . or great mental sympathy." Still yearning for
Salomé himself, Rée would warn her against each of the intellectuals he
brought to their salon, and many of the scholars and writers who gathered
there found themselves stymied by her lack of interest. With Ferdinand
Tönnies, a sociologist and follower of Nietzsche's, they achieved another
short-lived Trinity, as Tönnies traveled with them, but he was ultimately
disappointed when he never got any time alone with Salomé.

Salomé was not in contact with Nietzsche, but Elizabeth and others
began to agitate for her return to Russia—by force if need be. Feeling
that she would be less vulnerable to deportation if she had a profession
to support her, Salomé wrote an autobiographical novel, *In Struggle for
God*, which was published in 1884. The main character is a preacher's
son—clearly Nietzsche, his name disguised only anagrammatically—and
Salomé herself is rendered as the three different women the Nietzsche
character loved. The book dramatizes her struggles, both as the Nietz-
sche character and through him, with faith and love, and it describes
the danger of turning a person into a substitute for a lost faith, prefer-
ring independence and "mentally passionate nonmarital relationships"
to consummated affairs. Published under the nom de plume Henri Lou,
In Struggle for God brought Salomé a torrent of fan mail. Her fiction is no
longer generally read, but one critic described it as having "the effect of
hymns in the thunderous sounding of an organ. It rings out full and stir-
ring, and dies away in tones celestially light."

Salomé and Rée lived and traveled together from late 1882 to the end
of 1885, but they separated, for reasons she never documented: by the
beginning of 1886, Salomé only wrote that they were living "at opposite
ends" of Berlin "like children mad at each other." In the middle of 1886,
Rée moved to Munich to study medicine, while Salomé, now thirty-one,
remained in Berlin, entertaining suitors before she finally accepted a
marriage proposal.

Salomé met her husband in the pension where she lived after parting
from Rée. Fifteen years older than her, Fred Charles Andreas was giving
German lessons to Turkish officers there. Descended from a German-
Malayan mother and a princely Armenian father, Andreas had been raised
and schooled in Germany and then Switzerland, and after a doctorate
in oriental philology, he traveled to Persia in 1876 to study the historical
Zarathustra. Andreas remained in Persia for five years after the expedi-
tion was recalled, but when he returned to Wiesbaden for treatment for
his eyes in 1882, he was fluent in two dozen languages and dialects, and he
started to give private lessons, and then to teach at a military school. By
the time he met Lou von Salomé, Andreas was living an unconventional
life in Berlin—wearing Eastern dress, going barefoot, and brewing his
own strong teas—and he was due to begin teaching Persian to diplomats
and businessmen at the Seminar for Oriental Languages in 1887.

It is not clear what drew Salomé to this learned but brooding and hot-
tempered man—she left only the thinnest records of their forty-three
years together—but biographer Rudolph Binion notes distinct similar-
ities with Nietzsche, from his name (Salomé Germanicized Fred Charles
to Friedrich Carl) and his age (he was two years younger than Nietzsche)
to his bad eyes and his interest in Zarathustra. But as with Nietzsche,
Salomé wrote that her reaction to Andreas's passionate nature "was not
that of a *woman*: I remained as *neutral* in this respect as I had toward the
companion of my youth [Rée]." In her memoirs, she wrote that

> My love for my husband began . . . with an inner demand. This
> produced an attitude which was critical of him to the point of pain
> . . . There is a difference between looking for some friendly attach-
> ment and searching for a *wedded union*. In the latter case, not only is
> a distinctly higher profound fondness included, but also the desire
> and ability to relinquish one's individual being . . . It isn't a ques-
> tion of a committing but of being committed . . . Love itself is . . .
> not purely ideal . . .

The man I loved but did not criticize was Gillot, although I loved him truly—ideally, as I define it . . . In the later stages of youth whatever one strives for ideally incorporates itself directly in a person . . . Later, when people and ideas are more clearly differentiated, one no longer searches for a divine mortal; instead there is unity in a mutual, internal devotion to that which both revere and hold dear. No longer does one person kneel before another, but Two kneel together.

The "inner demand" was actually partly a threat: Andreas had a fiery temperament, and he threatened to kill himself if Salomé refused to marry him—he actually went so far as to thrust a knife into his chest, narrowly missing his heart. After he recovered, they married in June of 1887—with Hendrik Gillot presiding, at Salomé's insistence. Later in life, she wrote that she had tried to make Rée's "acceptance into our bond . . . a condition of the marriage"—a condition her husband accepted—but Rée broke with Salomé for good when he heard of the engagement. On finishing his medical degree, Rée worked in Tütz in northern Poland and ultimately died in a hiking accident in 1901.

Salomé—now Andreas-Salomé—described her marriage as something that was still waiting on the future: it was not "something we *have*, but something we *make*." In keeping with her relationship with Rée and Nietzsche, she made it out of physical antipathy: if Salomé refused to be responsible for Andreas's suicide, she refused to have anything to do with his sexual life as well, and by all accounts, the marriage was never consummated. On one occasion, Andreas-Salomé recalled, she woke up to the sound of Andreas gasping for breath as she strangled him, defending herself in her sleep. Nevertheless, they settled into the roles of Little Old Man (*Alterchen*) and Little Daughter (*Töchterchen*), and Andreas looked for intimacy in other places: in 1904, he would have a daughter, Mariechen, with their housekeeper, Marie Apel. Out of respect for his wife, Andreas never acknowledged Mariechen, but Andreas-Salomé respected his family as well, and allowed him to keep his unofficial family with him in his travels.

From their home in Schmargendorf, in the Berlin suburbs, Andreas-Salomé spent a lot of time in the city while her husband was teaching. She entered into circles of writers and dramatists, and she wrote a study, *Henrik Ibsen's Female Characters*, which was published in 1891. Following Nietzsche's breakdown in 1889, she spent 1893 and 1894 writing *Friedrich*

Nietzsche in His Work, which characterizes the titanic thinker as too frail to bear out his own philosophy. Presumably, she herself, by surviving him, retained an inner surplus that was equal to the "insurmountable obstacles" she would confront as she shaped her life for herself.

In 1892, five years into their marriage, she finally consummated a relationship with socialist newspaper editor Georg Ledebour, with whom she shared a mutual love. When Ledebour told her that he would not settle for an affair, though—he wanted her for himself—she wrote in her diary that she planned to give him no sign for a year while she left Andreas: her abandonment of Andreas would be her "final gift to him, my final proof of love." Andreas refused to grant her a divorce, though, and since he spoke, she said, "only with knives and tears," she ultimately relinquished Ledebour. At dinner, she wrote in her diary,

> I thought incessantly of the *knives beside the plates.* But . . . neither the horrors that could result if Fred lost all control as at home nor even our being already so frightfully compromised seemed to me the worst of it. The worst *for me* was Ledebour's irremediably altered conception of our marriage—the impossibility of my ever again making him see it with *my* eyes, think of it with *my* judgment.

Threats of violence notwithstanding, Ledebour left, and Andreas-Salomé set off to Petersburg, Paris, Switzerland, and Vienna. We do not have any record of how Andreas reconciled himself to her independence, for she consorted with artists and lovers throughout her travels, while he remained at home with his students. More than forty years later, she would describe the marriage as "the total freedom we each had to be ourselves," which was "something we both experienced internally as something *shared*." The marriage itself has been a source of mystery and speculation for biographers.

Georg Ledebour was Andreas-Salomé's last older lover: after him, her lovers were always younger, by eight to eighteen years. After Ledebour, she traveled with various escorts, but constant travels kept her from settling down with any one lover, and she would be on the move for the rest of her life, on a circuit that varied widely, according to her whims—typically she returned to Berlin, Munich, and Vienna, Peterhof in Finland, and Petersburg in Russia. She would stay in a place for six weeks or a few months at a time, but she never settled into a routine, as she entered the circles of leading writers and intellectuals wherever she went, and she engaged their work in her books, reviews, and articles, about theatre, art, and psychology. Andreas-Salomé would not write about any of these companions—only Rilke, and then Freud, who would both burnish her image as a muse to geniuses. The others were consigned, with Rée and Andreas, to minor notes in her journals, or minor characters in her novels.

In Vienna in 1895, dramatist Arthur Schnitzler recalled her "turning a bit female" and showing "the need to be desired," by poet Richard Beer-Hofmann, who broke with her on bad terms in early December of 1895. This flirtation paved the way for the relationship with Friedrich Pineles—Zemek—a medical student, eight years her junior, whom she met at Christmas 1895. After a week's hiking south of Salzburg, there is a four-month gap in her papers, during which time biographers speculate that she aborted a pregnancy.

Andreas-Salomé prevented Zemek, too, from making it into the record of her life, but after she spent the summer of 1896 with him, she began to take lovers for regular periods. Considering her relationships later in life, she would say that she "certainly 'abused' Z. and the others," but "it came to turnover, almost rhythmic turnover [in her relationships], because my strong subjectivity ever and again won freedom for solitude, for 'fructified peace.'" Typically Andreas-Salomé returned to her solitude and her marriage after nine months with a lover—biographers note the echo of parturition—and she did indeed break with Zemek after nine months, but she sought him out again in 1897, and they resumed their travels together.

Bound to a husband fixated on maintaining the marriage, Andreas-Salomé articulated a theory by which the "natural love-life . . . is grounded in the principle of infidelity," but this did not give her the right to keep multiple lovers simultaneously so much as it gave her the right to break faith with her lovers. But she was determined to create her faith for herself. In an attempt to reconcile her lingering sense of a grandfather-God with her disappointment in human people, Andreas-Salomé wrote an essay, "Jesus the Jew," which portrays Jesus as a human man who is utterly disillusioned when God refuses to save him on the cross. Dying in human pain, he resigns himself to a life without contact with divinity and creates a religion out of his own repletion: his desire to believe creates a god, even in spite of the lack of evidence for a divinity.

V.

By the mid-1890s, Andreas-Salomé's novels *In Struggle for God* and *Ruth*, in addition to her books on Nietzsche and Ibsen's heroines, had made her famous as a writer, and also notorious as a friend of the now-mad but still controversial Nietzsche. Rilke was only twenty-one when he met her at poet Jakob Wassermann's Munich dinner party, but he had been cultivating literary contacts in Prague and now in Munich, and he had been publishing poems in journals and magazines throughout Germany ever since he finished school at seventeen. He was anxious to avoid the "desolate counting house future" his family foresaw for him, so he had every reason to cultivate a relationship with Andreas-Salomé. He did not make his admiration known in person, though: he was not a handsome man—almost every photograph we have of him shows a dreamy face, with watery eyes and an indistinct chin, with facial hair making hesitant attempts around his mouth—and not being established yet, himself, he did not have anything to offer to a lover—so he wrote her a flattering letter the following day:

> Yesterday was not the first twilight hour I have spent with you. [Reading her essay "Jesus the Jew,"] a devout fellow-feeling walked ahead of me along this solemn path—and then at last it was like a great rejoicing in me to find expressed in such supremely clear words, with the tremendous force of a religious conviction, what my *Visions* present in dreamlike epics. That was the mysterious twilight hour I could not but be reminded of yesterday.
>
> You see, gracious lady, through this unsparing severity, through the uncompromising strength of your words, I felt that my own work was receiving a blessing, a sanction . . . for your essay was to my poems as reality is to a dream, as fulfillment is to a desire.

Born of similar disappointment and longing, the forsaken Christ of Rilke's *Visions of Christ* was cursed to die and be repeatedly resurrected, until Christianity should dissolve under the weight of its false piety.

Rilke's interest in Christ as a human martyr came from his experience as a sickly and weak student at military school. He would tell every lover and patron for the rest of his life about how traumatic this experience had been, but he would neglect to mention that he had chosen it for himself, in hopes that through military service he could win the promotion into the Austrian nobility that his father had failed to attain. Josef Rilke had once distinguished himself in battle, but he retired from the military at twenty-seven to become a railroad official. As a sensitive and fragile child, Rilke suffered enormously for having followed his father's footsteps to a military high school—so he had followed his mother's religiosity and sentimentalism instead, and turned his experience into poetry that treated suffering itself as a strength.

Josef Rilke's failure to be promoted was a source of bitterness and disappointment for his wife, Sophia (Phia) Entz. Her father, Carl Entz, was a wealthy Prague merchant who owned a color and chemical business and served as a director of the Bohemia Savings Bank: Josef's promotion would have elevated her wealthy family's status as well. His brother Jaroslav had recently been promoted, and Josef still hoped to be promoted when he met Phia: Prague had been a prominent city in Austria-Hungary, but German speakers had recently become an upper-class minority to the Czechs, and noble descent was an alluring possibility. Together the brothers pored over the family records, trying to establish a link to the thirteenth-century Knights of Rulko, but Josef was no longer a military man: living in Prague, he worked for the Turnau-Kralup-Prague railway, and his application for promotion was ultimately turned down on account of a throat illness.

Josef and Phia married in 1873, but when his promotion was turned down for good, the disappointment became a wedge between them. By all accounts, Phia gave off an aura of dissatisfaction and superiority for the rest of her life: when she found that her husband was not a dashing soldier but a conservative railroad official, she dressed in black, put on airs, and performed her Catholic rituals ostentatiously. René Maria Rilke, their only son, was born in 1875—later in life he sketched his family to a patron:

My father began the career of officer (following a family tradition) but then switched over to that of official. He is a railroad official, holds a fairly high post in a private railroad, which he has earned with infinite conscientiousness. He lives in Prague. *There* I was born … Of my mother's family I know nothing. Her father was a wealthy merchant whose fortunes went to pieces on a prodigal son. My childhood home was a cramped rented apartment in Prague; it was very sad. My parents' marriage was already faded when I was born. When I was nine years old, the discord broke out openly, and my mother left her husband. She was a very nervous, slender, dark woman, who wanted something indefinite in life. And so she remained. Actually these two people ought to have understood each other better, for they both attach an infinite amount of value to externals; our little household, which was in reality middle class, was supposed to have the appearance of plenty, our clothes were supposed to deceive people, and certain lies passed as a matter of course.

In 1884, Phia moved into her own place, taking Rilke with her, and he would later complain that she entrusted him, "for the greater part of the day . . . to a serving-girl, immoral and of few scruples," while she, "the woman whose first and most immediate care I should have been," went out, or to Vienna and a lover.

When it became inconvenient for René to continue living with Phia, Rilke's uncle Jaroslav, who had lost his own sons to illness, arranged a stipend for him to attend military school. Fired by visions of sabers and epaulets, the eleven-year-old René was anxious to win the promotion his father had failed to attain, and for the first four years, his evaluations were typically "very good" to "excellent," with notes that he was "quiet and good-tempered" and "industrious." In his final year, though, he fell from eighth in a class of forty-eight to eighteenth of fifty-one and then withdrew, citing his health—although he himself said later that he had been "more spiritually troubled than ill in body." Rilke would frequently rehearse the trauma of being the weakling in the class, but when he described the trauma to his first girlfriend, he said that he and a fellow student had attained

> a truly brotherly affection based on mutual sympathy, and with kiss and handclasp we sealed a bond for life. As children do. We understood each other well, and I blossomed out in the knowledge that the scarcely varied events of my soul were sounding and ringing on in the like-tuned soul of my friend . . . [but] later I learned that fellow pupils had dragged our pure bond into the mud . . . After that my heart never became attached to anyone again.

Still, Rilke seems to have expected to return to school: he wrote to his mother, "I have taken off the Emperor's uniform only to don it again before long—for always: and rest assured I shall wear it honourably."

Rilke never did go back to military school, but now his family expected him to embark on a career, so Jaroslav volunteered to pay his tuition at the Commercial Academy in Linz, south of Prague, where he would prepare to work in his law practice. After failing to win any acclaim in his father's line, though, Rilke found that his uncle's law firm was not a consolation. At the Commercial Academy, he retained his military bearing and background—but he used it to cultivate the dignified air of the class poet. He began to publish poems in 1892, and ended up second in a class of more than fifty. At this time he also began to take his future in his own hands: for four days in May of 1892, he ran off with Olga Blumauer, a children's nurse. They checked in to a hotel together in Vienna—but Rilke had chosen this destination with more than romance in mind: while they were in the city, he dropped off a book of poems with an editor who had published and encouraged him. The head of the academy ultimately had him recalled to Linz, where he apologized for the elopement, which he now called a "stupid flirtation," but he had already begun to proclaim that "there is no one like me, there never has been," and his stubborn preference for poetry over the law shows that he was determined to find the words that would give that statement some definite meaning.

Jaroslav Rilke died before René finished at the Linz academy, but his will ordered that René should be paid a stipend—administered through his two daughters, Rilke's cousins—for as long as he continued to study. Passing his final examinations in 1894, Rilke spent the winter of 1894–1895 studying not law but the history of art at Carl-Ferdinand University in Prague, and with his uncle's money, he paid to print and distribute volumes of his poetry: he gave some of these to the poor, and he tried to sell some, but he could never turn a profit from his poetry. He was still a concern to his parents, though, and even as he asserted himself, he lamented that

all I do is cost more and more money, and even with a doctorate, if I am not to starve as an assistant teacher, more money still will be required to gain me a professorship—a prospect which anyway has no appeal for me.

With every day that passes I see more clearly how right I was to resist from the start, with all my strength, the catch-phrase beloved of my relations: that art is just something for leisure hours after coming home from the office or whatever.—I find that a frightful statement. For me, it is an article of faith that he who does not devote himself to art with all his desires and everything in him can never reach the highest goal . . . [Art] needs the whole man! not just a few free hours of weariness.

Saved by his stipend from having to work, Rilke cultivated a circle of artist and writer friends, and he also sought out a new family through a girlfriend. Valery von David-Rhônfeld was an artistic young noble-woman, and her family took him in—as soon as he took his diploma, they were engaged. It was to Vally that Rilke had described his military school agonies—but now he described her as his salvation:

> [until] I met you, beloved, dearest Vally, when you strengthened, healed, comforted me and gave me life, existence, hope and future . . . My whole previous life seems to me a road to you, like a long unlighted journey at the end of which my reward is to strive toward you and to know you will be *all* mine in the near future.

Vally found money to publish Rilke's *Life and Songs* in 1894, but after two years of engagement, Rilke spent a summer vacation in the Baltics and there he wrote love poems to a doctor's daughter before returning to Prague to break off the engagement.

Making a career of poetry, Rilke started a journal, *Wegwarten* (Wild Chicory) with some friends, and by 1897, he had placed poems in a range of obscure journals. He cultivated a circle of literary friends and contacts, in Prague and then in Munich, where he had started to take art history courses at the university in September of 1896. But he was still printing his poems at his own expense, and while his plays were produced, none of them were critically praised, and Rilke's only assets remained his poetic promise, and his determination to write, and to make the right contacts, to see that his promise was realized. It was in this atmosphere that he attended the dinner party where he met Lou Andreas-Salomé.

VI.

The day after Jakob Wassermann's dinner party, Lou Andreas-Salomé responded favorably to Rilke's twilight hour note, and the two writers met for tea and the theater in the next few days. Having apprenticed in the role of lovelorn poet, Rilke spent hours wandering the streets of

Munich with flowers for her, hoping to see her before the time of their meeting. Even in the first few days of their affair, Rilke wrote to her, "At last I have a *home*," and when they traveled, two weeks later, to Wolfratshausen, eighteen miles south of Munich, they became lovers.

Andreas-Salomé went to Wolfratshausen looking for an escape from Munich for the summer—and she and Rilke spent much of that summer there together—but whatever passion they shared was continually interrupted by streams of friends and visitors. First to visit was a Russian friend and admirer of Andreas-Salomé's, then Andreas and others, and then Andreas-Salomé traveled on her own to see Zemek, who gave her advice about how to handle her new young lover. Having herself convinced René to adopt the stronger, Germanic "Rainer"—not as a nom de plume, but as his name—she nevertheless diagnosed his personality as "split up into two beings": on one hand, he was the poet, on the other, the hysterical one overcome by his fears.

At the end of the Wolfratshausen summer, Rilke abandoned *Wegwarten* and all the efforts he had been making to cultivate a literary circle in Munich, and he followed Andreas-Salomé and her husband to Berlin, where he rented a furnished room nearby and was a frequent guest in their home. During this first autumn, Andreas-Salomé wrote a short story, "A Decease," in which a poet's talent is not recognized until after he has died—as if poetic talent cannot be seen while a poet is still alive—or in a relationship—but Rilke was slow to be pushed into poetic recognition: it was only after Andreas-Salomé took him to hear Stefan George read poetry that he beheld for the first time a poet who wrote for himself, instead of for readers or critics. Rilke had always flattered editors into printing his verse before, but now he disowned the conventional verses he had published and the standard persona of the sentimental poet. He would have to judge the value of his writing himself, and now, following Andreas-Salomé (who was, in turn, following Nietzsche) he would have to hold himself to the highest standard: his life itself would have to be poetic in order to produce poetry. Andreas-Salomé would write in her memoir that Rilke's "whole tragic destiny is summed up in this tension between the exclusive grace of a creativity he considered to be holy, and the irresistible compulsion to imitate that state of grace, to 'ape' it, to project it even when it was absent."

Devoted now to art wholeheartedly, but painfully conscious of the gaps in his business-centered education, Rilke took up the study of Renaissance art through the winter of 1897–1898, and in the spring, he traveled

to Florence to see it firsthand. On Andreas-Salomé's instructions, he
kept a journal of his trip, which reads as an extended letter to her, but
she was hesitant to receive his strongly worded affections, so the "You"
he addressed was ostensibly God: "my joy will seem far-off and unfes-
tive," he wrote, "as long as You . . . do not share in it." When he defined
the ideal relationship, now, it sounded like her ideal of wise and generous
restraint: "artists shall avoid each other," he wrote, proving themselves by
withdrawing from each other, to devote themselves to art.

When Rilke returned to Schmargendorf in July and presented his
journal to Andreas-Salomé, he was deeply disappointed by her lackluster
reaction. She would confess to him in her memoir that she "couldn't mus-
ter any appreciation for your early poetry, in spite of its musicality"—but
he wrote a long complaint in which he said that he hated her as "some-
thing *too great*":

> I wanted this time to be the rich one, the giver, the host, the master,
> and You were supposed to come and be guided by my care and love
> and stroll about in my hospitality. And now in Your presence I was
> again only the smallest beggar at the outermost threshold of Your
> being . . . Every reunion with You made me ashamed . . . Once I
> came to You in such poverty. Almost as a child I came to the rich
> woman. And You took my soul in Your arms and rocked it . . . [but]
> I didn't want to be embraced by You, I wanted You to be able to
> lean against me when You are tired . . . however far I may go—*You*
> *are always there before me.*

Rilke could only see them united in the future, in art and devotion:
"be always thus before me," he said,

> You dear, peerless, sacred one. Let us go upward together, You and
> I—as if up to the great star, each leaning on the other, each repos-
> ing in the other . . .
> With each work that one raises out of oneself, one creates space
> for some new strength . . .
> As for ourselves: we are the ancestors of a god and with our
> deepest solitudes reach forward through the centuries to his very
> beginning. I feel this with all my heart!

This god would be the only child Andreas-Salomé and Rilke had together,
for when she became pregnant by Rilke in late 1897, she aborted in early

1898. Years later, in a letter that expressed sympathy with Rilke's need for independence for creativity, she would write, "I could say of myself that I (although no artist) have denied myself motherhood in response to the demands of both [life's art and art's life]."

Searching for the gods who would be their children, Andreas-Salomé and Rilke turned toward Russia, the land of her birth, where the people's religious customs had not yet been dragged all the way into the modern world. Throughout the winter of 1898–99, Rilke used his uncle's stipend to study Russian at the University of Berlin. For Easter of 1899, he and Andreas-Salomé traveled to Russia—with Andreas—to witness what Andreas-Salomé called "the [Russian] spiritual life, [which] remains innocent and childlike in its simplicity when compared to more 'mature' nations which focus upon personal love of a more 'egoistic' kind." They visited Tolstoy, who "vehemently warned us against participating in the superstitious customs of the peasants," Andreas-Salomé wrote, although they immersed themselves in the Easter celebrations nonetheless. Rilke was relegated to the role of traveling companion throughout this trip, and he lodged separately while the Andreases stayed with the Salomé family. Rilke occupied himself with a flirtation with his Russian friend Elena Voronin, whom he had met in Italy, but he would abandon Voronin when Andreas-Salomé beckoned.

This first trip marked a change in tone of Rilke's letters though, and now his writing treats Andreas-Salomé as "a far-off city . . . a word from you will be to me an island . . . but if you ask, you will see me hesitate: I don't know for certain whether the wood we walk through is not just a reflection of my own feelings." His journal also returned to the theme of solitude, and now he wrote that God "can only come to one, or to a couple between whom He can no longer distinguish." But by the end of the trip, God would have been able to distinguish between them: writer Boris Pasternak, who was ten when Andreas-Salomé and Rilke visited his father, recalled the poet traveling with a woman—"perhaps his mother or his elder sister."

Nevertheless, Rilke spent a second winter in Berlin, still a frequent guest in the Andreas house. The autumn of 1899 was highly productive for both of them: Rilke wrote *The Lay of the Love and Death of Cornet Christoph Rilke*—a romantic verse narrative that fulfilled Rilke's military dreams in the story of the Cornet's death in battle following a night of love: it would become his most popular work when he published it in 1907. He also wrote *Tales of God and Other Things*, a lighter work, and the first part of *The Book of Hours*—in which a monk essentially creates God through his devotion and longing. Many of these devotional poems can be read simultaneously as love poems, especially since the god Rilke was addressing was himself a human creation. For her part, Andreas-Salomé wrote a novel, *Ma*—about a mother who keeps her children close instead of relinquishing them to their own futures—and an essay, "Thoughts on the Problem of Love," which concluded that "two are at one only when they stay two."

That winter, Rilke began to translate Russian poetry and started to look for career opportunities in publishing translations in Germany. From May to August of 1900, he and Andreas-Salomé made another trip to Russia—this time without Andreas: they walked barefoot in the fields at dawn, ate porridge, and lived like peasants among peasants—and spent the rest of their time in museums, or studying in archives. They visited briefly with Tolstoy again, and they also visited with Spiridon Drozhzhin, the peasant poet whose verse Rilke had been translating. They traveled widely—from Petersburg south to Kiev, then down the Dnieper into the Ukraine, then overland to the Volga, where they took boats as far north as Nizhniy Novgorod before seeing Moscow and returning to Petersburg. Forever afterward, they would remember this trip as the moment of their greatest intimacy.

This luminous memory glazed over the "anxiety, almost states of terror," which crippled Rilke throughout the trip. When Andreas-Salomé left Rilke by himself at the end of the trip—while she visited family in Finland for three weeks—Rilke panicked for not hearing from her. He sent off a hysterical letter, in which he sounded, Andreas-Salomé said, "almost depraved on account of the presumption and arrogance of your Prayers." Filled to overflowing with things Russian, he was devastated by the need to create something that would give him the same sense of enduring reality. "Everything that is truly seen *must* become a poem," he wrote, but when he could not write the poem of each thing, he lamented that "to be awake and to be alive are deeds, not states. And I did not *do* them!"

VII.

The tensions between Andreas-Salomé and Rilke ran deep enough that she returned to Schmargendorf alone, while Rilke traveled on to an artists' colony in Worpswede, in northern Germany. There Heinrich Vogeler, a painter he had met in Florence and known in Berlin, was working on woodcuts to illustrate *Tales of God and Other Things*. Among artists his own age, now, Rilke found a kind of belonging. On long walks in nature, he could tell stories of Russia, and he could read his poems in the evenings. "If I can learn from people," he wrote,

> then surely it is from these people, who are so much like landscape themselves that their nearbyness doesn't frighten me away . . . How they responded to me as a counselor and helper. How requisite I was to them. And how I grew strong under the shelter of their trust to be everything they needed, to be their happiest one and the liveliest one among them.

Rilke was drawn to two women in particular, painter Paula Becker and sculptor Clara Westhoff. Becker was also the child of a railway official, and like Rilke, she had chosen art in spite of her father's insistence that she support herself. At first his journal celebrated the "white painter"—he referred to the sculptor as "Clara Westhoff" for a full month before she became simply "Clara." In September of 1900, he described Becker and Westhoff to Andreas-Salomé:

> How much I learn in watching these two girls, especially the blond painter, who has such observant brown eyes . . . How much mysteriousness invests these slender figures when they stand before the evening or when, leaning back in velvet chairs, they listen with all their aspects. Since they are the most receptive, I can be the most giving. My whole life is full of the images with which I can talk to them; everything that I've experienced becomes an expression for what lies deep behind experience.

Rilke was initially attracted to Becker, but she was in love with one of the other Worpswede artists, Otto Modersohn, whose wife had recently died, and when Modersohn and Becker announced their engagement, in October 1900, it was not long before Rilke and Clara Westhoff found each other. As with Vally, Rilke was taken by Clara's family as much as by her herself: her father was a wealthy merchant, who supported her studies in Munich and Dachau before sending her to Paris to work with Rodin. After visiting her family's house in nearby Oberneuland, Rilke told Clara that

Your home was for me, from the first moment, more than just a kindly foreign place. Was simply home, *the first home in which I saw people living* . . . That struck me so. I wanted at first to be a brother beside you all, and your home is rich enough to love me too and to uphold me, and you are so kind and take me in as a real member of the family, and initiate me trustfully into the abundance of your work weeks and holidays.

Scenting a change in Rilke, Andreas-Salomé called him back to Berlin, and on October 5, 1900, he left Worpswede suddenly, to resume his Russian studies and translations. To Andreas-Salomé alone could he describe the part of him that could not be touched or satisfied in society. As he explained later,

There is always only *one thing* in me, and I must remain locked up (that is, keep silent or prattle) or else open myself and make visible the single thing that inhabits me. This inner disposition of mine . . . excludes me from all legitimate exchange, since it leads only to disjunctions and misunderstandings and pushes me into unwanted relationships amid which I suffer and from which many dangerous reversals can occur . . . I have acquired all my "friends" by such illicit means and for this reason possess them badly and in poor conscience. Only thus is it possible . . . that I should have acquired a whole crowd of friends who could give nothing in return for my continual expenditure, and that at any rate no one *can* reciprocate me, since I give ruthlessly and brutally, without regard to others.

Even as he returned to Andreas-Salomé in Berlin, though, Rilke was making promises to Westhoff, assuring her that "Before you possessed me, / I didn't exist. But I remain now / when you no longer see me," and he was turning his feelings into stronger and stronger poetry: his Worpswede diary shows the first signs of the voice that would carry him for the rest of his life.

If Andreas-Salomé had wanted to keep Rilke close, it was not long before she was irritated by his supersensitive self-explorations. On New Year's Eve, 1900, she told her journal, "Just about all I want from the coming year, all I need, is quiet—more solitude, such as I had until four years ago"—before she met Rilke. Her journal entry for January 10, 1901, records that "I've certainly been horrid sometimes at home. Afterwards

I always feel terrible about it. I'd like to have oceans of love with which to extinguish it all. I'm a monster. (I was mean to Rainer too, but that never bothers me.)" By January 20, she was more severe yet: "to make Rainer go away, *go completely away*, I would be capable of brutality. (*He must go!*)" Clearly the relationship was over: Andreas-Salomé wrote to her friend Frieda von Bülow that Rilke "*has* at all costs to find support, and an exclusive devotion, if not with me, then elsewhere: better for him to lean on even the most unsuitable object than to have none. And so he will find what he needs very soon."

Rilke found what he needed very quickly indeed, and returning to Worpswede in early 1901, he became engaged to Clara Westhoff. He saluted her as "Beginner of my joys! First one! Eternal!" and in April of 1901—possibly with a baby on the way (a daughter would be born eight months later, in December)—Rilke and Clara were married at her parents' house, with no Rilkes in attendance. Rilke had gone so far as to leave the Catholic Church—repudiating his mother's faith—to marry into Clara's Protestant family.

Andreas-Salomé would later acknowledge that "for all the caring fervour of our relationship, I stood detached, outside the bond which truly links man and woman," but when she heard that Rilke was planning to marry, she sent him a letter with "Last Appeal" in place of a salutation. Citing Zemek's professional opinion, she described Rilke as prone to madness and at risk of suicide if he should abandon the poetry in which he had "stood before me sound," and she described her own progress, through their relationship, back "*into my youth!* [sic]" She invited him to "take the same path toward your dark god!" and she cast him off, although she reiterated what she had told him when he left Schmargendorf for Worpswede: that "if one day much later you feel yourself in dire straits, there is a home here with us for the worst hour."

Andreas-Salomé would later say of her affairs in general that she had an "obstreperously good conscience over brutal rupturing of relations etc." because she felt "compelled to do service be it in the hardest, most painful way (as, say, God compels man)"—she did concede that "This thought would ease my black egoist's soul"—but if she had already effectively relinquished Rilke, she was not yet prepared to be replaced by another woman. We can only guess, though, what her feelings must have been when she wrote this appeal, for she destroyed her journal pages from the end of January to mid-March, and she suggested that she and Rilke should burn their correspondence. When Rilke complied (she did not) she effectively relegated him to the minor relationships she would not record, as she had already struck Rée, her husband, and Ledebour and others from her life. By May, she was back with Zemek—whom she would also hardly record—and she resumed her travels, to Nuremberg and Wiesbaden, Russia and Sweden. In keeping with her image from the end of the "Last Appeal," she wrote an essay, "Old Age and Eternity," which described aging as the process of returning to a blissful childhood. In the five short stories she wrote at the time, only one of her young female protagonists was outraged to discover a friend's infidelity—the others drifted innocently and cheerfully toward maturity.

VIII.

Cut off from Andreas-Salomé, Rilke described himself as "shattered" or "swallowed" in an abyss—but when his daughter was born in December of 1901, he named her Ruth, which was also the name of the protagonist in Andreas-Salomé's autobiographical novel of 1895. That winter, isolated in Worpswede with his wife and their infant daughter, Rilke experienced something like the consummation he had been waiting for: he told a friend that he felt as spiritual as the Russian peasants, who were "linked in some way with God, that is, with the highest needs and unfolding of their existence . . . artists, they could be, led by some hidden impulse to a wise selection of realities and finding thus their own life, released from the confusions of the world." Nevertheless, it was not long before he was echoing Andreas-Salomé, writing to a friend that "it is an impossibility for two people to be *really together,* and if they appear so, it is a limitation, a mutual agreement by which one or both are deprived of their freedom and their development." At the same time, Paula Becker was criticizing Clara for having "shed much of your old self and spread it out like a cloak for your king to walk on."

Rilke turned down paid work in order to protect his solitude for writing, but he and Clara were very poor, and even with help from her parents, money was a constant problem—although they did not yet relinquish their servant. When Rilke found out that his cousins would terminate his uncle's stipend in the summer of 1902, though, he panicked. He started to look for work—as a reviewer, correspondent, or critic, lecturer or translator, anything to replace the stipend—but his first impulse was to cut costs by "dissolv[ing] our little household." "I am my own circle," he wrote to a friend, as he cut himself free of Clara, and he described a marriage where

> each could live his life according to his own work and its needs . . . That will make things much simpler, and advance us both, whereas this exhausting and anxious life together is a dangerous and hopeless standstill. I believe with all my heart that Clara Westhoff can reach the greatest heights as an artist, and it was in this conviction that I joined her, not to disturb her and turn her into a "housewife", but on the contrary to help her follow, quietly and securely, the road she had taken alone with such courage.

A year and a half into his marriage—and eight months after the birth of his daughter—Rilke left Worpswede for Paris, where he had arranged a commission to write a monograph on Westhoff's old teacher, Auguste Rodin. Abandoning Clara Westhoff—"of whose art," he said, "I expect the greatest things!"—he could no longer fulfill their marriage, since it had been made, he said, "in order that each might better help the other to his work and to himself . . . But Clara Westhoff . . . has to think of Ruth as well as of herself and her development." Clara ultimately left Ruth with her parents, and in October she followed Rilke to Paris.

In Rodin, Rilke found someone before whom he could prostrate himself, and now Rodin's old age and his authority inspired Rilke to turn industrious solitude into a religious devotion. At sixty-two, in 1902, Rodin was established with his long companion Rose Beuret—he had long ago concluded his passionate and disastrous affair with Camille Claudel—and Rilke was deeply encouraged by his creative lifestyle. He wrote to Clara that Rodin had told him,

> with wonderful seriousness . . . il faut travailler, rien que travailler. Et il faut avoir patience . . . Tolstoy's unedifying household, the discomfort of Rodin's rooms: it all points to the same thing: that one must choose either this or that. Either happiness or art. On doit trouver le bonheur dans son art.

With this philosophy of work, Rilke kept himself apart from Clara, and when Clara followed him to Paris in October, they lodged separately: they would be united only in working "as we have never worked before" to make the art that might one day support them.

Paris both knitted Rilke together and tore him apart. He had found a mentor in Rodin, but compared with Rodin's sculptures—and the physical conditions of Paris, which he experienced as terrifyingly filthy—Rilke's words did not seem to have the same enduring reality, and the rootless poet, who had given up wife and family for his work, experienced the city as a "vast screaming prison." Broken down by loneliness and isolation—unsure how he would ever make poetry under the conditions of his panic and dread, he fled from Paris to the Italian coast, and from there, in June 1903, he broke the two-year silence with Andreas-Salomé: he asked her for "just a single day" in which he might "seek refuge" with her—and Andreas.

While Rilke had been living in Paris and writing his monograph on Rodin—and then another on the Worpswede artists—Andreas-Salomé had been writing and traveling with Zemek, and in the summer of 1901, she appears to have aborted another pregnancy. She continued to travel with Zemek after she and her husband moved to Göttingen, in north-central Germany, in June 1903. Andreas had taken a professorship that would give him a steady income, high status, and freedom to teach in his own home, with refreshments of his own preparation, as was his custom. He created a close-knit community of students, and he became famous for his midnight seminars, where he would regale his devoted students with stories and Asian fare. But he never did complete the definitive work on Persian philology he was preparing—he could never stop researching, to produce a final draft, and his notes were only published by his students after his death. Andreas-Salomé had not been productive from 1901 to 1903, either: she was traveling more than she was writing, and she did not publish anything between 1901 and 1904.

In response to Rilke's request for a meeting in 1903, she said that he could "stay with us any time, in difficult as in good hours." But she was still seeing Zemek, and she proposed that she and Rilke "first reunite in writing. For two old scribblers like us there would be nothing artificial in proceeding this way." Rilke wrote back, describing his fears—of the street people, who had raised a fascination and a horror in him, and also of other, childhood terrors. "I can't ask anyone for advice but you," he wrote. "You alone know who I am. Only you can help me ... You can make me understand what baffles me, you can tell me what I need to do; you know what I *should* be afraid of and what I shouldn't—: *should* I be afraid?"

From her new home in Göttingen, Andreas-Salomé pointed out that instead of feeling fear, Rilke should feel joy, because now the street people "have you as their poet." She told Rilke that his long and detailed description of his horror was in itself evidence that he was "standing already where even in the best subsequent times you have only occasionally stood: undivided from yourself." Turning his hysteria into a sign of health, she told him that "the poet in you [has] created poetry out of the man's fears . . . You have never been closer to the health you wish for than now!" When he was afraid, she said, he should "write about how you feel and what's tormenting you—write it out of your system, as it were; this in itself may generate some curative strength."

Now that his fears had been soothed, and elevated, Rilke described the failure of his marriage:

> I used to think it would be better, if I would one day have a house, a wife and a child, things that were real and undeniable. I thought that I would become more visible, more palpable, more real. But, see, Westerwede [near Worpswede] was real. I really did build my own house and everything that was in it. But it was an external reality and I did not live and expand within it. And now that I no longer have that little house and its lovely quiet rooms, I know that there is a person still there. And somewhere a child in whose life nothing is closer than she and I. This gives me a certain assurance and the experience of many simple and deep things, but it does not give me the feeling of reality, that sense of equal worth, that I so sorely need: to be a real person among real things.

At the same time that Rilke was complaining that "no one can depend on me: my little child must live with strangers, my young wife, who also has her work, needs others to provide for her instruction, and I myself am no use anywhere and acquire nothing," he was also, in his decisions, effectively stating his devotion to Andreas-Salomé, who had predicted that he should keep himself aloof for art, and "take the same path" she had taken "toward your dark god."

Now that they were back in touch, Rilke asked Andreas-Salomé to "read [the monographs] . . . as you read these letters; for there is much in them that I wrote to you and with rich awareness of your existence." Her response to the books was a consummation of all his hopes—now he could see the very real effect of his writing in her response:

When your *Rodin* arrived and I gradually realized what was in it, I felt: it will be a long time now before I can write you! I wanted to retreat into long, uninterrupted stretches of calm and take my fill of this little book, which has the greatness of many thousand pages. It is unbelievably valuable to me, perhaps—no, beyond doubt—the most valuable of all your published books.

When she made her analysis, now, she described his poetry as separate from and even antagonistic to his physical health, and she described his creative urges themselves as demon lovers that "had to turn their energy against your own self, had, as it were, to hold in thrall *your own body* like a vampire." She celebrated his suffering:

> You have undergone such severe after-shocks, and yet only because so much that is completely new has been born in you. Therefore you suffer, and I rejoice: for how should I not rejoice when you reveal even in the expression of your suffering who you have become. This happiness that lies over your letters has not yet filtered down to you yourself: but it is indeed yours, and in its shade you will yet find sanctuary from everything that would cause you harm.

Now that he was suffering for the elevated purpose of art—now that his poetry had found its own object in his other self—not in her—her next letter had the effect of a wedding between them:

> You gave yourself to your opposite, your complement, to a longed-for exemplar,—gave yourself the way one gives oneself in marriage—. I don't know how else to express it,—there is for me a feeling of betrothal in this book,—of a sacred dialogue, of being admitted into what one was not but now, in a mystery, has become . . . I believe that in such experiences one touches the very limits of human possibility, one provides oneself evidence *of who one is*— . . . I for my part am certain now of what you are: and this is the most personal thing about this book for me, that I believe us to be allies in the difficult mysteries of living and dying, two people united in that sense of the eternal which binds human beings together. From this moment on you can count on me.

IX.

Andreas-Salomé and Rilke now began to exchange long, encouraging, and prophetic letters—which she never again asked him to destroy—which rhapsodized about the life that was an art, the art that was a life. While his letters to friends and patrons would describe his problems with jobs and money, or the logistics of constantly moving, his letters to Andreas-Salomé would simply contain his confessions and physiological torments: he would describe his psychological and physical ailments to her, then ask for her advice. Rilke's health was never, in fact, very good, but these long complaints also ultimately served as preparation for creative periods, as he cleared his correspondence and settled down to work. Later in his life, he would write as many as eighty letters in a month before sitting down to write poems, but no one else received letters with such detailed self-analysis.

Now that Rilke had witnessed Rodin's creative lifestyle, he began to quest for the uninterrupted time and quiet for writing poetry—but when this was hard to find, he began to use letters as a surrogate art form. When a young cadet, Franz Kappus, wrote to ask him for advice about poetry, Rilke's responses—which would be published posthumously as *Letters to a Young Poet*—echoed Andreas-Salomé in treating separation as a proof of devotion:

> To love is . . . good, for love is difficult. For one human being to love another is perhaps the most difficult task of all, the epitome, the ultimate test . . .
>
> Love does not at first have anything to do with arousal, surrender, and uniting with another being—for what union can be built upon uncertainty, immaturity, and lack of coherence? Love is a high inducement for individuals to ripen, to strive to mature in the inner self, to manifest maturity in the outer world, to become that manifestation for the sake of another. This a great, demanding task; it calls one to expand one's horizon greatly . . . It is the final goal, perhaps one which human beings as yet hardly ever seek to attain . . .
>
> The responsibility that the difficult work of love demands of our evolvement overwhelms us; it is larger than life. We, as yet beginners, are not equal to it . . .

We are just now reaching the point where we can observe objectively and without judgment the relationship of one individual to a second one. Our attempts to live such a relationship are without a model. Yet, there already exist within our time frame some things intended to help our faint-hearted beginner's steps.

Rilke took the same view of his marriage, for he wrote to his brother-in-law in early 1904 that

> Clara and I . . . have come to an understanding in the very fact that all companionship can consist only in the strengthening of two neighboring solitudes, whereas everything that one is wont to call giving oneself is by nature harmful to companionship: for when a person abandons himself, he is no longer anything, and when two people both give themselves up in order to come close to each other, there is no longer any ground beneath them and their being together is a continual falling.
>
> So whoever loves must try to act as if he had a great work: he must be much alone and go into himself and collect himself and hold fast to himself; he must work; he must become something!

At last Rilke began this work himself—not by returning to Andreas-Salomé or Clara, but by writing out his fears, and in Rome in 1903 and then in Sweden in 1904, he gave his anxieties a voice in his *Journal of My Other Self*—which would become *The Notebooks of Malte Laurids Brigge*. He described his terrors in Paris, and the freedom to indulge his inmost fears was both a relief and a way to give his existence solidity in itself.

Things that existed in their own right still terrified him, though—even his daughter: when he returned from Rome to Oberneuland and his in-laws for Christmas 1903, he wrote that two-year-old Ruth "already seems a complicated little personality of her own, and I shall have to go a long way, with great attention, to find her." Insufficient even to his infant daughter, the one thing Rilke wanted was to return to Andreas-Salomé. From Rome, he ultimately asked for permission to come live nearby in Göttingen. "I see for miles around," he wrote, "no other thought, no source of trust which I can truly believe might help me." Andreas-Salomé did not encourage him—she was still involved with Zemek—but one of her feminist friends stepped in to at least answer his question of where to go.

Andreas-Salomé had known Ellen Key since 1897, when she reviewed Key's feminist writings: Key was eleven years older than Andreas-Salomé, and deeply maternal—she loved "odd people," she said, and she became Rilke's first patron and supporter. She collected his writing, and she gave him the proceeds when she lectured on his work. Now she arranged an invitation to a vacant country house in Sweden, where Rilke spent six months of 1904, writing *Malte*. Andreas-Salomé had not yet allowed him to visit her, and she did not see Rilke when she passed through Copenhagen on her way to Russia and her family with Zemek, but Rilke continued to request a meeting into January of 1905—"a reunion with you is the single bridge to my future,—you know that, Lou," he wrote—before she finally agreed to a visit.

Before he saw Andreas-Salomé in Göttingen that summer, though, Rilke used some money that had come to him through Ellen Key to take Clara for a cure at the Weisser Hirsch sanitarium near Dresden. It was a luxurious way to spend the money, but it proved to be wise in the end, because with his unique combination of talent and diligence, grace and refinement—along with his bad health, helplessness, and poverty—he was an excellent candidate for the patronage of the aristocrats he met there. He already had Ellen Key's endorsement, and now when he met Countess Luise von Schwerin and writer Rudolf Kassner, he was taken up as a cause, and in the next few years, they would introduce him to patrons who would support him with money and estates to write in for the rest of his life.

By the time Rilke came to Göttingen in the summer of 1905, he brought with him the finished *Book of Hours*, the monk's love poems to God, now expanded to three parts of sensitive, devout love poems. After a visit consisting of barefoot walks in the woods and long conversations, Andreas-Salomé wrote to Rilke in her memoir that after *Book of Hours*,

> for the first time the "work" itself—what it would become through you, and what it would require of you—seemed to me to be your rightful lord and master. What more would it ask of you? . . . From that Whitsuntide on I read your work on my own, and not just when I was with you. I opened myself to it, welcomed it as an expression of your destiny, which was not to be denied. And in so doing I became yours once again, in a second way—*in a second maidenhood.*

As she entered her second innocence with Rilke, Andreas-Salomé was hardly a threat to Rilke's marriage; rather she was now a resource he wanted to share with Clara, and he wrote to her from Göttingen, wishing that "this person, who plays such a big part in my inner history, [might] be . . . indispensable and essential to you too." Westhoff and Andreas-Salomé did meet eventually, and a friendship developed between them, although when Rilke heard, a year later, that Andreas-Salomé had visited Clara—and that Andreas-Salomé had been critical of him for abandoning her—he wrote to cast their marriage in his own terms. From Capri in 1906, he asked Clara:

> how can the circumstance refute me that we must keep postponing our life together, which practically too is one of mutual support, since only with you two did my world grow into the nameless . . . If we are living thus separated from each other by days of travel, and trying to do that which our hearts require of us day and night (are we not turning away from the difficult for the sake of the difficult? . . .) tell me: isn't there a house about us after all, a real one, for which only the visible sign is lacking so that others do not see it?

Rilke and Clara would live nearby each other from time to time in their travels, but they would never return to a house together. Following the 1905 visit to the Weisser Hirsch sanitarium—and then the reunion with Andreas-Salomé—he began to draw close to other women, who would shed their selves like cloaks (to use Paula Becker's metaphor) only to find that he was only placing their admiration between himself and the ground. For Rilke did not become any more capable of supporting women over time. In two affairs in Paris, he let wealthy women draw close to him, only to withdraw into solitude and work. When one lover had a breakdown a year later, he told her brother that he could not help: "you overrate me . . . I am no support . . . I'm only a voice." "I *implore* those who love me," he wrote to the daughter of a patron, "to love my solitude."

Making his home in his work, Rilke returned to Paris in September 1905 to work as Rodin's secretary, but now, when Rodin dismissed him because of a misunderstanding, he was continuously supported by patrons. He kept rooms in Paris, he put the finishing touches on *Cornet*, and he wrote new poems, *The Book of Images*. In 1907, he went on a reading tour and wrote another book, *New Poems*, which saw things with sculptor's eyes, stripping away the poetic self to present the panther, the gazelle, a sculpted torso of Apollo as they might be to themselves. The following year, Anton Kippenberg, his publisher, acquired rights for his earlier work, and started to pay him a quarterly stipend, so that by the summer of 1909, Rilke had a secure income, and he could offer Clara a place to work in Paris—although Ruth still remained in Oberneuland with her grandparents.

Rilke's stipend was really an advance on installments, so now he needed to produce the longer work he had promised: he returned to *The Notebooks of Malte Laurids Brigge*, the narrative of a young Danish man who felt all of the sensitivities and anxieties Rilke had felt in Paris. *Malte* turned Rilke's sensitive longings and disappointments into the foundation for attentive spiritual devotion, for the book turned sensitivity to and unrequited affection for things into wealth and strength: "to be loved means to be consumed," Rilke wrote. "To love means to radiate with inexhaustible light. To be loved is to pass away. To love is to endure."

Finishing *Malte* in May of 1910, Rilke fell into a depression: externalizing his fears had left him not only exposed but creatively empty, and now he sought out the company of women as a balm. After a reunion with a lover in Janowitz, he set off to North Africa with a patroness, although he withdrew from the trip when he could not sustain the elevated tone of the affair. Like Andreas-Salomé, he would not preserve any record of his affairs—only those that elicited his most poetic letters—and his lovers are just as indistinct in his biographies as Andreas-Salomé's husband and lovers are in hers: anything that was not poetry fell away.

But there were details to be arranged nonetheless. In order to keep up with his aristocratic patrons, Rilke affected a fastidious appearance, and even though he was always running out of funds and begging his publisher for money, his helplessness continued to elicit support, from Kippenberg and others. He would continue all his life to make exquisite and thoughtful gifts to his patrons and friends, and he was always ordering and then abandoning books and furniture when he moved, but the persona of the poet—dedicated to his art above all things—was good publicity in selling his books, and in 1911, Rilke finally came into real financial stability, as Kippenberg, Kassner, and Harry Graf Kessler collaborated to give him an income that would cover his necessities—at least for the next three years. He would always overspend, though, and beg Kippenberg for advances—which were almost always paid, even though the sales of his books never kept pace with them.

Returning to Paris in 1911, broke and emotionally spent from the trip to North Africa, Rilke was looking for a single person to take him in. The woman he found was not a lover but a prostitute, eighteen-year-old Marthe Hennebert, whom he rescued from a brothel. Taking her up in her helplessness—providing the assistance she needed—he rallied his aristocratic supporters, and found her a home with artists who taught her a craft. They never became lovers, but Marie Taxis later said that he was "closer to this young girl than to any other woman."

While Rilke was making arrangements for Marthe Hennebert, though, Clara was finally liberating herself from their marriage: she had moved to Munich with Ruth, and she had been in therapy since the spring of 1911. By summer, she could no longer sustain the illusion of marriage, and she filed for divorce. Rilke was in favor of the divorce—he told Andreas-Salomé that "there is no ill will between us, but as my wife she does, so to speak, go around falsely labeled, is not with me and yet cannot move on to anything free of me"—but because of their numerous international relocations, in addition to gaps in the original paperwork, the divorce was prevented by bureaucratic difficulties. Rilke and Clara would spend a good deal of time and money on lawyers, but they would remain married until Rilke's death in 1926.

By the middle of 1911, in the creative vacuum after *Malte*, in the aftermath of his flight from North Africa, and now in the middle of complex divorce proceedings, Rilke began to despair. Andreas-Salomé had known Clara's therapist, Victor Emil von Gebsattel, since 1906, and now, at the end of 1911, Rilke thought that therapy might help him, and he asked Andreas-Salomé for Gebsattel's address.

X.

When Andreas-Salomé got Rilke's request for Gebsattel's address—and then his letters describing his ailments and fears—she was just coming back to life herself. She had split with Zemek in 1908—for reasons that are not recorded—and the period from 1906 to 1909 was more social than literary for her: she had traveled with Zemek, she had been frequently sick, and she had socialized in Berlin. But the record of her travels is sparse, and biographers can say nothing about her movements in 1907 and 1908. The record resumes in the summer of 1908, for an August tour of the Balkans with Zemek, before they split up. When a close friend of hers died in early 1909, Andreas-Salomé inquired to Ellen Key about poisons that might kill her painlessly, without leaving any trace—but she never followed up with her inquiry. Instead she met and befriended Ellen Delp, a young woman who had admired her novel *Ruth*, and now Delp traveled with her in Zemek's absence. Soon Andreas-Salomé began to refer to her as her daughter, and she would take on other "daughters" as travel companions over the years.

That May, of 1909, she, Rilke, and Clara had a reunion in Paris, with Rodin, and when Rilke sent her his new *Book of Images*, she had celebrated

how exceptionally life has favored you with this possession, Rainer. And, you know, this is surely one more reason why full human honesty in artistic matters is even more important than in relations with other human beings: without it, one would lose this refuge within oneself. The only undeceiving one.

I have been together with you so strongly during this entire time that it feels odd having to write.

Now, when Rilke wrote to ask for Gebsattel's address, Andreas-Salomé was strenuously opposed to therapy. She argued, as she had argued before, that he would always make himself both ill and healthy—although biographers point out that she must have wanted to keep Gebsattel from helping Rilke pry into her psyche. But Rilke was only flirting with analysis himself: he never followed through with Gebsattel, because he was afraid that psychoanalysis would be "too fundamental a help, it helps once and for all, makes a clean sweep of things, and to find myself swept clean one day might be even more hopeless than this disarray."

Apparently the combination of self-help and aristocratic support—in addition to the long self-exploring letters he wrote to Andreas-Salomé—created exactly the conditions he needed, for shortly after his flirtation with psychoanalysis, he retreated to the Adriatic coast, where Princess Marie Taxis had offered him Duino Castle, high above the sea. From this isolated castle, where he did not have to provide for anyone—on a day that likely brought letters from both Gebsattel and his divorce lawyer—Rilke wrote three poems and additional fragments of a ten-poem cycle that would constitute his master work. "Who, if I cried out, would hear me among the angels' / hierarchies?" he wrote, taking down the lines as if from dictation, from the voice he had always been waiting to be filled by. When he sent the poems to Andreas-Salomé, she responded that it was "the joyful cry of the consummate artist. It is no longer a question of his existence . . . Unity is achieved in the work itself; the angels are *created*." Like *Malte*, the First Elegy idealizes unfulfilled desire: "when you feel longing / . . . Sing / of women abandoned and desolate (you envy them, almost) / who could love so much more purely than those who were gratified." It would take Rilke ten years to finish the cycle of poems—but now his faith had been borne out: he could point to something on paper to show what his devotion and aspiration had created. Now there was something, not just an infinite expectation.

Having pointed Rilke away from psychoanalysis earlier in 1911, Andreas-Salomé attended the Psychoanalytic Congress herself in the fall. A new young lover, Poul Bjerre—a distant cousin of Ellen Key's, fifteen years younger than Andreas-Salomé, who had just turned fifty in February—took her to Vienna and introduced her to Freud. She had not published anything since 1909, but she had turned from fiction toward psychology, with essays on God and "the erotic effect," which celebrated the selflessness of the woman who gives her lovers, her children, and her creations to the world. She did not fully enter the psychoanalytic world in this visit, but she spent the intervening winter studying psychoanalysis, and when she returned to Vienna in 1912, she obtained Freud's permission to join his Wednesday meetings and his university course.

Andreas-Salomé did not devote herself to Freud without also cultivating a relationship with Alfred Adler, a recent defector from Freud's circle. Freud asked her to create "an artificial psychic split" for his sake, "never mentioning there your form of existence here and vice versa," and Andreas-Salomé soon deserted Adler, who wanted her to explore her role as a woman. She did not begin to practice or theorize psychoanalysis, though: she sought to befriend Freud personally, and in two meetings with him, she analyzed her own hatred for her mother as against her lifelong love for her father, attributing creativity to anal erotism—in which, Freud said, "we grasp a work of ours, something objectivized, as ourselves"—and love to infant narcissism, which she portrayed as the first psychic reality.

Andreas-Salomé found lovers from among the psychoanalytic circles, but she had taken so much of her own self-prescribed solitary independence that these men were merely companions who accompanied her back to her youth, and the greater part of these relationships passed in letters as she traveled. Generally these younger men saw her as a woman of boundless optimism, even of genius, but she always pushed them away—and asked them to burn her letters—before the relationships could demand too much from her.

Without any formal training, Andreas-Salomé took patients for psychoanalysis in Berlin starting in October 1913, and when she finally told Freud that she was practicing in 1917, he began to send her money to supplement her wage: she had been seeing patients for less than half the professional rate. Andreas-Salomé worshipped Freud as another father figure, although there is a certain wariness in his view of her imperturbable happiness: "even after we've talked about the most terrible things," he said, "you look like Christmas is coming." Unlike the journals she kept during her other relationships, Andreas-Salomé's notes from 1912 to 1913 were published as *The Freud Journal*, and she published an open letter, *My Thanks to Freud*, as her personal commentary on psychoanalysis—although it was not the academic article Freud and his circle had hoped she would contribute.

Except for some impromptu dream analyses, Andreas-Salomé did not analyze Rilke—she kept to her old formula of self-help through art as the answer for psychosomatic ailments—and when Rilke descended into despair again after writing the first of the *Duino Elegies*—he could never tell where he would ever find the peace and quiet in which to finish the series—she asked him to believe in the same fictional relationship he had asked Clara to see. From Vienna in January 1913, she said that "it should be possible for us to be together quietly and without any effort at all on invisible paths" instead of seeing each other in person. She celebrated the notion that he "*must* suffer, and that it will always be so" although she claimed that "a thousand maternal tendernesses are ripe inside me now for you and only for you," and she prophesied that "however long it may take to happen, we *will* rejoice in being with each other again, and will revel also in all the dangers that life, for each of us individually, has in store."

After having met Freud himself at the 1912 psychoanalysis congress in Munich, Rilke had professed "to be once more my own severest doctor: alone and quiet," but his solitude still bore the imprint of his first months with Andreas-Salomé: "long walks in the woods, going barefoot and letting my beard grow day and night, a lamp in the evening, a warm room." If Rilke remained true, all his life, to the abstract union he and Andreas-Salomé had always prophesied—and if he accepted as well that suffering was inextricably linked with writing—he was nevertheless still anxious for a companion who would accompany him through his torments and through his longing: he described himself in a letter to Andreas-Salomé as "always standing at a telescope, ascribing to every woman who approached a happiness that was certainly never to be found with any of them: my happiness, the happiness, long ago, of my most solitary hours." Two years, now, from forty, itinerant, half-divorced, and poetically still only half-begun, he confessed his insufficiency in love to Princess Marie Taxis:

> I've neither the experience which could help in a detached way, nor the love which can find inspiration in the heart. I can never be the lover, this touches me only from without, perhaps because no one has ever truly overwhelmed me, perhaps because I do not love my mother . . . For me all love is an effort, a task, *surmenage* [overwork]; only towards God have I a certain facility in loving.

XI.

For four months in the beginning of 1914, Rilke let himself believe that his hopes and expectations were being fulfilled, after he got a letter from Magda von Hattingberg, a concert pianist from Vienna, who was eight years younger than him. As usual, Rilke asked her to love his solitude, but after a month of elevated letters, he gave up Paris and a winter of planned work to move to Berlin, and then to travel with her. They could not sustain the intensity of their first letters, though, and while the correspondence would be published as a testament to their affection, they separated in May. Rilke described the affair to Andreas-Salomé in June:

> What finally turned out so absolutely to my misery began with many, many letters, light, beautiful letters that came rushing out of my heart: I can scarcely remember ever having written such letters before . . . if it is possible for someone inwardly turbid and muddied to become clear, that happened to me in those letters. The everyday and my relationship to it became to me in some indescribable way sacred and accountable, . . . so that for the first time I seemed to become the owner of my life.

Poetic intensity notwithstanding, this breakup was embarrassing for Rilke, since he had rhapsodized about Hattingberg to Princess Marie

Taxis, and now he could see his soured enthusiasm through her eyes, but if he became more and more self-aware, from relationship to relationship, the course of his affairs would never alter much. After a few passionate months came the "terror, flight, retreat back into the forfeited solitude," and when he reflected on his career as a lover, he could only console himself with the quality of the initial moments: "what at most I can have in common with others are just fleeting moments: meetings—but who can complain, when granted such encounters, that he is denied true contact."

Andreas-Salomé and Rilke were both in Germany when the Great War broke out in August of 1914—Andreas-Salomé in Göttingen, Rilke in Munich—and they both stayed in Germany for the war's duration. Rilke spent most of it in Munich—a center of antiwar activity—seeing a lover in between his travels to Berlin and elsewhere. Restricted in her travels during the war, Andreas-Salomé saw psychoanalytic patients in her home—and a few by correspondence—and she wrote about narcissism and infant sexuality, elaborating her psychoanalytic theories in essays that trace the infantile sense of unity with the world through artistic and psychosexual development.

By 1919, at age fifty-eight, Andreas-Salomé had been working as a therapist in Göttingen for almost five years—but she had once again returned to writing fiction, and she wrote that over "these three years past," her stories had become "as important to me as in my early youth." She visited with Rilke and his lover in Munich for two months of readings and conversations, after which she once again asked Rilke to believe in their abstract relationship:

> I must always remind myself that the magic of our subterranean connection does remain with me, and that it would persist even if neither of us were to be aware of it. But I didn't tell you even once what it meant to me to feel such connectedness enter my bright day, such hour-by-hour reality of knowing you were only a few streets away. When we went to the dance-recital that morning I was so close to being able to say it, and yet even then I *could not*.

After this visit, Rilke left Germany for the more stable economic and political environment of Switzerland. He would never return to Germany, and Andreas-Salomé, now nearing sixty, was no longer traveling as freely as she had. They would never see each other again, but of course they would continue to write to each other.

XII.

Try though he might to find a place where he could write out the remaining elegies in peace, safe from distracting lovers, Rilke could not resist entering into another affair, with Elisabeth (Baladine) Klossowska, a young painter who was separated from her husband, living with her two small boys. Rilke and Klossowska met in Switzerland in 1919, and corresponded until they became lovers in August 1920. Unlike almost all of his other lovers, Klossowska did not come to Rilke through his poetry—they met with exile from Paris in common—and this relationship proceeded on different terms than any of his other affairs. Having always been quick to use the familiar *tu* or *du* with women, he now retained the formal *vous* or *Sie*, and when his correspondence with Klossowska took place in French, he began to sign himself René again, dropping Andreas-Salomé's "Rainer." But Rilke undermined Klossowska even as he gave her a larger place in his life than many of his other lovers: in a letter to his longtime patron Marie Taxis—who had given Rilke the title "Doctor Seraphico"— he wrote that Klossowska saw his writing as the "work" of an "author" when he was trying to "create a universe."

Intimacy with Klossowska did not prevent Rilke from accepting another patron's invitation to spend the winter in solitude in a castle near Zurich, leaving Klossowska in Geneva with her boys. "But we are human beings, René," she objected, when he told her that he had left. He spent the winter of 1920–1921 alone in Berg, trying to finish the *Duino Elegies*, but when Klossowska and her boys needed to return to Berlin, to reclaim possessions abandoned during the war, he lost a good deal of his hard-won solitude in helping her make arrangements from his distance. Losing his solitude sent him into a deep depression again, during which he finally turned against love:

> For a spirit which finds fulfillment in [subordination to work], the state of *being loved* will perhaps always turn out a misfortune … Thus the love-experience appears like a stunted, unfit subsidiary form of the creative experience, almost its degradation—and remains incapable of achievement, unmastered and, measured against the higher order of successful creativity, impermissible.

For its isolation, though, Berg became another Duino, symbolizing the quintessential solitary, literary experience, and he began to look for "a second Berg" for the following winter. Klossowska entered the search with him, and that summer, traveling in Sierre in Switzerland, they found Muzot, a thirteenth-century stone manor house—final *t* pronounced, he would say. The building offered only primitive accommodations, but it would be a place of his own, and Rilke convinced a patron, Werner Reinhart, to buy, decorate, and repair the house, with the understanding that Rilke would live there when he was not traveling.

Rilke lived in Muzot for six months with Klossowska—him upstairs, her downstairs—and her presence touched off an extremely productive time for him. After more than a month of letter-writing, and then translation work, he finished the remaining seven *Duino Elegies* and wrote all fifty-seven Sonnets to Orpheus in a two-week creative burst in February 1922. After finishing the elegies, it was to Andreas-Salomé that he celebrated first: "now I know myself again. It was like a constant mutilation of my heart that the *Elegies* were not—here. They are. They are." Ready to share in the triumph of the love they had shared through his creativity, she wrote that she "sat and read and cried from joy and it was not just joy at all but something much more powerful, as if a curtain were being parted, rent, and everything were growing quiet and certain and present and good." Three weeks later, she wrote, "*I can never tell you*: how much this means to me and how I have unconsciously been waiting to receive what is *Yours* as also *Mine*, as life's true consummation. I will remain grateful to you for this until the end, until the new primal beginning, dear, dear Rainer." Rilke in turn responded with gratitude, "That you are there, dear, dear Lou, to seal it so joyously in my inmost heart with your response!" Andreas-Salomé went further than simply praising his work to him: she put his poems to use, and in 1923, she paid him the compliment of describing how his poems had brought her patients back to life, when they saw how alive things could be.

Rilke was eventually won away from Klossowska—who returned to Zurich while he wrote in solitude—by an epistolary correspondence with Marina Tsvetaeva, a Russian poet living in exile in Paris, but by 1923, his ailments were finally restricting his movements—the leukemia that would kill him was beginning to express itself—and they never met in person. He did make one flight to Paris, in 1925, where he had reunions with lovers and patrons in a whirlwind of readings and visits, but he ultimately retreated to Muzot and then to the Valmont clinic, where his illness was being treated.

Doctors did not understand leukemia very well in the 1920s, so when Rilke suffered sores on the inside of his mouth, in addition to pain and weight loss, Andreas-Salomé—the only correspondent to whom he described his health—attributed his symptoms, as always, to psychological causes. In a letter to her, he described his illness as an adverse effect of masturbation, which he had resumed at the time of his relapse.

> For two whole years I have been living increasingly in the very midst of an alarm, whose most palpable cause (a self-induced stimulation) I invariably, with devilish obsession, exacerbate just when I think I have overcome the temptation to indulge it. It is a horrible circle, a ring of evil magic that encloses me as into a picture of Hell by Breughel.

Without any medical knowledge, Andreas-Salomé attributed his sores to his creativity:

> The tipping-over into the realm of the tormented, the forsaken, the being at the mercy of one's own body,—it's not something you experience merely as a reaction after tension-filled creative work; on the contrary, it has been from the first *intrinsic to* that work: the reverse of the thing itself, and the devil merely a *deus inversus*.

Rilke made sure that no one who cared for him saw how sick he was— he confessed his feelings only to Andreas-Salomé. It was common practice at the time to keep information from patients, so he was never told of his prognosis, but he described his illness as "an inevitable mystery, which ought not to be analysed too closely." Still, he wanted Andreas-Salomé to know everything about him, and his friend and patron Nanny Wunderly told her that he had said "Lou must be told everything— perhaps she will know of some consolation."

Andreas-Salomé's last surviving letter to Rilke was written a year before Rilke died, although she got letters from his nurses right up until his death. Toward the end, a nurse wrote that when she had "asked him whether to write you again, he said *no*, with a wave of his hand." His last letter to her began and ended in Russian, recalling the period of their deepest intimacy: "farewell, my love," he wrote, and he died in his doctor's arms two weeks later, on December 29, 1926. Neither Andreas-Salomé nor Klossowska nor Clara Westhoff came to his funeral a few days later: only one of his ex-lovers joined patrons and friends to see him interred in Switzerland. Clara Westhoff, who had come to see him in his decline, had been turned away.

XIII.

A year after Rilke's death, Andreas-Salomé published her Rilke memoir, *You Alone Are Real to Me*, which reprised her portrait of Nietzsche in describing a creative genius whose body was insufficient to the demands of his art. She would outlive Rilke by just over ten years—she died a week shy of her seventy-sixth birthday in February of 1937—and she practiced psychoanalysis and wrote her memoirs until her deteriorating health prevented her working. In 1929, she was hospitalized with diabetes, and in 1930, three years after Rilke died, she was widowed when Andreas died of cancer. She started her memoirs in 1931, and there wrote that she had "held aloof from [her husband's colleagues], antagonized them, offended against all civility, twenty-seven years long, and now suddenly stood amidst their pure tenderness and warmth."

When Freud had not permitted her the same intimacy she had enjoyed with Nietzsche and Rilke, she befriended his daughter, exchanging visits and long letters. In her last surviving letter to him in 1935, she said that she wished she "might look into your face for but ten minutes—into the father-face over my life"—but Freud resisted her tendency to call him father, preferring to see himself as a brother, with the other analysts. In 1933, at seventy-two, she became a mother when she formally adopted her brother Sacha's son—her literary executor had fled Germany, and she wanted an heir—but when relations turned sour between them, she sought to undo the adoption, and found another executor, settling her estate three years before she died.

Andreas's daughter, Mariechen, acted as her primary caretaker when Andreas-Salomé went nearly blind from diabetes, and then had a mastectomy in 1935. By that time, she had added a confessional epilogue to Rilke in her memoirs:

> Even in that concerned and ardent closeness, I still stood outside the circle of that which fully links a man and woman . . .
>
> How many times I held my head in my hands back then, struggling to understand it myself. And how deeply disconcerted I was when, leafing through an old and tattered diary . . . I read the nakedly honest sentence: "I'll be true to my memories forever, but I'll never be true to other people."

XIV.

This determined disloyalty has made Lou Andreas-Salomé's legacy a controversial one. Generally she is celebrated, as she clearly wished to be, as the muse who inspired Nietzsche, Rilke, and Freud. Rilke seems to have shared her sentiment—he remained true only to his poetry, as well—but their marriages and their minor relationships alike show us human beings behind the relentlessly happy, or relentlessly elevated souls, who blithely—or in torment, respectively—considered every experience as an opportunity for art and devotion.

To tell the story of this man and this woman—to tell the detailed story of the present moments in which they lived, loved, and wrote—and to describe in detail the relationships and emotions they hid—from each other and from themselves—is to work against the grain of their writing—and of their relationship, where they consistently strove for a creative lifestyle that was not artistic but art itself. So long as they could consign their failed relationships to silence—so long as they could recast the injuries they suffered (or inflicted) as sacrifices they made for art (breakups they described as gifts, torments they described as encouragements), so long as they could turn solitude into love, and torment into devotion, they could still see their poems, their letters, and their relationships as artworks: everything else was left in the abyss, uncreated.

The artists who followed in their footsteps—keeping apart from marriage, holding tight to a transcendent bond beyond it, keeping faith in acts of creativity—would feel these same impulses: to turn life into art, to decide what was or was not to be included. The movement over the course of the twentieth century would be toward more and more detailed confessions of the difficulties entailed in creative marriages, but Andreas-Salomé and Rilke retain their relevance even to the present day. Steadfastly they insisted on the art experience in which human life is transformed into something eternal, beautiful to the point of being terrifying—even if it was also terrifying for the degree to which it just barely repressed the desires and dissatisfactions that keep art—and marriage—from ever being pure and complete works in themselves.

Chapter Two

Mutually Sustaining Visions

Alfred Stieglitz and Georgia O'Keeffe

⟨⟨⟨∞⟩⟩⟩

I believe it was the work that kept me with him, though I loved him as a human being. I could see his strengths and weaknesses. I put up with what seemed to me a good deal of contradictory nonsense because of what seemed clear and bright and wonderful.   Georgia O'Keeffe

My biography will be a simple affair. If you can imagine photography in the guise of a woman & you'd ask her what she thought of Stieglitz, she'd say: He always treated me as a gentleman.   Alfred Stieglitz

The relationship was really very good, because it was based on something more than just emotional needs. Each of us was really interested in what the other was doing. Of course, you do your best to destroy each other without knowing it.   Georgia O'Keeffe

I.

On New Year's Day 1916, Georgia O'Keeffe's art school friend Anita Pollitzer showed up at Alfred Stieglitz' gallery at 291 Fifth Avenue, with O'Keeffe's drawings in a tube under her arm. O'Keeffe had sent her friend the drawings from Columbia, South Carolina, where, at twenty-nine years old, she was teaching art to schoolgirls. O'Keeffe had not suggested that Pollitzer should ask Stieglitz for his opinion of the drawings. She only told her that she wanted to be rid of them: she said that she had expressed something so personal that she could not look at them anymore.

The abstract charcoals of seething, elemental forms marked the end

of a season of crisis for O'Keeffe. She had left her friends and the New
York art world behind her to take the job in South Carolina, but she did
not see herself as launching her career as a teacher. She had only taken
the job because it would pay her enough to get by and still leave her time
to paint, and the other teachers recognized that she was not one of them.
All fall she had been isolated, full of dread that she might never make
anything that would distinguish her as an artist.

O'Keeffe had been working hard at her paintings that term, but she had also been hoping that a man would give her some of the support and approval that would make her feel at home in the world, both as a woman and as an artist. She had taken a liking to Columbia University political science professor Arthur Macmahon over the summer of 1915, but even after she had spent four days in his arms over Thanksgiving, she told Pollitzer that she was unclear about where the relationship was heading—and even that she was becoming wary of love:

> I dont love him—I don't pretend to—sometimes when Im very tired I used to want him because he is restful—I probably will again—though—I doubt it.*
> He is nice to let go—and nice to keep—so I will do both—because he doesn't want to—go—We will always be friends
> I almost want to say—don't mention loving anyone to me
> It is a curious thing—don't let it get you Anita if you value your peace of mind—it will eat you up and swallow you whole.

While she was "nearer being in love with [Macmahon] than I wanted to be," she had begun a flirtation with Columbia College (South Carolina) sociologist Marcus Lee Hansen, as well, but she told Pollitzer that Hansen was another "man I don't know what to do with. If he were less fine—I would drop him like a hot cake—but he is too fine to drop—and too fine to keep—and he doesn't know how fine he is."

When Hansen did not make her choices any clearer—he only gave her another option not to choose—O'Keeffe put aside the oil paints she had been working with, and she stopped working with color altogether. In frustration and disappointment, she laid her drawing paper directly on the floor and made a series of abstract charcoal drawings that gave form to the overflowing feelings that none of her relationships had crystallized. Muscular and feminine, the swirling shapes suggest the internal state of desire, and express an in-folding, feminine place with fountains and phallus-shaped figures that suggest either a seething vacancy or the forms that might give it fulfillment.

These drawings were partly inspired by the modern art O'Keeffe had seen in Alfred Stieglitz' gallery, and in *Camera Work*, the journal Stieglitz edited. Stieglitz had made a name for himself as a photographer in the 1890s, but when he started to exhibit European Modernism at his gallery

---

* I have not changed O'Keeffe's unconventional punctuation.

at 291 Fifth Avenue, he had made a new name for himself as an ardent promoter of modern art—and of yet-undiscovered artists, as well. He was known to take artists under his wing, giving them shows at 291, and helping to cultivate audiences and buyers for their works. O'Keeffe had never explicitly asked her friend to show her work to Stieglitz, but she had written to Pollitzer, in the fall of 1915, that she

> would rather have Stieglitz like something I had done—than any-one else I know of—I have always thought that—if ever I do any-thing that satisfies me ever so little—I am going to show it to him to find out if its any good—Don't you often wish you could make something he might like?

Pollitzer found Stieglitz at 291 and told him that she had some draw-ings she thought he might like to see. Recounting the New Year's scene to O'Keeffe, she wrote that Stieglitz "looked . . . he thoroughly absorbed & got them—he looked again—the room was quiet—One small light . . . It was a long time before his lips opened—'Finally, a woman on paper'— he said." O'Keeffe had arrived: she had communicated a genuine and unique experience through her art—and Stieglitz had discovered a new talent—and a younger woman who might look to him for help starting her career.

Alfred Stieglitz was always looking for new American artists—and a female artist would be especially good for business—but Stieglitz was also looking for a lover. He had been separated from his wife for a long time now—she had never shared his passion for photography and art—and he had recently concluded an affair with another young painter, Kath-erine Rhoades, who had been twenty-six to his forty-eight when they had started seeing each other in 1912. Rhoades broke with Stieglitz in 1915, after he exhibited her work—she destroyed her paintings and left New York—and now, on New Year's Day 1916, his fifty-second birthday, Stieglitz had an eye out for another lover who would be sympathetic to his artistic ideas and lifestyle.

After she had heard from Pollitzer how Stieglitz had reacted to her drawings, O'Keeffe herself wrote to ask him for his impressions, and she and Stieglitz began a correspondence in which O'Keeffe tried to describe her work and Stieglitz encouraged her to keep making more of it. As they corresponded over the following months, Stieglitz was more and more impressed with both her personality and her work: by the spring of 1918, Stieglitz would write that O'Keeffe herself was the "spirit of 291—Not I."

O'Keeffe had practically offered herself to this abstraction. Ever since her family had begun to drift toward poverty in 1899, she had lost creative years to illness and making money, but she had never made commitments that tied her down, either to jobs or to lovers. She had staked all her hopes on art, and when she finally accepted Stieglitz' offer of a studio in New York in 1918, she chose Stieglitz over a younger photographer, Paul Strand, to whom she felt a stronger physical and even a stronger artistic connection, but by taking Stieglitz as her lover, she was securing a place for her artwork. Stieglitz was motivated by his own art as well, and he moved in with O'Keeffe two months after her arrival in New York: not only was she the new, up-and-coming artist for his gallery, but now she became his model and his collaborator as well.

Stieglitz had already spent years promoting the idea that art was a transcendent experience that lifted people beyond their particular lives. But if he and O'Keeffe were sympathetic to each other's art, they were still nearly twenty-four years apart in age, and they were profoundly different in their backgrounds and in their temperaments. They had very different ideas about how to spend their days, and the abstracting language of artistic vision would not always reconcile—or even conceal— their affairs and their profoundly different personalities. But in spite of their differences, and the crises they caused, art kept them together until Stieglitz' death in 1946.

II.

For Alfred Stieglitz, the art that gave unique expression to intense personal feelings was both an outgrowth of and a refuge from his childhood as the son of an overbearing and wealthy father. Edward Stieglitz had come from humble origins in Germany, but he made a fortune manufacturing surveying instruments and then woolen goods during the Civil War. He was twenty-nine in 1862, when he married eighteen-year-old Hedwig Werner, who brought a proud family heritage of Talmudic scholarship to her newly wealthy husband. When they celebrated Alfred's birth on New Year's Day 1864, and then his twin brothers' in 1867, she and Edward were still living close to their Jewish-German community in Hoboken, New Jersey, but in 1871, when Alfred was seven, Edward pulled up roots and moved to a fashionable address on East Sixtieth Street in New York City, where he could socialize with other wealthy New York families, free from the more restrictive conventions of his immigrant community.

Edward Stieglitz completed his social ascent by patronizing painters and musicians, and also by dabbling in art himself. As a self-made man who was creating his own society, Edward wanted to provide his children with luxuries, although he still half expected them to make their fortunes for themselves, as he had done. But in the absence of any traditional community, Edward's whims were the inviolable laws in the family, and Alfred grew up torn between his father's expansive wealth and his resentment whenever it seemed like Alfred himself was enjoying a liberty he had not earned.

Raised in the dissonance between the abstract promises of art and the realities of commerce, Stieglitz became sensitive to the contradictions in his position, and in his parents' expectations. Later in life, his lover Dorothy Norman quoted him as saying that

> because what I was promised stirred me, but then was nowhere to be found, I decided I must create a world of my own in which the preachments made in my youth might be put into practice. I have spent my life trying to discover what people really mean when they speak; when they claim to believe in one thing, yet do another; declare one set of values in public, another in private; make pompous resolutions, yet fail to live up to them.

Seeing two sides of people and words, Stieglitz was always looking for someone who could confirm his vision, and one biographer speculates that he needed people even more after his mother had given birth to twins when he was three: without a twin of his own, he would always be alone in his experience, anxious for a peer with whom to share it.

Stieglitz may have felt his experience keenly, but his parents nonetheless made his decisions for him. In the absence of a strong leaning in his son, Edward had enrolled Alfred in a German secondary school, and then in the mechanical engineering course in the Polytechnikum in Berlin* in 1886. Stieglitz obeyed his parents and enrolled, but he abandoned

---

* It is worth noting that Stieglitz was attracted to German universities because of their reputation, fostered by liberated Russian women like Lou von Salomé, for sexual and artistic license.

his engineering studies as soon as he discovered the camera. He had not been enamored of photography when he started at the Polytechnikum, and there is no evidence that he had ever picked up a brush in his father's quasi-artistic household, but photography was a new medium, and Stieglitz saw an opportunity. By mastering the technical details of making pictures, he could express himself in a new medium that was fundamentally different from his father's business accomplishments. With an art that was also a highly technical process, Stieglitz could choose everything, from what fell within the viewfinder to the mastery of the exposure and then the development of the plates. Then as a pioneer in the field, he himself could be the sole judge of what he had accomplished in a print.

Stieglitz found a mentor in a chemistry professor who had developed new photographic processes and allowed Stieglitz to skip his class, because he was already spending plenty of time in the laboratory and darkroom. Stieglitz refused to accept the limitations imposed by current techniques and materials, and he experimented with papers and films, exposures and developing baths, and he found new ways to capture sharp contrasts and the subtleties of textured surfaces. In the 1890s, photography was still a form of Victorian portraiture, and photographers were generally expected to doctor their portraits, refining them in the darkroom, but Stieglitz seized the high ground, claiming that his photographs were "straight, unmanipulated, devoid of all tricks, a print not looking like anything but a photograph, living through its own inherent qualities and revealing its own spirit."

As he mastered the techniques of exposure and developing, Stieglitz gained a vocabulary with which to describe a philosophy and a poetry, as well as a theory of perception, at a time when critics were just beginning to recognize that there were artistic possibilities in the camera. One contemporary critic noted that "in Stieglitz, there is no revolt: always a spontaneous acceptance—unquestioning—of what is there," but this acceptance was not only an application of new techniques. It was also a form of revolt against his parents' class prejudices, which saw things as symbols of wealth and status. It was a form of revolt as well against the dehumanizing "mechanicalization" of industrial culture, which Stieglitz felt was turning men into functions and nature into machines. Focusing on the realities that went unseen, Stieglitz used his camera as an act of devotion to the human qualities his culture overlooked.

"When I make a picture," he would later say, "I make love." Sex and art would always be intertwined for Stieglitz, for at the same time that he was discovering photography, he was also discovering the erotic freedom of the moneyed bachelor abroad, and in the same way that he insisted that his photography was art, he insisted on describing his relationships in his own terms. In his relationships in Berlin, though, Stieglitz was still following in his father's footsteps, for his father was well known for his womanizing—so notorious indeed that his reputation eventually prevented Alfred's younger brother Lee from being appointed to a residency at Mount Sinai Hospital. Stieglitz had condemned his father for affairs with servants and others, but now that he himself could afford to keep a lover, he set up housekeeping with a prostitute named Paula in 1886. But Stieglitz did not hide the relationship, as his father had hidden his affairs: he rebelled against conventional morality by living with Paula openly, and he answered any objections by claiming that she was "as clean as his mother." Later in life, he would say that this was when he was "happiest and freest," for in his relationship with Paula, he had all the freedom of a lover and all the stability of a married man. He balked at accepting the responsibility of a parent, though, and he ended the affair when Paula became pregnant. She was not the only woman to bear a child of his—there is evidence that he left more than one child behind him in Europe—but when he returned to America in 1890, he would continue to send her $150* a year for the child's expenses.

On his return to New York from Berlin, Stieglitz' freedom was curtailed by his family's scrutiny and control, and later in life he more than once recalled having cried himself to sleep every night "from a sense of overpowering loneliness. The spiritual emptiness of my life was bewildering." Determined to see him succeed in business, Edward installed him as a one of the directors of the Photochrome Engraving Company. For five years, Stieglitz ran the business with Joe Obermeyer and Louis Schubart, friends of his whom Edward had convinced to become his business partners. Stieglitz was not interested in this kind of success, though, so he neglected the business and continued to devote himself to photography, where his amateur work had begun to earn him a reputation as a diligent innovator, and in 1892 he began to publish articles that advocated the personal, cultural, and even national benefits of "straight photography"—as opposed to the shoddy evasions of sentimental retouchers.

Stieglitz may have tried to escape from his business responsibilities, but he could not escape pressure from his parents, and from his partner,

---

* About $3,500 in 2011 dollars.

Joe Obermeyer, to complement his business ties by marrying Obermeyer's sister. Emmeline Obermeyer was twenty when they married in 1893—Stieglitz was twenty-nine—and she had always been sheltered by her family's considerable brewery wealth, so they were incompatible from the beginning: Stieglitz had already lived with a prostitute, and Emmy was not his choice of wife. She had not met him on artistic grounds, and she refused to pose nude for him: by various accounts, they did not consummate their marriage for between one and four years.

Soon after he married, Stieglitz began to make his escape from the Photochrome Engraving Company. He had refused to conform to the standardized workday, and now he disavowed the privileged position of owner as well. He later made clear that "during the entire period of five years I did not draw one cent, either as salary, dividend or interest on the money invested by my father for me." In 1895, Stieglitz gave his share of the business to the workers, backed out of the partnership, and continued to live on an allowance from his and Emmy's families.

Withdrawing from the business, Stieglitz retreated from his marriage as well. He frequently left Emmy alone in their twelve-room New York City apartment when he went out to photograph, and when he took over editorial duties for the Camera Club of New York, he avoided his home as much as possible. As a photographer whose artistic work was already contributing to national conversations about individuality and society, photography and art—as a photographer who was still experimenting with problems of exposure and developing—as a practitioner of an art that was not recognized as an art, yet, Stieglitz could only ever be alienated from a wife who asked him, "Why do you always speak in that semi-abstract way?"

The birth of a daughter, Kitty, in 1898, did nothing to foster their affections, and Emmy's questions became even more pointed: "you cannot think how bad it is for me and what horrible thoughts I get. Have you ever thought it over what little joy you bring into my life? . . . You are either entirely taken up with your work and those interested in it or else in deep gloom." Three days later, she wrote him, "What good is the advancement of art or any other thing to a woman when she feels that it takes away the family life and all pertaining to it." Later in life, Kitty would reprise this sentiment as well. Dorothy Norman recorded her saying, "I wish father would speak of things about which people know something. He is always talking about art and life."

Miserable as a businessman and distant from his loveless marriage,

Stieglitz found his calling as an expert artist and promoter of the arts, and from 1895 to 1915—from age thirty to fifty—he hardly worked with the camera, but he gave his most productive years to the business of creating an intimate circle of artists who shared his values. Stieglitz unified the photography clubs in New York, and in 1902, he organized the "Photo-Secession" as an unofficial gathering of avant-garde photographers for whom the status quo was still too sentimental. Photography was finally—slowly—gaining acceptance as an art form, but by 1907, after other photographers had taken up his call for a straight photography that could be taught and learned, he leaped ahead again and began to defend the mystical experience of art, which he described as an inherent trait that could only be seen by those in the know. Distancing himself from the "Photo-Secessionists"—who by now were capitalizing on the title he had given them—he began to exhibit European avant-garde art. His business partner at 291, Edward Steichen, had traveled to Paris, where he had come into contact with European modern art as a frequent visitor to Gertrude Stein's salon. When he sent paintings to Stieglitz, 291 became the first gallery in America to exhibit Rodin's erotic watercolor drawings in 1908 and then works of Matisse and Cézanne in 1911.

Stieglitz did not seem to have understood the works of Matisse, Cézanne, and Rodin, but he seems to have promoted them even *because* he did not understand them: there was still a certain something that could serve as the basis for provocative conversation. Championing the idea of revolutionary artwork, he assumed the role of the savvy connoisseur who had the largesse to invite people into his galleries, the authority to educate or condemn their tastes, and the high principles to refrain from selling the art he hung. Stieglitz used the new modern art as a stimulant to conversation, and as a test of his visitors' ideas. By all accounts, he could be contentious and condescending toward his visitors, but he was also known to give a work away, if a visitor was sufficiently moved.

Sherwood Anderson paints a sympathetic picture of Stieglitz "in a room with paintings on the wall and facing the stupid, half-irritated people. You patiently explaining, over and over, trying to make all of the poor dears see the beauty you see." Visitors who were receptive to the art at 291 were welcomed into an elite circle. For those chosen few, 291 was a revolutionary meeting place and surrogate family, where Stieglitz fought to protect struggling younger artists from the ignorance and apathy of the public. For those who could show him the loyalty and appreciation he demanded, he even made the gesture of protecting them from himself.

As he told one visitor, "Don't let anything I have said affect you except insofar as it belongs to you personally and you can use it."

Three years before Anita Pollitzer showed up with Georgia O'Keeffe's charcoal drawings, Stieglitz turned away from European art—which was now beginning to sell—and he began to look for a native talent that would be purer, unsullied by commercialism. Since the time of the 1913 Armory show, European Modernism had become big business, but Stieglitz refused to run 291 for profit—he refused as well "to call these rooms a gallery. They are more like a laboratory in which we are testing the taste of the public." With the authority of 291 and his earlier photographic innovations behind him, he opened the Forum Exhibition of Modern American Painting in March of 1916, and he used this gallery space to promote a small group of American painters and photographers, beginning with watercolorist John Marin. Stieglitz would sell Marin's paintings in annual exhibits for the next twenty years, and he also supported Marsden Hartley, raising more than $5,000 by auctioning his work at a time when Hartley was broke. Along with painter Arthur Dove, photographer Paul Strand, and others, Marin and Hartley were the heart of Stieglitz' loyal following, and Stieglitz guaranteed them all his support, only infrequently bringing new members into the "family," as they came to be called.

Discussion at 291 centered on the elusive quality of "fineness," which implied "completion," and "refinement" as well as "finish." After Stieglitz' confirmation—"Finally, a woman on paper"—his assistant, Abraham Walkowitz, had looked at O'Keeffe's drawings and said simply, "Very fine." At its core, "fineness" consisted of a technical excellence in which intense experience and formal composition complemented each other: it was as much sex appeal as it was an antiauthoritarian insistence on the inexpressible aspects of human experience. Of one of his later galleries, Stieglitz wrote:

> Between man and woman there is this reaching towards the center of one another. But in the ecstasy of that touch is the desire to touch the center beyond. That is what the Room is. The Room is the search for this. There is a common desire for something that seems to be brought to life when two forces potentially meet. The Room is not only the meeting of these forces, but the extra straining to that point beyond.

By contemporary accounts, discussions at Stieglitz' galleries were often punctuated by snickers, as the mostly male crowd acknowledged their familiarity with the intimate secrets of life, art, and women. Stieglitz himself was still married, with a daughter, but he used the galleries to draw people into the sexual world beneath art's surface, and he was always open to the possibility of an affair. He no longer needed to outrage convention by living with a prostitute. With Katherine Rhoades and now with Georgia O'Keeffe, he used his position as a promoter of art to become intimate with the women who came to him looking for approval, exposure, or guidance.

III.

In the early 1910s, while Stieglitz was securing his reputation as a photographer and as an art promoter, Georgia O'Keeffe was just discovering her artistic voice. She had been working toward an artistic career since she was a small child, and her stubborn insistence on making a living from her artwork was a legacy of her mother's family's cultural pride.

Having married beneath her, Ida Totto wanted to provide her children with the cultural refinement she herself had grown up with in Madison, Wisconsin. Totto's parents came from Hungary—they claimed to have followed a Hungarian prince into exile—and they were proud of their aristocratic ancestry: by the time Ida was growing up, her family had done well enough for themselves to lease their farm in the country and live in town. When they arranged her marriage to Francis O'Keeffe, though, it was to unite the Totto farm with the neighboring O'Keeffe farm, for Francis O'Keeffe and his family of Irish immigrants had already been working the Totto farm in addition to their own. Francis was ten years older than his bride, but he could barely read and write, and Georgia and her siblings grew up in the dissonance between their mother's urban culture and their father's unlettered familiarity with the land.

O'Keeffe was born on November 15, 1887, as the second child and eldest daughter in a family that would expand to seven children. She was lost in the big family, but she was consoled for her isolation by a certain power. She was not as pretty as some of her sisters, so she was not groomed for marriage, but she was given responsibility for her younger siblings, which gave her authority and responsibility. Independent by nature, she developed a rich inner life, and her mother gave her the tools to express it when she paid extra to enroll her in art classes at the Sacred Heart Academy in Madison.

The O'Keeffe family's finances began to decline in the financial crash of 1893. Soon thereafter, Francis's father and two of his brothers died of tuberculosis, and Francis's last living brother, Bernard, developed a bloody cough as well. When he came to live with Francis and Ida in 1897, he turned the family out of the dairy business, since tuberculosis could be spread in contaminated milk, and Francis sold the farm in 1899 after Bernard died. In their ultimately hasty departure from Sun Prairie, Wisconsin, in 1902, the O'Keeffes left debts unpaid behind them in order to start a new life flush with cash in Williamsburg, Virginia.

Having just lost almost all of his family, Francis suffered one business loss after another—in a grocery and feed store, in real estate, in a creamery, and in manufacturing. In his last disastrous investment, in 1908, he and some partners undertook to build houses with concrete bricks made from seashells. When investors failed to materialize, the O'Keeffes moved out of their house and into the dank, dilapidated model. Ultimately Francis set out on the road to find employment and did not return, leaving his wife—who was by now tubercular herself—to provide for herself and the daughters who were still at home with her.

Once-proud Ida O'Keeffe took boarders to slow the dwindling of the funds from the Wisconsin farm, but she was still determined to provide some culture for Georgia, and in 1905 she paid for her tuition at the Art Institute of Chicago—just as impulsively, perhaps, as her husband had made his own investments. After O'Keeffe finished her program at the Art Institute, she supported herself solely through drawing and painting. She drifted between work and study, drawing lace for an advertising agency in Chicago and taking classes at the Art Students League in New York in 1907 and 1908, and then teaching in Amarillo, Texas, and Charlottesville, Virginia, before she returned to New York in 1914 to study at Teachers College, where she met Anita Pollitzer. O'Keeffe had progressed to advanced studies quickly throughout her schooling, but she had also changed schools so many times that she had to start with introductory classes again and again, and her art had developed by returning continually to the basics. When she came to Teachers College in 1914, she was twenty-seven years old, but she was taking classes with freshmen.

Having discovered the wealth of experience to be found in art, O'Keeffe was nonetheless still poor, and she protected her freedom fiercely. She was barely getting by while she worked at her own art, and the luxury to make decisions artistically was not something she could afford to let a man threaten, so love was not her top priority, although to be fair, she did not leave journals or letters that give us much insight into her feelings. This may explain as well why contemporary accounts of her frequently remarked on the contradictory juxtaposition of passion and reserve in her temperament, and even describe a quality of androgyny about her. O'Keeffe's Teachers College peers called her "Patsy," a nickname drawn as much from her stereotypically Irish wit as from her masculinity, for she dressed in "severely tailored" men's suits and expressed herself with a Midwestern, masculine directness.

Until she moved to New York in 1918, O'Keeffe had taken teaching jobs in culturally remote cities where she surrounded herself with students or with working people who did not appreciate the art that moved her. If she sustained herself with her correspondence, though, with friends like Anita Pollitzer in New York and her sisters in Chicago and Virginia, she was still waiting to live in her art. As she wrote to Pollitzer,

> I am disgusted with myself—
> I was made to work hard—and Im not working half hard enough—Nobody else here has energy like I have—No one else can keep up
> I hate it
> Still—its wonderful and I like it too
> At any rate—as you said in the fall—it is an experience ["to know tame people for a little while," Anita had written].

After 1914, O'Keeffe found sympathy, understanding, and encouragement in her correspondence with Pollitzer more than anyone else. After finishing at the Art Students League, Pollitzer had gone to work in women's rights advocacy, and in their correspondence, she played the role of the supporter who vicariously identified herself with O'Keeffe's heroic artistic isolation. Together they enthused about the art they found in *Camera Work*—they exchanged drawings, and they encouraged each other in their "arting." Shared understanding was essential for both of them: O'Keeffe longed to express the ache caused by physical beauty, and if the feeling itself could not actually be shared, she needed to know that she was not alone in feeling the ache of things—throughout her letters, Pollitzer was constantly assuring her that she knew how she felt. When

O'Keeffe went to Charlottesville to clean out after her mother's death in 1916, the issues of *Camera Work* Pollitzer sent her "excited me so that I felt like a human being for a couple of hours." From South Carolina, O'Keeffe wrote, "I haven't found anyone yet who likes to live like we do."

Art was such a personal language between O'Keeffe and Pollitzer that Pollitzer was taking a risk by showing the charcoal drawings to Stieglitz: O'Keeffe had sent them in personal correspondence, and even though she was frustrated with her isolation, she might have felt that Pollitzer was betraying her by sharing them publicly. When Pollitzer wrote with Stieglitz' reaction, she could not describe Stieglitz' admiration without reassuring O'Keeffe that her drawings were most important as an act of communication between friends: "they do it to me too, or I wouldn't give a hang."

IV.

After Pollitzer wrote to tell her about Stieglitz' reaction, O'Keeffe wrote to Stieglitz herself to inquire "what the drawings said" to him. With a mixture of flirtation, flattery, and praise, he wrote back to say that he could only convey his thoughts to her in person and alone: "it is impossible for me to put into words what I saw and felt in your drawings . . . I might give you what I received from them if you and I were to meet and talk about life. Possibly then through such a conversation I might make you feel what your drawings gave me." The correspondence affected O'Keeffe deeply, and within a few weeks, she wrote to him,

> I think letters with so much humanness in them have never come to me before. I have wondered with every one of them—what is it in them—how you put it in—or is it my imagination—seeing and feeling—finding what I want—they seem to give me a great big quietness.

O'Keeffe did not make a trip to New York to confirm her accomplishment in person right away. It was not until May that she got fed up with teaching, abruptly quit her job in South Carolina, and came to New York City, although even then, it was only to take the one class that would allow her to accept a position as the head of art at the West Texas Normal School in Canyon, Texas. And even though Stieglitz had already moved her with his letters, she did not seek him out until she heard that 291 had shown works by "Virginia O'Keeffe." It was, of course, an honor for her work to have hung at 291, but O'Keeffe resented Stieglitz' presumptuousness in hanging them without her permission. The drawings had already been taken down when she arrived at 291 to complain, though, so O'Keeffe had nothing to lose when she told Stieglitz how angry she was. Stieglitz defused her indignation, though, and convinced her that the drawings deserved a larger audience. To express his contrition, he gave her photographs of her drawings—photographs she later claimed to prize above the drawings themselves.

This first unofficial show hardly put O'Keeffe in any position to support herself with her art, yet, so as soon as she finished her last remaining course in New York, she left for Texas in the fall of 1916. Stieglitz' letters followed after her again, and after he gave her another solo show of new work in the winter of 1916–1917, she returned to New York for a ten-day visit in May of 1917. Stieglitz had just taken down the authorized exhibition by the time she arrived, but he hung the show again for her alone, and while neither of them left a record, biographers agree that they became lovers during this visit.

If O'Keeffe had gone to New York for Stieglitz in 1917, it was his new protégé, Paul Strand, whom she craved when she took the train back to Texas. Strand was a talented photographer, three years younger than O'Keeffe, and they were captivated by each other as soon as Stieglitz introduced them. O'Keeffe wrote to Pollitzer that she and her friend Dorothy True "both fell for him," and that she "almost lost my mind" over his prints. Speculation among O'Keeffe's biographers places their meeting a few days after Stieglitz and O'Keeffe had become lovers, so even though they began to resonate with each other's artistic visions, a certain awkwardness pervades their letters. O'Keeffe was corresponding with Stieglitz as well—and he had the power to bring her work to the widest possible audience—so she and Strand were not free to pursue each other without O'Keeffe risking her career.

Returning to Texas, O'Keeffe did not commit to Stieglitz or to Strand. Instead, she began to go around with Ted Reid, a student her own age—a fact she confessed to Strand, but not to Stieglitz. Reid's age notwithstanding, student-teacher relationships were forbidden, and a committee of concerned townswomen warned Reid away from her shortly before Reid shipped out to France as an aviator in the Great War. Left to choose between Stieglitz and Strand, O'Keeffe still did not make a decision.

Stieglitz was in a position to support her through 291, but he himself was almost twenty-four years older than O'Keeffe. He was shorter than her, and thin—not the strapping man O'Keeffe hoped would carry her on his physical strength.

If she did not yield to Stieglitz, O'Keeffe would not give herself to Strand, either. She wrote Strand that she had "wanted to put my arms around you and kiss you hard," but when he asked her why she had not, she wrote back that "so many people had kissed me in such a short time—" (biographers count only Stieglitz and Reid) "and I had liked them all and had let them all—had wanted them all to—it simply staggered me that I stood there wanting to kiss someone else." She explained to Strand,

> I some way seem to feel what [men] feel—never wanting to give all . . . As I see it—to a woman [commitment] means willingness to give life—not only her life but other life, to give up life—or give other life—Nobody I know means that to me—for more than a moment at a time. I can not help knowing that—the moment does not fool me—I seem to see way ahead into the years—always to see folks too clearly—
> It's always aloneness—
> I wonder if I mind.

Isolation and uncertainty had been productive while O'Keeffe was corresponding with Pollitzer from South Carolina, but now that she was back in Texas—now that Stieglitz' professional recognition had not solved her need for a partner—her need for expression began to stifle her. Nauseated by the wartime patriotism of the rural Texans, she almost ceased to paint, and by early 1918, she had contracted influenza and was on the verge of developing tuberculosis. During her illness, O'Keeffe found a sympathetic companion in Leah Harris, an independent woman of the Panhandle with whom she had a close—and, some biographers speculate, sexual—intimacy. Harris was a home economics teacher in Canyon, and she invited O'Keeffe to convalesce on her family farm in Waring, Texas, where O'Keeffe finally allowed herself the luxury of being taken care of. She wrote to Strand that she and Harris would curl up together to read in the evenings, but she also told Strand that she and Leah were two of a kind: "both cold women."

O'Keeffe's illness inspired an avalanche of concerned letters from Stieglitz and Strand, who were tormented by the idea of the talented artist languishing in illness, indecision, and obscurity in Texas. While she convalesced with Harris, Stieglitz and Strand both wrote urging her to return to New York, and O'Keeffe was starting to feel a protection in Stieglitz' understanding. In the winter of 1918, she acknowledged in a letter to Elizabeth Stieglitz, Alfred's niece—whom Stieglitz had enlisted in his campaign to entice O'Keeffe to New York—that Stieglitz "is probably more necessary to me than anyone I know." O'Keeffe added, though, that "I do not feel that I have to be near him. In fact I think we are probably better apart."

Two years ago, they might have simply maintained a passionately encouraging correspondence, but Stieglitz himself had fallen into a depression since closing 291, after the war had chilled the art market in 1917. In his withdrawal, Stieglitz turned O'Keeffe into a symbol of the spirit that would rejuvenate him. He wrote to Strand:

> She is the spirit of 291
> ——Not—I——
> That's something I never told you before. That's why I have been fighting so madly for her . . .
> Her health—just plainly *She*—These are the prime considerations—All else must be secondary.

Exasperated by her fragility, her helplessness, and her indecision, Stieglitz urged Strand to go and bring her back to New York. Arriving in Texas on Stieglitz' errand, Strand wrote to him, "If I had some money I might be able to help her—I know I wouldn't be afraid despite all the difficulties of living with such a person. But I haven't—so it is all very clear that I am not the one. Besides it is very clear to me that you mean more to her than anyone else." Stieglitz may have meant more to her than anyone, but Strand developed his own intimacy with her. He wrote to Stieglitz,

> The best way I can tell you how things are at the moment is that she lets me touch her—wants me to. But with me at least—no both—no passion—except in a far off—very far off potential. I never thought she would again—I don't think she did either—it was all a nightmare . . . I think besides she was unwell.

In another letter, Strand wrote,

I'm sure she has made up her mind to come to New York—all it needs is for me to say at the right moment—let's go. Of course, if you wrote to come, that would settle it at once—But it isn't necessary unless you want to do it.

I think before she could go with you there would be many things to be given up—very many.

I love her very much. You know my feelings for you.

But Stieglitz was not willing to take responsibility for O'Keeffe's decision, and he wrote back to Strand,

The coming or not coming is entirely in her hands—there must be no suggestion or interference one way or another . . . You have brought about a very essential thing & that is Georgia's becoming conscious of her actual feelings for Lea[h] . . . From this end, nothing can be decided.

If Stieglitz refused to consider either his or O'Keeffe's personal feelings as factors in the decision, he was nonetheless offering O'Keeffe his niece's studio, and he arranged for an anonymous donor to pay her rent. When she finally realized that the terms were too good to turn down, O'Keeffe allowed herself be carried by the man who had the most power to support her artistic vision, and she wrote to accept.

Once the decision was made, O'Keeffe and Leah and Strand enjoyed an idyllic time of creativity, with Leah posing nude for Strand and O'Keeffe both. Except for some abstract paintings of women in shawls and a rare portrait, O'Keeffe's watercolor nudes of Leah were the last figurative representations she would make of the human form.

V.

When O'Keeffe came to New York in 1918, Stieglitz installed her in his niece's studio. O'Keeffe was still weak from her illness, but Stieglitz himself became her caretaker. He wrote to his niece, "Why I can't believe she is at all . . . I never realized that what she is could actually exist—absolute Truth—Clarity of Vision to the Highest Degree and a fineness which [is] uncannily balanced." "She is much more extraordinary than even I believed," he wrote to Arthur Dove.

In fact I don't believe there ever has been anything like her—mind & feeling very clear—spontaneous and uncannily beautiful— absolutely living every pulse beat . . .

Sane madness—so damn sane that it sometimes frightens me. O'Keeffe is truly magnificent. And a child at that. We are at least 90% alike—She a purer form of myself.

O'Keeffe is a constant source of wonder to me—like Nature itself.

Having captured this force of nature by providing her with a studio and support, Stieglitz still wrote to his niece, "I can never quite accustom myself to the idea that I should have the privilege of meaning—being— anything to her . . . It's all intensely beautiful—at times unbearably so."

Stieglitz was O'Keeffe's most frequent visitor, and in her illness she relied on him for food and nursing, but as her health improved, she and Stieglitz resumed the affair that had started during her 1917 visit. Having chastised Stieglitz for hanging her drawings without her permission, O'Keeffe did not scold her new lover for being married. Unlike Emmy, she allowed Stieglitz to photograph her nude, offering both her body and their intimacy to his art. Shortly after she had arrived in New York in May, Stieglitz took her to his and Emmy's home to photograph her there, but when Emmy discovered them, she forced him to move out of the house. Stieglitz moved in with O'Keeffe, but he would not admit that he was having an affair. He wrote to his brother-in-law Joe Obermeyer that Emmy had misconstrued the relationship between photographer and model. "[Emmy] slandered an innocent woman—girl. It seems you can't understand any fine or decent relationship between man and woman."

Men had been photographing nude women since the invention of the camera, but Stieglitz was breaking new ground by taking a series of photographs in which O'Keeffe's personality was rendered as clearly as her body. His elaborate photo-portrait—which consisted of 310 mounted prints and numerous "snapshots"—has been described as a "collaborative performance," and when she wrote about the process of being photographed, O'Keeffe said that Stieglitz' instructions were precise and demanding. Each photographic plate needed to be mounted individually, and O'Keeffe needed to hold perfectly still for as long as the exposure lasted, sometimes three or four minutes at a time. The work was still rewarding, though: Stieglitz wrote to Strand that "whenever she looks at the proofs, she falls in love with herself.—Or rather her Selves—There are many." In addition to the tired, exulting, wry, comic, lazy, or intense selves Stieglitz portrayed, there was the figure of her body, which took wiry and portly, dynamic and inert forms through his camera. If Stieglitz flattered O'Keeffe by focusing his photographic eye on her, he also invited her into his unprecedentedly intimate artwork.

Posing for Stieglitz, O'Keeffe herself played a number of roles as well: she was the lover, whose sexual intimacy was assumed as a condition of many of the photographs; she was the fellow artist, who could understand and endure the "fusses" her lover was making for the sake of her own beauty and his art; she was the detached woman, who had nothing personal to lose in the photographs, which after all were only capturing her image; she was the sequestered woman, available at her lover's convenience, to pose when the light or the inspiration were right. It may be worth noting that the photo-portrait does not show O'Keeffe in daily routines in a recognizable world, though: the photos consist of either clothed shots, in which O'Keeffe is most often dressed in masculine black-and-white suits—or else nudes in which her face does not appear. When Stieglitz exhibited the photos in 1921, she gave her body to gallery-goers as well, with human grumblings about being on display, but with no objections to the artistic value of what he had created. If some visitors snickered to see their intimacy exposed, one visitor was reportedly reduced to tears, exclaiming "he loves her so."

Stieglitz' photographs would not fully describe the value of their intimacy, though—not until O'Keeffe had demonstrated her worth by expressing her own artistic vision—so Stieglitz was deeply supportive of her art, which would show the full extent of how his love comprehended and supported her. Soon after O'Keeffe arrived, she wrote that he had asked her, "If I could do anything I wanted to do for a year, what would it be." She "promptly said I would like to have a year to paint . . . he thought for a while and then remarked that he thought he could arrange that." O'Keeffe gave up her teaching post in Texas, and Stieglitz advanced her money against future sales of her work, inducting her into the family of artists who would depend on his galleries and his promotion for support. As long as she could endure the pressure to remain Stieglitz' upcoming star—as long as her paintings remained original and as feminine and as fine as the charcoal drawings Pollitzer had taken to 291 in 1916—O'Keeffe had the devout support of one of America's greatest photographers and art promoters.

VI.

Having closed 291 in 1917, Stieglitz was spared the overhead and the work of coordinating shows. He turned his attention to photographing O'Keeffe and used the studio he shared with her as his gallery. Now that he was inviting patrons and buyers for private viewings of both O'Keeffe's paintings and of his photographs of her, he gave up the role of public impresario and returned to living the life of the working artist, although he still acted as a gallery owner and private art expert, who could sell paintings and photographs that were unavailable to the common man.

This ability to start over time and again helps explain Stieglitz' hold over O'Keeffe, for now that he was living with O'Keeffe, he was no longer solely an art promoter, but with his photographic portraits, of O'Keeffe and then of others, he became an artist in his own right again. Having promoted the art of others for so long, Stieglitz now assimilated the technical achievements he had promoted, and O'Keeffe wrote to Sherwood Anderson, "His work is always a surprise to me—. One feels there can be nothing more for him to do—and then away he goes—shooting way ahead just like the last time."

As she recuperated, O'Keeffe began to enjoy the freedom to paint on her own schedule, but now that Stieglitz was comprehending her in his photographs, she was no longer wondering what it might be like to have his support and understanding. Stieglitz was surrounding her with affectionate devotion, and she was serving as Stieglitz' lover and his model, in addition to being his new up-and-coming artist: now she only needed freedom to pursue her own experience and her art. If Stieglitz was going to exploit whatever she showed him—whether it was her body or her paintings—and if he would make sure that it supported her, she nonetheless had to protect herself from absorption by Stieglitz' personality and by his own artistic needs.

O'Keeffe did not enjoy the overbearing atmosphere of combative conversation Stieglitz fostered in his galleries and in his talk, where he provoked and scolded, shocked and tested his visitors. Later in life, she would write to a friend that

> A[lfred] gets on a prickly edge ready to meet [his visitors]—He seems to become all different at the thought of having someone to talk to—so I don't feel pleased any more to be here . . . now there

will be talk—steady talk I suppose—and it all bores me so—No one will say anything except how awful the world is—and I know all those things they will say and don't see any sense in saying them—I would rather walk through the woods . . . or just look at the sky.

When, in the summer of 1919, Stieglitz brought her to meet his family at Lake George, it became customary for the family and their guests to discuss O'Keeffe's paintings as soon as they were finished. O'Keeffe reportedly "suffered while her paintings were being discussed," even though she appeared to be "as detached as though she had nothing to do with the paintings." In this atmosphere, O'Keeffe became even more removed from her paintings, and in public she would disavow their effect on people as being unrelated to the internal life that formed her own ongoing experience. "I think each painting very fine just after I've done it," she wrote. "But that wears off. It's just part of my daily life." When Stieglitz' promotion ultimately focused critical attention on her work, she began to separate her work from public commentary on it, and she asserted her independence:

> I get out my work and have a show for myself before I have it publicly. I make up my own mind about it—how good or bad or indifferent it is. After that the critics can write what they please. I have already settled it for myself so flattery and criticism go down the same drain and I am quite free.

Under the pressure of Stieglitz' critical explications, O'Keeffe's paintings did shift from representation toward a pictorial language that encoded her personal feelings. From one of Stieglitz' other artists, Charles Demuth, O'Keeffe learned to treat flowers and shells as "object portraits" of people. Demuth had used the calla lily to portray the combination of masculine and feminine qualities in his subjects, and now O'Keeffe adopted it as one of her signature portraits. In 1927, she would depict Stieglitz himself as the gleaming Radiator Building, hiding her actual feelings and her affections behind symbolic language that proclaimed them and hid them at the same time.

O'Keeffe may have been hiding her feelings from Stieglitz' exploitation, but her enigmatic and symbolic figures nonetheless helped him build a myth around her personality. In the first show of her paintings in 1923, his press releases and articles promoted O'Keeffe as the priestess of womanhood, the American Woman, a naive wonder who was unaware of the sometimes sexual content of her own paintings. Stieglitz had not shown O'Keeffe's work publicly for years after she moved to New York: he had sold her paintings directly out of the studio. But he had revealed her nude form in his 1921 show, so she was already somewhat infamous in advance of her first major show of one hundred paintings in 1923. Now her abstract flowers and object portraits, in addition to the subtle snicker in Stieglitz' billing, turned her into an enigmatic personality in the art world: her paintings may or may not have been revealing the most intimate details of their relationship.

Since 1918, Stieglitz and O'Keeffe had been living together in a workmanlike routine of painting and photographing and printing and meeting with artists and buyers, but once Stieglitz created the persona of the innocent woman genius, aloofness became part of her public identity. Critics were largely receptive to O'Keeffe's work, but as reviewers began to write about her personality and her art, she retreated from their speculations. "The things they write," she said, "sound so strange and far removed from what I feel of myself—They make me seem like some strange unearthly sort of creature floating in the air breathing in clouds for nourishment. When the truth is I like beefsteak and like it rare at that."

Stieglitz' publicity was effective—almost twenty of the hundred pieces sold in her 1923 show—and now they were bound to each other: O'Keeffe depended on Stieglitz and the public persona he created for her, even as she privately resisted his attempts to impose his narrative on her work. Stieglitz' publicity and the sales that resulted would allow her to continue to paint, but she treated even her success as a challenge to be overcome through the work of making art. "Whether you succeed or not is irrelevant," she would write to Sherwood Anderson,

> there is no such thing. Making your unknown known is the important thing—and keeping the unknown always beyond you. Catching, crystallizing your simpler, clearer vision of life—only to see it turn stale compared to what you vaguely feel ahead—that you must always keep working to grasp.

As early as 1920, though, O'Keeffe had begun to put physical space between herself and what could be overwhelming in Stieglitz' company, and in their summer visits with Stieglitz' family in Lake George. Daunted by the prospect of a second summer at Lake George, she accepted an offer to stay at an inn run by Stieglitz' friends at York Beach, Maine, where she painted the stones and seashells. Returning from Maine to Lake George late in the summer, she laid claim to an outbuilding, and when Stieglitz claimed that they could not afford the renovation, she solicited help from friends and visitors, who helped her transform the shack into her private studio. By all accounts, O'Keeffe enjoyed taking the work into her own hands, and now she had a studio of her own, where she could paint in the nude, as she had in New York when Stieglitz first began to photograph her.

VII.

Georgia O'Keeffe was not the only artist who had to escape from Stieglitz' powerful influence, although not all of Stieglitz' artists were as successful as she was. After he had brought his own breakthrough portfolio to Stieglitz in 1915, Paul Strand had not only been rewarded with a show: Stieglitz had given him free run of 291, so that he had become a trusted assistant and promising artist in his own right. But Strand was not independently wealthy—he was always looking for commercial work—so Stieglitz put him to work running errands and fundraising for the gallery. When painter John Marin's father had suggested that Marin take commercial work, Stieglitz had replied, indignantly, "that, sir, is like suggesting that your daughter be a virgin in the mornings and a prostitute in the afternoons," but by the 1920s, Strand had taken the job of Stieglitz' regular assistant.

When Paul Strand married Rebecca "Beck" Salsbury in 1922, Stieglitz continued to keep him busy, and Stieglitz and O'Keeffe took Beck to Lake George that summer without him. With Strand tied up in the city with commercial appointments, Stieglitz himself began to photograph Beck in the nude, making it impossible for Strand to feel that he was exploring virgin photographic territory in his own wife. Beck herself was complicit in the diminution of her husband, for she wrote to Stieglitz: "I knew very well that you have communicated much of your spirit to him, and I am therefore grateful to you, for you see, he expresses it to me." When Strand did finally photograph Beck nude, he only compelled Stieglitz to innovate again, and in 1923 Stieglitz began to photograph the clouds above the Lake George house, describing them as almost-musical "equivalents" for subjective experiences.

Beck Strand had artistic leanings herself, but she had been working as a medical secretary to help cover household costs, and she had been bored with the work. She was full of admiration for Stieglitz and O'Keeffe's artistic industriousness, and she returned from Lake George to the city at the end of the summer of 1922 simultaneously invigorated by her proximity to their creativity and depressed by her own lack of talent. When she traveled to Lake George again next summer, she took Stieglitz briefly as her lover. Stieglitz did not hide his enthusiasm about Beck—although he would not admit that he was having an affair—so O'Keeffe went to Maine for a month at the end of the summer again, in order to spare the household the unpleasant scenes that might have come about if she had stayed. By the summer of 1924, though, O'Keeffe and Beck and Stieglitz' old lover Katherine Rhoades were all at the house at the same time, and O'Keeffe was more vocal in expressing her discomfort. Stieglitz distanced himself from Beck, and even though Beck continued to make annual visits, after 1924, Stieglitz' letters to Beck became more and more nostalgic.

Beck's brief affair with Stieglitz did not keep her from acting as O'Keeffe's assistant, scouting locations and bringing her apples, branches, leaves, rocks, and bones to paint. For a time this created an extremely harmonious working relationship between the two women, but if distance had allowed the correspondence between O'Keeffe and Anita Pollitzer to preserve the impression of artistic equality when O'Keeffe was still unknown, now O'Keeffe hardly made any attempt to sustain the egalitarian illusion. She was the artist, and in spite of Beck's dreams about her own artistic talents, it was clear that she was the assistant. O'Keeffe would place other artistic friends in this role, some of whom she would refer to, even in public, as her "slaves."

VIII.

Stieglitz fostered O'Keeffe's and his artists' dependency on him so extensively that critics and biographers and even the artists themselves invariably revert to describing him as a father to many children, but when O'Keeffe pressed Stieglitz to have a child in the early 1920s, he refused. He was nearing sixty, and he may not have wanted O'Keeffe to be consumed with caring for a child. He resisted the idea, and his opposition was bolstered when his daughter Kitty was hospitalized for postpartum depression after giving birth to her first child in 1923. Stieglitz himself had developed an elaborate pictorial vocabulary for articulating his depressions and his sense of alienation, but he could not imagine Kitty working herself out of her depression, he could only imagine sterilizing her. "If I had the power," he wrote to his brother, "I'd pull up by the roots every bit of 'feeling' she has for either me, her mother, or uncle Joe." Stieglitz' reaction to Kitty's depression was compounded by the fact that the rest of the family held Stieglitz himself responsible for her breakdown and hospitalization.

Now when O'Keeffe wanted to have a child, Stieglitz argued that she could not realistically take care of a child because she needed long hours of undisturbed creativity. A poet, she herself would later say, could be interrupted, but a painter would have to be with the paint until it dried. If paintings were going to have to remain O'Keeffe's only children, the debate about whether to have children did bring out a certain childish helplessness in Stieglitz, who was getting older and beginning to require more care himself. Instead of a child, it was Stieglitz whom O'Keeffe began to refer to as a "little thing" who still had to make a place for himself in the world. When they were moving out of Stieglitz' brother Lee's house in 1924, she wrote to Sherwood Anderson:

> It seems we have been moving all winter. Stieglitz has to do every-
> thing in his mind so many times before he does it in reality that it
> keeps the process of anything like moving going on a long time—It
> really isn't the moving with him. It is many things within himself
> that he focuses on the idea of moving—He has to go over and over
> them again and again—trying to understand what it is that he is
> and why—in relation to the world—and what the world is and
> where it is all going to and what it is all about—and the poor little
> thing is looking for a place in it—and doesn't see any place where
> he thinks he fits.

Stieglitz may have refused to have children, but he insisted on marrying O'Keeffe three months after his divorce from Emmy came through in 1924, the year Stieglitz turned sixty. He and O'Keeffe had been living together for six years, but O'Keeffe was still only thirty-seven in 1924, and if Stieglitz was anxious about the possibility of being replaced by a younger man, marrying would assure him that he himself would have O'Keeffe's companionship until death. O'Keeffe had already become the caretaker at the Lake George farmhouse, and when she agreed to marry him, she effectively became Stieglitz' caretaker as well, although she herself would be compensated by the right to inherit his property, which by this time included a large collection of modern art and photography. They were married by a justice of the peace in New Jersey, without ceremony, although a minor car accident after the service was a slightly ominous portent as they were returning to New York and their work.

IX.

In 1925, Stieglitz and O'Keeffe moved into a suite in the Shelton Hotel, where they were completely relieved of housekeeping responsibilities. They took their meals in the eighteenth-floor cafeteria, and their elevation above the city prompted O'Keeffe to paint cityscapes for the first time since she came to New York. Stieglitz was apprehensive about her painting the city—he wanted her to remain the feminine genius of flowers and landscapes—but O'Keeffe persisted in exploring the city as a subject in spite of his opposition. She worked alongside Stieglitz, though, and when he opened another gallery—the Intimate Gallery, where he would return to the role of art impresario—she helped him with the business of hanging shows.

Now that O'Keeffe had a secure place inside of Stieglitz' circle, she reveled in his attention to her work. In 1926, she wrote to journalist Blanche Matthias that "since the 291 exhibitions I haven't had anything so sympathetically cared for—Being Stieglitz' own place the things feel at home." Now that Stieglitz was actively engaged in the role of advancing an artistic vision through a gallery again, O'Keeffe was in awe once more. Her letter to Matthias continued,

> Stieglitz always seems more remarkable—and he brings remarkable things out of the people he comes in contact with. I feel like a little plant that he has watered and weeded and dug around—and he seems to have been able to grow himself—without any one watering or weeding or digging him—I don't quite understand it.

As an artist in his own right, Stieglitz was deeply reverential of the human impulse that led to the creation of art, which expressed profound truths that were only visible through the artist's unique combination of vision and technical talent—but as a gallery owner, he had to be responsive to the market for paintings. Starting in 1924, Stieglitz focused this generous attention on the work of seven artists: the American Seven, which consisted of Marin and O'Keeffe and himself in addition to Arthur Dove, Marsden Hartley, and Paul Strand—and the last position was kept open for different artists from year to year. Stieglitz tried to present the seven artists as a movement from year to year, but O'Keeffe could not see herself as part of an aesthetic group with the others. "Stieglitz liked the idea of a group," she would say. "I didn't." Stieglitz always looked at O'Keeffe's paintings with an eye to the market and the persona he had created for her, and she had to resist his judgment every time she innovated. With her large flower series, with her cityscapes, and then with her shells and stones, and again with the series of bones, she had to elude Stieglitz' ideas about her painting, leaping beyond him to define her own enigmatic, coded art.

Throughout the 1920s, Stieglitz promoted O'Keeffe as the remote priestess of American art, and as she retreated from this image, the aloof and enigmatic persona he created became a self-fulfilling prophecy. Stieglitz continued to promote and support her work, but as they approached ten years of living together, her paintings—particularly her shell series from 1926, and then the bones she painted in New Mexico after 1929— began to define closed, internal, or absolute spaces and shapes. O'Keeffe may have depended on Stieglitz for promoting her paintings or for support in her day-to-day life, but in her paintings, a sense of mutuality is almost nonexistent, as things themselves are presented solely as they appear to her and the only relationship is between self and object. Everything else is encoded in the gesture of painting, where any relationship has to be gleaned from the act of choosing a subject, the act of painting it, or the act of disposing of the painting—by selling it, giving it to friend as a gesture, or giving it away—or even, occasionally, destroying it.

If O'Keeffe filled large canvases with small flowers and bones as a form of resistance against Stieglitz' vision, she also diminished him with humor, since he was tenacious in argument, and outright opposition was unthinkable. More and more, over the course of their marriage, her letters take a bemused and slightly condescending tone with regard to Stieglitz. When he was hospitalized for a kidney attack in 1926, she wrote to a friend that "it has been very painful for him and the poor little thing is quite wore out."

Stieglitz found ways to get what he needed in spite of O'Keeffe's reserve, as well: he found other people whom he could keep close to him, and he began a relationship with Dorothy Norman, who was unhappily married to Edward Norman, the heir to the Sears & Roebuck mail order business. Norman was twenty-one when she came to Stieglitz' gallery for the first time in the spring of 1927, and she described being impressed with what she overheard of his conversation. "'You will discover,' he remarked,"—to another visitor, explaining, ironically, Georgia O'Keeffe's art—

> "that if the artist could explain in words what he has made, he would not have had to create it" . . . It was the sole occasion on which I had heard an older person communicate with someone younger about art without using tutorial, pedantic language; without failing to take into account the potential growth or development of the other.

Norman wrote that she was drawn to Stieglitz' "magnetism," as she put it, "the way he saw it, said it, spoke his life out loud. Confronting the world without mask." When she returned in November of that year, Norman recorded the following encounter with Stieglitz:

> I go into the Room once more. Stieglitz is alone, looking far into space. He asks if I am married, if the marriage is emotionally satisfying… "Yes, I'm in love with my husband and we have a new baby." "Is your sexual relationship good?" Talking about such matters is of vital importance, in spite of my inability to be totally honest. Stieglitz inquires, "Do you have enough milk to nurse your child?" Gently, impersonally, he barely brushes my coat with the tip of a finger over one of my breasts, and as swiftly removes it. "No." Our eyes do not meet.

"As soon as Stieglitz spoke to you," she wrote, elsewhere, "you felt freed of all your burdens and secrets; his understanding freed you." Norman was a socially minded philanthropist, who was well positioned to help Stieglitz subsidize his galleries—she was willing to be governed by his tastes, and she was sympathetic to the seemingly endless energy he spent on others, so she began to bathe Stieglitz in admiration, and soon she began to perform secretarial and administrative work at the gallery.

When Norman helped Stieglitz find funding for the Room, though,

Stieglitz himself would not admit any obligation, to Norman or to anyone. As Norman wrote in her biography of Stieglitz, "Either one worked with Stieglitz in perfect trust or not at all . . . No matter what you wanted to do for Stieglitz, it seemed always that he did more for others than anyone possibly could do for him and he asked nothing." Stieglitz would not allow Norman to tell him who was funding the gallery lest a sense of obligation compromise his independence or his authority. Nor would he accept gifts when they were offered, if he thought that the gift entailed obligations. O'Keeffe once attempted to repay her debt to him by giving him a painting, *Red and Brown Leaf,* which was an object portrait of the two of them, but Stieglitz hung the painting for sale, price $600. O'Keeffe "exclaimed," but he answered that "no one picture was his, all the pictures had been painted for him and for others, and he had to undergo the discipline of giving people the opportunity of carrying away even 'his' picture."

After 1927, Stieglitz did not turn to O'Keeffe but to Dorothy Norman for intimacy, as her admiration rekindled his sexual passions, but O'Keeffe described his attentions to Norman as more pathetic than threatening: she wrote that Norman "was one of those people who adored Stieglitz, and I'm sorry to say he was very foolish about her"—but she did not fight him in his infatuation. Hardly naming her jealousy, O'Keeffe expressed her discontent in geographical terms: "the city's very hard," she told an interviewer, before she spent most of the summer of 1928 traveling to Wisconsin to visit her sister and other relatives. By the winter exhibition season of 1928–1929, Stieglitz and Norman had become lovers, and O'Keeffe wrote to a friend that her work that winter was "mostly all dead for me."

Neither Stieglitz nor O'Keeffe would name Stieglitz' affair with Dorothy Norman as one of the factors in O'Keeffe's departure—they only described their needs in geographical terms. By 1928, O'Keeffe was beginning to chafe against the routine of living together half the year in New York and half in Lake George. Her health and their marriage were both suffering, but Stieglitz could only say that O'Keeffe was unhappy with the geography of Upstate New York, which she had never painted. He wrote to a friend that "I oftentimes—most times—feel like a criminal . . . in being the cause of keeping Georgia from where she really naturally belongs."

Having spent much of the summer of 1928 traveling, O'Keeffe disregarded Stieglitz' opposition the next summer as well, and she traveled to

Taos, New Mexico, for an eight-week-long visit to Mabel Dodge Luhan. O'Keeffe had heard about Taos and its community of writers and art- ists from Paul and Beck Strand, and from other artists who had passed through Mabel Dodge Luhan's ranch there, and O'Keeffe herself had been impressed by what Mabel had written about another painter in 1925. "I wished you had seen my work," O'Keeffe wrote her. "I thought you could write something about me that the men cant."

The trip to New Mexico in 1929 rejuvenated her, and it also resulted in a number of affairs. Primarily, O'Keeffe fell in love again with the flat, dry, and empty landscape she had loved in Texas: "I am West again and it is as fine as I remembered it—maybe finer—There is nothing to say about it except that for me it is the only place." Sunbathing nude together, she and Beck either became or simply acted like lovers that summer (biog- raphies differ), and after a short period of intimacy with Beck, O'Keeffe moved into Mabel's bedroom at night, then into Mabel's husband Tony's bedroom when Mabel went north to have a hysterectomy.

With liberty to draw close to lovers of her own, O'Keeffe could clarify what had been bothering her about Stieglitz' affair with Norman and come to her own peace about it, even indirectly. She wrote to Mabel,

> Right now as I come fresh from six days mostly spent with your Tony—I want to tell you that next to my Stieglitz I have found nothing finer than your Tony . . . I feel you have got to let him live and *be* his way—however much it might hurt you . . . I feel that you haven't any more right to keep Tony utterly unto yourself than I have to keep Stieglitz—Even if he goes out and sleeps with someone else it is a little thing. If Tony happens to go to women with his body, it is the same thing when one goes out for a spiritual debauch.

In New York, Stieglitz was still openly going about with Norman, but he wrote to his niece that he was "going through a kind of crisis" in O'Keeffe's absence. Stieglitz may have been panicking about the possibil- ity that she would desert him, for he could not depend on Norman for the same kind of support he got from O'Keeffe. He wrote O'Keeffe as many as fifteen letters a day and lamented the possibility of being forgot- ten. "The cunt has no memory," he complained to a friend. Stieglitz had turned sixty-five on January 1, 1929, and that summer his crisis mani- fested itself in a conflagration. He purged his papers, destroying clippings as well as early prints, which he called the "diapers of my children" and the "dreams of youth." "That's death riding high in the sky," he would say of that summer's "Equivalents." "All these things have death in them . . . ever since I realized O'Keeffe couldn't stay with me."

But Stieglitz also described himself in a letter to his niece as "finally beyond all Hurt," and when he wrote to Mabel, he said that art compensated his jealousy. His letters turned O'Keeffe into an ideal, though abstract partner: "my photographs—the Equivalents—are what that Self is—as Georgia's paintings are what she is." To his niece, again, he insisted on the language of unity: "I had a marvellous wire from Georgia this morning—she feels as I feel—Exactly . . . She feels a greater & more wonderful togetherness—the first coming together in purity on a much higher plane!"

At the end of that summer, O'Keeffe's return to New York was a joyous occasion. To Mabel, she wrote that

> it is wonderful to be here and be with my funny little Stieglitz—
> He is grand—so grand that I dont seem to see [his] family about
> or anything else—I just seem to think—to know—that he is the
> grandest thing in the world—and wonder how I ever was able to
> stay away from him so long . . . He seems to me the most beautiful
> thing I ever knew . . .
> The summer had brought me to a state of mind where I felt as
> grateful for my largest hurts as I did for my largest happiness—in
> spite of all my tearing about many things that had been accumu-
> lating inside of me for years were arranging themselves—and re-
> arranging themselves—The same thing had been happening with
> Stieglitz—and as we meet—it is quite difficult to tell how—it seems
> the most perfect thing that has ever happened to me—Maybe you
> understand it without understanding it—as I do.

The summer of jealous anxieties did not disturb the functional, public relationship between herself and Stieglitz, but now that she had tasted the freedom—and the arrival—of traveling to New Mexico, reconciling their personal lives was going to be more difficult. O'Keeffe continued to travel during the summers, and in 1932, she again used geographical terms to express the tensions in her marriage. She wrote to Russell Vernon Hunter that the migration between New York and New Mexico made her feel "divided between my man and a life with him—and something of the outdoors . . . that is in my blood and that I know I can never get rid of—I will have to get along with my divided self the best way I can."

X.

The opposition of powerful erotic and geographic tensions played itself out in 1932, when Stieglitz' forty-year retrospective placed early nudes of O'Keeffe—who was now thirty-four, and childless—alongside newer nudes of Norman, with whom Stieglitz had been going about openly since 1931. That season, Paul Strand also parted ways with Stieglitz, and he and Beck divorced as well. Beset by her own difficulties with Stieglitz, O'Keeffe could only console Beck by writing that "I think of you and think of you and wish I could think of something to say to you and I cannot—It just seems that what is going to hit us has hit you first."

What struck Beck as a divorce hit O'Keeffe as a nervous breakdown the following year. As early as 1930, as Stieglitz' infatuation with Norman entered its third year, O'Keeffe had been starting to rely on him less and less, emotionally and then professionally. She expanded her sphere of associations with galleries, museum, and dealers, and she cultivated a relationship with the Museum of Modern Art, whose curators had always been enemies of Stieglitz'. When she accepted a commission from the Rockefellers, though, to decorate the ladies' waiting room of Radio City Music Hall, Stieglitz felt threatened enough that he started almost immediately to undermine the project. He railed against O'Keeffe's judgment, and he enlisted his friends to try to talk her out of it. The possibility of losing Stieglitz' support—at a time when she had already lost his erotic interest—increased O'Keeffe's anxiety to such an extent that when she found pieces of canvas separating from the walls during her initial inspection of the room, she resigned the commission. Stieglitz wrote to Radio City to explain her withdrawal, citing the wall's unreadiness, and then her health as reasons, threatening to sue if they would not release her from the contract. The crisis ran deeper than just this project, though, and in February 1933, O'Keeffe was hospitalized for depression and anxiety and uncontrollable fits of weeping.

O'Keeffe's hospitalization jarred Stieglitz out of his infatuation with Norman, and the affair cooled down as he devoted himself to O'Keeffe's care and then he began to purge old prints and papers again. In March of 1933 O'Keeffe left the hospital to convalesce in Bermuda with her friend Marjorie Content, but she really only began to regain her health toward the end of 1933, in a brief intimacy with Jean Toomer, the author of *Cane*, a 1923 prose poem of the African American experience. When Toomer

visited her in Lake George in December, he worked on a novel while
O'Keeffe convalesced. On the winter solstice, he wrote to Stieglitz,

> For the first ten days I was sort of in the house by myself . . . Now
> it is inhabited by someone else, by an extraordinary person whom
> I've hardly more than peeped at from the outside (and how she can
> keep people outside!) whom now, however, I'm beginning to see
> and feel—if not understand! . . . I'm impressed by the way she has
> of remaining always herself.

Toomer left O'Keeffe on December 30, but O'Keeffe remained at Lake
George, and she did not attend Stieglitz' seventieth birthday in the city
on New Year's Day 1934. Dorothy Norman had already claimed the day
for herself, and she had organized a party and a Festschrift for Stieglitz,
with essays from many of his artists, but nothing from O'Keeffe.

Toomer may have rejuvenated O'Keeffe, but he did not resolve her
need for intimacy. "What you give me," she wrote to him after his depar-
ture, "makes me feel more able to stand up alone—and I would like to
feel able to stand up alone before I put out my hand to anyone." She had
been moved by Toomer's physical beauty, as well as his refinement and
understanding, but she told him that she saw herself moving "more and
more toward a kind of aloneness—not because I wish it so, but because
there seems to be no other way." After he left, she wrote:

> The center of you seems to me to be built with your mind—clear—
> beautiful—relentless—with a deep warm humanness that I think
> I can see and understand but *have not*—so maybe I neither see nor
> understand even tho I think I do—I understand enough to feel I
> do not wish to touch it unless I can accept it completely because it is
> so humanly beautiful and beyond me at the moment. I dread touch-
> ing it in any way but with complete acceptance. My center does not
> come from my mind—it feels in me like a plot of warm moist well
> tilled earth with the sun shining hot on it—nothing with a spark of
> possibility of growth seems seeded in it at the moment—
>
>   It seems I would rather feel it starkly empty than let anything
> be planted that can not be tended to the fullest possibility of its
> growth and what that means I do not know
>
>   But I do know that the demands of my plot of earth are relent-
> less if anything is to grow in it—worthy of its quality

Maybe the quality that we have in common is relentlessness—
maybe the thing that attracts me to you separates me from you

If the past year or two or three has taught me anything it is that
my plot of earth must be tended with absurd care—By myself first—
and if second by someone else it must be with absolute trust—their
thinking carefully and knowing what they do—It seems it would be
very difficult for me to live if it were wrecked again just now.

As with her relationship with Mabel Dodge Luhan, though, her time with
Toomer made it possible for her to articulate her needs to Stieglitz, and
now she was more appreciative of his consideration. After her reunion
with Stieglitz in New York in the winter of 1934, she wrote to Toomer,
"there were talks that seemed almost to kill me—and surprisingly strong
sweet beautiful things seemed to come from them."

In the spring of 1934—in spite of her reunion with Stieglitz and in
spite of Stieglitz' renewed opposition—O'Keeffe went west again for
inspiration and recuperation. She did not return to Mabel and Tony
Luhan's ranch, though, but in 1934 and then again in 1935, she spent
six months at the Ghost Ranch resort in Abiquiu, where she met and
developed a friendship with Elizabeth Arden, who commissioned her
to decorate the Elizabeth Arden spa—a $10,000 project that offered a
kind of redemption for her failure at Radio City Music Hall.

Now that Stieglitz was into his seventies, O'Keeffe was more and more
independent of him, and between Stieglitz' old age and the sympathy
he had developed for O'Keeffe during her breakdown, he no longer had
as strong a desire to oppose her independence. His health and strength
began to decline, and in 1938, he had a heart attack from which he spent
six months recovering. There would be six more heart attacks before
his death in 1946, but after the first one in 1938, he no longer had the
strength to work with the camera, and he ceased to take pictures. After
1929, O'Keeffe had established part-time residence in New Mexico with
extended visits, but in 1938 her departure was delayed by Stieglitz' heart
attack, and in 1939 she did not go west at all, but she stayed in New York
to nurse him. O'Keeffe was not always in New York when Stieglitz had
his angina attacks, though, and while she herself obeyed the instinct that
took her back to New Mexico, she arranged for him to be cared for by
his doctor brother, Lee, and his friends, as well as hired nurses. Stieglitz
had always made the living arrangements for the two of them, but now,

through her connection with patron Elsie de Wolfe, O'Keeffe secured a large penthouse apartment for their winters in the city.

Stieglitz was lonely without O'Keeffe, but her independence was an outcome of his own very carefully executed publicity plans. Stieglitz had manipulated the art market so that sales of her paintings had begun to outpace even the revenues from his photography. In 1930, the first year of the Great Depression, he had issued a press release stating that six of O'Keeffe's paintings had sold for the astounding sum of $25,000.* The paintings had not been sold—they had in fact been lent on commission—but after the press release and the resulting publicity, the price for O'Keeffe's paintings increased as collectors felt safe investing in her beautiful, valuable canvases. By the end of the 1930s, the Great Depression notwithstanding, O'Keeffe's paintings were selling steadily for large sums, and O'Keeffe could begin to provide for her siblings and their children, in addition to providing the space and independence she needed for herself.

In 1940, O'Keeffe bought an adobe house on eight acres at Ghost Ranch, where she began to spend more and more of each year. The place "has such a clean untouched feeling," she said, "I never get over being surprised that I am here—that I a house and I can stay." She even had a brush with motherhood during her first summer there, when a baby was born to the girl she had hired to cook and clean for her. The girl would not name the man who had abandoned her, so O'Keeffe took her in, and together they cared for the baby until the end of the summer, when O'Keeffe finally extracted the father's name from the girl. She wrote to him and she drove the girl and her baby to Colorado, where she made all the arrangements for the girl's wedding.

O'Keeffe also met and began an enduring friendship with Maria Chabot, another independent woman who fixed up the house and managed O'Keeffe's affairs. Chabot lived and worked with O'Keeffe for ten years, but she described herself as "the second of O'Keeffe's slaves. Beck Strand was the first." In 1945 O'Keeffe bought another house, in Abiquiu, and she entrusted Chabot with renovating the buildings and farming the land, while she herself took part in the subsistence routines of gardening, canning, and baking bread between painting.

Now that she was assured of an income from her painting, O'Keeffe's

---

* Roughly $325,000 in 2011 dollars.

work evolved toward the landscape and the bones and plants that repre-
sented it, all of which she continued to use as object portraits and even
self-portraits, abstracting certain elements even as she rendered the sky
or landscape or the bones in fine detail. If her experience still moved
her deeply, her expression was still largely private, encoded in her paint-
ings. In a letter to art critic Henry McBride, she wrote that her visions
shamed reality:

> If I could just get down all Im thinking about while Im sick those
> calla lilies would look like a mere speck—and my New Yorks would
> turn the world over—but—fortunately—or unfortunately—I lose
> a lot of it before I can do anything about it—so it is usually only
> remnants that finally appear.

Even in spite of herself, O'Keeffe seemed to be fulfilling the prophecy
Stieglitz had made—the same prophecy she had resisted—of a self so
pure and remote that her experience itself, of the landscape or of things
themselves, seemed both to require and to compensate her loneliness.

Now that Stieglitz had already successfully cultivated a public for
O'Keeffe's paintings—now that he was no longer inspiring her with his
own innovations—the correspondence between them tended toward
a nostalgic formality. In 1937, O'Keeffe wrote from New Mexico, "you
sound a bit lonely up there on the hill—It makes me wish I could be
beside you for a little while—I suppose the part of me that is anything
to you is there—even if I am here." In 1940, when she left to fly to New
Mexico, Stieglitz made her departure bearable by abstracting their dif-
ferences, describing an essential unity:

> I greet you on your coming once more to your own country. I hope
> it will be very good to you. You have earned that. A kiss. I'm with
> you wherever you are. And you ever with me I know.
>
> Incredible Georgia—and how beautiful your pictures are at the
> Modern—I'm glad. I'm glad we were there this morning . . . Oh
> Georgia—we are a team—yes a team. Can't believe that you are to
> leave and that you are reading this in your own country.
>
> It is very hard for me to realize that within a few hours you will
> have left . . . But there is no choice. You need what "Your Place" will
> give you. Yes you need that sorely. And I'll be with you, Cape and all.
> And you'll be with me here and at 59 [East Fifty-fourth Street].

Self-sufficient and independent in the landscape she loved, O'Keeffe continued to correspond from New Mexico with the nurses and friends who had been taking care of Stieglitz starting in 1940, and they organized a joint retrospective together in 1941.

Stieglitz may have tried too often to use his health as a reason to bring O'Keeffe back to New York, because O'Keeffe became wary of making the long trip by train, and even when his condition was becoming genuinely grave, she delayed, waiting for more information. When she heard that he had suffered a massive stroke in 1946, she ultimately missed his death, arriving in New York hours after he had died. She remained in the city for the next three years, though, to dispose of Stieglitz' estate, and she distributed his papers and his pictures, as well as his extensive art collection, to museums and libraries.

XI.

After she returned to New Mexico in 1949, O'Keeffe moved in to the recently restored Abiquiu house full-time. She exchanged visits with her sisters and with other artists, and she traveled widely—to Mexico to see the work of muralists Orozco and Rivera, and to France, then to Peru, Japan, and Morocco, among other places. She frequently traveled with or visited friends, but she did not draw close with anyone romantically for a long time. She maintained close, almost sisterly relationships with her assistants, but in addition to describing her assistants' deep loyalty to her, contemporary accounts of these working relationships often described fierce bickering as well as tempestuous departures, which sometimes lasted for years before the working friendships resumed.

With John Marin, O'Keeffe tried to keep Stieglitz' gallery open, and she showed some of her New Mexico paintings there in 1950, but she closed the gallery after the show. She found a dealer who would handle her paintings, and now she could live in New Mexico and ship her paintings east to be sold in New York. In 1961, O'Keeffe broke with her dealer and started to have her works shown in the warehouse where they were kept, further bolstering the myth Stieglitz had shaped, of the remote priestess of art. The myth was only partly accurate, though, for her Abiquiu house came with water rights—which the Ghost Ranch house did not have—and the ability to irrigate crops allowed her to hire on locals to help her maintain a large garden and grounds. Integrating herself into the community, O'Keeffe contributed to the schools and subsidized college costs for local children. She remained a painter and a foreigner, though, and an enigma to the locals, and she sometimes icily refused to see the young artists who made pilgrimages to her house.

O'Keeffe's letters pondered her remoteness even as she retreated into it. In 1955 she wrote to Anita Pollitzer,

> It is a week or more and I do not write you. Now you must realize that I am old enough so that people I have called friends have died—but my dogs are here . . .
>
> Friends—maybe the best—and very beautiful too—Maybe the man who gave me the dogs is my friend—He knew their parents and grandparents—He knew they were good
>
> I am old enough so that my friends children bring their new husbands and wives—and then their children.
>
> Is the man who brings me a load of wood my friend—I pay him—and then because the wood is good I give him a loaf of bread I've made because I know the bread is good—I know he cooks for himself and he will know the bread is good and I want to give him something because the wood is good—Sounds funny doesnt it.
>
> Are any Texas neighbors across the River friends—Is Jackie [Suazo—a young man and petty criminal with whom she was involved at the time] my friend? I call him my darling and tell him my idea of a darling is someone who is a nuisance—he has been the horror of the community . . .
>
> Is my framer my friend? he has been a great help to me for many years—Is the young man who sends me a tub of salt herring because he likes it—my friend— . . .
>
> Is the woman who gets me to go to Europe [Betty Pilkington] my friend?
>
> I consider my doctor and her family my friends
>
> I once had a cat that was my friend. The people I visited often in N.J. when N.Y. broke me down were certainly friends
>
> I have a new woman here to take care of me and tend to the many things that have to be done—I've had her 2 weeks and my life is so much easier that maybe such a one is a friend—I dont know— she may not stay—The term "friend" is an odd word—
>
> Names of interest are what would interest most people I

suppose—It is another sort of human quality of human nearness
and usefulness that has made what I call my friends
    Goodnight Anita
    I am sleepy and a little cold
    G

Pollitzer herself wrote a short piece about O'Keeffe in 1950, and then
turned her piece into a full-length biography. O'Keeffe and her dealer
both helped her write and research, but O'Keeffe was too severe with
herself to let Pollitzer publish the draft she finally submitted in 1959.
"You have written your dream picture of me," she wrote her. "It is a very
sentimental way you like to imagine me—and I am not that way at all.
We are such different kinds of people that it reads as if we spoke different
languages and didn't understand one another at all." O'Keeffe withdrew
her consent from the project, and the book was not published in Pol-
litzer's lifetime.* Even without Pollitzer's contribution, O'Keeffe lived
long enough to witness her own canonization, with honorary degrees,
election to the American Academy of Arts and Science, and retrospec-
tives at MoMA and the Whitney in New York in addition to art museums
in Worcester, Massachusetts, and Fort Worth and Houston, Texas.

XII.

At the age of eighty-five, O'Keeffe was revitalized once more by Juan
Hamilton, a transient twenty-seven-year-old potter who showed up at
her ranch shortly after her secretary had quit in 1973. He started doing
odd jobs for her, and then when her eyesight began to deteriorate, he
became indispensable to her. As with Anita Pollitzer, Beck Strand, and
Maria Chabot, O'Keeffe drew Hamilton into her life by encouraging his
work, but soon she demanded so much from him that his own artwork
became impossible, and O'Keeffe enlisted him in the labor of writing—
dictating and typing, then reading and revising—her own autobiography.
Hamilton became O'Keeffe's private secretary, and he acted as her gate-
keeper to the rest of the world, with power to determine which letters
she heard and which visitors saw her. An attraction developed between

---

* *A Woman on Paper: Georgia O'Keeffe* was published in 1988.

them in spite of his drinking and his angry outbursts, and as O'Keeffe's eyesight and then her health began to fail, she gave her private life with him priority over the public life with dealers and old friends who could not tend to her daily needs the way he could. Forced to choose between old allegiances and her present caretaker, she honored Hamilton's influence in the face of her dealer's lawsuits, and the desertions of friends and assistants.

Hamilton took a wife in 1980, but it is not clear whether he may also have staged a wedding ceremony with O'Keeffe. In the same way that O'Keeffe was far from Stieglitz when he died, Hamilton was in Mexico when O'Keeffe died in 1986 at the age of ninety-eight. He became the heir and executor of O'Keeffe's estate, but O'Keeffe's relatives would contend in court that Hamilton had exercised undue influence over her. The court settlement gave him property and paintings, but it also provided for the majority of her artwork to be distributed to museums and libraries by a committee that paired him with her relatives.

XIII.

If old age allowed Georgia O'Keeffe to exercise what her sisters would call poor judgment in her choice of partners, her relationship with Juan Hamilton was perfectly in line with her lifelong desire to feel her experience resonate in someone who had the strength to carry her—in spite of her poverty, when she was young, and in spite of her celebrity when she was older. O'Keeffe always felt her own experience sharply, but she never found a partner who could share the full depth of her feelings. If Stieglitz' expert promotion allowed her a greater and greater freedom of experience over time—and if her paintings attained a certain fineness of expression—her art and her marriage alike remained incomplete consummations of her powerful drive toward beauty and experience. This drive was at the heart of Stieglitz' life as well, even at the heart of his definition of marriage, which he described as a companionship in which each preserved the other's drive toward self-fulfillment. "If it is real," he wrote, marriage "must be based on a wish that each person attain his potentiality, be the thing he might be, as a tree bears its fruit."

In all their time together, Stieglitz and O'Keeffe promoted each other's artwork—Stieglitz through his galleries, O'Keeffe by offering herself to Stieglitz' camera—but in their daily lives, Stieglitz and O'Keeffe valued very different things. O'Keeffe never felt that her paintings were more than rough approximations of what she felt, but the act of painting and the daily work of running a household and working the land were their own consolations, even their own form of work. In her love for such daily work, though, O'Keeffe found herself temperamentally opposed to Stieglitz, who thrived in argumentation and debate, and who needed to see the effect his ideas and his visions had on the people around him.

If they compromised—if O'Keeffe kept house for Stieglitz' family's social vacations at Lake George each summer, or if Stieglitz ultimately relinquished O'Keeffe to Maine or New Mexico—their shared purpose also allowed them to defer any resolution of their most pressing differences. Stieglitz' affairs might never have been spoken about, but O'Keeffe did not let his opposition keep her from getting what she needed for herself either: she simply packed up and left when he was infatuated with Beck Strand or then with Dorothy Norman.

O'Keeffe and Stieglitz hardly addressed the serious differences that set them against each other, and they never reconciled them, but they continued to live and work together nonetheless. Throughout their correspondence, they expressed a faith in the impersonal process of making art, and they trusted their work either to provide a fulfillment that could occasionally compensate their pains or to contain, or compose, the feelings they could not reconcile. So long as they continued to make art, they had a bond they could trust, and it allowed them to endure—and even to inflict—real sufferings. "You must not let the things you cannot help destroy you," O'Keeffe wrote to a friend, when Stieglitz was starting his affair with Dorothy Norman. "I am so sure that Work is the thing in life—We mustn't let the human problems kill us . . . Do save your strength and energy for creating—don't spend it on problems and situations you can't help."

Intellectuals in Love

Jean-Paul Sartre and Simone de Beauvoir

The only sort of person in whose favor I could ever wish to surrender my autonomy would be just the one who did his utmost to prevent any such thing.   SIMONE DE BEAUVOIR

I'm a genius because I'm alive . . . Oh I wish others could experience my life as I do, overflowing, tumultuous . . . If only I could express it, tear it out of myself. Then I'd be in reality the genius I'm entitled to be. Only one man is alive for me: myself . . . and I cannot believe I am going to die.
                                          JEAN-PAUL SARTRE

With Sartre, too, I have a physical relationship, but very little, and it is mostly tenderness, and—I'm not quite sure how to put this—I don't feel involved in it because he is not involved in it himself.
                                          SIMONE DE BEAUVOIR

I.

In July 1929, Simone de Beauvoir joined Jean-Paul Sartre and René Maheu's study group for the last two weeks of preparation for the prestigious *agrégation* exam in philosophy. With seventy-three other students, they would be competing for thirteen of the highest-ranked positions in the philosophy departments of French public schools. If they passed, they would be more than well-paid civil servants with plenty of time on their hands for writing: they were going to use the prestige of their positions to fashion themselves as the new authorities on how to live in a culture that was spiraling deeper and deeper into crisis.

Beauvoir wrote in her memoir that she and Sartre grew up in "a world that was without God, yet where our salvation still remained at stake." Between the horrors of the Great War and the Communist revolution

in Russia—between the advent of Darwinian evolution, Freudian psy-choanalysis, and nihilistic modern philosophy, not to mention all the turmoil of industrialization and modernization—Sartre and Beauvoir and the students in their circle felt that their parents' generation's bour-geois social conventions no longer had any value. Sartre and Beauvoir had come to philosophy by way of the contemporary literature of dis-quiet, weltschmerz, and ennui—and they and their friends were going to use philosophy to rebel against their inherited culture: they wanted to describe reality, even if it was tumultuous, vulgar, contradictory, or painful.

When Beauvoir joined Maheu's study group, she was still relatively inexperienced, and she wrote in her memoir that she felt Sartre, Maheu, and their friend Paul Nizan "had all explored much more fundamentally than I had the consequences of the inexistence of God and brought their philosophy right down to earth." Irreverent and cocky, they seemed to be studying Descartes and Spinoza, Leibniz and Kant, Hegel, Schopenhauer, and Nietzsche—the past in toto—for the sole purpose of defining their own philosophies. They were confident that they themselves would one day explain, in their own terms, how to live in the violent chaos of the twentieth century—without recourse to God or absolutes. They believed that "man was to be remolded," Beauvoir would later write, and now that Sartre and Maheu absorbed her into their group, she felt that "the process would be partly our doing." In their writings and in their experiences, they were going to bear witness against their parents' artificial culture and testify to the complexity of real life.

Sartre and his friends quickly nicknamed Beauvoir the Beaver—both for how hard she worked and because of *beaver*'s resemblance to *Beauvoir* in English—and when the *agrégation* test results came in, Sartre had placed first, Beauvoir a close second, Nizan third. Maheu, Beauvoir's favorite, had failed—he and Nizan left Paris immediately after the exam, but Sartre stayed in Paris and took Beauvoir under his wing. Beauvoir had not originally been impressed with Sartre, but she had been sheltered in her Catholic girls' school, and now he enjoyed showing her the world. He bought her books, he took her to cowboy films, and he delighted her by inventing songs and poems extemporaneously. They would talk for hours, she wrote,

> about all kinds of things, but especially about a subject which inter-ested me above all others: myself . . . Sartre always tried to see me as part of my own scheme of things, to understand me in the light of my own set of values and attitudes. Not only did he give me encouragement but he also intended to give me active help in achieving this ambition.

Liberated from the stifling atmospheres of their conventional families' values—delighted in their newfound independence, they extrapolated rebellious philosophical systems from each other's words and gestures, and they prophesied the books they would write, the philosophical systems they would build their careers on. Having just passed the test that would free her from all dependence upon her family and its tradi-tions, Beauvoir wrote that "there were no scruples, no feelings of respect or loyal affection, that would stop us from making up our minds by the pure light of reason—and of our own desires. We were unaware of any cloudiness or confusion in our mental processes; we believed ourselves to consist of pure reason and pure will."

That summer, Sartre and Beauvoir became inseparable. When she left Paris with her family to vacation at her father's family's estate, he came to stay in a nearby hotel, and they spent time together in the fields, mocking at society and encouraging each other to live philosophically genuine lives. Beauvoir's father asked Sartre to leave—not because he was concerned about Beauvoir's reputation, which was already beyond repair at that point, but because the neighbors were talking about them, and he was concerned that gossip would ruin Beauvoir's cousin's reputation on the eve of her wedding—but Sartre refused to go. He and Beauvoir just took their conversations to more remote arbors, where Beauvoir continued to thrive on his attention. In early September, Beauvoir wrote in her journal that it was "not an overwhelming passion . . . but it's happiness . . . Never have I loved so much to read and think. Never have I been so alive and happy, or envisaged such a rich future."

Back in Paris in October, Sartre clinched their philosophical interrelationship in a landmark three-hour discussion in the Luxembourg Gardens. With his nearly nihilistic willingness to trust his own chaotic experience—and to jettison all absolutes and external authorities—he "demolished" Beauvoir's "carefully assembled . . . pluralist philosophy," which she said had "authorized me to look upon my heart as the arbiter of good and evil." Even that, Sartre said, smacked of sentimentalism, and Beauvoir wrote in her memoir that she knew she had been beaten: she acknowledged his intellectual superiority and had to admit that she lived in the chaotic, contingent world he described, where nothing was settled and even her heart had no moral authority. As she wrote later in her memoir, she realized that "many of my opinions were based only on prejudice, dishonesty, or hastily formed concepts, that my reasoning was at fault and that my ideas were in a muddle."

This demonstration of philosophical superiority was an act of dominance that bound Sartre and Beauvoir to each other for the rest of their lives. Beauvoir would henceforward trust Sartre to show her the meaning of her feelings and the consequences of her actions, and Sartre would be guaranteed a devoted listener who was both intelligent enough to appreciate the philosophy of his everyday life and individualistic enough to use his theories as she searched for her own philosophy. Trained in the same philosophies, rebelling against the same culture, they felt they were developing a single philosophy together.

When they became lovers in mid-October, they even began to describe themselves as one person. Beauvoir had finally moved out of her parents' house into a room in her grandmother's boarding house, and there in her rented room, free from parental scrutiny, she and Sartre consummated their discussions. They were still determined to respect the chaos of experience, though, and they wanted to outrage their parents, so they refused to be married. As Beauvoir recounts their decision in her memoir, Sartre had said that he was

> not inclined to be monogamous by nature: he took pleasure in the company of women, finding them less comic than men. He had no intention, at twenty-three, of renouncing their tempting variety.
>
> He explained the matter to me in his favorite terminology. "What *we* have," he said, "is an *essential* love; but it is a good idea for us also to experience *contingent* love affairs." We were two of a kind, and our relationship would endure as long as we did: but it could not make up entirely for the fleeting riches to be had from encounters with different people. How could we deliberately forego that gamut of emotions—astonishment, regret, pleasure, nostalgia—which we were as capable of sustaining as anyone else? We reflected on this problem a good deal during our walks together.

Sartre suggested that they "sign a two-year lease," during which time they would live together in Paris, then travel separately to teaching positions abroad. They would then return to one another, and "for a longer or shorter period, live more or less together. We would never become strangers to one another, and neither would appeal for the other's help in vain; nothing would prevail against this alliance of ours." To guarantee their essential love, they proposed one additional pact: "not only would we never lie to one another," Beauvoir wrote, "but neither of us would conceal anything from the other." With visions sharpened by philosophy, they would look their desires in the face and they would describe them in their writing—unlike Beauvoir's father and Sartre's grandfather, who had hypocritically lied about their affairs.

Sartre and Beauvoir joked that they were making a "morganatic marriage"—a marriage in which partners come from different social classes and one cannot inherit the wealth of the other: together they renounced everything they might have inherited from their families. Beauvoir could not refuse Sartre's unconventional proposition: she herself had expressed disdain for the double standard by which men were permitted casual affairs while women were bound by a much stricter morality, and now she was determined to be as free as any man. Sartre's refusal to make an exclusive commitment himself—and his refusal to let her bind herself to him—actually testified to his genuineness.

Their unconventional lease promised them both a radical new liberty at the same time that it confirmed their rebellion against bourgeois society. For the rest of their lives, they would encourage each other to take lovers when they wanted to have the experience of intimacy with another person, and they would edit each other's novels and the philosophical works in which they crystallized the truth of their "contingent" experiences. Refusing to rest in secure bourgeois comforts, they suffered—and they made their lovers suffer—for their insistence on contingency, but they did not insist on reconciling their actions with conventional morality. Even if they ultimately devised "temporary moral codes" to justify the lies and half-truths they told to their lovers, they held each other to the most scrupulous standards in their creative, political, and philosophical writings.

II.

For Jean-Paul Sartre, the radical liberty of his relationship with Beauvoir was an antidote to the stifling pleasantness of his childhood household, and the overbearing presence of his highly cultured grandfather, Charles Schweitzer, who was the head of the house. Sartre's mother, Anne Marie Schweitzer, had fled from that home in 1904 at twenty-one, when she married Jean-Baptiste Sartre, a naval officer she had met through an older brother. Less than three years later, though, Jean-Baptiste died of enterocolitis, and she came back home with her eighteen-month-old infant. In his autobiography, Sartre wrote that in her parents' house, "Anne Marie, chilled with gratitude . . . became a minor again, a stainless virgin" who "gave herself unstintingly, kept house for her parents" and was always "under surveillance . . . obedient to everyone." When mother and son were lodged in the same room—which was called "the children's room"—he took her to be a sister: "my mother and I were the same age and were always together. She called me her knight attendant, her little man. I told her everything."

Charles Schweitzer, Sartre's grandfather, was fifty-six when Anne Marie brought her infant home. An immigrant from Alsace, he had opened the Modern Language Institute in Paris to teach French to foreigners, and he had written a series of readers for teaching, the royalties from which supported a comfortable existence. Schweitzer resumed the breadwinner's role and began to teach again after Sartre and his mother returned, but he was not intent on playing the part of the father again—he preferred to be entertained by his grandson. As soon as Sartre learned to read, Schweitzer proclaimed him a genius, and Sartre, catching on to his grandfather's game, began to seek further praises by reading the most difficult books he could find. Young Sartre delighted his family with precocious sayings gleaned from his readings, and thus gained a reputation as a prodigy. According to Sartre's autobiography, this image was constantly reinforced by his grandfather, who saw in Sartre the image he wanted to see of himself, of the immigrant whose brilliant progeny had mastered the high literature of his adopted culture.

When Sartre reached school age, Schweitzer tutored him himself—the practice was not uncommon at the time—and he employed tutors only occasionally. When Schweitzer did finally send Sartre to school, his teachers took him to task for his unorthodox spelling, and Schweitzer pulled him out after the first day. Accustomed to a steady diet of his grandfather's approval, Sartre later wrote that "my failure had not affected me: I was a child prodigy who was not a good speller, that was all." Petted and spoiled—lacking any external standard of judgment—Sartre learned only slowly to distrust his family's praises, and to see that he was just a pawn in a game designed for their self-satisfaction. As he wrote in his memoir, "Whether the adults listen to my babbling or to *The Art of the Fugue*, they have the same arch smile of enjoyment and complicity. That shows what I am essentially: a cultural asset."

Trying to give her child something like a normal childhood, Sartre's mother bought him adventure books, infuriating her father for corrupting the prodigy's literary tastes, but these books gave Sartre the images and narratives by which he could cast himself as a hero or a martyr, someone who was important because of his actions. He began to invent trials and adventures for himself, and he began to write them down in stories that were based on, if not outright copied from, his adventure books—or from the encyclopedia, when he needed hard facts. He himself was both adventurer and author, and his exploits were always heroic. "Since nobody laid claim to me *seriously*," he wrote, "I laid claim to being indispensable to the Universe." Freed from his grandparents' unreal praises by his imaginary exploits, Sartre discovered the terrifying freedom of the author who can imagine anything he likes—but whose personal experiences nonetheless do not exist until they are written down.

When Sartre was finally enrolled in school full-time at age ten, he did not vault to the top of his class, but he was not daunted: he was "too loved to have doubts" about himself. He only began to be constrained in earnest at age twelve, when his mother married Joseph Mancy, an engineer who moved the family to La Rochelle, in the west of France. There Sartre lost his mother's attention to Mancy and his grandfather's to the distance, as he entered into battle with what he would later call his stepfather's "physicist's temperament, pessimism, underhandedness, bitterness."

Sartre was also up against the reality that he was physically different than the other children: at age four, he had contracted leucoma in his right eye, which impaired his vision and caused his eye to wander, and he would reach an adult height of only five foot one. Sartre was beaten up frequently by the rougher country boys, but he had already created a personality that could endure the abuse: he was going to be a famous writer, and these were just the indignities the famous writer had to suffer in his youth. Sartre did not believe that he was ugly until he and his classmates began to notice girls, but by the time he learned to see himself through other eyes, he had already turned to language—and to his imagination— to compensate. Among the other boys, he assumed what he would later call an "odd tone and role . . . among groups of men: a pathetic sort of guy, ugly . . . his ideas somewhat revolting, but making people laugh anyway, stirring them up a bit." Even though Sartre was short and weak, he acquired a reputation for creative and exacting brutality in his insults, and so shifted the contest from brute strength to a game he would ultimately win by becoming a famous writer.

At sixteen, Sartre enrolled in the Lycée Henry IV, Paris' most prestigious high school, where he became fast friends with Paul Nizan, the dandyish son of an engineer, who was also slightly cross-eyed. Sartre and Nizan were soon inseparable—so much that they came to be known as Nitre and Sarzan—and in an autobiographical sketch from 1940, Sartre wrote that

> what had changed profoundly since my arrival in Paris was the fact that I'd found comrades and a friend. Friendship was the main thing. It's something which appeared in my life with my sixteenth year and Nizan, and which, in different guises, hasn't left it since . . . What friendship brought me—far more than affection (whatever that may have been)—was a federative world, in which my friend and I would pool all our values, all our thoughts and all our tastes. And this world was renewed by ceaseless invention. At the same

time, each of us buttressed the other, and the result was a *couple* of considerable strength . . .

What it comes down to is that, since my seventeenth year, I've always lived as part of a couple . . . I was engaged in a kind of radiant, and somewhat torrid, existence—without any inner life and without any secrets—in which I felt the total pressure of another presence constantly upon me, and in which I hardened myself to endure that presence . . .

From that period on, a pitiless clarity ruled over my mind: it was an operating room, hygienic, without shadows, without nooks or crannies, without microbes, beneath a cold light . . . Until the present war, I *lived publicly.*

Sharing with Nizan a deep appreciation for role-playing and wordplay—or for anything that provided them with evidence of their originality—Sartre could feel wholly accepted at the same time that his close friendships—with Nizan and then with fellow student Pierre Guille and then with Beauvoir—made it possible for him to experiment with expressing a self that was still in the making. Living from his imagination, he fostered so many possibilities that he could not commit himself to any one role or identity. "I became a traitor and have remained one," he wrote in his autobiography.

Though I throw myself heart and soul into what I undertake, though I give myself up unreservedly to work, to anger, to friendship, I'll repudiate myself in a moment, I know I will, I want to, and I'm already betraying myself, in the heat of my passion, by the joyful presentiment of my future betrayal. On the whole, I fulfill my commitments like anyone else; I am steadfast in my affections and behavior; but I am unfaithful to my emotions.

Overflowing with his own freedom, Sartre was always looking for partners, comrades, and philosophical co-conspirators who were free enough in their views to see the chaotic contingency of the sensations and impressions that were never fully organized by cultural conventions.

After a few chance encounters and visits to bordellos had initiated him into sex, Sartre's first relationship was with a woman he met at a cousin's funeral in 1925, at age twenty. An independent woman of twenty-two, Simone Jollivet was effectively a courtesan who used her beauty and her eccentric personality to elicit money, gifts, and devotion from her suitors. Sartre spent four passionate days with her before he returned to Paris, and while he did not see her again for six months, he wrote her long letters, professing his love and describing the books he planned to write. Jollivet was more intent on being courted than on giving herself up to a "federative" relationship, though, and when Sartre came to Toulouse to see her, she made him sleep in the park until she could sneak him into her room, and even after she finally let him in, she struck poses and played games, eluding him with mysterious protestations and explanations.

In spite of—or perhaps because of—her elusiveness, Sartre saw something more than a courtesan in Jollivet. He tried to talk his way into her confidence, and this gave him the opportunity to exercise his ingenuity and understanding as he tried to fathom her resistance. As she continued to elude him, he projected his faith in himself onto her. He loaned her books and engaged her in philosophical conversation, trying to correct her little faults as he urged her to make art out of her experience. He counseled her—she said he lectured—not to write him that she felt sad: "you might as well tell it to the League of Nations . . . Stand erect, stop playacting, get busy, *write*: that's the best remedy for a literary temperament like yours." He extended his intelligence to her—"Why should you have less ability to see than I?" he wrote. When she resisted him, he chastised her, "Who has made you what you are? Who is trying to keep you from turning into a bourgeoise, an aesthete, a whore? Who has taken charge of your intelligence? I alone."

Sartre's affair with Jollivet cooled in 1927, when she left him for wealthier suitors, but they rediscovered each other early in 1929. Sartre had been briefly, unofficially engaged to a grocer's daughter in the interim, but the engagement was broken when he wrote too ambitious an essay and failed the *agrégation* in his first attempt in 1928. By 1929, Jollivet had established herself in Paris as the mistress of Charles Dullin, a theater director, and she and Sartre resumed their relationship there, but only casually: Jollivet did not plan to leave Dullin—they would eventually marry—so Sartre was unattached when Beauvoir joined his study group.

III.

Years before Simone de Beauvoir met Sartre—years before she ever described herself as one with him—she was emerging from a family environment in many ways similar to his. If Sartre had been preparing to redeem his family's smug bourgeois culture by living a great writer's life, so too had Beauvoir, and if she ultimately took Sartre's freedom as her measure, her family had already prepared her to believe that literary greatness was possible for her as well.

Beauvoir was raised in a combination of aristocratic ease and bourgeois self-satisfaction. Her father, Georges de Beauvoir, was the youngest son in a wealthy aristocratic family. In her memoir, she wrote that he "appreciated elegant gestures, charming compliments, social graces, style, frivolity, irony, all the free-and-easy self-assurance of the rich and well-born." An actor by temperament but not by trade, he surrounded his children with the arts, but Simone wrote that he was "contemptuous of successes which are won at the expense of hard work and effort," and he disdained "the more serious virtues esteemed by the bourgeoisie."

Françoise Brasseur had blossomed when she married Georges de Beauvoir in 1906, and Simone, their first child, was born in the first flush of her mother's freedom from her own strict bourgeois family. Beauvoir wrote that her "first memories of her are of a laughing, lively young woman," but Françoise could still be harsh in her judgments, and Beauvoir learned to dread her condemnation that something was "ridiculous," or just "wasn't done," so she learned to censor herself to fit into a regulated household. She wrote in her memoir that "the ability to pass over in silence events which I felt so keenly is one of the things which strike me most when I remember my childhood." Nakedness was forbidden—"in our universe, the flesh had no right to exist"—and time and money were measured severely, to provide the impression of a "world free from all irregularities."

The combination of aristocratic freedom and bourgeois formality allowed Beauvoir to feel, from an early age, that she was one of the elite, the correct, the privileged. If she and her sister Hélène were "forbidden to play with strange little girls" in the Luxembourg Gardens, it was "obviously because we were made of finer stuff." As the older sister, Beauvoir must have been made of the finest stuff of all: she taught Hélène to read and to count, and her sister became her "alter ego, my double; we could not do without each other." In all her play, she wrote, "even when I was just doing transfers or daubing a catalogue with water-colours I felt the need of an associate."

Beauvoir was always an excellent student—she made good grades and was praised—but her parents and her teachers' approval was not always enough, and even when she was playing with her sister, she wrote that she was always watching herself as if from outside. She realized that she was not like other girls, and that no one felt her experience as sharply as she did—she concluded that if she did not describe it, no one would ever know that her experience was in any way special. To justify her uniqueness, she began to write. "If I was describing in words an episode in my life," she wrote in her memoir, "I felt that it was being rescued from oblivion, that it would interest others, and so be saved from extinction."

Beauvoir's aristocratic privilege collapsed in 1917, when she was nine, and her father lost a good part of his fortune when the Bolshevik revolution rendered his Russian investments worthless. He went in as co-director in his father's shoe and boot factory, but when the factory went into decline around 1920, he took work as an advertising salesman. Beauvoir wrote that "the trade bored him and brought in very little money. To make up for that he now went out in the evenings much more than formerly, to play bridge with friends or in a café." Over the next decade, the family was embarrassed to move into smaller and smaller apartments, and as Beauvoir's parents quarreled about their newly straitened circumstances, her father began to find female companionship in brothels and bars.

Neither Beauvoir's father's financial troubles nor his affairs released her from the strict dictates of proper bourgeois society, though: rather they trapped her in an impossible position. Her father was embarrassed by his inability to provide his daughters with dowries—and thus with good marriages—and he was humiliated by the fact that they would have to work for a living. He began to resent Beauvoir, who, as the eldest, seemed to incarnate his failure, and he began to criticize her for not being capable of making a proper marriage. Beauvoir took refuge from his criticisms in her studies, but this only made her even less marriageable, since society women were not supposed to be bookish, and the books only made her question the value of social conventions. Soon she was beyond marriageability altogether. "My mother dressed me badly," she wrote,

and my father was always reproaching me with being badly dressed: so I became a slut. They were not attempting to understand me: so I took refuge in silence and odd behavior. I wanted to make myself impervious to my surroundings. At the same time I was warding off boredom. My temperament was not suited to resignation; by taking to inordinate lengths the austerity that was my lot, it became a vocation; cut off from all pleasures, I chose the life of an ascetic; instead of dragging myself wearily through a monotony of days, I set out in stubborn silence, with set face, toward an invisible goal. I wore myself out with work, and my exhaustion gave me a feeling of fulfillment.

Beauvoir's younger sister sympathized, but Hélène remained on good terms with her mother, and as Beauvoir entered the awkward period of adolescence, her father transferred his affections from Simone to Hélène. As Beauvoir became more and more isolated in her family, she turned against her mother's Catholic values, and she ceased to believe in God. When she saw her mother suffering because of her father's affairs, she recognized the double standard in bourgeois sexual mores, and ceased to believe in her parents' authority altogether. She could not have supported herself respectably on her own, though, so she never left, but she remained at home as an outcast in her own family.

Beauvoir found an ally in her slightly older cousin, Jacques Laiguillon, whose family had come down in the world as well. Jacques' father had died and his mother remarried a man from a lower class—but Jacques still dreamed about restoring the family's fortunes. In his frustration with the slow pace of redemption, Jacques had discovered the books of Gide, Cocteau, Claudel, and Montherlant—books Beauvoir called the "literature of Disquiet"—who collectively skewered the absurdity and the pretense of bourgeois conventions, urging their readers to "live dangerously. Refuse nothing." If Beauvoir was partly trying to impress Laiguillon by devouring the books he lent her on his breaks from his secular lycée, she was also acquiring the tools with which to oppose her parents:

> Apart from . . . rare exceptions . . . I regarded works of literature as historical monuments which I would explore with more or less interest, which I sometimes admired, but which did not concern me personally. But now, suddenly, men of flesh and blood were speaking to me with their lips close to my ear; it was something between them and me; they were giving expression to the aspirations and the inner rebellions which I had never been able to put into words, but which I recognized. I skimmed the cream of the Sainte-Geneviéve library; with fevered brow, my brain on fire, and my heart pounding with excitement, I read Gide, Claude, Jammes. I exhausted the resources of Jacques' private library . . . I found release in reading

as once I had done in prayer . . . The books I liked became a Bible from which I drew advice and support . . . they rescued from silent oblivion all those intimate adventures of the spirit that I couldn't speak to anyone about; they created a kind of communion between myself and those twin souls which existed somewhere out of reach; instead of living out my small private existence, I was participating in a great spiritual epic. For months I kept myself going with books: they were the only reality within my reach.

Laiguillon's books showed Beauvoir the limitations of the education she was receiving at Cours Désir, her private Catholic school: her teachers were no longer "the august high-priestesses of Knowledge but . . . comical old church-hens" whose "qualifications were Christian virtues rather than degrees and diplomas." Having found authors who "thought their lives out," she began to be more outspoken and rebellious. Her parents even tried to forbid her seeing Laiguillon, but this did not prevent her from making a self-righteous crusade against stupidity—or from insisting that she would do better to trust herself than her parents. She stayed in school, and she anchored herself in literature and then in philosophy— where principles and abstractions framed her experiences in universal terms that transcended her parents' narrow, hypocritical authority.

While Laiguillon was away at school, Beauvoir shared her rebelliousness with a good friend from Cours Désir, Elizabeth Le Coin, who went by Zaza. Zaza came from a large Catholic family, but as she was the third child and second daughter, her impulsive personality had largely escaped parental scrutiny, and Beauvoir was impressed by how, "in everything she did, [Zaza] displayed an easy mastery which always amazed me." Together Zaza and Beauvoir dreamed of marrying for love, although as they approached marriageable ages, their mothers began to censor their correspondence and their reading, banning forbidden books and banishing progressive friends. Zaza was the first person for whom Beauvoir felt deep affection, but Zaza was not in the same state of rebellion against her parents. She still loved them and respected their authority, and Beauvoir was frustrated that Zaza could not see the full extent of her solitude. She felt that she herself "did not entirely correspond to the person [Zaza] took me for, but I couldn't find a way of . . . revealing my true nature to Zaza; this misunderstanding drove me to despair."

Isolated in school, lonely in her family, and desperate for a sympathetic affection, Beauvoir tried to imagine marrying Laiguillon, but he saw marriage as "a solution and not as a point of departure," and Beauvoir came to believe that it was "not possible to reconcile love and disquiet." On the eve of his departure for military service in Algeria in 1928, he took her out drinking, introducing her to his favorite bars, and now whenever her parents went out for an evening, Beauvoir would go to the bars, "hunting secretly for extraordinary experiences." She learned to find "comfort in the warmth of a strange hand on the back of my neck, stroking me with a gentleness which resembled love." Sometimes alone, sometimes with her sister, she would roam the streets, hitching rides from strange men, but eluding the kisses they felt they deserved. Completely naive in sexual matters, she later recalled being only confused when she was groped in a movie theater: "I didn't know what to do or say: I just let [the hands] go on."

Trapped without guidance between her bourgeois sense of owning the world and her family's straitened finances—stuck between her aristocratic sense of her own innate perfection and now her attempts to debauch herself—Beauvoir was in crisis. Her parents, her teachers, and the church were conspiring to force her into the role of bourgeois wife and mother, disregarding her own reality as an independent and unhappy young woman. Except for her good marks in school, though, and her sense of her own uniqueness, Beauvoir had nothing with which to oppose them. Her rebellion was still unfocused, and she became so independent and outspoken that "there was talk of sending me abroad," she wrote. "All sorts of people were asked for advice and there was a general panic."

It was only in her reading that she found the "people who, without cheating, looked this all-consuming nothingness in the face." When she graduated from Cours Désir—and then, in June of 1926, completed her *baccalauréat* at the Institut Sainte-Marie in Neuilly—she told her parents that she wanted to take a doctorate in philosophy at the Sorbonne. Her teachers—who, she said, "had given their lives to combating secular institutions"—saw a state school as "nothing better than a licensed brothel," and they disapproved. Her parents opposed her as well, because "to train for a profession was a sign of defeat" for their aristocratic lineage—but so few women had doctorates in philosophy that Beauvoir would gain a notable degree of distinction by passing the *agrégation*, which might in its way redeem the family's lost fortune. Beauvoir's parents ultimately allowed her to study at the Sorbonne, and in her second year, she even gave up her "life of debauchery" when one of her classmates disapproved of the time she spent looking for excitement in the bars.

Zaza had fought her parents for the right to study philosophy as well, but even though she had followed Beauvoir to the prestigious Institut Sainte-Marie for the *baccalauréat*, her parents refused to enroll her at the Sorbonne. Her family was so conservative that when Zaza met and fell in love with one of Beauvoir's classmates, her family hired an investigator to dig up skeletons in his family's closets. They still expected to arrange her marriage themselves, and in the fall of 1928 they sent her to Berlin for a year to get her away from Beauvoir and the Sorbonne's secularizing influence. In November 1929, though—only a month after Sartre and Beauvoir became lovers—Zaza died of meningitis—or encephalitis, her doctors could not say which: Zaza had been so upset about her parents' opposition to her love that her headaches and other ailments had not been seen as symptoms of a disease.

In her memoir, Beauvoir said that Zaza's death made it impossible for her to compromise her own liberty. She and Zaza had rebelled together against the "revolting fate that had lain ahead of us," and now that she and Sartre had just consummated their radical relationship, Beauvoir was only more determined to defy her parents and her teachers' outdated beliefs. More than anything else, she resolved to write the books that would "succeed in laying bare reality without either deforming or minimizing it."

IV.

In Sartre, Beauvoir had found a powerful new ally against conventions and limitations. Beauvoir wrote that "one single aim fired us, the urge to embrace all experience, and to bear witness concerning it . . . When we were together we bent our wills so firmly to the requirements of this common task" that they "found themselves bound as closely as possible." Until they wrote their books and published them, though, their relationship itself—their sense of their "perfect agreement"—would be their only claim to a truly genuine existence.

If Sartre and Beauvoir were confident that their free association was a bold step toward a new way of living, the result was certainly not a closer relationship with their parents—none of whom approved of their relationship. Beauvoir recalled her father saying that she would "never amount to more than a Worm's whore"—and Sartre's stepfather considered Beauvoir a loose woman and would not allow her into his house.

Not having made a conventional marriage, they were still treated like children. Even in 1939, ten years into their relationship, Sartre would write that his parents

> sadden me . . . they surround me with their image of me, and I of course must play that image, bend to it somewhat, under threat of conflicts. I feel I'm a decent lad (perhaps even a "good sport"), a little crazy, with a bit of the devil in me (not too much, just enough . . .), but who adores his mother. An honest lad too, who messes around some with ideas—small wonder, he's still young—too clear-sighted to be a communist, but a nice little anarchist surrounded by his books, basically very serious-minded, a young teacher of merit. Someone who still has a lot to learn from life but is starting out well. And he writes, in his free time. He turns out nice little stories, and more serious articles on philosophic questions. A nice amateur talent. I swear to you, my darling Beaver, that it even takes away my desire to write.

But Sartre and Beauvoir had not started to write their books in the months immediately following the exam. For the first year after the *agréga-tion*, Beauvoir scraped together a living by teaching psychology at a girls' school in Neuilly, relishing the freedom to come and go at leisure—or not to leave her room at all, if she felt like reading all day. To make ends meet, she sold her books "and all the smaller jewelry I had been given as a young girl, which greatly shocked my parents." In November of 1929, Sartre began his mandatory eighteen months of military service in a meteorological unit his friend Raymond Aron had recommended to him. He hated the conformity of military life, but Saint-Cyr was not far from Paris, and he saw Beauvoir as often as his leaves permitted.

Beauvoir found such pleasure in her liberty that she still did not start to write until Sartre reproached her for resembling "those heroines of Meredith's who after a long battle for their independence ended up quite content to be some man's helpmeet." Stung by this reproach, Beauvoir did not bother to start with short stories, but she threw herself into a novel that fused her philosophical and her literary reading with her experience of being tormented in love. She wrote in her memoirs that "the opening chapters" of her metaphysical melodramas "held up pretty well," but even if she wrote that they soon "degenerated into a mere shapeless hodgepodge," she was still spending her days writing.

When Beauvoir finally assumed a teaching position in Marseille, on the Mediterranean coast, in October 1931, she "felt I had played a practical joke on someone" when she received her first paycheck. Teaching was a sham obligation—sixteen hours a week of a subject she knew so well that she did not need to prepare for her classes. "I discharged the duties of a philosophy teacher without really being one," she wrote. "I was not even the grown woman that my fellow teachers saw; I was living out a private and individual adventure to which no categories had permanent relevance."

Sartre was still the only person who understood Beauvoir, and their separation began to take its toll in the fall of 1931, when Sartre was posted to teach in Le Havre in the north. When Beauvoir was upset about parting for the school year—she was still teaching in Marseilles—Sartre offered to marry her, although the tie would still not have any special meaning: they would only get "the advantages of a double post." Beauvoir wrote that she was "not for one moment . . . tempted to fall in with his suggestion." She had a strong aversion "to the common customs and observations of our society," and she "felt such absence of affinity with my own parents that any sons or daughters I might have I regarded in advance as strangers; from them I expected either indifference or hostility—so great had been my own aversion to family life." Instead of settling down anywhere, Sartre and Beauvoir lived the lives of isolated writers, investing themselves more in their correspondence with each other—and in the progress of their writing—than in the day-to-day business of teaching or in the comforts they could afford with their salaries.

As soon as Sartre had finished his military service in the spring of 1931, he began his first novel, which would not be published until 1938 as *Nausea*. The book described the unsettling strangeness of a human existence in which the constant stream of sensations and thoughts could not be anchored by any absolutes. In his autobiography, he said that he used the main character

to show, without complacency, the texture of my life. At the same time, I was *I*, the elect, chronicler of Hell, a glass and steel photomicroscope peering at my own protoplasmic juices. Later, I gaily demonstrated that man is impossible; I was impossible myself and differed from the others only by the mandate to give expression to that impossibility, which was thereby transfigured and became my most personal possibility, the object of my mission . . . Fake to the marrow of my bones and hoodwinked, I joyfully wrote about our unhappy state . . . I built with one hand what I destroyed with the other, and I regarded anxiety as the guarantee of my security.

Committed to anxiety instead of to comfort, Sartre and Beauvoir never set up housekeeping together—or even really for themselves: they would not even have their own apartments until 1948. Throughout the 1930s, they moved from one teaching post to another, living in hotels, eating in restaurants, working in cafés. When Beauvoir was posted to Rouen in the fall of 1932, she was only a short distance from Sartre in Le Havre, but then Sartre went to Berlin in 1933, before returning to Le Havre in the fall of 1934. It was only in 1937, when he was posted to Neuilly, in the Paris suburbs, that they moved into the same hotel together, although even then they lived on different floors, an arrangement that Beauvoir said "had all the advantages of a shared life without any of its inconveniences." In spite of their refusal to settle down, Beauvoir wrote that by the mid-1930s, their "illegitimate relationship was regarded almost as respectfully as though it were a marriage." The inspector general even considered them together for teaching assignments.

Having refused the comforts of a conventional relationship, they had not hesitated to have "contingent" relationships. When Beauvoir had made a motoring trip through the south of France with Sartre's friend Pierre Guille in the summer of 1931, Sartre knew that they had slept together. When Sartre traveled to Berlin in the fall of 1933—where Raymond Aron had helped him get a fellowship to study Husserl at the French Institute—his German was not good enough for flirting with local women, so he had a brief affair with a Frenchwoman whose husband was also studying at the Institute. Beauvoir wrote in her memoir that Sartre's affair with Marie Ville

neither took me by surprise nor upset any notions I had formed concerning our joint lives, since right from the outset Sartre had warned me that he was liable to embark on such adventures. I had accepted the principle, and now had no difficulty in accepting the fact. To know the world and give it expression, this was the aim that governed the whole of Sartre's existence; and I know just how set he was on it. Besides, I felt so closely bound to him that no such episode in his life could disturb me.

Beauvoir knew that Sartre and Ville had "agreed there could be no future in this relationship," and she claimed that the affair caused her no jealousy, but she nonetheless risked her teaching position by faking illness to travel to Berlin in order to meet Marie for herself and assert her essential claim.

Later in life, Beauvoir would publish an interview in which she asked Sartre what he found particularly attractive in the women he had affairs with. "Anything at all," Sartre answered her.

As I saw it you possessed the qualities, the most important qualities that I could ask of women. That therefore set the other women free—they could be merely pretty, for example. What happened is that since you represented far more than I wanted to give to women, the others had less and so they committed less of themselves.

When she pressed him to describe the appeal of other women, he replied,

Sartre: Most of the time a woman had emotional and sometimes sexual values; and it was that aggregate which I drew toward myself because I felt that having a connection with a woman like that was to some extent taking possession of her affectivity. Trying to make her feel it for me, feel it deeply, meant possessing that affectivity—it was a quality I was giving myself.
Beauvoir: In other words, you asked women to love you.
Sartre: Yes, they had to love me for that sensibility to become something that belonged to me. When a woman gave herself to me I saw that sensibility on her face, in her expression; and seeing it on her face was like taking possession of it.

Having since adolescence considered himself terribly ugly, Sartre had learned to use language and philosophy to inspire an unconditional loyalty and affection in Beauvoir—and now his conditional, "contingent" relationships renewed his confidence, again and again, that he could draw people toward himself notwithstanding his looks.

If Sartre and Beauvoir were each enlarging their own experience by having love affairs, they were enlarging the world for each other as well, for when they described their lovers in letters, the affairs became a source of intimacy between them. While they were still living separately in the

1930s, Beauvoir wrote that in their correspondence, they "set about turning [their lovers and acquaintances] inside-out . . . to produce our own definitive portrait of them." They had always been determined to expose the fallacies or deceptions, hypocrisies or defects in conventional ideals and customs, and now they used their friends and lovers as material for their theories about freedom and authenticity, or about the bad faith by which people misrepresented their lives to themselves. Even as they enjoyed their lovers, they described their affairs in extensive detail, undercutting any threat of betrayal or jealousy by maintaining a deep complicity in their letters, which reaffirmed their superiority over each other's lovers.

V.

The potent combination of their own essential relationship and their love affairs could not always obscure the reality that Sartre and Beauvoir were both still provincial schoolteachers. They were still writing, but "like every bourgeois," Beauvoir wrote,

> we were sheltered from want; like every civil servant, we were guaranteed against insecurity. Furthermore, we had no children, no families, no responsibilities: we were like elves. There was no intelligible connection between the work we did . . . and the money we got for it, which seemed to lack all proper substance.

For five years, now, they had been encouraging each other to create a new philosophy of living, but neither their books nor their contingent relationships had confirmed their uniqueness yet.

In 1934, still anxious for genuine experiences, Beauvoir started a relationship that fundamentally modified her "essential" tie with Sartre. Olga Kosakiewicz was a quiet student of Beauvoir's—she was high-strung and inconsistent, and she did not always turn in good work, and sometimes she failed to turn in any work at all. But when she submitted an excellent essay on Kant, Beauvoir saw signs of intelligence and started a conversation with her student. When Olga confessed that she admired Beauvoir—and that she was terrified of disappointing her—Beauvoir was moved by Olga's mortification. She began to meet with her privately, and she was impressed by what she called Olga's "eager and indiscriminate appetite for things and people"—as well as by the "fresh, childlike quality about her enthusiasms" and by "her impetuous, whole-hogging nature," in which Beauvoir saw her own desire to possess the world.

Like Beauvoir, Olga had grown up in the gap between aristocratic ideals and tight finances. Her father had been a high-ranking official in Russia, and her mother was a French governess, and when they bought a mill in Normandy after fleeing to France in 1917, they were proud of their foreignness and of their aristocratic status. Beauvoir wrote that Olga's parents had "first filled her up with hatred of all the traditional French virtues—conventional virtues, pious shibboleths, and general stupidity—and *then* . . . [abandoned her] to the ridiculous discipline, routine, and old-fashioned ideas prevalent in any girls' boarding school." Disregarding Olga's "dream of becoming a ballet dancer," they enrolled her in medical courses, but Olga loathed her work—and school and then the world—for failing to fulfill her parents' aristocratic promises. Having disdained any rigorous training throughout her childhood, she was helpless to fulfill those dreams for herself. Too insecure to complete her schoolwork, she nonetheless did not hesitate, with Beauvoir, to condemn the artificiality of society as a whole.

Sympathizing with Olga's rebellion, Beauvoir wrote that she felt "admirably placed to come to her aid, being nine years her senior, endowed with the authority of a teacher, and possessing the prestige conferred by culture and experience." She took Olga under her wing—she approved of Olga's vision, and "promised her she would blaze her own trail" into the future. Offering encouragement, Beauvoir found that "the sense of private solidarity, and everything else which, grudgingly at first, I gave her—was what she needed most of all." They became co-conspirators, staying out all night at shady bars, where "chronic fantasy flourished," and soon Beauvoir turned upon Olga the same close attention that Sartre had paid to her. Over the summer of 1934, she wrote to her,

> I want you to know that there is not one of your facial expressions, not one of your feelings, and not one incident in your life that I do not care about. You can be certain that when you sit down to eat, there is someone who would be extremely interested in knowing what kind of soup you are eating. Naturally this someone would love to get long and detailed letters.

Deeply similar in their rebellions, Beauvoir and Olga may or may not have become lovers (biographies disagree) but in March of 1935, Beauvoir introduced Olga to Sartre, who was in dire need of new influences himself.

Sartre was not immediately anxious to meet Olga. For the past three years, he had isolated himself in his writing, and when he had still failed to make any breakthroughs, Beauvoir wrote that he "shrank from burdening a stranger with the company of this pitiable neurotic (which was how he saw himself)." In his frustration with the slow progress of his writing and in search of new experiences to be nauseated by, Sartre had allowed a doctor friend to give him an experimental shot of mescaline in February. Instead of friendly visions, though, he had seen ominous fish and vultures, and for weeks afterward, he felt he was being pursued by lobsters. Doctors insisted that anxiety and overwork, not the mescaline, were causing the sustained hallucination, and they recommended society.

Olga's violent swings between crippling insecurity, aristocratic disdain, and attentive observation distracted Sartre from his dread. "For the first time in my life," he wrote, "someone could make me feel humble and disarmed. I wanted to learn from her." He too saw intelligence, and even a method, in Olga's assertions—that "music bores me; I only enjoy sounds," for instance. At the same time that he tried to mold her to a philosophically genuine life (just as he had with Jollivet and Beauvoir) Sartre allowed her to mold him as well with her sulks and whims and fears, which he accepted as fair critiques of his too-settled lifestyle. Beauvoir wrote that "instead of concentrating on a black spot that danced about at eye level, Sartre now began to devote . . . fanatical attention to Olga's every twitch and blink, from each of which he inferred whole volumes of meaning."

To assure the insecure Olga that they were genuinely interested in her life, Sartre and Beauvoir extended their pact of openness and honesty to include her, and now they described their relationship as a "trio." In the atmosphere of their admiration, which forced Olga into the role of youthful inspiration for her teacher, Beauvoir wrote that Olga "became Rimbaud, Antigone, every *enfant terrible* that ever lived, a dark angel judging us from her diamond-bright heaven," condemning Sartre and Beauvoir alike for having betrayed their artistic values by settling into regular writing and teaching routines. When Olga failed her medical exams—twice, in July 1935 and again in October—Beauvoir and Sartre convinced her parents to let them support her. She took a room in Beauvoir's hotel in Rouen, where Beauvoir gave her lessons in philosophy, and from time to time she and Beauvoir would visit Sartre in Le Havre.

Even when Beauvoir was alone with Sartre, though, they would spend hours talking about how to mold Olga, how to give her encouragement, and how to learn from her anarchic whims. This obsessive concern for Olga began to elicit a deep resentment in Beauvoir, especially when Sartre became determined that "no one should mean as much to Olga as he did," and started trying to "bring [his relationship with Olga] to a climax." Beauvoir sympathized with Olga's willfulness, though, and she had committed herself to accept Sartre's insights into her life, so she had forbidden herself "any expression of reserve or indifference." She could not object to Olga's whims without appealing to conventions of polite behavior—all of which had been forbidden—but she could not ignore her frustration when Olga ruined their plans with her whims, and she could not help but feel threatened when Olga appeared to be displacing her in Sartre's esteem. She tried to let Olga's sulks expose the limitations in her views, but now she was suffering her own mood swings as well, which were all the more troubling because they were irrational, and did not fit with her sense of the rational openness and honesty of the trio.

If Beauvoir was tortured by the trio, Olga was in a difficult position as well. She was taking her lessons directly from Beauvoir, but without other students to work with, she paralyzed herself with sulking and dreaming, and therefore failed to make any progress. Intimidated by Sartre and Beauvoir's apparently undeserved interest in her, she tried to manipulate them: she tried to win their approval by charming them, or else she bullied them with her bad moods. She resisted Sartre's attempts to seduce her, and when she angered him, Beauvoir generally took her side, widening the gulf between herself and Sartre. These struggles undermined Beauvoir's faith in her fundamental unity with Sartre, and she wrote in her memoir that "when I said 'We are one person,' I was dodging the issue. Harmony between two individuals is never a *donnée*; it must be worked for continually." But if Beauvoir suffered when she was beginning to ask herself "whether the whole of my happiness did not rest upon a gigantic lie," she still did not have any grounds for terminating the trio. When she was posted to Paris in 1936, she offered to bring Olga with her, half hoping that Olga's parents would refuse, but they allowed it. Sartre and Beauvoir were supporting her, after all—and Olga moved into the Royal Bretagne hotel with her.

Events conspired to end the trio nonetheless. In early 1937, Beauvoir's sense of dread and crisis probably contributed to her life-threatening case of pneumonia. She would not seek medical attention until one of her lungs collapsed, and when stretcher-bearers came to take her to the hospital, she saw that a crowd had gathered around the ambulance: she realized that she herself had become one of the "other people" to whom things happened. Her lifelong self-centeredness—which since 1929 had included Sartre inside herself—was suspended, and now she could admit that she and Sartre were separate people, with different temperaments and feelings: they could feel different things without her being split within herself. Beauvoir's illness had a sobering effect on Sartre as well, as his solicitude for her tempered his obsession with Olga, with whom he had been losing patience anyway.

But Beauvoir's pneumonia was only one of several influences that dissolved the trio. It also broke up because after Olga failed to make any progress in philosophy, Sartre and Beauvoir had encouraged her to take acting lessons with Charles Dullin and Simone Jollivet, who were by now running a theater company together in Paris. Jollivet, Sartre's ex-lover, claimed Olga as her "daughter before Lucifer" when she met her, and when Olga achieved a moderate success in the theater, Sartre and Beauvoir could feel that they had finally launched her into the world. Olga continued to need endless amounts of encouragement, but she was starting to make a life for herself, and now she could even begin to repay Sartre and Beauvoir by taking them to the Café Flore and introducing them to actors and directors—more characters to turn inside-out.

The trio had been so close that it took still two more influences to unravel it. One was a student of Sartre's in Le Havre, Jacques-Laurent Bost, who was the son of his school's chaplain and younger brother to Pierre Bost, a well-known author. Little Bost, as he was known, had, in Beauvoir's words, "no ambitions, but a number of small, obstinate desires instead . . . He did not possess an original mind . . . On the other hand he was both quick-witted and droll." Like Olga—and about Olga's age—he "personified youth for us," in Beauvoir's words. The other person—another friend of Sartre's—was Marco Zuorro, an opera singer Sartre knew from university. Zuorro was a gossiping troublemaker, whom Beauvoir said possessed a "satanic sense of humor," and when he saw Sartre's interest in Olga, he drove Sartre mad with jealousy by devoting himself to Olga as well. Zuorro took a genuine amorous interest in Bost, and when Bost and Olga both started to hide together—from Zuorro and from Sartre respectively—an affection developed between them, and soon Zuorro reported having seen Bost and Olga, through a keyhole, embracing and kissing.

After two years as part of a trio, Sartre and Beauvoir were free of Olga by March 1937. They returned to each other, and in the fall of 1937, Sartre finally joined Beauvoir in Paris, where they both resumed their writing. Beauvoir's third attempt at a novel, *When Things of the Spirit Come First*, had been turned down with an encouraging letter, and now, when Sartre suggested that she write a book that proceeded from her own experience, she used the trio with Olga to explore the philosophical problem of living in the world with other people. Opening with an epigraph from Hegel—"Each conscience seeks the death of the other"—*L'Invitée* (*She Came to Stay* in English) dramatizes the trio in Françoise, a writer; Pierre, a director, her lover; and Xavière, the student they adopt. In reality, Beauvoir remained close with Olga all her life, but the book concludes with Françoise turning on the gas in Xavière's room, murdering her while she sulks, framing her death as a suicide. Beauvoir acknowledged in her memoirs that the murder was excessive, but "by killing Olga on paper," she wrote,

> I purged every twinge of irritation and resentment I had previously felt toward her, and cleansed our relationship of all the unpleasant memories that lurked among those of a happier nature . . . The paradoxical thing is that to do so did not require any unpardonable action on my part, but merely the description of such an action in a book.

The book mirrored life even further, for in same way that Françoise has an affair with Gerbert—Pierre's acolyte, who had become Xavière's lover—Beauvoir would indeed start an affair with Bost, Sartre's student, even after he had already started seeing Olga.

VI.

In 1938 Sartre finally burst into public existence as a writer: he had published short philosophical treatises, and in 1936 a book of five short stories, but now his novel *Nausea* was considered a favorite for France's prestigious Prix Goncourt, and he began to be seen as a rising literary star. He could finally start to be judged not on his teaching career, but on his ideas about human existence, which were already starting to define their trajectory. As he explained to his editor,

> I contemplated doing a brief preface to explain that I was not "playing around in the muck" etc. and that the stories represent a precise moment in a general plan. *Nausea* defines existence. The five stories describe the various possible escapes from it ("The Wall": death—"Erostratus": the gratuitous act, crime—"The Room": imaginary worlds, madness—"The Childhood of a Leader": privilege, the social) showing the failure of each, with "The Wall" to mark their bounds. No possible escape. Then I'll offer a glimpse of the possibility of a moral life at the core of existence and with no escape, the life I want to define in my next novel. I've had enough of being called deliquescent and morbid, when I am precisely the opposite.

Redoubling their literary efforts, Sartre and Beauvoir continued to experiment with contingent relationships as well. While Beauvoir was out of Paris in the summer of 1938, hiking with Bost, Sartre wrote to tell her about his affair with a young actress, Colette Gibert:

> I had two beautiful and tragic nights with her that plainly moved me, and I'm left with the slightly bitter regret of having absolutely no place for her in my life. The sad part is that she had begun to love me passionately . . . and she wanted to give me her virginity . . . You will say that the whole thing was imprudent. On the contrary. Everything's settled; she left cheerfully and without the slightest hope.

"You're very sweet to have told me the whole story in such detail, my love," Beauvoir wrote to him, five days after his letter. She went on to write,

> I slept with little Bost three days ago. It was I who propositioned him, of course. Both of us had been wanting it . . . He was tremendously astonished when I told him I'd always had a soft spot for him—and he ended up telling me yesterday evening that he'd loved

me for ages. I'm very fond of him. We spend idyllic days, and nights of passion. But have no fear of finding me sullen or disoriented or ill at ease on Saturday; it's something precious to me, something intense, but also light and easy and properly in its place in my life, simply a happy blossoming of relations that I'd always found very agreeable.

Bost was still seeing Olga, but if Beauvoir was revenging herself on Olga for the trio, she also became genuinely attached to Bost, for after nine years with Sartre, the sensuality and passion had ebbed out of their "essential love," and Beauvoir wrote to Bost that "I have only *one* sensual life, and that is with you, and for me it is something infinitely precious, and serious, and weighty, and passionate."

Beauvoir was not Sartre's only reason for keeping Gibert at a distance. He did have room in his life for a lover, but that place was already occupied by Olga's younger sister, Wanda. When Sartre had finally given up trying to seduce Olga, he had turned his attentions on Wanda, who was twenty years old—to Sartre's thirty-three years—when she came to visit Olga in Paris in 1938. Wanda, Sartre would write, "feels in a sharper, fuller way than her sister, but ultimately senses her situation in the world very strongly, though hazily." She too was prone to rages, sulks, and whims, and when she resisted Sartre's advances, he pressed even harder, thrilling in the chase. As he wrote to Beauvoir, "it takes the violence of arguments or the touching quality of reconciliations for me to feel alive." Even as he was coming to life in this way, though, Wanda's fits diminished the relationship in Sartre's eyes, so that when he wrote to Beauvoir, he could still reassure her of her primacy. "I do miss you," he wrote. "I much prefer the life of the mind to personal obsessions"—which were not exactly unpleasant, he said, but "on the insipid side." More and more consumed by his writing, Sartre did not have time to devote the same kind of intense attention he had paid to Olga. He was not as open with Wanda as he had been with Olga, either. He never told her the true nature of his relationship with Beauvoir, but he wrote to Beauvoir that Wanda had "undertaken to gradually tear down the 'friendship' I bear for you. It's rather amusing."

In the fall of 1938, at the same time that Sartre was seducing Wanda, Beauvoir met another promising student, Bianca Bienenfeld, whose parents had emigrated from Poland. Bienenfeld was seventeen, and she would write in her memoir that she was overwhelmed by Beauvoir's "obvious beauty" and by her "brilliant, piercing, bold intelligence." She wrote that "the power and speed of her comprehension was startling, her thirst to read unquenchable." Beauvoir was captivated by Bienenfeld as well, and they became lovers, although Beauvoir wrote to Bost that "I think ultimately that I'm not a homosexual since sensually I felt almost nothing, but it was charming and I love being in bed in the afternoon when there is lots of sunshine outside."

Beauvoir eventually introduced Bienenfeld to Sartre, who did not tell Wanda—whom he was still courting—that the three of them started a second trio. Sartre began to seduce Bienenfeld—soon he slept with her as well—and in his affectionate letters he tried to mold the girl's ideas. He wrote her that he and Beauvoir had "agreed that we should dissuade you from your rationalism because you have the optimistic tendency to believe that it is possible to confront irrational objects with rational conduct." Sartre and Beauvoir were more reserved in how much time they devoted to this second trio, though, for between their teaching and writing and other affairs, their time was becoming more and more precious.

VII.

Even as they were getting close with Bienenfeld, Sartre and Beauvoir were both also spending more and more time trying to establish their personal relationships with the political events that were leading Europe into the Second World War. The French reserves were called up on September 1, 1939 when Germany invaded Poland, and Sartre was posted to a meteorological outfit in Alsace, behind the Maginot Line fortifications. This separation returned Sartre to Beauvoir, for she alone, of all his women, could maintain the voluminous daily correspondence that kept his interest—just as he alone could serve as a witness to her thoughts, decisions, and actions. Neither of them broke off their relationships—with Wanda or Bienenfeld or Bost—but between the General Mobilization in September and the invasion of France in the spring of 1940—a time they called the Phony War—their letters returned very tenderly to the insistence that they were one person. Two weeks into September, Sartre wrote,

I've never felt so intently that you are me. That has deeply moved me over these past two days. I love you so, my darling Beaver. Besides, when two people have lived together for ten years, and thought with each other and for each other, without anything serious ever coming between them, it has to be more than love.

"Write me everything in detail," he urged her. "The smallest detail of your life is terribly precious to me." In answer to Beauvoir's long, detailed letters about goings-on in Paris, Sartre wrote long descriptions of his work and of his meteorological stations in Alsace. (When Wanda wanted a letter, though, he complained, "It's a terrible bore, but I'll have to write her a letter filled with detail. How to make it picturesque? A table, a typewriter, some paper, surrounded by jerks: that's all there is.") No one wrote Sartre better letters than Beauvoir, and he gave her pride of place, writing to her first of all his correspondents. October 1939 was the ten-year anniversary of their morganatic marriage, and Sartre wrote to "immediately renew the lease for ten years."

Sartre and Beauvoir were also united by the fact that the Phony War was an extraordinarily productive time for Sartre. Beauvoir was less productive in Paris, because it took her a little while to adjust to Sartre's absence, but Sartre's official duties could be performed in only a few hours each day, and he was free to spend a great deal of time writing in the barracks. Between his second novel, *The Age of Reason*, which used the trio with Beauvoir and Olga as one aspect of a story about political commitment and liberty—and the notes that would become *Being and Nothingness*, a foundational text for existential philosophy—his letters and Beauvoir's are full of reactions to and commentary on his unfolding ideas, which sometimes consumed an entire ink cartridge in only a day and a half.

The war was changing Beauvoir nonetheless. She felt "less in my life and more in things"—and instead of thinking of herself as privileged, she was now "a rootless being—without either a home or expectations—absorbed in a tragic collective history." When she wrote to Sartre that "my life's full but terribly barren, with abrupt fissurations of pain," she did not neglect to say that it was "more for Bost than for you, actually"—for Bost had been posted to the infantry, close to the front, where it was easier to imagine him coming back crippled—or simply not coming back—whereas Sartre seemed "close, not really lost at all."

Isolated in completely male and philosophically unsympathetic company, Sartre depended on the mail for all of his relationships. He suffered when Wanda did not write for days at a time, and then he suffered when she wrote to tell him that she had been spending time with an actor named Roger Blin. Blinded by jealousy, Sartre was too far away to do anything except console himself that "her life is me—less perhaps through the tenderness I inspire in her than through the intellectual and material need she has for me." (Whether or not this consoled him, he repeatedly asked Beauvoir to recover from Wanda the parts of his novel he had sent her.)

While Sartre was discovering his jealous side, Beauvoir's affairs were also becoming more complicated. She was furious to discover that Bienenfeld "envisaged . . . [the trio] as an exact tripartite division," and so thought she deserved equal time with Sartre when he came to Paris on leave. She later acknowledged that Bienenfeld "really could have reproached us . . . with not having made things clear," but she continued to "be melting" with her. She also discovered a "hint of depravity" in herself, as she had the "vague, lousy idea . . . that I should at least 'take advantage' of her body . . . It was the awareness of having a sensual plea-sure without affection—something that has basically never happened to me." But Beauvoir was still aware of the fact that she was missing her primary love. "My love, what barren nourishment," she wrote to Sartre, "all these people who aren't you!"

In addition to Bienenfeld, Beauvoir had begun a flirtation with Nath-alie Sorokine—another student of exiled Russian parents. Sorokine, she wrote to Sartre, "gives me what used to be precious about [Olga] Kos.—in a more facile way this time, but also more pleasing. Namely, a new percep-tion of the world, a world rethought in an absolutely unexpected way by an original little consciousness." Again like Olga, Sorokine was an enfant terrible, who would lie in wait outside Beauvoir's classroom or hotel, with gifts or with interesting stories, but she would also sulk and refuse to leave when Beauvoir asked her to, and several times Beauvoir had to throw her out of her hotel room by force, although even then, she would typically find her in the morning, curled up asleep on the stairs.

For students like Bienenfeld and Sorokine, to be accepted by Beau-voir was a singular honor. She was one of the rare women who possessed France's highest degree, she had a deep confidence that her philosophy benefited her in her life, she was relentless in fostering her own freedom, and her open relationship with Sartre—who was already a recognized author—had made them both infamous. When she focused her atten-tion on her students, she was effectively inviting them into the exclusive society of philosopher-writers. Bienenfeld later wrote that Beauvoir "had regard for the brilliant students, the elite capable of taking an interest in philosophical discussions. She felt biting disdain toward the others." Beauvoir's confidence and approval gave Bienenfeld and Sorokine confidence to rebel against their bourgeois parents, much the same way Beauvoir had rebelled against hers. But Beauvoir was not offering encouragement alone: her salary allowed her to offer material support as well. In Sartre's absence, she was collecting and cashing his paychecks, and on both of their behalf, she subsidized hotels, meals, and studies for her sister, Olga, Wanda, Bienenfeld, and Sorokine—all of whom came to be known collectively as the Family.

If Beauvoir was the elder and the teacher in almost all of her relationships, she was not always completely in control. When Sorokine pressed her for embraces and kisses before her philosophy lessons, Beauvoir reluctantly let herself be charmed. "I feel a bit like some clumsy seducer," she wrote to Sartre, "confronted with a young virgin, as mysterious as all virgins are. Only the seducer at least has a clear mission . . . to pierce the mystery. Whereas in my own case, I'm simultaneously the prey." By mid-December, she wrote, "I'll have to sleep with her, there's no help for it. I'm quite put out—and pretty well smitten—by this little personage," and, when they slept together in January 1940, she reported that "it interested [Sorokine] as an experience more than it gave her pleasure, since she was paralysed by shyness . . . There was no question of mad passion— she was mainly happy because it seemed 'really intimate', and she'd like the most complete intimacy." Soon Beauvoir was writing to tell Sartre that she had developed "a very keen taste for her body, and find these moments extremely pleasing—especially her expressions, which are ever so moving—and her tenderness, all trustful but without surrender."

At the end of many of her stories about the girls—whom Sartre called her "harem of women"—Beauvoir often complained that her relationships were not providing her with the kind of trusting, egalitarian liberty she shared with Sartre. Lacking any rigorous philosophical training or any deep commitment to their own philosophies, Olga, Wanda, Bienenfeld, and Sorokine alike lacked restraint in making their demands on Sartre and Beauvoir. "Either [Sorokine] *exacts* promises, and then feels I'm keeping them out of duty," Beauvoir wrote, "or else she doesn't demand anything, but then she's consumed by fears." If Beauvoir invited her lovers into the life of the mind, she was disappointed when they lacked the courage—or the authority—to press her about her life. She complained to Sartre that Bienenfeld would never ask a question about, for example, my real feelings for Kos., or my relations with Sorokine, or what kind of state I'm in regarding your absence. She never for a single instant strives to know me, but takes me for granted—like a mathematical postulate—and builds *her* life upon that.

In February of 1940, she wrote in her journal that Sartre's "consciousness is such an absolute for me that this morning the world seems utterly empty when I think of the substitutes: Olga, Bianca, it makes me sick."

In November 1939, Beauvoir demonstrated her commitment to Sartre—and her daring, as well as her superiority over Sartre's other lovers—by coming to visit him at his post, in defiance of the prohibition against conjugal visits. None of Sartre's lovers dared attempt this: as children of immigrants, they all had difficulty obtaining the identity cards that would let them travel. Not to be kept from Bost, either, Beauvoir planned ten "conjugal days" with him in March of 1940, although they were discovered by the military police almost as soon as she arrived, and so did not spend much time together before she was sent back to Paris. Beauvoir and Bost were not the only ones having affairs: Olga had an affair and an abortion of her own while Bost was serving.

Waiting in Paris for the war to begin in earnest, Beauvoir had to fight to protect her solitude from her lovers. She persuaded Bienenfeld "as far as possible to accept a life without us . . . to make her solitude into a strength and seek an emotional independence." She suggested that she should "theorize *her life* rather than us." In February 1940—probably at least partly because of Beauvoir's complaints about Bienenfeld—Sartre broke off with her himself, although when Beauvoir found her feeling hurt and betrayed, she wrote that Bienenfeld "blamed us—myself as much as you, actually—in the past, in the future, in the absolute: the way we treat people. I felt it was unacceptable that we'd managed to make her suffer so much."

Hurt feelings notwithstanding, Sartre and Beauvoir were using their affairs and their lovers' stories in their writing. Beauvoir was working on her novel about the Olga trio, and in between taking weather readings, Sartre was using things Olga had told him about her childhood in Russia as he developed the characters in his new novel. He was using Bienenfeld's life and her stories as well—which caused her to complain in her memoir that one character's name, "Birnenschatz is strangely similar to Bienenfeld; my sister's name is Ela; Ella's father [in the novel] is a diamond merchant, while my father sold natural pearls." Sartre and Beauvoir both shared their works in progress with their lovers, but they reserved to themselves the authority to make editorial changes: when Sartre finished *The Age of Reason* in the spring of 1940, he gave Beauvoir "carte blanche to cross out, erase, strike anything you like."

VIII.

In March of 1940, only months before real fighting broke out, Sartre's peace was shattered by a purely personal crisis. Wanda had heard from a friend about his affair with Colette Gibert, and she sent him an outraged letter. Sartre's affair with Gibert had not in fact overlapped with his courtship of Wanda, but he wrote an open letter to Gibert, making it clear to Gibert—and to Wanda, who was to read the letter before she posted it for him—that

> I never loved you, I found you physically pleasant though vulgar . . . In your own romantic head you spun an entire pretty fiction of mutual love, which was alas forbidden by a prior vow, and I let you have your own way because I thought it would make the breakup less painful for you. But the reality was much simpler. During September I was already a bit bored with you . . . My letters, which were exercises in passionate literature . . . gave the Beaver and me many a good laugh.

Sartre did not laugh for very long. Even by the next day, he wrote that he was "very profoundly disgusted with myself." Didn't he simply want, he asked Beauvoir,

> to play the neighborhood Don Juan? And if you excuse me because of sensuality, let's just say, first of all, that I have none, and that minor skin-deep desire is not an acceptable excuse, and secondly that my sexual relationship with her was disgraceful . . . It seems to me that up to now I've behaved like a spoiled brat in my physical relationships with people. There are few woman I haven't upset on that score . . . As for you, my little Beaver, for whom I've never had anything but respect, I've often embarrassed you, particularly in the beginning, when you found me rather obscene. Not a satyr,

certainly. That I'm quite sure I'm not. But simply obscene . . . The atmosphere of sadistic dirty-dealing . . . comes back to me now and disgusts me.

What bothered him even more was that when Wanda had accused Sartre of feeling "mysticism" for Beauvoir, he had gone so far as to denigrate Beauvoir to her. Sartre wrote to Beauvoir:

Today I wrote: "you well know that I'd walk all over everyone (even the Beaver) despite my 'mysticism' to have a good relationship with you." The end justifies the means, but I was not proud to have written that. Because of you as well as because of her.

Conclusion: I've never known how to lead either my sexual or my emotional life properly; I most deeply and sincerely feel like a grubby bastard. A really small-time bastard at that, a sort of sadistic university type and civil-service Don Juan—disgusting. That has got to change. I've got to swear off (1) vulgar little affairs: Lucile, [Gibert], etc—(2) big affairs undertaken lightly. I'll keep [Wanda] if it clears up because I'm fond of her. But if it doesn't clear up, it's all over, my career as an old rake will be over, period. Tell me what you think of all this . . .

Underlying all this is the fact that I thought nothing could ever tarnish me, and I now realize it isn't true.

In spite of his disgust with himself, he resolved in his next letter not to break off with Wanda:

My feelings for [Wanda] include nothing very elevated, but they *exist*, I rage when she bawls me out, I worry about her, I'm moved when she is tender, etc. And to be sure, it is profoundly regrettable that I put things on such a footing that to express a moment of strong affection I'm obliged to say, "I love you passionately." And it's too bad I have to lie to her about you, etc. But all full of sneaky little ways and fibs as it may be, this affair is right, because I am fond of [her]. The war has . . . taught me that I must not be negligent or casual toward you, since our love is so strong and noblesse oblige. But next it showed me, slight though this may be, that I have strong feelings for [Wanda], and it is so seldom that I have deep feelings that they have become precious to me.

Even as he decided to honor his feelings for both Wanda and Beauvoir, Sartre renounced "that shifty sort of generosity that has me spending hours and hours with people who aren't worth a damn to me, under the pretext that 'it would be just too rotten to hurt them.'" This still did not resolve the issue, but a "severe letter" from Beauvoir put him through the ringer again.

> I've never been this uneasy with myself . . . I'm afraid I must seem slightly underhanded to you with all the lies I'm entangled in . . . I'm afraid you might suddenly ask yourself . . . isn't he perhaps lying to me, isn't he telling me half-truths? My little one, my darling Beaver, I swear to you that with you I'm totally pure. If I were not, there would be nothing in the world before which I would not be a liar, I would lose my very self. My love, you are not only my life but also the only honesty of my life . . . What particularly struck me was your saying that I grant myself an advantage over people and that I find that what is lying for me is actually good enough truth for them. That is *absolutely true.*

Seeing his contrition, Beauvoir largely forgave him, but Sartre's extensive introspection only settled the issue for a little while, for when Wanda was being x-rayed for a lesion in May of 1940, Sartre found it "*very* disagreeable to know that she's panic stricken." He told Beauvoir,

> It's odd, she is becoming more and more "my child," as [Olga] was at one time for you . . . I've just written to her that if she wants it, and if the delays aren't too great, I was ready to marry her to get three days of leave. I don't imagine that will be very nice for you; though it's purely symbolic, it does make me look committed up to my ears. I for one don't like it at all, not so much because of that, but because of my family, from whom I must hide it and who'll surely hear about it someday. But I've told you and my mind's made up: I want to do everything I can for [Wanda] from now on. In exchange, I'll still take a little day to see you.

By that evening's letter, though, Sartre would be appalled again, and he wrote to Beauvoir to say he would "slam the brakes on marriage." He charged Beauvoir with finding out the details of Wanda's illness, and after it came out that Wanda was not very sick—only afraid and alone—Sartre never raised the idea of marrying her again. He did not disavow Wanda, though, and if Beauvoir felt betrayed, she did not try to drive Wanda away. The letters Beauvoir got from Sartre were so detailed and so full of literary and philosophical material that she could tolerate his insipid obsession, with confidence that she herself received his most serious attentions.

IX.

Soon after this frenzied exchange of letters, Germany invaded France in May 1940, and Sartre and Beauvoir's affairs were held in suspension as they looked at their lives through the lens of the war. Their familiar routines fell apart: Beauvoir fled Paris with Bienenfeld and her family, and when France capitulated a few days after Hitler entered Paris on June 14, Sartre was taken prisoner. Beauvoir returned to occupied Paris almost immediately, hoping to get word of Sartre's location and condition, but when he failed to materialize—it was weeks before she would even get a postcard from him—she soon resigned herself to write in spite of her despair. It might be senseless to write during a war, she told herself, but if she survived, she would at least have put the time to good use.

Teaching and writing in occupied Paris, Beauvoir's affairs simmered down. Bost was invalided back to the city—having been wounded by shrapnel in the first fighting—and he and Beauvoir resumed their relationship, but in October 1940, Beauvoir finally broke with Bienenfeld, who began to see one of her classmates, Bernard Lamblin, whom she would eventually marry—but only after her parents decided not to marry her to an American in order to get her out of France. As a Jew in Vichy France, Bienenfeld was deeply anxious about her safety, but when Beauvoir saw her, later in the war, "suffering from an intense and dreadful attack of neurasthenia," she wrote to Sartre that "it's our fault I think. It's the very indirect, but profound, after-shock of the business between her and us. She's the only person to whom we've really done harm, but we have harmed her." Beauvoir also continued to see Sorokine, but Sorokine too had found a boyfriend, and now Beauvoir had more freedom from the students she had called her "charming vermin."

Sartre returned to Paris in March 1941, after having forged the papers that let him escape from the detention camp in Germany. He could have returned earlier, but the situation of the prison camp and his status as one prisoner among others had inspired him to do something that would express the solidarity between them, so at Christmas he had written a nativity play that used the Roman occupation of Jerusalem as a metaphor for the German occupation of France. Having written, produced, and acted in his own play, Sartre returned to Paris determined not to collaborate—or even compromise—with the occupation forces. If his situation as a freethinking son of bourgeois parents had led him to live a genuine life in defiance of convention, and if his friendships—with Nizan and Guille and now Beauvoir—had always involved him in couples—now, as a French citizen in an occupied city, he felt a deep solidarity with his fellows, and he wanted his writing and his visions of liberty to inspire a resistance against Nazi oppression. Beauvoir did not immediately understand Sartre's transformation from individualism to commitment, but soon she shared his views, and together with Bost and some others, they founded a resistance group called "Socialism and Liberty." Sartre and Beauvoir even made a trip together to the Free Zone, in southern France, to talk with André Malraux and André Gide, two veterans of the Spanish Civil War. Sartre wanted to find out about how he could form an armed resistance, but Malraux and Gide trusted more in American tanks than in writers with weapons, and they did not give him any connections.

Back in Paris, Sartre and Beauvoir used their writing and their ideas about rebellion and liberty to encourage their fellow Parisians. Sartre dramatized Orestes' murder of Clytemnestra and Aegisthus in *The Flies* as a way of encouraging Parisians to rise up against their oppressors. Beauvoir came to grips with the occupation by writing *The Useless Mouths*, in which the soldiers in a besieged town plan to kill all those incapable of combat, and the noncombatants offer to die fighting instead of allowing the town to be morally blighted by their murder. These plays—in addition to Sartre's *No Exit*, in 1944—established Sartre and Beauvoir's credentials as committed resistance intellectuals, whose art was inextricable from their political situation.

In spite of their activity in literary resistance groups, it was only because of their love affairs that Sartre and Beauvoir ran into trouble with the Vichy government. When Sorokine's mother got wind of some stories about Sartre and Beauvoir in 1943, she filed a complaint with the Ministry of Education, accusing Beauvoir of seducing her daughter and procuring other young women, in addition to her daughter, for Sartre and Bost—both of whom had slept with her as well. The police interviewed everyone involved, but they had all coordinated and rehearsed their stories, so the case was dropped. Beauvoir was nevertheless not reappointed to teach in the fall, and Sartre found her a job producing radio shows about traditional French culture. Beauvoir was not terribly inconvenienced by the loss of her position—not only because she and Sartre had always shared their finances, but because *She Came to Stay* had been published in 1943, and now she was beginning to be recognized as a talented new author in her own right.

The end of the war marked a turning point for Sartre and Beauvoir. Sartre was forty and Beauvoir was thirty-seven, and for the moment, they were free of other attachments, for Sartre had split up with Wanda after Wanda had had an affair with Albert Camus in 1944. Sartre and Beauvoir had worked in small circles for all their adult lives, but now that they were famous authors in postwar France, the rest of their work would be done in the glare of international political and intellectual attention. They were thrust into the cultural spotlight both by a French government that had only cultural assets to export—its material resources having been destroyed—and by a public that was hungry for their humanist ideas, which described how to live without God in a postwar wasteland.

In their novels and plays, and now in lectures, editorials, and articles, Sartre and Beauvoir were espousing the philosophy they had first developed as irreverent students, but instead of rebelling against bourgeois traditions and keeping themselves almost furiously open to the contingencies that were always seething beneath conventions, Sartre was now proposing—more publicly than Beauvoir—that the world be rebuilt based on a philosophy that used the uniqueness of each individual as the basis for commitment and solidarity between individuals. His philosophy was centered on the idea that in the absence of God or absolutes, men alone created their reality, and in the postwar atmosphere, his existential philosophy became a political ideology by which Europeans hoped to save themselves from the excesses of both capitalism and communism. While Sartre's vision of solidarity would yield to Cold War militarism in the mid-1950s, this philosophy was in high demand throughout the late 1940s. When in 1945 Sartre gave a lecture entitled "Existentialism Is a Humanism," some of the members of the standing-room-only crowd had forged their tickets to get in.

As Sartre's partner—and as an author in her own right, who had only recently published a thinly veiled account of their ménage à trois—Beauvoir became a celebrity as well, and she and Sartre started to be surrounded by photographers and autograph-seekers. The books they had written during the war were read widely—Beauvoir's *She Came to Stay* and *The Blood of Others* and Sartre's *The Age of Reason* and *Being and Nothingness.* Their plays—Sartre's *The Flies* and *No Exit*, Beauvoir's *Useless Mouths*—were performed in Paris and New York, and soon Sartre had written new plays, *The Respectful Prostitute* and *Dirty Hands*, in which Wanda enjoyed a considerable success in leading roles.

Having rebelled against institutions all their lives, Sartre and Beauvoir—along with Albert Camus and Arthur Koestler, among others—used their newfound cultural capital to found an institution of their own, in the form of a literary magazine. *Les Temps Modernes* served as a platform for the existential project of finding philosophical meanings in the details of modern life. Sartre also founded the Democratic Revolutionary Assembly, in an attempt to prevent Europe from becoming the battleground for the war that seemed imminent between America and Russia.

X.

After the war, Sartre and Beauvoir were consumed by their editorial and political responsibilities, and consequently had less free time for flirtations and seductions. Fame did not stop them from taking contingent lovers, but after the war, there would be much less time for seduction and its accompanying intellectual and epistolary fireworks. They would just take lovers who sought them out, or who simply crossed their paths—and they would conduct their liaisons within their rigid schedules.

When Sartre sailed to New York in 1946, as part of a cultural delegation—Beauvoir would soon be off to lecture in Tunis and Algeria— he met and began an affair with Dolores Vanetti, a French-speaking American journalist who showed him around the city he had always idealized as the home of jazz and modern innovation. For the first time, Sartre's deep involvement with a woman made Beauvoir profoundly uncomfortable. As she wrote in her memoir,

> According to his accounts, she shared completely all his reactions, his emotions, his irritations, his desires. When they went out together, she always wanted to stop, to go on again, at exactly the same moment he did. Perhaps this indicated a harmony between them at a depth—at the very source of life, at the wellspring where

its rhythm is established—at which Sartre and I did not meet, and perhaps that harmony was more important to him than our understanding.

Dolores' own marriage was dissolving at the time, and she became determined to win a place in Sartre's life, but even though he more than once allowed her to extend her visits to Paris—even though he even proposed to marry her at one point—the relationship always remained impossible. Sartre wrote Beauvoir that "Dolores' love for me scares me. In other respects she is absolutely charming and we never get mad at each other. But the future of the whole thing is very grim."

If their relationship's future was grim, it was really only because Sartre could not imagine continuing to love her. He was not, however, unwilling to support her, as he had supported his other lovers. Ever since he and Beauvoir had started receiving their teaching salaries in the early 1930s, he had been generous with his money, and he supported more than one of his ex-lovers. Even after they split up, he wrote several plays for Wanda, and he would always insist that she perform in the leading roles, even when directors and critics told him that she was insufficient to the parts. He would support Wanda for the rest of his life, and when he returned from America in the spring of 1946—even as he anticipated Dolores' visit—he started an affair with Michelle Vian, the young and beautiful wife of novelist Boris Vian—and even though their romantic affair would end a few months later, Sartre would support her for the rest of her life as well. Sartre might have supported Dolores, but she considered his offer an insult, and when they split up in 1950, after her divorce had finally come through, she went her own way without him.

In 1947, after lecturing in northern Africa, Beauvoir followed in Sartre's footsteps, flying to New York as part of another lecture tour. She met Dolores herself and wrote to Sartre that she "found her exactly as I'd imagined. I like her a lot, and was very happy because I understood your feelings—I could appreciate them, and honored you for having them—and at the same time didn't feel the least bit embarrassed." From New York, she traveled across the country, lecturing and visiting for two months, until, on the eve of her return, Sartre wired to ask her to delay her arrival in Paris, since by that time Dolores had come to see him, but Dolores had delayed her own departure, and she was still in Paris.

Hungry for male attention, Beauvoir returned to a writer she had met in Chicago at the beginning of her travels. Nelson Algren had made his career writing stories of the Chicago slums, and he took her out with him, to strip clubs and seedy bars. He did not speak French, but Beauvoir got by with her English, and when he kissed her after hardly paying her any attention at the bars, it was with a passion Beauvoir had not experienced before. As she wrote in her novel *The Mandarins*, which fictionalized the relationship:

> His lust transfigured me; I who for so long had had no taste, no form, I again possessed breasts, a belly, a sex; flesh. I was nourishing like bread, I had smells like earth. It was so miraculous that I didn't think of measuring time or place. I only know that when I finally drifted off, one could hear the feeble trills of dawn.

In spite of this new fulfillment—Algren almost immediately asked her to marry him—Beauvoir refused from the beginning to leave Sartre and Paris. Algren still felt a strong attachment to Chicago's slums, and he refused to relocate to France, so in spite of the fact that Beauvoir described Algren as "the only truly passionate love in my life," for the next five years, the relationship's future remained as grim as any other of her or Sartre's affairs had been. Ultimately Beauvoir urged Algren, in Engish, to take other lovers:

> I love you too much, in a physical, sexual way too, not to feel any jealousy. I think I should have to be very cold blooded to be able to fancy you kissing a girl, sleeping with her, and not to feel a bad pang in the heart. But this kind of animal instinct does not matter very much . . . next time when you are tempted by a woman, just do what you please, take her to Wabansia home if you like. I really mean it. You have not to be afraid of hurting me by doing so. I just wish she'll be away when I come, and never too deep in your heart. In this matter, the chief question is rather: take care the girl will not be unhappy if you drop her afterwards.

Beauvoir made several trips, between 1947 and 1951, to live a "conjugal life" with Algren, generally at the same time that Vanetti would travel to Paris to be with Sartre. Still, she wrote to Sartre, "I can't regret this affair being dead, since its death was implied in the life I've chosen—which you give me." It was the same for Sartre and Dolores, and starting in 1947, Beauvoir would encourage him to "extract yourself as best you can from your own troubles."

Beauvoir's relationship with Algren began to deteriorate as early as 1948, when Beauvoir cut short their visit in order to rush back to Paris, to help Sartre with a screenplay—and to help him evade Dolores, who was still insisting on a conjugal life of her own. Algren realized that Beauvoir was not going to be the full-time companion he needed, and when he met his ex-wife in Hollywood prior to Beauvoir's next trip to Chicago in 1949, he began to court her again: they remarried in 1953, after he and Beauvoir split up in 1951. They would divorce again soon afterward, and Algren would rediscover Beauvoir briefly in 1960, but neither of them could agree to move for the other, and the relationship remained as impossible as ever.

In their time and their travels together, though, Algren had opened Beauvoir's eyes to her commonality with other women. Beauvoir had always thought of herself as herself—never explicitly as a woman—but her only income after the war was a stipend she got from Sartre, through *Les Temps Modernes*, so she began to write an essay on women in an attempt to make some money at the same time that she explored her own womanhood. What began as a short essay turned into *The Second Sex*, a two-volume landmark of modern feminism, which compiled far-reaching historical and mythological examples into a catalog of the reasons why women have been subordinated to men. With faith in the possibility that each individual woman could find an existential self-fulfillment of her situation, Beauvoir concluded that woman's "apprenticeship in abandonment and transcendence: that is, in liberty" was only beginning, and that "the free woman"—the woman who can find liberty in her existence as a woman, and who can express that liberty in works and in art—"is just being born." She herself, of course, with her intellectual and erotic freedom, was serving as a path breaker and role model.

Throughout the late 1940s and early '50s, Sartre was applying his philosophy to actual lives as well. He spent a great deal of time writing editorial pieces or speaking at rallies or trials, or traveling with Beauvoir to Russia or Cuba or China for Communist Party meetings. In the contest between capitalism and communism, he had ultimately endorsed Russia's Communist government, and he would support it until Russian forces invaded Hungary in 1956. But he was also devoting his attentions to *Saint Genet*, a biography of writer and convict Jean Genet, which was published in 1952. In 1955 he started to work on *The Idiot of the Family*, which attempted to render a full account of Gustave Flaubert's life. Sartre only completed three of the planned four volumes, but with the Flaubert project, he spent the last twenty-five years of his life trying to express the tumult and contingency of lived experience—and the purposeful work that organized it.

By the late 1950s, Sartre and Beauvoir were beginning to offer up their own lives as existential literature. When Beauvoir's *Memoirs of a Dutiful Daughter* came out in 1958—*The Prime of Life* followed in 1960, *The Force of Circumstance* in 1963, and in 1964 Sartre's *The Words*—some of their lovers were outraged to find that their identities had not been completely hidden by pseudonyms. Beauvoir had remained close with Algren after their relationship dissolved, but he broke with her permanently when he saw what she had made of their relationship in print. He complained to Beauvoir that "the big thing about sexual love is it lets you become her and lets her become you, but when you share the relationship with everybody who can afford a book, you reduce it." Beauvoir was still determined to deflate sentimentalities and idealisms, and to bear witness to reality, so if she published her intimacy with Algren, she did not neglect to include her own despair about their break:

> The pain and the pleasure of writing would not have been enough to settle the memory of my last few days in America . . . wouldn't it be better to give up the whole thing? I asked myself that question with an anxiety that bordered on mental aberration. To calm myself, I began to take orthedrine. For the moment, it allowed me to regain my balance; but I imagine that this expedient was not entirely unconnected with the anxiety attacks I suffered from at the time. Since they were founded in reality, my anxiety could at least have been discreet in its manifestations; but it was in fact accompanied by a physical panic that my greatest fits of despair, even when enhanced by alcohol, had never produced . . . suddenly I was becoming a stone, and the steel was splitting it: that is hell.

Beauvoir was not alone in relying on pills and alcohol. In the period after the war, when there was such an urgency in injecting existential humanism into the debate between capitalism and communism, Sartre had begun to take stimulants in order to generate as much writing as possible, and soon he was taking a whole bottle of corydrane every day, which he said tripled the speed of his writing, so that he was generating around twenty pages each day. He would take stimulants for much of the rest of his life—with ever larger doses of alcohol in the evenings to slow him back down—and he only finally cut back when his doctors warned him that his attempt to increase his output was threatening to curtail his output by killing him.

Writing remained a central occupation for Sartre and Beauvoir both. From the end of the 1940s, they were supporting themselves solely with their books, articles, and lectures, and through the 1950s, their lovers and lovers-turned-companions were scheduled in around blocks of writing time. In addition to his afternoons with Beauvoir—when they would meet for literary feedback and political consultation—Sartre was scheduling a few evenings each week for Wanda and for Michelle Vian in addition to other, incidental women. In 1952, after she split up with Nelson Algren, Beauvoir started an affair with a journalist from *Les Temps Modernes*, Claude Lanzmann, who was seventeen years her junior. Lanzmann moved into Beauvoir's small apartment, but he would acknowledge that there was never "the slightest question of rivalry with Sartre." After working with Lanzmann all morning, Beauvoir would still meet Sartre to edit and consult in the afternoons. Sartre and Beauvoir generally accepted each other's lovers as part of the Family—and some of them actually were family: for not only had Sartre and Beauvoir taken Wanda and Olga as lovers, but over the five years when Beauvoir was seeing Lanzmann, Sartre was also seeing Lanzmann's sister, Evelyne Ray, who had played Estelle in *No Exit*.

In spite of these other relationships, though, it was Beauvoir alone who accompanied Sartre to his public appearances. A number of women depended on Sartre at any one time—Wanda and Michelle, Evelyne Ray, and Sartre's Russian interpreter, Lena Zonina, among others—and even though he concocted the idea of a "temporary moral code" to explain the half-truths and lies he would resort to when he needed to resolve a conflict between his women, he nonetheless strove to be scrupulously moral in his writing, and he and Beauvoir continued to edit each other's writing, working together to express their ideas about political solidarity and existential genuineness. Even when Sartre was writing his *Critique of Dialectical Reason*—which Beauvoir said she "could hardly understand"— she continued to give him feedback on the manuscript.

None of the women to whom Sartre had proposed marriage challenged his relationship with Beauvoir as much as Arlette Elkaïm, an Algerian Jewish philosophy student, who was nineteen when Sartre took her, briefly, for a lover in 1956. When Sartre discovered in 1958 that Michelle Vian was betraying him with another man, he began to spend more time with Elkaïm, and after Elkaïm failed her exams, he bought her an apartment and a country house and supported her entirely. Having offered to marry Beauvoir and Wanda, among others, when it would have been bureaucratically useful, Sartre adopted Elkaïm in 1965 when she was threatened with deportation back to Algeria, although the adoption served several other purposes as well: Elkaïm would serve as his heir, preventing his papers from reverting to his stepfather's estate when he died, and in the act of adopting his onetime lover, Sartre also showed that he was just as willing to outrage bourgeois morality in his old age as he had been when he and Beauvoir had declined to marry. Sartre had always been anxious to preserve his youthfulness—he was sixty-three during the protests and turmoil of 1968, and now he gave up the customary shirt and tie of the traditional intellectual and assumed the casual language and dress of the insurgent students.

These kinds of gestures had merely reaffirmed Sartre's rebelliousness, but his adoption of Elkaïm threatened Beauvoir's place in his life, for now he had given a much younger woman a legal authority Beauvoir did not have. Beauvoir and Elkaïm stayed on fairly good terms—Elkaïm was, by all accounts, a passive, deferential woman, who coordinated Sartre's weekly schedule with his women—but by the 1970s, Sartre was slipping away from Beauvoir. His health was in decline—he had been hospitalized with heart trouble in 1958 and a stroke in 1971, and in 1973 another stroke took his eyesight—and Beauvoir had less and less access to him. She would read to him in the mornings before she left him in Elkaïm's or Michelle's or Wanda's care for the rest of the day, but she still relied so much on Sartre's presence as a fact in the world that she needed to keep him healthy, and when she tried to enforce his doctors' proscriptions of work, smoke, and drink, she only drove a wedge between them, for Sartre's other women and visitors would indulge him with hidden bottles, even as he was becoming weaker.

Beauvoir could only care for Sartre when he would let her, about three nights a week: she could not keep him from coming under other people's influences. She tried to stop a journal from publishing an interview he gave to his secretary, an Egyptian Jew named Benny Lévy. Beauvoir felt that the interview had misrepresented Sartre's life's work, but Sartre insisted that the interview be published, even over her objections. After the incident, Elkaïm wrote a public letter denigrating Beauvoir, and when Sartre died in 1980—predeceasing Beauvoir by six years—Elkaïm and Lévy locked Beauvoir out of Sartre's apartment and took possession of all of his papers. In response, Beauvoir made a monument to her lifelong relationship with Sartre by publishing Sartre's *War Diaries* and two volumes of his letters, *Witness to My Life* and *Quiet Moments in a War*, in addition to her *Letters to Sartre*. Nelson Algren had already seen his affair with Beauvoir in print, but now Bianca Bienenfeld and others realized that Sartre and Beauvoir had been in league together throughout all their affairs.

After Sartre's death, Beauvoir adopted an heir of her own. After Lanzmann had fallen in love with another woman and ended his affair with Beauvoir in 1958, Beauvoir does not appear to have taken new lovers, but in 1960 she befriended Sylvie Le Bon, a young philosophy student who had written to her while she was preparing for the *agrégation* in 1960. Beauvoir found an attentive and perceptive companion in Le Bon, who passed her exam in 1965 and became a philosophy teacher herself, resisting Beauvoir's offers of full financial support. Throughout the 1960s, Le Bon became a closer and closer friend, accompanying Beauvoir in her travels. Beauvoir wrote in *All Said and Done*—the last volume of her memoir, which she published in 1972—that Le Bon

> is as thoroughly interwoven in my life as I am in hers. I have introduced her to my friends. We read the same books, we see shows together, and we go for long drives in the car. There is such an interchange between us that I lose my sense of age: she draws me forward into her future, and there are times when the present recovers a dimension that it had lost.

Le Bon said in an interview that "the Beaver often used to tell me that she had been very cautious with me. She felt she had made mistakes in the past"—although this had not kept Beauvoir from encouraging her to have an affair with Bost in 1968.

As Sartre's health had deteriorated through the 1970s, Beauvoir had begun to describe her relationship with Le Bon in the same terms she had once used to describe her relationship with Sartre: "it is an absolute relationship, because from the beginning we were both prepared to live in this way, to live entirely for each other." After Sartre died, she adopted Le Bon officially, allowing her to inherit her works, and Le Bon edited Beauvoir's letters to Sartre, Algren, and Bost for publication.

XI.

In the publication of their letters to each other, Sartre and Beauvoir's lives assumed the intimacy they themselves had always been working toward. They had become celebrities in postwar European culture, and their relationship was treated as a model by students and feminists: their letters revealed a complex web of fidelities and infidelities, and their morganatic marriage and their existential openness and honesty gave lovers in Europe and America a philosophical justification and a vocabulary with which to rebel against their own traditions.

In the affairs they used as raw material for their theories about human existence, Sartre and Beauvoir redefined partnership as a form of complicity in witnessing and suffering the infidelities that proved the chaotic nature of the world and the disloyal—even dishonest—nature of the human heart. But if they have since come to be seen as manipulators and liars for their "temporary moral codes," Western culture has still not found more forthright chroniclers of the intersection of erotic freedom and intellectual and creative commitment.

Chapter Four

The Sacred Monsters

Diego Rivera and Frida Kahlo

❧

I am not merely an "artist" but a man performing his biological function of producing paintings, just as a tree produces flowers and fruit.

DIEGO RIVERA

I will not speak of Diego as "my husband", because that would be ridiculous; Diego has never been, nor will he ever be, anyone's "husband".

FRIDA KAHLO

The most joyous moments of my life were those I had spent in painting; most others had been boring or sad. For even with women, unless they were interested enough in my work to spend their time with me while I painted, I knew I would certainly lose their love, not being able to spare the time away from my painting that they demanded. When I had to interrupt my painting to spend days courting a woman, I would be unhappy for losing the never-to-be-recovered time. Therefore, the women who were best for me were those who also loved painting. DIEGO RIVERA

Whenever you feel like caressing her, even if it's just a memory, caress me instead and just pretend it's her, eh?

FRIDA KAHLO TO ALEJANDRO GÓMEZ ARIAS

I.

When Diego Rivera moved to Paris in 1909, he was still an unknown painting student. He was twenty-two years old, he was tall and grossly overweight, and he rarely bathed, but he was precocious and talented, a prodigy. He had been painting ever since the age of ten, when his father

147

had enrolled him full-time in the San Carlos Academy in Mexico City, and for the past two years, since 1907, he had been studying in Spain with funding from the Mexican government. Rivera was highly successful as a painting student—his bursary would be continuously renewed from 1907 until 1914—but his sponsors had not wanted to help him develop a unique personal style: they wanted him to glorify the Mexican state by bringing the skills of the European masters to Mexican painting.

In 1909, Rivera was still some years away from acquiring the techniques that would mark his mature style, and he had still not had any substantial experience with women, but shortly after he moved to Paris, he set out to travel in northern Europe with painter friends, and at a rooming house in Bruges, he met and fell in love with a Russian painter. Angelina Beloff was slender and beautiful by all accounts, and she too had been living in Paris and painting before setting out to tour northern Europe with painter friends of her own. Beloff turned thirty years old that summer—she was seven years older than Rivera—but their parties merged, and Rivera and Beloff visited museums and sketched together, communicating in an ersatz mixture of Spanish, French, and Russian. By the time they reached London, an intimacy developed between them, and Rivera declared his affections and began courting Beloff—"so fervently," she said in her memoir, "that I felt under too much pressure . . . So I decided to return to Paris, to reflect in peace." When Rivera returned to Paris full of hope for a life together, Beloff wrote that she was "prepared to become his fiancée" and that she "thought that [she] would be able to love him." While biographers cannot find a record of their marriage, by 1911, they were living together—and speaking of each other—as husband and wife.

Love was a new experience for Rivera, and it changed how he saw his paintings. He had received prizes for mastering drawing techniques, but now he made an emotional connection with the paintings he had always studied and copied technically. In 1910, he wrote from Spain, describing his new feelings to Beloff, who was still in Paris:

> I was feeling more or less destroyed by my reaction to Velázquez but I looked ahead with my eyes and inside with my spirit, and slowly I began to see ahead . . . So, my wife, in that moment I realised that my soul was feeling something new. I realised that in truth I had been passing in front of these pictures like an uncomprehending admirer, that I had failed to understand their soul.

El Greco, the most sublime of painters, the greatest in spirit, had been until then unknown to me . . . Everything that one might feel or desire to feel was there in the pictures of El Greco, whose colours I knew inch by inch but which I did not really know at all. And then, girl, the *Pentecost*, the Descent of the Holy Spirit! I felt a spirit descend on *me* which filled me with the fire of a great beauty, of the highest feelings, from beyond. And I realised that I was understanding El Greco's *Pentecost* because your high spirit had descended on my soul. It was a stronger emotion than I have ever felt before a work of art, unless it was when I stood beside you in front of Rembrandt, in front of Turner, in front of Botticelli and Paolo Uccello and Piero della Francesca, but the feeling was even stronger this time because you were not only beside me, you were within me.

Even with Beloff's spirit inside him, it was still some time before Rivera began to make paintings that expressed a unique individuality. He exhibited traditional landscapes in the 1911 Salon des Indépendants, but he did not arrive at his own style until 1913, when two painter friends—Dutchman Piet Mondrian and fellow Mexican Angel Zárraga—introduced him to Cubism, which had been gaining in popularity. Cubism was a geometrical and hypertheoretical style for which Rivera's education had prepared him well, and now as he began to make Cubist canvases, he distinguished himself among painters who did not have his thorough academic training. By 1913, he was living on the sales of his paintings, and when his state bursary ended in 1914, he was twenty-eight years old, and he was supporting himself completely with his brush.

Success was a big change for Rivera. By 1913, he had already been with Beloff for more than three years, but now that he was selling avant-garde paintings, he became a character in Parisian bohemian society. His status allowed him to create a new identity, and now his obesity, his ugliness, and his Mexicanness were no longer reasons for insecurity. In the carnivalesque atmosphere of prewar Montparnasse—where art had become outrageous and abstract and incomprehensible, and artists were recognized as much by their personal eccentricities as by their painting—his peculiarities all became points in his favor. Rivera was already a diligent painter, with the confidence that came from having been supported by his government, but now he befriended Picasso, a fellow Spanish-speaker whose paintings had been fascinating and eluding the bourgeoisie. Rivera and Picasso exchanged pranks and fabulous stories—and they traded images and themes in their paintings—and soon Rivera began to supplant his bourgeois childhood by telling outrageous stories—of having been suckled by a goat, of having harangued his aunt's Catholic congregation with an atheistic tirade at age six or of having had his first—adulterous—sexual experience at age nine. Capitalizing on his exotic Mexicanness, he claimed to have practiced cannibalism as a student—the flesh of young women is best, he would say; it is succulent, like roast pig.

In this bohemian atmosphere, where every bourgeois norm was openly flouted, sex was a form of rebellion, and also of networking. To have a brief affair with a painter, model, or dealer was a way of associating with other artists, and now Rivera's talent made him attractive—even in spite of his appearance—to a Russian painter and model of Picasso's. When Rivera met her in 1915, Marievna Vorobiev was twenty-three years old, six years younger than Rivera, who was twenty-nine, and still living with Beloff, who was now thirty-six. Art critic Ilya Ehrenburg described Vorobiev as a "badly trained tigress" and Rivera would describe her in his autobiography as a "'she-devil' not only because of her wild beauty, but also because of her fits of violence." Nevertheless, by this time, Rivera had acquired such clout that Beloff recalled him being "interested in launching her as a painter," and Vorobiev even lived with the couple for a time. But when Beloff got pregnant in 1915, Vorobiev herself wrote that she was "caught up in a dangerous game, and instead of avoiding Rivera because of his wife's pregnancy, I allowed myself to come closer and closer to the man who frightened and fascinated me."

Sexual charades may have been standard fare among the Montparnasse artists and models, but in her memoir, Beloff confessed that she was hurt by Rivera's affair. Vorobiev, she wrote, was "a young woman who called herself a friend and who I had welcomed into my home," and now Beloff left the house, feeling twice betrayed. After she gave birth, she stayed with a friend with her baby for about six months while Rivera's passion for Vorobiev cooled. When Rivera ultimately returned, Beloff took him back, but she could never force him to break with Vorobiev. She could not afford to give him an ultimatum: she was thirty-seven years old and responsible for an infant, and if she still loved Rivera, she and her baby also needed his financial support. Having cornered Beloff, Rivera went back and forth between the women, and by allowing this, Beloff essentially gave him the freedom to keep the two relationships simultaneously. All of his future relationships would put women in one or the other of these two roles: the dependent wife or the seductive girlfriend who threatened to take her place.

In late 1928, when she met Diego Rivera, Frida Kahlo was returning to society after almost three years spent recuperating from a bus accident that had crippled her, but she was also single for the first time since 1923: she had finally ceased to write pleading letters to her first love, Alejandro Gómez Arias, who had just married a friend of hers that June.

Kahlo and Arias had met in Mexico City at the Preparatoria school, as fellow members of "the Cachuchas," a small gang of friends known for their jaunty caps and their pranks. Kahlo had enjoyed a reputation for outrageous and daring behavior ever since a bout of polio at age six had withered and shortened her right leg: her personality had expanded to compensate her debility. Her illness also bonded her closely with her father, a German freethinker, who had been epileptic since a childhood accident of his own. Illness gave her a peek behind bourgeois conventions, and also an affinity with street urchins and the poor: she learned to curse colorfully, and to hold polite society at an ironic distance, if not in contempt. When her parents enrolled her in the prestigious Preparatoria in 1922, recent reforms in the Mexican education system were being criticized by students and politicians, and Kahlo took part in revolts and demonstrations that protested the obsolescence of the faculty and the irrelevance of the course material. She and the Cachuchas disrupted what they felt was a pedantic academic routine with pranks that involved fireworks, bombs, or, in one case, riding a burro through the halls.

As circumstance would have it, Rivera himself was painting a mural at the Preparatoria when Kahlo was in school there, and while they would not meet for another six years, Rivera's obesity and his reputation for womanizing made him a prime target for the Cachuchas' pranks. Kahlo herself was reputed to have soaped the stairs where Rivera was painting— although the school's rector, not Rivera, was the one who eventually slipped—and she called out false warnings when Rivera's wife was coming in, to give the impression of an illicit encounter between the painter and his model. As a student, Kahlo had not been interested in Rivera except as someone to prank. She fell in love with Alejandro Gómez Arias, and their relationship involved a degree of daring: Kahlo herself had helped her elder sister Matilde elope, and she knew that her parents held to a strict morality, so she had to invent stories and alibis to make time for Arias.

Kahlo was one of only two girls in the gang of nine, and while she projected an outrageous personality in school, she prostrated herself before Arias in private. Her letters show her practically begging for his affection at the same time that they use self-mocking humor to defend against any appearance of emotional neediness. "For my part," she wrote him, "I wish to be with you very much, but who knows if it bores you a lot to talk with this *novia* of yours who loves you very much but is a bit of a dunce." Kahlo was nonetheless willing to take a small place in his life, and on Christmas of 1924—nine months before the bus accident—she wrote to him:

> Sometimes I'm very afraid at night and I would like you to be with me so you wouldn't let me be so fearful and would tell me you love me as before, as last December, though I'm an "easy thing," right Alex? You have to start liking easy things . . . I would like to be still easier, a tiny little thing you could just carry around in your pocket for ever and ever . . . Alex, write me often and even if it's not true tell me you love me very much and can't live without me.
> Your child, *escuincla** (or woman or whatever you want).
> Frieda

In spite of her apparent dependence on Arias, Kahlo herself was not a faithful lover. When she applied for a job at the Ministry of Education library in the summer of 1925, she was seduced by a female employee there, and her parents made a scandal when they found out. When she took a paid apprenticeship with an engraver at the end of the summer, he taught her to draw and she took him briefly as a lover as well—this time in private. It is not clear how much Kahlo and Arias even expected fidelity of each other, for when Arias confessed his own attraction to a girl Kahlo knew, Kahlo embraced his attraction, offering herself not as an alternative but as a stand-in for the other girl. On New Year's Day 1925, she had written to him:

> Concerning what you say about Anita Reyna, naturally I wouldn't be angry in the least, firstly because you're only telling me the truth, that she is and always will be very pretty and very lovely, and secondly

---

* Hairless Mexican dog.

because I love everyone you love or have loved (!) [*sic*] for the very simple reason that you love them. Nevertheless, I didn't much like that part about the caresses, because even though I understand that she is very lovely, I feel something like . . . well, how can I put it? like envy, you know? but that's only natural. Whenever you feel like caressing her, even if it's just a memory, caress me instead and just pretend it's her.

In September of 1925, within a month or two of her encounter with the engraver, Kahlo and Arias were on their way home from school together when their bus was hit by a trolley. Arias suffered relatively light injuries, but Kahlo was crushed. Her shoulder, spine, leg, and foot were fractured in multiple places, and her pelvis was pierced by a handrail.* Kahlo was eighteen years old, but now instead of working at her studies, she was suddenly learning how to endure constant pain—not only the physical pain of her injuries, but the desolation of knowing that she would probably be crippled for good. To alleviate her boredom when she was still confined to bed after being released from the hospital—and to give her some outlet for her emotions—her father gave her paints, and her mother had a special easel built. Painting in bed, she began to make portraits of herself and of her family members to pass the time.

Kahlo was up and about within three months, and if she was still in pain, now she began to suffer further, because Arias seems to have found out about her affair with Fernando Fernández, the engraver. He complained about her loose morals, and they quarreled. In her letters she complained that she had "such a bad reputation" and while she defended herself against Arias' criticisms, she did admit that she had "said I love you to many, and I have kissed or been given ribbons by others, at the bottom of my heart I have loved only you."

They reconciled when she gave Arias her first mature self-portrait, but her pains returned, and they could never resume their relationship on the same footing. Kahlo's bones had not set correctly—her doctors did not know that her right leg was already shorter when they set the fractures, and because of her family's lack of money, she had not had the x-rays that would have revealed the full extent of her injuries. When she was bound in a plaster corset and kept at home, Arias came only rarely

---

* Kahlo would claim that the handrail exited her body through her vagina, but Arias and others have contended that this was an invention intended to add drama to the story, and primarily to explain the loss of her virginity to her parents.

to see her. Desperate and bored, forsaken in the suburbs, Kahlo could no longer use her coy and self-deprecating letters to hide the fact that she was asking Arias for more than he could give her. Between their quarrel and the fact that her parents' house was an hour's bus ride from the city, they effectively stopped seeing each other, and then Arias' family, who already disapproved of Kahlo, sent him to Europe to study. Arias left without saying goodbye—he said he did not want to create a scene—and then his four-month trip stretched to eight months. Kahlo wrote him long letters throughout his travels, but by the time he came back in November of 1927, the relationship was over, although Kahlo still did not relinquish him. Even after he married a friend of hers, Esperanza Ordóñez, in June of 1928, Kahlo pleaded, "In your heart, you understand me; you know why I did the things I did! What's more, you know I adore you! That you're not only something of mine, but my very myself! [. . .] Irreplaceable!"

If Kahlo was still yearning for Arias, she had been sobered by her suffering and her losses, and in Arias' absence, her new friends drew her into a circle of artists and students. Tina Modotti, a model and artist in her own right, hosted a salon that had become the center of a bohemian society much like Rivera's Montparnasse, although political assassinations and domestic terrorism—combined with the threats and promises of Russian-style communism—added an atmosphere of political danger to the air of artistic radicalism. Kahlo joined the Young Communist League and then the Mexican Communist Party, and in this new society, her talent for profanity, her tolerance for pain-killers, and her ability to drink—"like a real mariachi," in Rivera's ex-wife's words—made her an outspoken and colorful person, someone who could be appealing to a rebellious painter twice her age.

After he returned to Mexico in 1921, Rivera had married a model, Guadalupe Marín, but they had divorced in 1927 after Rivera had had an affair with Tina Modotti. Rivera and Kahlo both frequented Modotti's salon, and Rivera may have met Kahlo there when he asked her to model for the *Insurrection* panel in a mural that depicted the history of Mexico. But Rivera and Kahlo began to be intimately acquainted when she called him down from his scaffold in early 1929 and asked him for his opinion of her paintings. She had been painting for three years since her accident, and she wanted to know whether she should try to support herself as a painter.

In his otherwise fanciful autobiography, Rivera takes a less fantastic tone when he describes this interview with Kahlo. He recalls that she was quite direct, even defensive, about courting the opinion of one of the most famous muralists in her country—she had already asked Orozco and other painters for their opinions—and he recalls that he responded to her work, but because of his bad reputation, he could not express the warmth of his reaction.

> Why, I asked her, didn't she trust my judgment? Hadn't she come herself to ask for it?
> "The trouble is," she replied, "that some of your good friends have advised me not to put too much stock in what you say. They say that if it's a girl who asks your opinion and she's not an absolute horror, you are ready to gush all over her. Well, I want you to tell me only one thing. Do you actually believe that I should continue to paint, or should I turn to some other sort of work?"

When he told her that "no matter how difficult it is for you, you must continue to paint," she offered to show him further paintings, but now, he wrote, he was afraid that "if I showed my excitement she might not let me come at all." She was open to his attentions nevertheless, and they kissed just a few days after he came to her house to see more paintings. If they were genuinely attracted to each other, Kahlo's receptivity may also have been influenced by her pressing medical bills, which had been straining her family's finances, and by Rivera's reputation as a famous and wealthy artist. Kahlo may have been outspoken, exotic, dramatic, and irreverent in her behavior, but she was hardly independent, and with her crippling injuries and doctors' bills, she was indeed so dependent that Rivera must have seen that she would tolerate his affairs, the same way Beloff had.

Neither Rivera nor Kahlo ever wrote about their decision to marry— they did not, like Sartre and Beauvoir, or Miller and Nin, proclaim that their relationship was a brave new form of love—so we do not know whether Kahlo believed the she would keep Rivera from straying, or whether she had resigned herself to his affairs and already planned to take lovers of her own. We can only deduce from their actions, and the letters that touch their marriage and their affairs: they do not seem to have been head-over-heels in love—but they seem to have believed that they were making a good, even radical, match.

Nevertheless they were married within a few months of their first kisses, and as soon as they were married, Rivera paid off her parents' mortgage. He paid for her medical bills as well, but he never ceased to take lovers, and while Kahlo would make attempts at independence through-out their marriage, she would never really break with him over his affairs. She was resigned to stay with him, and when Lupe Marín, Rivera's second wife, saw that Kahlo was not going to replace her as his muse, she offered to help her. With Marín's assistance, Kahlo learned to take care of Rivera. She would out-flirt the lovers who threatened her, whenever she could, and if women took him away from her, she learned to act as if they were only spicing up their marriage.

II.

After Diego Rivera became famous in the early 1910s, he jettisoned the papers from his youth, so very little information exists about his child-hood or the atmosphere of his parents' household. In his autobiography, Rivera described himself as a "sacred monster"—a childhood atheist, insurrectionist, and cannibal—but surviving accounts describe a preco-cious artist—even a prodigy—who got all the support he needed from his parents and teachers as he was schooled in the craft of painting.

Not much is known about Don Anastasio de Rivera, the painter's paternal grandfather, beyond the fact that he immigrated to Mexico—probably from Spain—and that he invested in a silver mine that thrived until it flooded and caved in. Don Diego, the painter's father, was the first of Don Anastasio's nine children, and he grew up well-off in Gua-najuato. He had gone to school for chemistry and then tried assaying and prospecting before he wrote a textbook for teaching Spanish grammar and took a job at a normal school that had been founded by the widow Doña Nemesia Rodríguez de Valpuesta. Don Diego was thirty-three—he was fifteen years older than his bride—when he married Doña Nemesia's eldest daughter, María del Pilar Barrientos, in 1882. Soon thereafter, he became a member of the Guanajuato municipal council and founded his own normal school. Throughout the 1880s, he worked his way up in the educational administration, and he was eventually appointed a school inspector, which let him start a family in security and comfort. In 1886, after losing a number of pregnancies, María gave birth to Diego—and a twin brother, Carlos, who died in infancy. Diego was followed by a sister, María, in 1890.

Marriage did not resolve the significant differences between Don Diego and María's cultures, for he was an educated Freemason and an atheist, and she was a fervent Catholic. She had her way, at first, in little Diego's education—he was taught by priests in Catholic schools—and she had her way as well in deciding where to live. In 1902, when Diego was six years old and her husband was away on an inspecting trip, she packed up the house and fired the servant—without her husband's knowledge—and she moved with the children to Mexico City. Don Diego's investments in silver and his school inspection tours were no longer profiting the family, so she left a note instructing Don Diego to sell the house and join them when he returned. María may have moved to Mexico City because she stood a better chance of finding work there as an obstetrician—a trade she had acquired after Carlos' death—but one biographer speculates that she may have been eluding debt collectors as well. María seems to have felt that she made immense efforts on her son's behalf, for in 1917, when Diego's first son turned one year old, she wrote her grandson a letter in which she referred to the painter as her "dearly beloved but extremely ungrateful son . . . who will never be able to make up to her through filial love for the immense sacrifices and conjugal humiliations which his poor mother suffered in order to save her children from the slightest unpleasantness."

When Rivera reached the age of ten in 1896, Don Diego made his own unilateral decree, and he decided that the boy should be enrolled at the Colegio Militar, to be prepared for a career in the government bureaucracy. When Diego showed no interest in military or government work, his father enrolled him in the San Carlos Academy for art, where Diego fostered his talent in drawing by painstakingly copying the European masters as he acquired technical skills and a trade. Kahlo would write, on the occasion of his 1949 retrospective, that "images and ideas flow through his brain at a different rhythm than usual and thus his intensity of fixation and his desire always to do more are uncontainable"—and while Rivera was indeed a prodigy who learned quickly, there are no records indicating that he was a troublemaker or independent thinker as a student. He was always praised highly by his teachers, though, and in 1906, at age twenty, he was granted a state bursary to study painting in Spain. In his autobiography, Rivera omitted any mention of his obligations to the state, but in Spain he was heavily invested in the art career his father's connections had helped him launch, and in spite of the tall tales to come, he was by all accounts a shy, quiet, serious, and talented young painter—an insecure, overweight prodigy who had not yet expressed his own personality in his work.

Even a few years after he had moved to Paris—after he had been noticed and taken in by Beloff—he had not yet been noticed by the international art community: his patrons were the only ones who saw value in his work. When Rivera returned to Mexico for the hundredth anniversary of Mexico's independence from Spain in 1910, he was feted as a hero by his sponsors in President Díaz' government, and Díaz' wife purchased one of his paintings. Rivera was offered commissions for portraits, buyers for his landscapes, and an administrative sinecure, but in 1911, he declined these comforts for the chance to return—still funded—to Beloff, who saw him as an individual, and to Montparnasse, where painters were living unconventional lives as they experimented with new forms and theories of representation.

Beloff was an expatriate herself—she too defined herself through her painting more than through any family connections—but she was older than Rivera, and she nurtured him while he was led to Cubism. As he began to paint in what he would later describe as an overintellectualized bourgeois form of easel painting, he began to be more and more widely known—for his talent and now for his personality—and in 1913, he began to win some renown. Critic and writer Guillaume Apollinaire announced that Rivera was "by no means negligible," and art dealer Léonce Rosenberg added him to a stable of painters that already included Picasso and other prominent Cubists: now Rivera was painting on demand for a dealer instead of sending his canvases to his patrons in Mexico. Rosenberg recalled that Rivera "was always one of my most prolific painters... [he] did about five major pictures a month for me, not counting sketches, pastels, water colors, etc."—and when his state bursary ceased in 1914, he was respected enough that he could support himself with his sales.

Now that he had gained entrance into the most fashionable circles in the Paris art world—now that he had befriended Picasso, the inventive master of the Modernist renaissance—Rivera used his exotic origins and his self-mythologizing stories to draw people into his studio, and then shock or entertain them. He distanced himself from Mexico and from his family, and he began to speak about his bourgeois parents with a disdain that only became more and more inventive and contemptuous over the course of his life. His letters from Paris record his mother's surprise visits with a mixture of contempt and hilarity, as he and Beloff joke about struggling to come up with boat fare to send her back home. When his mother visited him in Spain in 1915— she thought she might escape from Mexico and her marriage and practice as a midwife in Europe—he arranged for the Spanish government to repatriate her against her will.

Rivera was redefining himself, but he was still living in a conventional marriage with Beloff, so when Beloff became pregnant in 1915, he supplemented his credentials as an artist by starting an affair with Marievna Vorobiev. Beloff moved out with the baby, when it came, but she took Rivera back when his interest in Vorobiev waned, and she did not break with him even though he continued to see the younger woman for a time. But even when he finally stopped seeing Vorobiev, he only began a new affair with Maria Smvelowna-Zetlin, a Russian woman known to collect artists as well as their work. If Rivera began to take lovers with flamboyant recklessness, he asserted his independence in other ways as well, sometimes with a callousness close to cruelty. In 1918, when his son Dieguito was dying of pneumonia in Rivera and Beloff's underheated apartment, he stayed out late at the cafés with friends, leaving Beloff alone with the dying child. When Vorobiev herself gave birth to a daughter, Marika, in 1919, he refused to acknowledge the child, although he would occasionally send her money for the rest of his life.

When Rivera was ultimately condemned for his faithlessness, it was in regard to his art, not his relationships, for after the Great War, Cubism itself underwent an identity crisis, and as Paris polarized into Cubist and anti-Cubist camps, Rivera was accused of using Cubist techniques—which other painters had pioneered—for profit but not for his own artistic growth. There were heated articles, confrontations, and even a fist fight—all of which only increased Rivera's renown—but Rivera ultimately walked away from the controversy. In her memoir Beloff recalls that one day, Rivera saw a stack of ripe peaches that caused him to exclaim, in disgust, "Look at those marvels, and we make such *trivia* and nonsense."

If Rivera was a victim of the critical conversation that was separating Cubism proper from Cubist imitators, now he was back to his old starting point: full of talent, he did not have a style to call his own. But he was fortunate in his timing, for in 1919, Mexico was emerging from civil war, and Álvaro Obregón, the new president, began a crusade to throw off European influences and return to traditional values and customs. The Great War in Europe and the Communist Revolution in Russia seemed to presage the collapse of industrial capitalism and European modernism, and indigenous Mexican arts and culture promised to harness industrial culture without succumbing to the corruptions of European and American capitalism. This Mexicanismo movement was influenced by Gerald Murillo—who had changed his name to Dr. Atl, a painter who had preceded Rivera by ten years in his studies at the San Carlos Academy, and then in Europe. Dr. Atl had returned to Mexico in 1914 to study and then promote the murals of the ancient Mexican Indians, and now that the revolution was over, as the director of the Fine Arts Institute, he advocated mural projects in the new schools and public buildings that were being built around Mexico. At the same time that Rivera was beginning to be criticized as an interloper in European Cubism, he was being courted by Obregón, Atl, and others as a Mexican artistic resource. He had turned his back on Mexico in 1907 and again in 1910, but now the Mexicanismo movement was more than a chance for commissions: it was an opportunity to treat his extensive academic background—as well as his highly professional experience as a Cubist—as mere preparation for the mural paintings he would call his true art.

In 1920, painters, writers, photographers, and intellectuals were flocking to Mexico, where the government was funding the public arts projects that were going to be instrumental in the culture that used modern machinery and workers' collectives to keep workers close to the land and allow them an unprecedented liberty in addition to native integrity and beauty. In this new society, easel paintings were going to be relegated to the history of bourgeois pastimes as art became part of the workers' everyday lives. Many art critics, including Rivera's friend and mentor, Élie Faure, were making revolutionary claims for the future of architecture and architectural arts like murals. When Rivera described his vision of mural painting in his autobiography, he was echoing Faure's prescriptions:

I foresaw a new society in which the bourgeoisie would vanish and their taste, served by the subtleties of cubism, futurism, dadaism, constructivism, surrealism, and the like, would no longer monopolize the functions of art.

The society of the future would be a mass society. And this fact presented wholly new problems. The proletariat had no taste; or, rather, its taste had been nurtured on the worst esthetic food, the very scraps and crumbs which had fallen from the tables of the bourgeoisie.

A new kind of art would therefore be needed, one which appealed not to the viewers' sense of form and color directly, but through exciting subject matter. The new art, also, would not be a museum or gallery art but an art the people would have access to in places they frequented in their daily life—post offices, schools, theatres, railroad stations, public buildings.

As soon as Atl, Faure, and others convinced Rivera that murals were the art of the future, he traveled to Italy to study frescoes from December 1920 to April of 1921, and then he returned to Mexico, where he was put to work for José Vasconcelos, the minister in charge of the mural projects. His first mural was more universal than Mexican in its themes or colors, but during a 1921 trip to the Yucatan Peninsula, he witnessed a celebration of liberated slaves, which gave him both indigenous and Communist themes for his new work, and on a wall at the Preparatoria school, he began to paint a distinctly personal vision of Mexican culture, celebrating Mexicanismo in a palette of colors and forms that were uniquely his own.

Painting murals in Mexico gave Rivera new technical opportunities: curving walls and huge spaces that were vastly more complex than the easel painting at which he had always excelled. It also gave him another new role to play, for as a fresco painter, he required a team of assistants to prepare the wall, mix plaster, grind colors, and apply preparatory layers of plaster through the night, as well as teams of models and visitors who would surround him as he painted all day. The collaborative nature of mural painting allowed Rivera to proclaim that he was doing his work for the masses as a worker among workers, but at the same time, he himself had complete responsibility for and control over the design and execution of the mural. Rivera frequently had it both ways, for as he claimed that the murals belonged to the people, he repeatedly defied both public opinion and his patrons in order to include controversial themes, portraits, and figures.

Now that he was a painter for the Mexican masses, Rivera joined the Mexican Communist Party in 1922, and he began to use the vocabulary of class struggle in describing his purpose as an artist, although he did not submit himself to the political party without yet again asserting his independence. With muralists Fernando Leal, David Alfaro Siqueiros, and Xavier Guerrero, he founded the Syndicate of Technical Workers, Painters, and Sculptors, an independent union within the party. In spite of his stated commitment to camaraderie, though, Rivera frequently took over his projects, painting so efficiently and quickly that he often filled in walls that had been promised to other muralists, and he was even known to banish ambitious assistants to whom he had promised walls of their own. Rivera may have been painting his murals for housepainter's rates, but he supplemented his income with lucrative easel paintings, and he was still a celebrity artist, whose projects were closely followed in the press. The mural projects were not always popular, though, and when Rivera and other muralists' work attracted vandals and protestors, Rivera began to carry a revolver. He claimed that he needed to protect himself against assassination attempts, but his pistol, his cartridge belt, and his wide-brimmed Stetson hat all gave dramatic emphasis to the radical political pronouncements and fabulous stories he delivered from the scaffold.

Ever since he had befriended Picasso in Paris, Rivera had outraged and delighted people with his stories, and now that he was one of Mexico's most prominent muralists, he told ever more far-fetched stories of his adventures to an audience of assistants, models, and spectators. His stories were oftentimes deliberately untrue, and anyone familiar with his actual childhood would have known as much, but he told them nonetheless, casting himself as a heroic sea captain, a Communist revolutionary, a rebel prophet. One of his assistants' wives would later say that "there was something hypnotic about him. Even when you knew he was fantasizing, you listened." Later in life, Kahlo would describe his storytelling for his retrospective. "His alleged lying," she wrote,

is in direct relation to his powerful imagination, that is, he lies as much as poets do, or children who have not yet been idiotized by school or by their mothers. I have heard him tell all kinds of lies: from the most innocent ones, to the most complicated tales of characters that his imagination combines in fantastical situations and behavior, always with a great sense of humor and a marvelous critical sense; but I have never heard him tell a lie that was stupid or banal.

If Rivera revised his early life in his stories, he wrote Angelina Beloff out of his life as soon as he returned to Mexico. In Paris, he had told her that he would go to Mexico in advance, and send for her later, but when he cabled her from Mexico to say that she should come, he neglected to send any money, so she had no way of coming. None of Rivera's surviving letters suggest that he ever had qualms about abandoning Beloff, but she was traumatized. In 1922 she pleaded,

I have become terribly "Mexicanized" . . . it seems to me that I will feel considerably less foreign with you than in any other land whatsoever. The return to my own home is definitely impossible, not because of political events, but because I cannot find myself among my compatriots.

In the same letter, she even offered him his freedom:

> I often think, too, that perhaps the supposed difficulties and com-
> plications of a life à deux frighten you to a greater degree than the
> phantom of a certain imagined responsibility holds you back. I have
> thought of that often, but I believe that in your country, where we
> have never lived together, one might build a life for oneself in which
> more would not be given by one to the other than could be given
> readily. I imagine that with me earning my own living as much as
> possible (and consequently being quite occupied) and with you
> working as you work now, we would meet, with a little good will
> on both sides, on the ground which is common to us, and only on
> that ground.

Beloff remained in Paris for years afterward, and while she would move
to Mexico later in life, there is only one recorded meeting between them,
but not until she was an old woman, when she asked Rivera to sign some
of his paintings that she had acquired.

Having erased his past and made himself at home in Mexico, Rivera
began to get close with one of his models, Guadalupe Marín, whom pho-
tographer Edward Weston described as "tall, proud of bearing, almost
haughty, her walk was like a panther's." Lupe, as she was called, came from
what Rivera's biographer Patrick Marnham called "a family of bourgeois
respectability," but now Rivera painted her both as Woman (nude) and
as Song (in a red robe) in his Creation mural at the Preparatoria. With
a personality closer to Vorobiev's fiery temper than Beloff's forbearing
patience, Marín was intuitive, spontaneous, and willing to slash a canvas
to make a point. Rivera describes her in his autobiography as a

> beautiful, spirited animal, but her jealousy and possessiveness gave
> our life together a wearying, hectic intensity. And I, unfortunately,
> was not a faithful husband. I was always encountering women too
> desirable to resist. The quarrels over these infidelities were carried
> over into quarrels over everything else. Frightful scenes marked
> our life together.
>
> One night, for instance, Lupe served me a dish of fragments of
> some Aztec idols I had just bought. She explained that, since I had
> spent my money on the idols, there was none left to buy the food.

Supporters and critics alike testified to the energy and fertility of imagination with which Rivera matched Marín's intensity. After his first 1922 Creation mural—and then with *The Bathers of Tehuantepec*, which demonstrated the convincing Mexicanismo he would be known for—Rivera was constantly busy with murals. He became Vasconcelos' favorite muralist, and as his work began to be followed closely, he became such a culture-hero in Mexico that when he used fermented cactus juice as a paint binder in his frescoes, he was celebrated for having "rediscovered one of the ancient secrets of the Aztecs." Even in the mid-1920s, when Rivera's murals and the mural project in general had become symbols of Obregón's now-unpopular government—when his walls were defaced and his work was attacked in the press—even when other muralists stopped painting after Vasconcelos was forced out of office in 1924—Rivera ingratiated himself with the incoming ministers and continued to paint at the Ministry of Education in addition to other projects.

Rivera earned a reputation as a tireless worker—putting in long days at the scaffold and then making watercolors and oil canvases at night between political meetings—but he continued to foster his reputation as an "incorrigible philanderer" as well, even though Marín brought him a "hot lunch" at the scaffold in order to discourage other women. This was effective so long as Rivera was painting in Mexico City, but when Marín became pregnant in 1926, he took a commission for a desanctified chapel outside of Mexico City in Chapingo, and there he started an affair with Tina Modotti, who had come to fame as a model of photographer Edward Weston's.

Modotti had remained in Mexico after Weston returned to the States, and she had become a photographer and a local personality. Modotti had become friends with both Rivera and Marín, but more than the double betrayal—by husband and friend—Marín was insulted when Rivera gave Modotti a prominent place in the Chapingo mural. She and Rivera fought and separated, but his affair with Modotti lasted until June of 1927, shortly after Marín gave birth to their second child. When Marín would not return to the marriage, Rivera left Mexico for almost a year, accepting an invitation to Moscow to be an honored guest for the tenth anniversary of the 1917 October Revolution. (He passed through Paris on his way to Russia, but there is no evidence that he saw either Beloff or Vorobiev.)

Rivera had been invited to Russia as a prominent Communist painter, but he could not suppress his artistic independence, and when Stalin clamped down on dissenters—Rivera was still in Russia when Trotsky was exiled in January 1918—he associated himself with a group of dissident artists and wrote a letter that appeared in the opposition review *Revolution and Culture*. While his opinions resulted in his expulsion from Russia, the incident did not diminish his celebrity when he returned to Mexico in June of 1928—rather it attested to his genuineness as a free-thinking artist who was willing to speak up against totalitarianism.

Rivera's marriage to Lupe Marín had ended with his affair with Tina Modotti and then with his departure for Russia, but now that he was back in Mexico, he was free to take lovers whenever he wanted. He would continue to support Marín and their two children—and he would occasionally send Vorobiev money for Marika as well—but at forty-two years old, he was at a transition point in his painting career. After he finished the Preparatoria murals in November of 1928, he took a break from painting—he could afford to, as his easel paintings were being exhibited in Los Angeles and New York—and in the winter of 1928–1929, he worked for José Vasconcelos' presidential campaign. He had been painting and exhibiting and selling paintings for fifteen years, and his reputation—as an artist, as a personality, and as a Communist—was established in Mexico and internationally. He still had to answer the question of how and where he would work, but now he could choose the venues that would give him the best opportunities for artistic expression—in addition to the greatest potential for erotic freedom.

III.

In late 1928, when Rivera returned from Russia and began to campaign for Vasconcelos, one of the beautiful young women he met in the Communist artistic circles and salons was Frida Kahlo, who was twenty-one years old and a painter herself. Kahlo had just spent three years recovering from her crippling bus accident, and she was still recovering as well from the end of her four-year relationship with her lover, Alejandro Gómez Arias. Kahlo had been desolated by the breakup—and she had been utterly broken by the accident and her extensive injuries—but she was compensating both of her losses with new a social life and new political activities. By all reports, she conducted her new life with a vivacity that turned every healthy day into a celebration: a Surrealist art critic would later describe her "theatrical quality, a high eccentricity. She was always very consciously playing a role and her exoticism immediately attracted attention."

Needless to say, this was not typical behavior for a girl from a respectable middle-class family, but Kahlo had left her family's values behind. She never wrote a substantial biographical sketch of her family or her childhood, but we do know that her parents came from very different cultures, the same as Rivera's: her father was a German-Jewish émigré, and her mother was a Mexican Catholic. Kahlo's father had been born in 1872, as Wilhelm Kahlo, to Hungarian-Jewish parents in Germany. He had been forced to quit school in Nuremberg at age eighteen after a head injury left him with epilepsy: when his mother died and his father remarried a woman he did not get along with, he sailed to Mexico in 1891 and changed his name to Guillermo. His parents had run a jewelry shop in Baden-Baden, and in Mexico, he worked in a jewelry shop again. He married and had two daughters, but his wife died, and then he married Frida's mother, Matilde Calderón y González, who was the daughter of a Spanish general and a Mexican Indian photographer. With his wife's father's equipment, Guillermo left the jewelry shop, and with contacts from his wife's mother's family, he received a commission in 1904 to photograph Mexico's architectural heritage in advance of the 1910 anniversary celebrations.

Guillermo and Matilde had four daughters—and one son, who died in infancy before Frida was born in 1907. Frida herself was the third of the surviving children, and then came Cristina, the last, in 1909. Starting in 1904, Guillermo and Matilde had prospered in Casa Azul, the house Guillermo built in Coyoacán outside of Mexico City, but when the Mexican Revolution broke out in 1910, Kahlo lost his lucrative commissions from aristocrats and government officials. Casa Azul was close to some of the fighting, and as a child, Kahlo herself witnessed gunfights outside of the house. But the Kahlo family felt the Revolution most strongly in their declining finances, and Guillermo and Matilde retreated separately—into pessimistic Germanic atheism and Mexican Catholicism, respectively.

Frida's sisters were not sent to school, but when her father encouraged her ambition to become a doctor, it was not because he was fond of her, and wanted her to have a career, so much as because he expected that she would have a difficult time marrying, on account of her withered leg. Frida assumed the role of potential wage-earner—she even dressed in a man's suit for a family portrait—and to protect herself from her disappointments—in polio, in her family's finances, and then in her marriage prospects—she affected the tough, irreverent personality that made her the *novía* of the Cachuchas' leader.

It is not clear from their letters that Kahlo and Arias ever expected to marry—Kahlo merely prostrated herself before him and took refuge from the question in irreverence and adoration. But if Kahlo was already unmarriageable because of her polio, her 1925 bus accident ruined any prospect of a normal life for her, and now her body itself became an obstacle and a hindrance in her relationship with Arias. Her family came to Mexico City to take care of her while she was in the hospital—even her banished sister Mati came when her parents were not there—but when Kahlo went home, she still had to remain immobile for another two months, and she chafed against her immobilization. She began to paint in bed, but painting was not a consolation: within a month, she wrote to Arias, who was still recovering from his own injuries, that she was "beginning to grow accustomed to suffering," and her letters began to repeat the refrain "I have no choice but to endure it."

The accident did not just strain the family's finances—it taxed Kahlo's sense of the family itself. "No one in my house believes that I am really sick," she wrote to Arias, "since I cannot even say so because my mother, who is the only one who grieves a little, gets sick, and they say that it was because of me, that I am very imprudent, so that I and no one but I am the one who suffers." To compound her misery, her parents' house was an hour's bus ride from her free-ranging friends, and their irreverent pranks and revolutionary attitudes were not welcome in the Kahlo household. She had to beg Arias to come see her, and she complained in many of her letters of having been effectively abandoned. Full of anxiety about her condition, about doctors' bills and her family's finances—and also about her parents' health—Kahlo developed an acute sensitivity to her body and all of her pains. She did not trust her doctors, since nothing they did removed her pains, but her body healed on its own, and after three months of recuperation, Kahlo was able to go to Mexico City and start working part-time jobs that would help pay off medical bills. Her relationship with Arias seemed to weather the crisis when he found out about her affair with Fernández, but their reconciliation was not strong enough to survive when Kahlo's injuries confined her to her parents' house again, as she had to be bound up in what became a series of plaster corsets. With Arias' departure for Europe in early 1927, the relationship was over.

By the end of 1927, Kahlo had spent two years encased in one plaster or steel corset after another, and she reached a crisis: her letters began to express the desire to die if she did not start to get better. Finally she healed enough to believe that she might outlast her pains, and chose invalidism and a life of constant suffering over death. She was compensated with a new vision that depressed her but also made her newly sensitive to the world. In September of 1927, she wrote to Arias in Europe,

Why do you study so much? What secrets are you looking for? Life will reveal it to you all of a sudden. I already know everything, without reading or writing. A little while ago, almost a few days ago, I was a little girl who walked through a world of colors, of hard and tangible forms. Everything was mysterious and concealed something; I took pleasure in deciphering, in learning, as in a game. If only you knew how terrible it is suddenly to know everything, as if a flash of lightning lit up the earth. Now I live on a dolorous planet, transparent like ice; but which conceals nothing, it's as if I had learned everything in one second, all at once. My girlfriends, my companions have slowly become women, I grew up in a few instants and today everything is pliant and lucid. I know there is nothing behind, if there were I would see it.

Exasperated with doctors whose expensive treatments never gave her relief, desolated by her abandonment and by her broken body, Kahlo learned to trust herself first. Her leg and back told her what she could and could not do, and with the help of painkillers and alcohol, she could get around most of the time. When she felt like asserting her independence, she would occasionally do more than her body allowed—even if she had to suffer further confinements as a consequence.

Kahlo did not console herself solely with drinking and outrageous behavior, though. She had begun to pass her time in bed painting portraits of herself and her family, and as she later explained in a letter,

From that time [of the accident] my obsession was to begin again, painting things just as I saw them with my own eyes and nothing more . . . Thus, as the accident changed my path, many things prevented me from fulfilling the desires which everyone considers normal, and to me nothing seemed more normal than to paint what had not been fulfilled.

She painted herself more than anyone else—"because I am so often alone, because I am the subject I know best," she said—but her paintings also reflect a newly awakened sensitivity to art, which she had never studied formally, her apprenticeship with the engraver notwithstanding. Her self-portraits reveal the influence of Botticelli—whose Venus floats in her own smoothed, unreal perfection, on legs that are not positioned to support her—as well as of Modigliani, whose elongated figures are also free of physical existence. She drew from the apocalyptic work of William Blake and Hieronymus Bosch, and locally from *retablos*, the small tin plate paintings Mexican Catholics would commission to express gratitude for a divine favor. Combining this popular art form with the more bourgeois and personal self-portrait, Kahlo's paintings depicted the self who endured her sufferings at the same time that they ritualistically prayed for and even tried to prophesy her survival of agonies nothing had yet saved her from.

Having painted throughout her confinement, Kahlo made new friends in Arias' absence. She became close with Germán de Campo, who was a friend of Tina Modotti's lover, Julio Antonio Mella, and now that she could finally get around, she began to spend time in Modotti's salon. Throughout 1928, Kahlo worked with Modotti, de Campo, and Mella to campaign for José Vasconcelos, and she agitated as well—in protests and demonstrations—for university autonomy from the government, a cause they would win in 1929, after Vasconcelos was defeated by the dictator Calles' puppet, Pascual Ortiz Rubio.

But in spite of her new political activities, Kahlo still needed to answer the question of her vocation. She was not in school any longer—so she had abandoned her plan of becoming a doctor—but she had been painting for more than two years now, and since there was still funding for the arts, she called Diego Rivera—the most famous muralist in the country—down from his scaffold to ask him for his opinion about her work and about her prospects.

IV.

The story of Rivera and Kahlo's first meeting is surrounded in mystery, for Rivera and Kahlo told the story a number of times in a number of different versions—and they were both renowned for shaping their stories to their listeners' expectations and desires. But it is generally accepted that they met for the first time in Tina Modotti's salon in 1928. Kahlo recalled later that it was only after Rivera had made the dramatic gesture of shooting a phonograph during an argument that he had caught her attention, but Rivera nevertheless depicted Kahlo as a comrade distributing arms in a mural of Mexican political history. She was not a muse for him, though, and he painted her fully clothed, in the Communist uniform of red shirt with red star, and black slacks. When Kahlo modeled for his mural, Rivera was reputed to have told her that she had a dog's face, but she fired back that he had a frog's face, and she would call him by the nickname toad-frog—*sapo-rana* in Spanish—throughout their relationship. When Kahlo asked Rivera in 1929 for an appraisal of her work—and for advice about making a living with it—Rivera came to her house to give her his opinion. They kissed soon afterward, and then they married, so any value she saw in her work as artwork was intertwined with the value she gained as an object of his desire, and Kahlo would never afterward describe her paintings as more than a hobby.

Kahlo's parents were less than happy with the match, for Rivera was twenty-one years older than Kahlo, who was only twenty-two herself. Guillermo Kahlo made sure that Rivera knew that Frida was "*un demonio oculto*" and an invalid, but while he allowed the marriage, he was reputed to have walked out of the civil service after asking, "Gentlemen, is it not true that we are play-acting?" The wedding reception itself was carnivalesque—Lupe Marín reportedly insulted Kahlo, Rivera got drunk and broke a man's finger when he drew and fired his pistol, and Kahlo left in tears—but shortly after the wedding, Rivera paid off the mortgage on Casa Azul and Marín befriended Kahlo. She arranged for her brother to act as Kahlo's doctor, she taught Kahlo how to cook Rivera's favorite meals, she sympathized with her over his stubborn or childish behavior, and she helped her endure his affairs.

Having courted Rivera with her paintings, Kahlo ceased to paint in the months after their marriage, as she adjusted to Rivera's demanding schedule of work and meetings. She cooked for him and managed his correspondence with patrons and friends, and almost immediately after their marriage, she helped him through a major crisis. Having identified himself with the dissidents and Trotskyites in the Communist Party, Rivera ran into opposition from Mexican Stalinists, who were trying to consolidate their control over other factions. With his free ideas and unpredictable behavior, Rivera had become a liability to the party, and while his expulsion from Russia had bolstered his artistic reputation, when he was expelled from the Mexican Communist Party in 1929, he suffered a personal crisis. He lost his position in Mexican—and international—society, and he lost the overarching context of class struggle that had given his work the sense of purpose that hid his consistent womanizing and bohemian peculiarities. "I did not have a home," he wrote later, "the Party having always been my home." Kahlo was still in good standing with the party, but she quit as well, in solidarity, making her home with her family—with whom she was still close—and with Rivera.

If Rivera no longer had a home, he nonetheless still had murals to paint, and a month after he was expelled from the Mexican Communist Party, he received a commission from the U.S. ambassador to Mexico to paint in Cuernavaca. Instead of a class struggle between proletariat and bourgeoisie, though, Rivera now painted the dispossession of the indigenous Mexicans by Europeans, and his Cuernavaca mural turned the Palace of Cortés—which Cortés himself had erected in triumph over the defeat of the Mexican Indians—into a graphic demonstration of the cruelty and brute power of the Spanish forces. Rivera ran a certain risk by painting this portrait—he was effectively defacing the victory monument, and rewriting history—but his patrons did not intercede, and his reputation as a daring and outspoken artist of Mexicanismo was preserved in the absence of his communism.

Kahlo lived in Cuernavaca with Rivera while he painted, and she followed Rivera's new Mexicanismo with an adaptation of her own, for now instead of the strict Communist uniform of pants and a worker's shirt, she donned traditional Tehuana garb, which Rivera idealized. "The Mexican women who do not wear it," Rivera wrote later, "do not belong to the people, but are mentally and emotionally dependent on a foreign class to which they wish to belong, i.e., the great American and French bureaucracy." Kahlo's Tehuana costume hid her bad leg—she would write later that "I must have full skirts and long, now that my sick leg is so ugly"—but it also did for her what Rivera's return from Europe did for him: it let her escape her origins in the bourgeoisie and associate herself instead with *las indígenas* whose identity was culturally genuine and physically robust, for the region of Tehuantepec was reputedly run by strong women.

In addition to wearing traditional dress, Kahlo learned to be outspokenly, theatrically Mexican in order to out-flirt potential rivals, and she sang bawdily and drew attention to herself, winning Rivera to her as often as she could. In spite of all her efforts, though, Rivera refused to give up his affairs. From Cuernavaca, he still commuted back to Mexico City, where he maintained relationships with his American assistant

Ione Robinson and his model Dolores Olmedo—who was actually from Tehuantepec. Rivera began further affairs after he completed the Cuernavaca mural and left Mexico at the end of 1930. When he traveled to San Francisco to paint two frescoes in the Pacific Stock Exchange, he began an affair with his model there as well, the tennis champion Helen Wills Moody.

Kahlo affected to tolerate Rivera's affairs, and Rivera's assistant Bertram Wolfe paraphrases her, in his biography of Rivera, as saying that because of "his great gifts, great indulgence was in order." But if she claimed that she "couldn't care less," she was often hurt, and she had what Lupe Marín described as "desperate nights" when Diego did not come home. She began to conduct affairs of her own, though, and when she traveled to San Francisco with Rivera, she began an affair with Cristina Cassati, the Italian wife of one of his assistants, John Hastings, and she also began a secret affair with Nickolas Muray, a Hungarian photographer whom she would see again in the late 1930s. But as Rivera spent time with other women, Kahlo also returned to her painting, and she devoted herself to new portraits—of herself and Rivera, of Luther Burbank, and of her doctor, surgeon Leo Eloesser.

Primarily Kahlo devoted herself to being Rivera's wife, and her theatrically Mexican dress and behavior, combined with Rivera's contradictory political sentiments—his willingness to paint the indigenous history for the conquerors—turned the husband-and-wife painters into an attractive package for American patrons. After the Cuernavaca mural and the Pacific Stock Exchange mural, Rivera accepted a lucrative commission for a retrospective at the Museum of Modern Art in New York in 1931. Painting murals in New York—in the very heart of capitalism—Rivera was criticized by the Marxists as a sellout, and American capitalists saw him as a Communist, but the catalogue for the MoMA opening downplayed his politics, saying that "Diego's very spinal column is painting, not politics." Rivera said that he and Kahlo were "feted at parties, dinners, receptions" and in spite of his politics, the vernissage at MoMA was attended by the wealthiest of New York financier patrons, including the Goodyears, Rockefellers, and Blisses, in addition to celebrities Edward G. Robinson, Greta Garbo, Hedy Lamarr, Paul Robeson, and Georgia O'Keeffe.*

After the retrospective at MoMA, Rivera and Kahlo moved to Detroit

---

*Kahlo later said that she and O'Keeffe had been intimate at around this time, but except for Frida's one statement, there is no evidence of an encounter.

in April of 1932, where Rivera received more than $20,000* to paint murals at the Detroit Institute of Arts. In the depths of the Depression, Rivera's reputation was so desirable to patrons that even in spite of his losses in the 1929 financial collapse, Henry Ford's son, Edsel Ford, provided many of the costs himself. Rivera repaid him with an optimistic mural that portrayed the ingenuity and the potential for harmony in machine culture. Rivera still insisted on a Communist perspective—after touring the Ford factories, he wrote that "Henry Ford made the work of the socialist state possible"—but he was an international artist, now, and his work was not explicitly political, so much as it portrayed an optimistic vision of industry's possible benefits.

Now that Rivera was taking lucrative commissions, Kahlo could afford to consult with armies of doctors, who offered a range of surgical solutions for the pains in her foot and back. Many of their treatments required further surgeries—but many of these only further complicated her injuries, and Kahlo was disheartened when her injuries did not respond to treatment and her pains continued. In the technological culture of American industry—which her husband was celebrating—pains like hers were meant to be cured by innovative treatments and machines. The fact that she continued to suffer only made her homesick for Mexico, where her suffering did not undermine a culture of progress.

While Rivera was painting or meeting with patrons or lovers, Kahlo was often left alone and without a purpose. She did not need to support herself, but her idleness magnified her pains and disappointments. At first, she was isolated by her lack of English, although in only a few years, she was writing to patrons and friends in serviceable English prose. But in her solitude, she began to turn her homesickness into paintings like *My Dress Hangs There*—in which she painted her exotic Tehuana dress without herself in it—and *Self-Portrait on the Border between Mexico and the United States*. These paintings surpassed the self-portraits she had done from her sickbed, for now she used symbolic imagery—very much the way Rivera did in his murals—to depict her entire cultural situation, not just her own appearance and feelings.

While Rivera was painting his homage to machine culture in the Detroit Institute of Arts murals, Kahlo made her first serious attempt at an organic production of her own. Having aborted once shortly after their marriage, in 1930, she was pregnant again when she arrived in

---

* Roughly $300,000 in 2011 dollars.

Detroit in April of 1932. She was twenty-five years old, now, and she was determined to have a child—even though she conceded in a letter to a friend that "I don't think Diego is very interested in having a child, since what preoccupies him most is his work and he's perfectly right about that. Kids would come in third or fourth place." Kahlo had been told that childbirth could kill her, but now her doctors told her that she might deliver by cesarean section. Her doctors could only make this promise if she would abstain from alcohol and take bed rest, though, and when she did neither of these things, she was virtually courting the miscarriage that came in July: Rivera came home from painting and found her in a pool of blood.

"I was so excited about having a little Dieguito that I cried a lot," she wrote in a letter, "but now that it's over there's nothing to do but grin and bear it . . . After all, there are thousands of things that remain forever cloaked in the most complete mystery." To compensate her loss and to penetrate that mystery, she obtained a graphic medical book and painted *Henry Ford Hospital*, which depicted her in bed, with a number of umbilical ties—to a fetus, a medical model, a snail, a pelvic bone, and a machine. She also painted *My Birth*, which depicted her own adult head emerging from between her mother's legs. Rivera celebrated Kahlo's courage, and to promote her paintings, he announced that "never before had a woman put such agonized poetry on canvas as Frida did at this time in Detroit."

V.

Shortly after her miscarriage in 1932, Kahlo was called back to Mexico— her mother was ill, and she arrived just a few days before her mother died. Left on his own in Detroit—working relentlessly to finish the murals in time to begin another commission in New York—and another after that in Chicago—Rivera took a drastic diet of citrus fruits and lost a hundred of his three hundred pounds, although this only launched a period of kidney and glandular problems that would plague him until 1936, when his doctors would ultimately prescribe that he should be "reinflated and not disinflated again under any circumstances."

In March of 1933, after her mother's funeral, Kahlo rejoined Rivera in Detroit, and they traveled to New York, where the Rockefellers had asked him to paint a mural in one of the nineteen skyscrapers they were building in Midtown Manhattan. Rivera had found a sensitive and politically tolerant listener in Abby Rockefeller, John D. Rockefeller's wife, but he may have felt some pressure to make a political statement, as fellow Mexican muralist David Siqueiros had just been banished from Los Angeles at the end of 1932 for attacking U.S. imperialism. Perhaps, after his celebration of the industrial process in Detroit, he may have felt that he needed to assert his Communist credentials in the heart of capitalism, but regardless of his motives, when the developers saw his portrait of Lenin—in a mural that adorned the entryway to a building full of corporate capitalist clients—they claimed that he had broken the contract and dismissed him and his assistants from the scaffold. When controversy had swirled around the Detroit murals, Edsel Ford himself had defended Rivera, and a delegation of workers had even stood watch to defend against vandals, but in New York, Rivera did not have any protectors, and his half-hearted offer to balance the head of Lenin with a bust of Lincoln was rejected. He himself was not in a position to compromise, for his assistants were all committed Communists, and they threatened to strike if he altered the portrait of Lenin. The mural was abandoned—it was eventually destroyed in early 1934—and with the destruction of the mural, Rivera lost his reputation as a fashionably outrageous muralist. More importantly, at age forty-six, at the height of his career, he lost his ability to command large fees for his controversial works, as his commission to paint at the World's Fair in Chicago was canceled as a result of the controversy.

Kahlo took Rivera's side in the RCA building debacle, but she was becoming miserable in New York, and she pressed him to return to Mexico. Rivera had felt that New York's modern industry was going to give him essential imagery for prophesying a new world order, but even though he had brought his fate upon himself by adding Lenin to the mural at the RCA building, when he agreed to return to Mexico, his assistant Lucienne Bloch said that "he feels he must go back there for Frieda's sake, because she is so sick of New York." Rivera and Kahlo left New York for good in December of 1933, and returned, practically broke, to Mexico—where, Kahlo wrote, "the people . . . always respond with obscenities and dirty tricks . . . [Rivera] has only to arrive and they start attacking him in the newspapers."

Rivera was miserable about returning home. His health was still bad as a result of his extreme weight loss, and he was not painting while he recovered, but he was not happy about having to submit to being taken care of by Kahlo. He already blamed his frustrations on her, but now he rebelled against her care by starting an affair with her younger sister, Cristina. Cristina was Frida's closest sister—she had nursed her after her accident—but ever since Cristina had been abandoned by her husband in 1930, she had been taking care of her children by herself at Casa Azul, and now Rivera found her receptive to his advances. If Kahlo had abided Rivera's affairs in the past, now she, like Beloff and Marín, was twice betrayed, and after Rivera set Cristina up in an apartment—and then bought her a house in Coyoacán—Frida and Rivera separated at the end of 1934. Rivera and Kahlo had just built a house together—begun in 1931, the San Angel house was actually two houses, connected by a bridge— but Frida found an apartment in Mexico City center for herself and one of her spider monkeys. In the aftermath of the RCA mural, Kahlo had not painted at all in 1934—she had suffered her own crises in the shape of another abortion and two further hospitalizations—but in 1935, she turned her own emotions into paintings that marked a new direction for her work: a *Self Portrait* in which she appears in Western dress and uncharacteristically short, curly hair, and *A Few Small Nips*—which illustrated a scene she gleaned from the newspapers, in which a man who had stabbed his lover twenty times claimed that he only gave her a few small nips.

Separated from Rivera, Kahlo was just as homeless as Beloff had been when Rivera returned to Mexico in 1921. She wrote in English to Bertram and Ella Wolfe (Rivera's assistant and his wife),

Here in Mexico I have no one, I had only Diego, and the members of my family, who treat the matter in a Catholic way, and I am so far from the conclusions they draw that I can count on nothing from them. My father is a magnificent person, but he reads Schopenhauer day and night and doesn't help me in the least . . .

In the end any attempt on my part is ridiculous and idiotic. He wants his complete freedom. A freedom he always had and would have had now if he had acted sincerely and honestly with me; but what makes me saddest is that now not even the part of being friends that there used to be between us exists anymore. He's always telling me lies and he conceals every detail of his life from me as if I were his worst enemy . . .

But now I see I have no more than any girl disappointed in love whose man has left her; I'm worthless, I don't know how to do anything, I'm not sufficient unto myself; my situation seems to me so ridiculous and so idiotic that you cannot imagine how I dislike and hate myself. I've wasted the best time living at the expense of a man without doing anything but what I believed would help him and be useful to him. I never thought of myself, and after six years his response is that fidelity is a bourgeois virtue and only exists to exploit and gain economic advantage.

Rivera's fortunes did not improve during his separation from Frida. After the RCA mural had been destroyed in February 1934, he had re-created it in the Palacio de Bellas Artes in Mexico City, but the effect was hardly the same outside of the capitalist context of Manhattan. He ceased to paint public murals in Mexico for some time, and even the private mural he painted next—the outlandish and acerbic *Burlesque of Mexican Folklore and Politics* at the Hotel Reforma—was not displayed because it was judged too critical of Mexican politicians and American tourists alike.

In July of 1835, Kahlo traveled to New York with two women friends, and now she offered Rivera the same freedom Beloff had offered from Paris thirteen years earlier:

Why must I be so stubborn and dense as not to understand that the letters, the skirt-chasing, the "English" professors, the gypsy models, the "good will" assistants, the disciples interested in the "art of painting", and the "plenipotentiary envoys from distant parts", only signify amusements and that at bottom you and I love each other very much, and even if we go through countless affairs, splintered doors, insults and international acclaims, we shall always love each other, I think what it is, is that I'm a little stupid and just a bit of a dissembler, because all these things have happened and happened again for the seven years we've lived together and all of the rages I've gone into have only led me to understand better that I love you more than my own skin, and though you don't love me the same way, in any case you love me somewhat, no? Or if that's not true, I'll always have the hope that it may be, and that's good enough for me.
Love me just a little. I adore you.
Frieda

VI.

When Kahlo came back to Mexico later in 1935, she was resigned to Rivera's affair with Cristina, and she did not have any expectation that his other affairs would end. But even though Rivera concluded his relationship with Cristina at the end of the year, the betrayal and the separation had changed the nature of their marriage, and now Kahlo began to conduct affairs of her own, with more independence. By one biographer's count, she had at least eleven lovers between 1935 and 1940, although many of these were not well documented. In a letter to Lucienne Bloch—Rivera's apprentice and her confidant—she reported,

> I've painted, which is something after all, since I've spent my life until now loving Diego and deluding myself about work, but now I keep loving Diego and, also, I've started seriously to paint my little figures. Worries of a sentimental and romantic nature . . . there have been some, but they haven't been more than amusements.

In addition to giving her access to a wider range of affections, Kahlo's affairs won her a certain respect from Rivera, for now she was proving that she was hard-hearted enough to take her own lovers. Sculptor Isamu Noguchi later described his relationship with Kahlo by saying that he

> loved her very much . . . [Frida] was a lovely person, absolutely marvelous person. Since Diego was well known to be a lady chaser, she cannot be blamed if she saw some men . . . In those days we all . . . horsed around, and Diego did and so did Frida. It wasn't quite acceptable to him, however . . . I knew Frida well during an eight-month period. We went dancing all the time. Frida loved to dance. That was her passion, you know, everything that she couldn't do she loved to do. It made her absolutely furious to be unable to do things.

Rivera generally laughed about Kahlo's encounters with women, but her affairs with men threatened him. She had to conceal her affair with fellow (rival) Mexican muralist Ignacio Aguirre, but when Rivera found out about Noguchi, he warned the sculptor away with his pistol.

After his affair with Cristina Kahlo ended, 1936 was a year of poor health for Rivera—partly because of the lingering effects of the drastic diet he had started in Detroit, partly because of his depression. He spent time in the hospital with kidney problems—and then for operations on his eyes—but he returned to politics by joining the Trotsky-affiliated International Communist League. After what he had seen of Stalin's repressive techniques in Russia, he turned his loyalty to Leon Trotsky, who opposed the consolidation of power in the Russian bureaucracy. Trotsky himself had been staying in France and then Oslo after his 1928 exile from Russia, and when he was threatened with yet another deportation in 1937, Rivera arranged for the Mexican government to let him stay at Kahlo's parents' house. Trotsky arrived in December of 1936, and after he was safely installed in Casa Azul, he returned Rivera's admiration. He told Rivera that his murals described "the hidden springs of the social revolution," and he wrote that a Rivera mural was "not simply a 'painting,' an object of passive aesthetic contemplation, but a living part of the class struggle."

Trotsky was attracted to Kahlo's sister Cristina when he first arrived in Coyoacán, but when he had difficulty eluding his guards, he found it easier to begin an affair with Kahlo herself, slipping notes into books he shared with her. Kahlo was twenty-nine years old to Trotsky's fifty-seven; she painted his portrait and then, when she used Cristina's house for rendezvous, she turned her sister into a confidant, reclaiming her from her role as Rivera's mistress. The affair with Trotsky did not last long, though. When word started to get out, his advisers warned him that a scandal might damage his political situation at a time when he was trying to clear himself of Stalin's charges. Trotsky's wife had also learned about the affair and was getting depressed, so Kahlo broke off with the older man, although soon she began an affair with his secretary, Jean van Heijenoort.

Rivera did not know about Kahlo's affair with Trotsky right away, but starting in 1937, as she painted prolifically—both for self-expression and in the hope of independence—he helped her turn her paintings into a means of financial support. With his help, she exhibited paintings in a group show in Mexico City in April of 1938, and when New York gallery owner Julien Levy saw them there, he invited Kahlo to exhibit at his gallery in New York. That summer, she made the first major sale of her work, to a collector, for good money, and when André Breton—the leader of the French Surrealists—saw her work, he offered her a show in Paris as well.

Kahlo's trip to New York was a professional success—she showed her work to some acclaim at Julien Levy's gallery in New York in 1938, and the Museum of Modern Art commissioned a painting for their collection—and from there she sailed to Paris in January of 1939. Breton had seen a Mexican Surrealism in paintings like *Henry Ford Hospital, Memory,* and *My Dress Hangs There,* and while Kahlo accepted the show, she rejected the Surrealist title. "They thought I was a surrealist," she said, "but I wasn't. I never painted dreams. I painted my own reality." Whereas French Surrealism distorts and juxtaposes images in order to emphasize the incomprehensible nature of everyday life, Kahlo's paintings are surreal only insofar as she had had to invent a visual vocabulary to represent the reality of her experience: she created a language in which her face on the body of a deer pierced with arrows would be an emotional reality, not just a disturbing dream-image. Surreal or not, Kahlo's shows in New York and Paris were critical successes—and the crowd in Paris, she wrote, "is very fond of me and all of them are exceedingly kind." She had to cancel her next show, in London, though, because the prospect of war was taking the steam out of the art market, and also because she came down with the flu.

Now that Kahlo was exhibiting and selling paintings on the international scene, she had evidence that she was independent of Rivera, and she used her new freedom to conduct a number of affairs—with Breton's wife Jacqueline in Mexico in 1938 and then again in Paris; with Julien Levy in New York, and also with a refugee from the Spanish Civil War—but these were all passing encounters. In New York on her way back to Mexico, though, she renewed her contact with Hungarian photographer, Olympic fencer, pilot, and patron of the arts Nickolas Muray, whom she had met in San Francisco in 1931.

Now that they found each other again, their relationship turned deeply affectionate. "Like you I've been starved for true affection," Kahlo wrote to him, and again, "I have no words to tell you what a joy [your letter] gave me. I adore you my love, believe me, like I never loved anyone—only Diego will be in my heart as close as you—always." Kahlo was not going to leave Rivera, but while she was in Paris, she imposed some restrictions on Muray: "you can only kiss as much as you want Mam. Don't make love with anybody, if you can help it. Only if you find a real F. W. [fucking wonder] but *don't love her.*" They spent some months together in New York before she went to Paris, and they saw each other in Pennsylvania on her return, but then the affair broke down, ostensibly under the pressure of her marriage to Rivera. After Kahlo left for Mexico, Muray wrote that "of the three of us there was only two of you," and he thanked her for the happiness "the half of you so generously gave me," but he said could not continue.

At the same time that Muray was relinquishing Kahlo to Rivera, though, Rivera was already planning a divorce. He had learned of Kahlo's affair with Trotsky while she was in Paris, and he had immediately invented a quarrel and split with Trotsky and the ICL. Once more, Rivera lost, as Trotsky had warned Kahlo he would, "a milieu of understanding and sympathy not only as an artist but as a revolutionary and as a person."

Kahlo did not come home in a conciliatory mood, either. She had left Muray's understanding arms, and she had only found out after her arrival in Mexico about Muray's April 1939 marriage. Under these circumstances, she was only in a position to need more from Rivera, not less, and their marriage came apart under the strain. While Rivera seems to have grown exasperated with Kahlo's interminable needs, in his autobiography, he frames the questions beneath their divorce solely in terms of his own freedom:

> We had been married now for thirteen years. We still loved each other. I simply wanted to be free to carry on with any woman who caught my fancy. Yet Frida did not object to my infidelity as such. What she could not understand was my choosing women who were either unworthy of me or inferior to her. She took it as a personal humiliation to be abandoned for sluts. To let her draw the line, however, was this not to circumscribe my freedom? Or was I simply the depraved victim of my own appetites? And wasn't it merely a consoling lie to think that a divorce would put an end to Frida's suffering? Wouldn't Frida suffer even more?

VII.

Rivera and Kahlo divorced in 1940, in a flurry of contradictory justifications. Rivera claimed in one interview that "there is no change in the magnificent relations between us. We are doing it in order to improve Frida's legal position . . . purely a matter of legal convenience in the spirit of modern times." On another occasion, he claimed that "I am already old and no longer have much to offer her." For her part, Kahlo said that they had divorced because "he likes to be alone and he says I always want to have his papers and other things in order and he likes them in disorder." Rivera wrote in his autobiography, perhaps most tellingly, that he "dreaded a long, heart-wrenching discussion so much that I impulsively . . . fabricated a stupid and vulgar pretext" to stop seeing each other, and Kahlo was so hurt by the story he invented that she agreed to the divorce.

Divorce, however, was as vague a term as marriage as had been, for the relationship did not change much, as they continued to spend their time together in the two bridged houses at San Angel. Rivera lived in other apartments as well, and he continued to have affairs, but he also continued to need Kahlo's companionship: she alone, of all of his women, warranted enough respect that he would take her advice about politics and painting.

Now that Kahlo had proven that she could conduct affairs of her own, Rivera even helped her make conquests. Whereas he had previously entertained Kahlo with stories of his own affairs, now he brought her lovers, to assure their mutual independence and also to distract her from her dependence on him.* One of his assistants, Heinz Berggruen, later wrote that Rivera

> took me to the hospital and I will never forget the way he looked at me when, just before we went into Frida's room, he said, "You are going to be very much taken by Frida." He said it in a pointed way. Diego was extremely perceptive and intuitive; he knew what would happen. Perhaps he even wanted it to happen. There was something diabolical in him. He led me on. He took me by the hand.

Kahlo took Berggruen for a lover, briefly, and as she became more self-sufficient—she wrote to Muray that since the divorce, "I don't accept a damn cent from Diego"—Rivera found it easier to speak of her as a beloved. Divorced though they were—involved as she was with the assistant he had introduced her to—he wrote to one of her doctors "that her life is of more value to me, much more than my own. She crystallizes in herself, in one human being, possessing artistic genius, everything that

---

* One of Kahlo's biographers, Hayden Herrera, writes that he was trying to distract her from her dependence on alcohol as well, for as Kahlo had continued to suffer with her back and foot, Herrera records that "by the end of 1939 . . . she was drinking a full bottle of brandy each day."

there is in the world, that interests me, that I love, and that gives any sense to me of why I live and struggle."

Rivera did not stay in Mexico for long, though, to take care of Kahlo. When fellow muralist Siqueiros made an attempt on Trotsky's life in 1940, Rivera fled from Mexico. He arranged a visa to paint in America, and with model and actress Paulette Goddard, he left Mexico to paint a mural at the Golden Gate International Exposition in San Francisco. Goddard became Rivera's lover during the project, and the mural portrays her looking at him longingly while he sits with his back to Kahlo, while on one side Goddard's husband, Charlie Chaplin, plays an absurd Hitler from his film *The Great Dictator*.

Through sales of her paintings, Kahlo was able to support herself in Mexico while Rivera was painting in San Francisco. Unlike Rivera, who courted commissions through a public process of proposals and bids that were assessed and accepted by committees, Kahlo had always treated her patrons as friends who were doing her a personal favor by asking for a painting. But after 1937, when Rivera had begun to publicize her work—and after the Surrealist exhibition in Mexico City, and shows in New York and Paris—Kahlo's work had finally begun to sell on its own. She was still spending a good deal of time in hospitals and then in bed, though, recuperating from operations, and she was never able to paint as prolifically as Rivera, so he himself would occasionally purchase her paintings, in order to provide her with money, although she was both outraged and deflated when she learned this:

> When I found out that you had in your possession the first self-portrait I painted this year . . . I realized many things . . . I've continued living off you, creating illusions for myself of other things. The conclusion I've drawn is that all I've done is fail. When I was a little girl I wanted to be a doctor and a bus squashed me. I live with you for ten years without doing anything in short but causing you problems and annoying you, I began to paint and my painting is useless but for me and for you to buy it, knowing that no one else will. Now that I would have given my life to help you, it turns out other women are the real "saviors". Maybe I'm thinking all this now that I find myself fucked up and alone, and above all worn out from interior exhaustion. I don't believe any sun, anything I'm supposed to swallow or any medicine will cure me; but I'll wait longer to see what this mood depends on; the bad thing is that I think I already

know and there's no remedy. New York no longer interests me, and all the less now with the Irenes, etc., there. I don't have the slightest desire to work with the ambition I would like to have. I'll continue painting only so that you'll see my things. I don't want exhibitions or anything. I'll pay what I owe with my painting, and even if I have to eat shit, I'll do exactly what I feel like doing when I feel like doing it. The only thing left to me is to have your things close to me, and the hope of seeing you again is enough to keep living . . .

I beg you not to leave this letter lying around because all my other ones were put with many others accompanied by notes from Irene and other whores.

Rivera and Kahlo nevertheless continued to depend on one another, and the divorce lasted only slightly more than a year. Trotsky was assassinated in 1940, and after she was roughly questioned about the murder, Kahlo came to San Francisco for surgery. When she rejoined Rivera at his mural for the Golden Gate International Exposition, Rivera himself had begun to petition Kahlo for remarriage, even in spite of his ongoing involvements with Paulette Goddard and model Irene Bohus. Kahlo wrote that he "wants me to [remarry] because he says he loves me more than any other girl." Rivera recruited Kahlo's surgeon to help give a medical basis to the reunion, and Dr. Eloesser wrote to Kahlo on his behalf:

Diego loves you very much, and you love him. It is also the case, and you know it better than I, that besides you, he has two great loves—1) painting 2) Women in general. He has never been, nor ever will be, monogamous, something that is imbecilic and anti-biological.

Reflect, Frida, on this basis. What do you want to do?

If you think that you could accept the facts the way they are, could live with him under these conditions, and in order to live more or less peacefully could submerge your natural jealousy in a fervor of work, painting, working as a school teacher, whatever it might be . . . and absorb yourself until you go to bed each night exhausted by work [then marry him].

One or the other. Reflect, dear Frida, and decide.

Kahlo accepted these terms, and on December 8, 1940—Rivera's fifty-fourth birthday, Kahlo was thirty-three—they remarried. Her health was their ostensible reason, regardless of the fact that Rivera's exasperation with her perpetually bad health was one of the factors that led to their divorce.

It was not long before they resumed their old relations, with her managing his correspondence and cooking for him, and listening to the stories of his affairs as if they were only spicy gossip. On its face, Rivera and Kahlo's second marriage expressly forbade any expectation of sexual fidelity—and any inquiries about affairs—although Kahlo's journals suggest that they continued to sleep together nonetheless. Rivera's biographer Patrick Marnham writes that in spite of their remarriage, in the 1940s, Rivera slept with "the film actresses Dolores Del Rio and Paulette Goddard . . . Linda Christian and the film actress María Félix, whom he painted and seduced in 1948"—although Marnham also notes that "María Félix, Dolores Del Rio and Pita Amor became the lovers of both Rivera and Frida."

In July of 1941, Kahlo described the marriage to Dr. Eloesser: "the re-marriage is working well. Few quarrels, greater mutual understanding, and on my part, less bothersome inquiring into the question of other women who suddenly occupy a preponderant place in his heart." And in 1944 she wrote to Bert and Ella Wolfe that the marriage was "better than ever because there is mutual understanding between the spouses, without impairment of the just freedom in such cases for each one of the consorts: total elimination of jealousy, violent arguments and misunderstandings. Great quantity of *dialectic* based on past experiences."

VIII.

If there was greater dialectic, it was partly because starting in the 1940s, Kahlo's injuries and her hard living were starting to catch up with her. Her surgeries had never really corrected her injuries—her body had always been slow to heal, but she had never had the patience to convalesce completely, either—and now she was laid up even more frequently. She had begun to teach painting classes in 1942, when she and Rivera were both appointed to the Seminario de Cultura Mexicana, but her health forced her to cut her schedule after 1944, when she was fitted with the first of another series of orthopedic corsets. She returned to painting for herself, and she recorded her pains in 1944 in *The Broken Column*, in which her spine is visible as a broken stone column through her corset, while tears run down her face, and her nude form is tacked with nails of pain. In 1945, further operations led her to paint *Without Hope*, a self-portrait in which she reclines in bed with a funnel projecting a gory scream from her lips—or else preparing the gore to be poured into her. In 1946, her pains took the shape of *The Little Deer*, in which her head appears on a deer which is pierced with nine arrows, in a forest of decaying trees.

An operation in 1946 fused five of Kahlo's vertebrae, but after eight months recuperating in a metal corset, she could not paint for more than three hours before she had to stop because of her "shooting pains." She had hoped that this surgery would give her relief, but the incisions became infected, and when they were reopened, it became clear that the surgery had only further compounded the original problems. Now that Kahlo needed additional surgeries—to reduce pains that had become almost unbearable—she was given such large doses of morphine that she developed an addiction to painkillers that would last for the rest of her life.

As she suffered more and more, all of her relationships changed, not just her marriage. Her body's deterioration shifted her attention from sexual to mystical connections, which she tended to describe in maternal terms. To one lover, José Bartolí—a Spanish painter whom she would see from 1946 until 1952—she wrote:

The atoms of my body are yours and vibrate together for us to love one another. I want to live and be strong to love you with all the tenderness you deserve . . . Near or far, I want you to feel accompanied by me, to live intensely with me, but never for my love to encumber you in your work or in your plans, I want to form such an intimate part of your life, that I become your very self, that if I care for you, it will never be by demanding anything of you, but by letting you live freely, because all your actions will have my complete approval. I love you as you are, your voice makes me love you, everything you say, everything you do, everything you project. I feel I have always loved you, since you were born, and before, when you were conceived. And I feel at times you gave birth to me. I would like all things and all people to care for you and love you and be proud, as I am, to have you. You are so fine and so good that you do not deserve to be wounded by life.

In 1947, she found a similar, cosmological love in Mexican poet Carlos Pellicer: "I feel that we have been together from our place of origin, that we are of the same matter, of the same waves, that we carry the same sense inside . . . Thank you for receiving [me], thank you for living, because yesterday you let me touch your innermost light, and because you said with your voice and your eyes what I had been waiting for all my life."

When Kahlo could not give herself physically, she gave herself abstractly, and she began to create a new vocabulary, casting the word *sky*, for instance, as a verb that meant "to shelter, include, arch over." Now when Kahlo wrote passionate, mystical, or maternal letters, though, she was writing to Rivera's mistresses as often as she was writing to her own lovers. To Emmy Lou Packard, she wrote, "I entrust the big-child to you with all my heart, and you don't know how thankful I am that you are concerned and taking care of him for me. Tell him not to have too many tantrums and to behave himself."

While Kahlo was growing more and more abstract in her relationships through the 1940s, Rivera had been anchoring himself in Mexicanismo. Ever since his return from Europe in 1921, he had identified himself with the Mexican people and the pre-Columbian cultures, and when he was offered a mural at the National Palace in 1941—after seven years without a mural in Mexico—he glorified Mexico's indigenous cultures without seeking controversy. He had been collecting pre-Columbian artifacts since the 1920s, and now he also began to build Anahuacalli, an immense stone building of his own design, which would serve as his studio and also as a museum for his pre-Columbian artifacts.

Rivera turned sixty in December of 1946, and while he was cementing his legacy and building his monument to Mexico, he was given a retrospective in Mexico City in 1949, to mark a painting career of forty years. When Kahlo wrote a "Portrait of Diego" for the retrospective, she described him as a force of nature:

> Diego exists to one side of all personal, limited and precise relations. Contradictory like everything that moves life, he is at once an immense caress and a violent discharge of powerful and unique forces . . .
>
> I don't believe the banks of a river suffer from letting it flow between them . . . In my role, difficult and obscure, as ally to an extraordinary being, I enjoy the reward of a spot of green in a mass of red: the reward of *equilibrium* . . . If I have prejudices and am wounded by the actions of others, even those of Diego Rivera, I accept responsibility for my inability to see clearly, and if I don't

have them, I have to accept that it is natural for red blood cells to fight against white ones without the slightest prejudice and that this phenomenon only signifies health.

In her paintings from this period, Kahlo began to combine her face with Rivera's. She painted him as a baby in her lap, and several times she placed his face in the position of her third eye. For his part, Rivera described Kahlo as "the greatest proof of the renaissance of the art of Mexico," but when he included her in his mural at the Hotel del Prado, he too portrayed himself as a child, with a snake in one pocket and a frog in his hand, holding hands with skeleton death while an adult Kahlo stood behind him, with her hand on his shoulder and a yin-yang in her other hand.

So long as Rivera was relying on Kahlo's management and her guidance, she was safe from the threat of being replaced, but Rivera never ceased to take lovers, and this did not alleviate the tensions in the marriage, for a second divorce was still sometimes hinted at. It never came to pass, though, for when Rivera talked about marrying María Félix in 1949—after Kahlo had undergone yet another operation—Kahlo painted *Diego and I*, which showed her own face in tears, Rivera's face in the position of her third eye, and another eye in the position of Rivera's third eye. Kahlo overdosed on drugs after she finished the painting, and while the gesture brought Rivera back from Félix, it did not diminish his exasperation with the constant burden of Kahlo's injuries, nor hers with his affairs.

While she was suffering more and more, Kahlo insisted on the distinction that she was broken, not sick. She refused to let any but her closest friends see her pains, though, so she turned her suffering into an irreverent performance, and she comforted her friends before they could comfort her. To one patron, Eduardo Safa, she wrote,

> You suffer a lot in this goddamned life, brother, and even if you learn, you really feel it in the long run, and for all I do to give myself strength, there are times when I'd like just to kick the bucket, like a real man!
>
> Listen, I don't like you to sound so sad, you know there are people in this world, like me, who are worse off than you, and they keep tugging just the same, so no getting down in the dumps.

As her health declined—she was hospitalized for most of 1950, and her toes and then her right leg were amputated in 1953 when they developed gangrene—she could not keep her spirits up. In his autobiography, Rivera wrote that "following the loss of her leg, Frida became deeply depressed. She no longer even wanted to hear me tell her of my love affairs, which she had enjoyed hearing about after our remarriage. She had lost her will to live."

Kahlo did continue to paint, though, and in the early 1950s, she said that "many things in this life now bore me. I am always afraid that I will get tired of painting. But this is the truth: I am still passionate about it," and as her health deteriorated, she began to paint still lifes—which began to show the influence of painkillers. She also identified herself more and more as a Communist, hoping that her work could be "something useful" for bringing about a revolutionary society. By the early 1950s, Kahlo's work—and her sufferings—were famous, and on the occasion of her one-woman show in Mexico City in 1953, she was judged too ill to attend, but she arrived in the gallery in her bed—heavily medicated—to be greeted by throngs of admirers. Still, she could not always withstand her pains—or her desperation over Rivera's affairs—and throughout the early 1950s, she made more than one additional suicide attempt.

As Kahlo's health declined, Rivera was with her constantly—unless he was painting, or out with another woman. But as Kahlo spent more and more time in the hospital, Rivera began to search for another wife who would keep his affairs in order and also suffer his affairs, and in 1946, he began an affair with his dealer, Emma Hurtado, whom he would marry a year after Kahlo's death. He left Kahlo in care of her sister Cristina and a group of devoted friends and nurses. While her friends recalled that "there was a party on in Frida's room every day," as the pains in her back and legs increased, Kahlo pined for death. "They amputated my leg six months ago," she wrote in her journal.

> They have given me centuries of torture and at moments I almost lost my "reason." I keep on wanting to kill myself. Diego is the one who holds me back because of my vanity in thinking that he would miss me. He has told me so and I believe him. But never in my life have I suffered more.

There is uncertainty as to whether Kahlo's death, at age forty-seven, in July of 1954, was the result of a deliberate overdose. Her last diary entry was "I hope the exit is joyful—and I hope never to come back—Frida."

IX.

Flouting his repeated promises not to make a political statement, Diego Rivera turned Frida Kahlo's 1954 funeral into a Communist demonstration, draping her casket with the Russian flag while it stood in state at the Palacio de Bellas Artes. Government officials were displeased, but they did not try to remove the flag by force, and the stunt won Rivera his readmission into the Communist Party—on his fifth application since his 1929 expulsion. More than five hundred people followed the procession to the crematorium, and Rivera alone stood in front of the oven as Kahlo's body was put into the flames. He reportedly ate a handful of Kahlo's ashes as they came out, although other accounts have him sketching frantically as her skeleton retained its shape in ashes for a few minutes before collapsing.

In 1955, Rivera married Emma Hurtado, his dealer, although almost immediately after the wedding, he moved in with Dolores Olmedo, who was Kahlo's executrix and a collector of Rivera's easel paintings. When he contracted cancer that year, he traveled to Russia for treatment, and during his convalescence, he reflected on his marriage and his behavior:

> Too late now I realized that the most wonderful part of my life had been my love for Frida. But I could not really say that, given "another chance," I would have behaved toward her any differently than I had. Every man is the product of the social atmosphere in which he grows up and I am what I am.
>
> And what sort of man was I? I had never had any morals at all and had lived only for pleasure where I found it. I was not good. I could discern other people's weaknesses easily, especially men's, and then I would play upon them for no worthwhile reason. If I loved a woman, the more I loved her, the more I wanted to hurt her. Frida was only the most obvious victim of this disgusting trait.
>
> And yet my life had not been an easy one. Everything I had gotten, I had had to struggle for. And having got it, I had had to fight even harder to keep it. This was true of such disparate things as material goods and human affection. Of the two, I had, fortunately, managed to secure more of the latter than of the former.
>
> As I lay in the hospital, I tried to sum up the meaning of my life. It occurred to me that I had never experienced what is

commonly called "happiness." For me, "happiness" has always had a banal sound, like "inspiration." Both "happiness" and "inspiration" are the words of amateurs.

When Rivera himself died in 1957, at age seventy-one, he left very little to Emma Hurtado or his daughters, or his other surviving ex-wives. To the state of Mexico, however, he left Anahuacalli, which was full of the preconquest artifacts he had collected, and Casa Azul, which he had turned into a museum of Kahlo's life and art. Rivera stipulated that his ashes should be mingled with Kahlo's, but after he had defied them for decades with his murals, Mexican officials finally revenged themselves by deciding that his remains should glorify the state instead, and they interred his ashes in the Rotunda of Famous Men in the Civil Pantheon of Mourning.

X.

Starting in 1946, Gladys March, one of Rivera's assistants, had been recording Rivera's stories as he told them—word for word, supposedly— and in 1960, his fantastic and self-congratulatory adventures were published under his name as *My Art, My Life*. In this "autobiography," Rivera adopts what seems to be a fanciful tone—he even seems honestly self-critical—when he describes the pains he caused Kahlo and the other women in his life. But he ultimately portrays himself—as Kahlo had already portrayed him—as a force of nature, as if his seductions were simply as inevitable as Kahlo's suffering. Kahlo herself seems to have accepted them as such in the end, and if she also reported having seen a stubborn or childish will behind the facade of cosmic machinery—if she loved Rivera and tried to elicit his love in return, and if she suffered when he showed no regard for her feelings—she nonetheless found a place for herself in his disregard. If she collaborated in painting the portrait of him as a sacred monster, perhaps she was using her injuries and her sufferings to define her role as his sacrificial victim. If he inflicted upon her one humiliation and insult after another, she was already enduring, in her injuries, more than anything he could have done to her. Using their art as well as the injuries they both of them suffered and inflicted, Rivera and Kahlo painted a picture of their marriage as a tough and vivacious bond, and the portrait never changed. They were both forces of nature, and they never changed the story, even when it was clear that they were deciding to live as they lived—even when they started to see that they were choosing their suffering, even when they were making art in frenzies of creativity that they hoped would give them some justification for everything they endured.

Chapter Five

The Miracle Accomplished by Blood and Joy

Henry Miller and Anaïs Nin

⸎

Henry has found himself because I have not made a slave of him. I have respected his entity—he feels I have never encroached on his liberty. And out of this his strength was born. And with this strength he loves me, wholly, without war or hatred or reserve. It is strange how to Henry I have been able to make the greatest gift: that of *not holding*, of keeping our two souls independent yet fused. The greatest miracle of *wise* love. And it is this he gives me, too.   ANAÏS NIN

I am saying to myself "here is the first woman with whom I can be absolutely sincere." I remember your saying—"you could fool me. I wouldn't know it." When I walk along the boulevards and think of that. I can't fool you—and yet I would like to. I mean that I can never be absolutely loyal—it's not in me. I love women, or life, too much—which it is, I don't know . . . Oh, it is beautiful to love and be free at the same time.
                                      HENRY MILLER

The journal is a product of my disease, perhaps an accentuation and exaggeration of it. I speak of relief when I write; perhaps, but it is also an engraving of pain, a tattooing on myself, a prolongation of pain.
                                      ANAÏS NIN

I.

When Anaïs Nin met Henry Miller at the end of 1931, she had been toying with the idea of finding sexual satisfaction outside of her marriage for

195

more than a year. She and her husband Hugo Guiler had been in Paris for six years, and while they lived comfortably on Guiler's banker's salary, they were both miserable with desires they were too timid to express. They were starting to consider "parties, orgies," brothels, and affairs— as well as "fulfillment in other directions"—but Nin had also begun to distinguish her own satisfaction from Guiler's: "I love my husband," she wrote in her journal, "but I will fulfill myself." She took Spanish dancing lessons, and she flirted with her instructor and a musician, then engaged in some preliminary embraces with a publisher's assistant, and again with her husband's college professor, John Erskine. She was not ready for a full-blown infidelity, but she was preparing herself: when Erskine introduced her to D. H. Lawrence and modern literature, in the spring of 1930, she started to write a book about sex in Lawrence's novels.

By the end of 1931, the book was starting to expand her horizons. Her husband had asked Richard Osborn, an American lawyer, to write the publishing contracts, and when Osborn saw that Nin was writing about sex, he offered to introduce her to his friend Henry Miller, an American writer who had also been writing about sex in modern culture. Miller had fled from a sex-drenched life in New York: his wife there, a taxi dancer and gold digger, had tortured him with jealousy over her admirers, patrons, and lovers. Now that Miller was alone in Paris—now that he was free from his wife's schemes—he had been writing regularly, working on a blasphemous book that used deliberately vulgar language to proclaim his freedom from a world that was dying of repression, false respectability, and senseless industry.

Miller had arrived in Paris without any money, and while he had been staying with Osborn for free, he was still always looking for free meals and supportive patrons, so Osborn was doing Miller a favor by introducing him to Nin, who had herself been cultivating a circle of artists, dancers, and writers. When Osborn brought Miller to lunch at Nin's house in the suburb of Louveciennes, Miller played the part of the coarse, bohemian artist for Nin and her banker husband, but if Nin was awed by the ease with which Miller discussed sexual topics, she was put off by his vulgarity. "I would never let Henry touch me," she wrote in her journal. "I can only find [the reason] in his own language. 'I just don't want to be pissed on.'" Nin may not have felt an attraction for Miller, but she was willing to play the role of patroness for his writing, so she invited him back a second time, and it was only when Miller returned with his wife, who was visiting from New York—it was only when Nin met June Mansfield that she finally felt safe to give herself over to her erotic urges.

By all accounts, June Mansfield was a beautiful and beguiling woman who held people close with a combination of sexual thrall and fascinating, evasive stories. Before she married Miller, she had worked as a taxi dancer, making a living on her looks, but she had supplemented her income by wangling gifts and money from patrons, with nebulous promises of sex and intimacy. June was always telling intriguing and frequently contradictory stories about her travels, plans, experiences, and affairs, and now Nin had the same reaction Miller had had when he met June in 1923: she half wanted to follow June into her fantasies, but some truth-seeking impulse made her want to penetrate to the heart of June's lies, and to know her for who she really was.

Miller had been married to another woman before June, but his first wife had nagged him about money and respectability, and if June's sex appeal and her chaotic stories and lifestyle had freed him, he had also thrown himself into the gutter to follow her. Now Nin thought about throwing herself at June's feet as well, and she took June shopping and spent her allowance on gifts for her. By the time June returned to New York in January of 1932, she and Nin had only exchanged kisses and a few embraces, but Nin had been swept away. June, she said, was "the only woman who ever answered the demands of my imagination."

June had reasons of her own for flirting with Nin: she had sent Miller to Paris for the sake of his writing, but she did not want to let him get too far away, and now she wanted to meet his new patroness. If June could make Miller jealous by stealing Nin's affection—even better, if she could throw Miller's manhood into question by having an affair with her—she could reassert her hold on him, for even though he had effectively pimped for her, and tolerated all of her affairs, he had a stability and respectability that awed her—and he had always promised to become a famous writer and immortalize her in his writing—so she wanted to keep her hold on him. But she could not make any money in Paris, so she returned to New York and her patrons after only a six-week stay.

Shortly after June sailed back to New York, Nin went to Switzerland for a vacation with her husband, but she was smitten by June, and now she turned to Miller for information. Miller had been fascinated with June himself—ever since he had read Proust, he had treated June as his Albertine, his obsession—and he was happy to write long letters that tried to express his love for her, as well as his exasperation. At first, Miller and Nin's letters traded theories about June's personality, but soon Nin began to appreciate Miller's voracious appetite for literature and life: here was a fellow writer whose novel in progress was describing the decay of his culture and the liberating power of sex. Responding to one of his letters, Nin exclaimed,

> God, Henry, in you alone I have found the same swelling of enthusiasm, the same quick rising of the blood, the fullness, the fullness.
>
> Before, I almost used to think there was something wrong. Everybody else seemed to have the *brakes on*. A scene in a movie, a voice, a phrase was not for them volcanic. I never feel the brakes. I overflow. And when I feel your excitement about life flaring, next to mine, then it makes me dizzy.

Now they exchanged their writing as well: Miller sent Nin his first novel—*Crazy Cock*, about his life with June—and Nin found parts of it "*éblouissants*, staggeringly beautiful." She sent Miller her book on Lawrence in return, in addition to her childhood journal, and Miller was unstinting in his praises. "Nobody has ever told us how and what women think," he raved, and later, "nobody else is doing anything like this. Ecstatic. Wonderful." Now that they had shared their writing, they began to share their reading as well, and soon they were discussing Spengler, Joyce, and Unamuno's *The Tragic Sense of Life* together—in addition to Jung and Freud. Suddenly their correspondence was far beyond June, and together they pried into questions of freedom, sex and art, madness, illness and death, cultural decay and renewal, and even though neither of them had been published or recognized as writers, soon they were both a little drunk for recognizing each other's genius, and for being recognized, themselves, in each other's eyes.

Once Nin saw what kind of contribution Miller was going to make to modern literature, she started to help him materially. She spent her allowance on books, food, and wine for him; she lent him her typewriter while his was being repaired; and she got her husband to arrange a teaching job for him in Dijon. Miller continued to send her long letters from Dijon, and when he found out that he would not be getting paid, she rented an apartment for him and a friend in Clichy. Within a few days of Miller's return from Dijon in March, they became lovers, and by April, Miller was promising to treat her to what he called—with studied crudity—"one literary fuck fest—that means fucking and talking and talking and fucking . . . with a bottle of Anjou in between, or a Vermouth Cassis." After all of her preparations, Nin had found a man who would tell her that he was "going to open your very groins." "You're food and drink to me," Miller wrote to her, "the whole bloody machinery, as it were. Lying on top of you is one thing, but getting close to you is another. I feel close to you, one with you, you're mine whether it is acknowledged or not."

Neither Miller nor Nin were ready to acknowledge their love publicly, although they did use this language, of marriage that was real in spite of being unacknowledged. They were both still married, and Nin refused to let Miller reveal the affair to her husband—nor could she give up her husband's substantial income, not when Miller himself was broke and her husband alone made it possible for them to spend their days together, making love, drinking, talking, and poring over each other's manuscripts.

Neither Miller nor Nin needed to break up their marriages to be together: they were married as writers, they could allow each other their smaller, human marriages. Their writing already exempted them from normal life: they described their love as inhuman, diabolical and infernal, monstrous and heroic by turns. Marriage did not apply to them—they were writers: they were married without having married. As Nin wrote in her journal,

I really believe that if I were not a writer, not a creator, not an experimenter, I might have been a very faithful wife. I think highly of faithfulness. But my temperament belongs to the writer, not to the woman . . . Subtract the overintensity, the sizzling of ideas, and you get a woman who loves perfection. And faithfulness is one of the perfections. Perfection is static, and I am in full progress. The faithful wife is only one phase, one moment, one metamorphosis, one condition.

As diabolical writers, Miller and Nin encouraged each other to have other experiences—with their spouses—or with whores, in Miller's case—or with June, in Nin's. Their love was going to consist of allowing each other their freedom, and they would show their fidelity by using their sexual experiences—even their infidelities—in their writing. Their honesty about the voracious nature of desire intoxicated them both. "This is a little drunken," Miller wrote to Nin.

I am saying to myself "here is the first woman with whom I can be absolutely sincere." I remember your saying—"you could fool me. I wouldn't know it." When I walk along the boulevards and think of that. I can't fool you—and yet I would like to. I mean that I can never be absolutely loyal—it's not in me. I love women, or life, too much—which it is, I don't know . . . you seem to urge me to betray you. I love you for that. And what makes you do that—love? Oh, it is beautiful to love and be free at the same time.

Miller had been married twice, and he had consorted with prostitutes for long enough that he already had a casual relationship with sex, but Nin was no less eager than Miller to use her new freedom. "What I have found in Henry is unique," she wrote. "It cannot be repeated. But there are other experiences to be had." Soon she was making love enthusiastically—and skillfully—with her husband, and when her homosexual cousin convinced her to go into therapy, she seduced him as well, and then she began a slow seduction of her therapist, which culminated in clandestine meetings in a hotel.

Nin hid each of these affairs from her husband, but she told Miller all the details, and now in addition to being sexually enthralled with each other and in love, Miller and Nin shared the conspiratorial intimacy of writers who shared a secret: that monogamy was an artificial, bourgeois convention, a symbol of a decaying world. "We are living something new," Nin wrote, and as long as their experiences—as long as their love, their affairs, and even their jealousies could still feed their writing, they were confident that they shared the most exclusive, most courageous, most self-aware intimacy possible. Nin recorded having told Miller that "'The mountain of words has sundered, Literature has fallen away.' I meant that real feelings had begun, and that the intense sensuality of his writing was one thing, and our sensuality together was another, a real thing."

Neither Miller nor Nin, though, ever expressed a desire for an exclusive union or a conventional, settled lifestyle, where they would be primarily responsible for each other's material needs. They were still making sacrifices and compromises while they waited until their work was published and recognized, and they were content to straddle the worlds in which they were married and the worlds they were creating through their writing. In between lovemaking, they helped each other put the finishing touches to their books, and they told each other that once they were published—once the world saw the courage and genius they themselves already saw in each other's writing, they might make an entirely new kind of union, based on complete erotic and artistic freedom. But neither one of them could provide for the other yet, and neither one of them minded the other's marriage, so they continued to depend on the money Nin took from her husband, and as long as Guiler was still supporting them—as long as they could hide their affair from him, there was plenty of time to work on their writing, and to make love in preparation for that new world.

II.

For Henry Miller, the celebratory outrageousness of fuck fests with a beautiful and talented writer who was also a reputable banker's wife was a rebellion against the success his parents had always expected of him. Success and self-cultivation were practically a religion for Miller's Lutheran parents, who raised their first son on a strict diet of respectability and hard work. This formula had worked for Miller's grandfathers, who had emigrated independently from Germany to New York in 1862. Valentin Nieting, Miller's maternal grandfather, had learned his trade in London after fleeing from his conscription into the Prussian military. In London he made clothing for wealthy clients on Savile Row, and when he emigrated to New York, he succeeded so well that he installed his family in a fashionable German-American enclave on the Upper East Side of Manhattan.

That was where his twenty-year-old daughter Louise met twenty-four-year-old Heinrich Miller, whose father was also a tailor. Miller's father had not worked for the same wealthy clientele as Nieting, though, and after Heinrich and Louise were married in 1890, the gap between the fathers' statuses became a rift between husband and wife. Louise Nieting did not let her husband forget that in the pecking order of German-American families, her father had a higher status than his, and Heinrich never attained his father-in-law's degree of success: when the couple moved to Brooklyn, in 1892—and again when they moved to Bushwick in 1900—they were moving into apartments Nieting owned. According to biographies and Miller's own autobiographical accounts, Louise was critical of her husband's poor business instincts, and she generally resented his easygoing good fellowship and camaraderie, which turned into a drinking habit when he began to find it unpleasant to go home, and soon after they were married, he began to prefer the fellowship of the salesmen, suppliers, and customers to his wife's.

Louise Nieting Miller ran a strictly regulated household, and when Henry, her first child, was born on the day after Christmas in 1891, she was determined to make him a paragon of virtue. His talents and precociousness were going to compensate her disappointment in her husband, whose lack of ambition was already exasperating her. Young Henry was always the best dressed child in his class, and he got so much attention that he felt he should really have been born on Christmas Day, a new Messiah. He felt so privileged and generous that he would forego gifts, or give his toys away, in order to share his good fortunes with others. (Intent on preserving the family's distinction, though, Louise once took him by the ear to retrieve the gifts.) Henry did not grow up with art and literature, but photographs of his mother's family, many of whom were still in Germany, were hung prominently in their apartment, and their images invoked the authority of the Old World in a yet-uncultured America. Louise and Heinrich were not lettered people themselves, but the American religion of self-cultivation dovetailed with their German respect for learning, so that Henry was given books as gifts, and he had piano and zither lessons from the age of ten.

In spite of his culture, Miller would later describe his family as an insane asylum—and not entirely without cause, for insanity ran in his family. His mother had taken responsibility for her own parents' house-hold when her mother, Emilia Insel, "went crazy" and was "taken away," in Miller's words. Miller recalled that his mother had "*had* to be the autocrat to keep her sisters in line." When Miller's younger sister, Lauretta, was born in 1895 with a birth defect that kept her from developing intellec-tually, Miller recalled his mother "[throwing] her hands up in despair. 'What did I do to deserve this?' she would ask me, as if I were God and had all the answers, *me*, a little boy!" Miller had a certain affection for his sister nonetheless—he called her "a sort of harmless monster, an angel who had been given the body of an idiot"—but his mother was not so for-giving, and Lauretta's deficiencies did not exempt her from her mother's strict rules, so that she was severely punished when she failed in her les-sons or chores. In addition to his sister's debility, Miller's mother's sister, his aunt Melia, "went crazy" after her husband left her. As a young man himself, Miller was entrusted with the task of taking her to the asylum, leaving her there with the attendants, and walking away when she ran to the fence, crying for him not to leave her.

The Miller household was organized around the principle that young Henry was being raised to discipline himself and to succeed, but in light of his sister's debility and punishments, he resented the strict atmo-sphere, and while he sometimes allied himself with his mother against his easygoing father, he would later condemn her as "sober, industrious, frugal." He got good grades in school, but he said that "it was all too easy for me. I felt like a trained monkey." When nothing he did could avert his mother's rages at his sister or his father, though, he ultimately ceased to respect his parents' authority altogether. He rebelled and became a disciplinary problem in school, although he continued to earn his good grades easily.

When he could not escape from the scenes of his mother berating his father or beating his sister, Miller learned to live in his imagina-tion. He read voraciously, finding a better society in romances and tales of chivalry, where the man was a savior and protector. Like his father, Miller also escaped by spending his time outside of the house: he and the neighborhood boys roamed the streets, which were peopled by bums and drunks, and enlivened by wars between gangs of boys as well as occa-sional domestic scenes. This gave Miller a delicious sense of freedom—he recalled the years between ages five and ten as the best time of his life—but in 1900, when he was eight, the family moved to Bushwick, which was a less rowdy neighborhood than Williamsburg. If Miller's parents were happy with their rise in society, Miller himself was only stripped of his friends at a time when his sister's disability was creating a greater and greater tension in the family, and Miller immersed himself in books to replace the colorful life of the street, and to liberate himself from his family. From romances like *Ivanhoe* and *Robinson Crusoe*, he learned to idealize the chivalry in which a man should be a restrained gentleman, who provides for and protects his woman, although on the streets, his friends described sex as a trap in which men were caught and consumed by nagging wives. Miller idealized the camaraderie of friends, but he also retained a romantic sentimentalism, and when he fell in love at age thirteen, his first love, Cora Seward, was someone whom he "never thought of fucking": she remained an ideal in his heart, and in his memoir, *First Love*, he called her "the unattainable one." Recollecting his stories of his childhood in her journals, Anaïs Nin wrote that instead of a sublime love, Miller found "his first sexual experience at sixteen in a whorehouse and caught a disease."

If Miller saw love as beyond him, when he failed to win a scholarship at Cornell after graduating second in his high school class, he put worldly success out of reach for himself as well. In 1909, he took classes at City College, but he dropped out after only one term, and then gave up on schooling entirely. He poured his energies into his friendships, and he joined the Xerxes club, a group of musicians with whom he would meet regularly until 1925. He took a job as a filing clerk in a cement company and supplemented his paycheck by giving piano lessons.

Instead of a career, Miller began an affair with the thirty-two-year-old mother of one of his piano pupils. In his memoir, Miller described Pauline Chouteau as

> delicate, petite, beautifully proportioned, always of a cheerful nature. Uneducated but not stupid . . . she had taste, discretion, and a sound understanding of life . . . she had been deprived of a sex life for a number of years. She had never remarried, and, so far as I knew, had had no lovers. We were both hungry for it. We fucked our heads off.

"Not only was Pauline my mistress," Miller elaborated, "she was also my mother, my teacher, my nurse, my companion, everything rolled into one." This affair separated Miller from the boys his age, since he was already taken seriously as the lover of a woman fifteen years his senior, and it drove a wedge between Miller and his mother, who hated the fact that her prized child was scuttling his ambitions for a divorcée almost twice his age.

Having ceased to respect his parents' authority—having chosen a dead-end job and a futureless relationship instead of making the effort to advance himself through hard work, Miller was soon disillusioned about the virtues of employment, and he ceased to respect authority altogether. By eighteen, he was grubby and seriously devoted only to avoiding senseless work, although he saw his laziness as a rebellion against the contradictions, the absurdity, and the futility of everything, and he undertook this rebellion mainly by undermining his own prospects. He still nursed the sense that he was special and different—he still felt that he had some unique purpose—but he could not point to any work that distinguished him, and he courted failure instead of risking success. Even when his parents could finally pay to send him to Cornell, he took their money and squandered it with Pauline instead.

After four guilt-ridden years, during which Miller would neither marry Pauline nor leave her, he finally left New York looking for adventure in 1913 at age twenty-two, but when he took a job not as a cowboy, as he had hoped, but as a picker on a lemon ranch, he found that the hard work and the camaraderie of rough ranch hands was no substitute for books and the relationship he had left behind in New York, and he came back home. Returning to New York, Miller was returning to Pauline as well, but for the aimless layabout with still-groundless dreams of artistic glory, the older woman who asked "What good is all that reading going to do you?" was not the best fit. Miller felt that he bore "a tremendous moral obligation" toward Pauline, but when he told his mother that he intended to marry her, he wrote that she threatened him with a carving knife, and he never pressed the issue any further.

Miller began to work with his father, who had bought a half share in a tailor shop after inheriting money from his mother's father. There Miller was in charge of minding his father—primarily of retrieving him from the bars—but he also wrote scathing if not outright libelous letters to the firm's debtors. He was still drifting, but he told a friend at the time that he had had

> the devil's own torments lately from imagining that I have something in me to give to the world. I can't quite believe that I am capable of writing anything worthwhile and yet, for the life of me,

I can't repress the desire to put my thoughts on paper . . . If there is one thing worse than having an artistic temperament, it is thinking you have one.

After his return from California, Miller been reading voraciously in anarchist philosophy and literature, and he attended concerts at Carnegie Hall when his father's clients could get him tickets. Miller's father's clients introduced him to a world of class and refinement and culture—in spite of his grubbiness—and Miller wrote that Welsh poet John Cowper Powys was "like an oracle to me" for introducing him to Dostoevsky and Russian literature, at a time when Miller himself was still not producing anything but tremendous imaginary dialogues.

At a wedding in 1915, Miller met a good-looking twenty-three-year-old named Beatrice Wickens, who was a year younger than him, and a professional pianist, which gave her respectability in Miller's eyes. He engaged her to give him piano lessons, and then set about seducing her, and soon he was consumed by his new affair with Beatrice. When he finally broke off with Pauline, he wrote in *Book of Friends* that he "felt so ashamed" that "I never looked her up, never phoned her, never saw her again."

The affair with Beatrice might not have lasted, but when Miller was drafted in 1917, he proposed marriage in order to defer his conscription. He wrote later that "I got myself married overnight, to demonstrate to all and sundry that I didn't give a fuck one way or the other." Miller and Beatrice began to bicker almost immediately after they were married: Miller was still working for his father, but Beatrice took over the household finances, leaving him with no more than he needed for each day, and now Miller revenged himself on his wife's strict rules by bringing home friends and keeping odd hours. He passed his time at burlesque shows, where sex was treated openly and men idled together—and the shows were a relief from Beatrice, who was still a novice in sex, and guilty. As Miller later wrote, "the better the fuck, the worse she felt afterwards."

Miller had kept many of his childhood friends from Brooklyn, and his personable manner was always bringing new friends to him, so that he was surrounded by boisterous people whom he would outrage with his reading and his contentious, almost nihilistic views about work, sex, and society. From this time until the end of his life, Miller would call his good friends "Joey," after his friend Joe O'Reagan, who would stay with him and Beatrice from time to time. Miller would rely on any number of foils and friends to play his personality against, and if Beatrice objected to his friends' constant presence, her objections were only more strenuous after September of 1919, when their daughter, Barbara, was born: now Miller was either disturbing the baby, by debating or carousing with his friends, or else he was never home.

When Miller's father quit drinking in 1920, Miller was no longer needed to watch him, so he gave up working at the tailor shop and began to write short essays, which he submitted to a small literary magazine that paid a penny per word. This was not going to support him at all, and when Beatrice nagged him about getting work, he applied for a job as a Western Union messenger. He was turned down, but he was indignant about his refusal, so the next day, he put on his best suit and went to the corporate office to appeal to the president. He met with a vice president—whom he impressed with his articulate critique of the hiring process. A number of internal power struggles at Western Union made a fresh-faced, articulate, German-American father an attractive prospect in a company that was wary of hiring too many Jews. After spending a month on the street as a messenger, to learn the business, he was given a three-phone desk and power to hire and fire messengers himself.

Miller tried to take the job seriously at first, but when he saw that the company did not care about the messengers, he lost interest. His position practically invited him to be a tyrant, though: the applicants were such a range of hopeless characters—and turnover was such a relentless problem—that he let himself be corrupted by his authority over the applicants. He began to hire and fire them arbitrarily, in addition to demanding payment for favors. He ceased to keep regular hours, and he loitered with the messengers in brothels, flophouses, dance halls, and bars, where he both debased himself in an attempt to debase the system he worked in and exalted himself in all-night conversations with fellow dropouts who failed—or refused—to be part of the system.

The marriage Miller was supporting with this job was not a happy one. At one point, he tried to pawn his wife off on a musician who was boarding with them, but the boarder took offense at his offer and returned to the Midwest. Miller and Beatrice separated in 1921—she took their daughter to stay with an aunt in Rochester, New York—but she returned after two months, and when she got pregnant again, he had to borrow $100 from a lover to fund her abortion. In an attempt to reconcile, Beatrice made Miller a gift of Knut Hamsun's novel *Hunger*. She suggested he try his hand at writing, and in 1922 he took three weeks off and wrote

Clipped Wings, a novel about his experience in the messenger service, where he told his friend Emil Schnellock had that he felt like "a gaily caparisoned cacique among cormorants, like a bashaw among bastinadoes." Miller was too anxious to prove the breadth and depth of his learning and his rebelliousness, and the novel was disorganized as a result. "It was a crushing defeat," he said, when the novel was rejected. "But it put iron in my backbone and sulphur in my blood. I knew at least what it was to fail."

Reconciliations with Beatrice notwithstanding, Miller was always on the lookout for new lovers, and when he met June Mansfield in a dance hall—she overheard him talking about Pirandello with one of the other dancers—he was captivated by her first "knowing, mysterious, fugitive" smile, as he later described it. At twenty-one, June was stunningly beautiful, with dark hair and pale skin. Born Juliet Edith Smerth in Austria-Hungary, she had arrived in America with her family in 1907, and now her conflicting stories about herself—and also about the mysterious men who loved her—drew Miller in. He was driven by the urge to protect her—and to *know* her—and when he traveled to her house and wrote her long letters, he was so lovestruck that when she did not answer, he only wrote more. When she finally spent a night with him, her sexual openness was only satisfying for a short time before he found himself in the torturous position of the lover who can all too clearly imagine the scenes in which his beloved must have learned to be so open. This insecurity may have been torture, but it was good for producing literature, and now Miller had an ideal occasion to write diatribes, complaints, declarations, narrations, explanations, and reconciliations.

In order to end his marriage—which was now an impediment to his new love—Miller staged a scene in which Beatrice would catch him in bed with June, but even though this gave Beatrice grounds for divorce, she and Miller did not ultimately separate until December 1923. Miller oscillated between June and Beatrice for a time, and June finally won a commitment from him when she fired his passion by making him jealous with tales of her previous lovers. Miller and June married June 1, 1924, and when Miller finally walked off his job at Western Union at the end of 1924, he was already on the verge of being fired for irregular work and attendance. Sympathetic with his disgust about working, June resolved to make him a writer: she agreed to make all their money herself, in order that he should have time to write, but she installed them in an apartment they could not afford in a nice section of Brooklyn Heights. They were behind on the rent almost from the first month, but June represented a defiance, a chaos, and a wildness Miller appreciated. She helped him rebel against everything his wife and child symbolized: bourgeois respectability, industriousness, progress, and success, so he relinquished himself to her care.

If Miller felt that he might be saving June from herself, one of their schemes for making money was to open a basement speakeasy in their New York brownstone, and he ended up essentially pimping for her, serving drinks and food to her "friends" in the front of their flat while she entertained patrons individually in a back room. Miller seemed to welcome her affairs, though, as long as he continued to be the one in whom she confided. As he wrote in *Sexus* years later, "The more lovers she garnered the greater my own personal triumph. Because she did love *me*, that there was no doubt about."

In order to support herself and Miller, June ultimately quit the dance hall to work in a tea lounge, where men would sit for a long time with the women, buying expensive drinks. June was convinced that she might be an actress, and she fostered the illusion that she would make a great stage personality one day, and now that Miller was writing, he was deep in his own grand ideas, so they only encouraged each other to believe in their talents and the promising futures they had in store. But the truth was that they were only barely getting by, and they spent a great deal of time dreaming up creative ways to make money without really having to work. In his "misery over June's golddigging, which constantly preys on my mind"—in his disgust with the world that did not recognize his genius—in his despair over his own passivity and failure, Miller turned his weakness into what he called "purposeful, literary buffoonery."

If he was not actually writing, he was at least living something closer to the life of a rebellious, bohemian writer. He began to see everything as possible material for a book: he began to travel around the city, composing pieces about neighborhoods, people, and history, while June brought her patrons around to meet him. When the rejections piled up, Miller resolved to publish himself, and he and June printed up short pieces on heavy paper. They did not have much success selling them door-to-door, but when June took them to the cafés, she would sometimes sell out her entire supply, although it was never clear that the writing was anything more than an excuse for June to tell her own stories in person, and even to sell herself to patrons. Eclipsing her husband in sales, June eventually proposed that they remove Miller's name altogether and print her name on the cards instead, in hopes that she could make better money if it looked like she was selling her own work. Miller never let June print her name on his work, but the two of them kept trying different schemes—they sold candy out of a suitcase at bars and cafés, they sold mezzotints—but the schemes all ended up the same way: June was the better salesman, and when she took over the selling, she came back with more money than she could have possibly made from her wares, and now Miller had to wonder what else she was selling, or promising, to her customers.

In spite of all their schemes, there was never enough money. Miller was not making his alimony payments, and he was afraid that he would be imprisoned for failure to pay. After a trip to Florida to cash in on a real estate bubble that had already burst, Miller returned to New York to find that he and June had been evicted. She returned to her family, but he returned to live with his parents and his sister, where he had to hide in the closet when his parents had visitors. After further schemes to escape from the "dopes" and "saps" who were always offering June money, Miller tried to write city sketches and stories for magazines, but nothing sold, and he and June had to rely on her talent for wangling money from "supporters." When Miller finally took a job because they needed the money, June discouraged him, and he quit after the first day, putting himself entirely back in her hands.

June eventually came to loathe Miller for not fulfilling the promise of becoming a famous writer, and in 1926, she met Jean Kronski, an artist who had succeeded the way June had hoped Miller would succeed. June brought Jean to live with them in their apartment, and she humiliated Miller by sharing Jean's bed, throwing both his art and his manhood into question with her lesbian passion for Jean. Anaïs Nin would describe their living conditions in her journal:

> Bed unmade all day; climbing into it with shoes on frequently; sheets a mess. Using soiled shirts for towels. Laundry seldom gotten out. Sinks stopped up from too much garbage. Washing dishes in the bathtub, which was greasy and black-rimmed. Bathroom always cold as an icebox. Breaking up furniture to throw into fire. Shades always down, windows never washed, atmosphere sepulchral. Floor constantly strewn with plaster of Paris, tools, paints, books, cigarette butts, garbage, soiled dishes, pots. Jean running around all day in overalls. June, always half naked and complaining of the cold.

Miller was spiraling into depression, and after he overheard June telling Jean that "my love for Val [Miller went by his middle name, Valentine] is only like that of a mother's for a child," he made a half-hearted attempt at suicide. He took some pills his psychiatrist friend had given him, but they were only mild sleeping pills, and Miller did not accomplish the dramatic scene he might have hoped for, although he did get to try his hand at writing a suicide note.

In February 1927, Miller spent ten days in bed in nervous distress, with hemorrhoids and general misery, but he also read Proust, whose Albertine gave him a model for writing about June. In Proust, Miller found a kind of engine for converting memories and experiences into literature, without the complicated plotting and framing that might have required him to assume one narratorial persona or another, and to tell a structured story. Miller found that he was already the person whose life he could write about.

June and Jean left for Paris together in the spring of 1927, shortly after a friend had found Miller work in the Brooklyn Parks Department. With regular employment—and with June and Jean out of town, Miller had time to think about writing again, and one night after work, he made some thirty pages of notes that would later become the heart of the *Rosy Crucifixion* trilogy, which would narrate his life with June and Jean as a story of great love and great betrayal. He also started *Moloch*, a novel that told the story of his first marriage, and while the novel would only be published posthumously, the effort of organizing and recording his recollections galvanized him, and he began to work in earnest. He had material, and he had already been so humiliated that now he had nothing left to lose by continuing to fail. When June returned from Paris, she was alone—Jean gone off with an Austrian writer—but even though June promptly convinced Miller to quit his job, now he had a plan for a book, and he was more determined to write than ever.

Shortly after her return, June showed Miller's writing to "Pop" Freedman, a patron who was impressed by *Moloch*, which he believed was her writing. Pop offered to pay June a regular stipend provided she show him fresh pages every week. This gave Miller license to write, and when the novel was finished in the spring of 1928, Pop approved the manuscript. With the money—which was supplemented with other money June brought in on her own, Miller and June traveled to Quebec. Then in the summer of 1928, they went to Europe, touring by bicycle and train. Back in New York, Miller began another novel about himself, June, and Jean. While Miller was writing *Lovely Lesbians*—or *Crazy Cock*, as it would eventually be published, again posthumously—June began to use cocaine and alcohol, with the result that her stories became more and more disordered, and now Miller had to spend more time tracking her down in bars, or trying to piece together the truth of what she told him.

In February 1930, Miller left for Paris again, this time alone. He only had $10 with him, but June was supposed to wire him money as she got it from her patrons, and Miller was optimistic. Changes were in the air: Beatrice had remarried, so he was no longer worried about being jailed for abandoning her, and Jean had returned to New York and killed herself in an insane asylum. In Paris, Miller met Alfred Perlès, the Austrian writer whom Jean had gone off with—as well as Richard Osborn, a friend from New York. Perlès and Osborn helped him look for work and patrons, and he also met American poets Walter Lowenfels and Michael Fraenkel, who introduced him to a theme he would use in *Tropic of Cancer*: that the world was decaying toward death. More importantly, Fraenkel led Miller to the breakthrough that would produce his most famous works: write as you talk, he urged him.

Now Miller started writing in earnest, keeping a notebook and writing short pieces about his wanderings in Paris. He was in a state of ferment: "the sap is running," he wrote in a letter to Emil Schnellock, "I wake up with semen in my hand, I get ideas in the toilet, on the Metro, in the telephone booths, etc. Good sign. Great tidings." He was writing constantly, translating his wanderings into epic letters of up to twenty pages that were full of outrageous and detailed observations of Paris. These letters were undisguised first drafts of articles, sketches, stories, and pieces he would do for magazines and journals as well as pieces that would eventually become part of *Tropic of Cancer*. Soon his sketches—on the bike races and on the Cirque Medrano, and on Parisian prostitutes and Luis Buñuel's films—started to be accepted in the Paris *Herald* and Samuel Putnam's *New Review*, and now Miller began to gain some notoriety in the Paris cafés, as a bohemian writer of promise.

June arrived in September 1930 for a short stay, and by November, Miller was considering returning to New York, except that Richard Osborn, who worked in the Paris branch of the National City Bank, offered him a rent-free accommodation. Miller stayed on and continued to write. He still did not have any money, but he kept a long list of friends he could call on for small favors—never putting himself too much in any one person's debt—and he told Emil Schnellock that he had even befriended a prostitute who liked him so much that she did not charge him for sex. He maintained a list of friends from whom he could expect a good meal, and by careful rotation, he could subsist on at least one good meal a day. With his main expenses taken care of, he was free to find good fortune in small turns of events, and now his long-practiced poverty started to seem inspired, even sacred. Miller was becoming a personality in Montparnasse, and he was written up in a gossip column in the *Herald Tribune*. Through Alfred Perlès, he found part-time work proofreading financial reports at the *Herald Tribune* in August 1931, but when June came in October, she convinced him to quit his job once more. She was losing her hold on him, though, and she returned to New York without him again.

In the summer of 1931, Miller finished *Crazy Cock* and started what he called his "fuck everything" book, *Tropic of Cancer*, which was a plotless narrative full of sex, drinking, and disgust for every bourgeois custom and restraint. The book was not a novel but a surreal memoir, full of vitriolic writing about the uselessness of labor in a culture where getting ahead was a form of insanity. Miller was finally turning his own life into literature, catalyzing his failures and humiliations. He had happened upon a new approach to literature—a literature so structureless and honest and self-revealing that it amounted to personal destruction, which left him completely exposed as an author. He told Schnellock that the book "will further alienate the reader. It's almost as though I had made up my mind to prevent people from liking me," although as his writing gained momentum, he was beginning to find patrons more and more willing to support him and his writing. In October 1931, Miller wrote to Schnellock that he needed "a little peace now, a little security in which to work. In fact, I ought to stop living for a long while, and just work. I'm sick of gathering experiences." In this new atmosphere of literary purpose, Miller told Schnellock that he saw love as "a world on which I have slammed the door and I will never try to open that door, but I must confess that sometimes, in the night, I go back and I stand wistfully before the door, knowing that I have left behind me one of the most cherished, precious gifts."

So when Miller accepted Richard Osborn's invitation to dine with a banker's wife who had written a book about D. H. Lawrence, he was still only looking for interesting personalities and free meals from supporting patrons. He was playing the role of the bohemian, and his sexual crudity and coarse language were deliberately out of place in his patrons' polite households. When he met Nin, she was put off by his crude talk and sexual banter, and stories of street life, but she found him to be someone "whom life made drunk." When Nin and Guiler invited him back again,

June had just arrived from New York. She was jealous of Miller's pretty new patron, and when she invited herself along, she liberated Nin from the repression of her desires, and she gave Miller and Nin the grounds for conversations that would open up into profound literary and sexual intimacy.

III.

In 1923, at the same time that Miller was just beginning his self-destructive battle with June, Anaïs Nin, twelve years younger, was getting married at the age of twenty, and beginning a life of financial security. Her own family was fairly poor, but in spite of her relative poverty, Nin had presented a wealthy and cultured appearance to her new husband. Her mother, Rosa Culmell, was the oldest daughter of a distinguished merchant whose Danish family had ties to the Cuban sugar plantations, and Nin's father was a distinguished and highly cultured concert pianist, so Anaïs had been raised in high style in cities all over Europe.

Rosa Culmell was the eldest daughter in a large family, and she had acted both as her father's social secretary and as a foster parent to her eight younger siblings after her mother—Anaïs' grandmother—had left her family. Rosa gained a great deal of freedom and authority by coordinating her father's busy social calendar, and even after three of her four sisters had married, she still preferred her independence in her father's household to acting as a wife in her suitors'.

At age thirty, though, Rosa was drawn to a dashing twenty-two-year-old young man whom she saw playing piano in a music store. Joaquín Nin y Castellanos had been born in Cuba, but he was baptized in Spain, which set him apart in the class-conscious circles of Cuban high society. He had recently fled from Spain back to Cuba, though, after having been threatened with a whipping by the father of a young girl he was courting, and now he saw an appealing prospect in Rosa Culmell—not only because she herself was attracted to him, but because her wealthy family would be able to support him in grand style. Rosa's family actually forbade the union at first, but Rosa succeeded in bringing Joaquín into the house for singing lessons, and after a year's courtship and preparation, they gave a concert together in 1902 and married shortly thereafter. They then traveled to Europe, where her family supported them while they gave the concerts and lessons that launched Joaquín's career.

Her family may have helped launch her husband's career, but when Rosa gave birth to Anaïs, their first child—born in February of 1903—he refused to be bound to his family. On tour, Anaïs would write that her father was always "pampered by women," and this made Rosa jealous, but if he was "a prince, wonderfully courteous" in public, Anaïs described him as "crude, very different" in private, and he complained about his daughter's fussiness and bad health. When her brothers were born—Thorvald in 1905 in Havana and Joaquín in 1908 in Berlin—all three children felt their father's disapproval in the form of beatings. If Rosa objected to Joaquín's criticisms of her—or his overtures toward her sister Juana, among other women—he would lock the children up while he beat her, or else he would lock her up while he beat the children, torturing her with their cries.

Later in life, Nin herself described the beatings as occasions for sexual abuse, although her accounts are uncertain. After a journal entry that described a sex act with her father in graphic detail, she wrote: "I believe this really happened. I do not believe my father penetrated me sexually but I believe he caressed me while or instead of beating me." While she herself does not confirm that she was sexually abused, evidence from her journals and novels, as well as from her actions, has led her biographers to speculate that she probably was. Whether or not he had sex with his daughter, Anaïs recalled that her father always treated her as an ugly child, although he sought her out with his camera nonetheless, photographing her nude in her bath. Joaquín photographed all of his children in the nude—he believed in the beauty of the human form—but when Anaïs tried to figure out what pleased her father, her nudity was what distinguished his affection from his disapproval, and later in life she wrote that "he always wanted me naked. All admiration came by way of the camera." The rest of the time, her father was critical and harsh. "My father did not want a girl," she wrote in her journal. "He said I was ugly. When I wrote or drew something, he did not believe it was my work. I never remember a caress or a compliment from him, except when I nearly died at the age of nine. There were always scenes, beatings, his hard blue eyes on me."

If the combination of beatings and sexual attention were not disturbing enough, Nin was devastated in 1914 when her father abandoned the family to court a wealthy student, Maruca Rodriguez, who was only six years older than Anaïs herself. Anaïs could not be convinced that she was not responsible for her father's departure, and for a long time, she believed that some actions or virtues of hers could convince him to return. But she was terrified of further abandonments, and her mother recalled her sobbing inconsolably each time her mother or grandparents left the house on errands, certain they would not return.

When Rosa's father had died in 1906, the executors of his estate had determined that she and her husband had already received more than a fair share of the estate, so when Joaquín abandoned her for Maruca, she could not go home to her family: she took the children to live with her husband's parents in Spain instead. The move did nothing to reconcile them—Joaquín did not write to Rosa with anything but demands about how she should raise the children—but he did write tender notes to Anaïs, urging her to cultivate an artistic sensibility and an appreciation for fine things. Anaïs and her mother and brothers may have been living in Spain with his family, and she may have been speaking Spanish in her daily life, but her father asked her to write to him in French—which was the language he used in his musical career—so Anaïs began a journal in her own phonetic French, and for a long time, she identified with all things French in loyalty to her father.

Just months before the Great War broke out, Rosa took Anaïs and her brothers back to New York to stay with her sister, Anaïs' aunt Edelmira, and another sister, Anaïs' aunt Antolina, gave Rosa money to buy a building. By this time, Anaïs had grown up in a number of European cities—the family had moved to Berlin in 1905, Brussels in 1909, then Spain and now America in 1914—and her education had been irregular, but as a European in New York, she was different from the American students, and she capitalized on her exoticism: she adopted dramatic costumes, which she said in her journal "created a void between me and other people." But Nin was a wayward student who did not like school or the discipline of academic work. She preferred her own view of things: in school, she said, "I learn things that I don't want to learn, and sometimes I am afraid of losing entirely the delicate and exquisite mental picture that I have of the beauty of things around me." This mental picture resided primarily in her journal, where she recorded everything that happened to her, in addition to trying out different aspects of her personality: throughout her teens, she described herself as alternatively the jilted lover and the self-sacrificing mother, and also as the dutiful wife, the devoted daughter, the seductive mistress, the rebellious iconoclast, and the independent modern woman.

In New York, Rosa gave some concerts, but her singing was not good enough to support her, and she ended up renting rooms in her house to musicians, so that Nin grew up surrounded by artists, and with Rosa's sisters nearby, she was filled with stories of wealthy relations as well. Rosa made some money as a purchasing agent for her sisters and then other wealthy Cuban families: she would send down the latest New York fashions and take a 10 percent commission. In 1919, when Nin was sixteen, her father finally demanded a divorce, though, and at the same time, the Cuban sugar industry collapsed, wiping out Rosa's purchasing business. When Rosa began to struggle financially, Anaïs convinced her to let her drop out of school, and she helped her mother run the boardinghouse. She picked up additional money by modeling costumes and fashions for artists and illustrators, an occupation that let her "sit there hour after hour," she wrote, "so quietly, so still, I can dream, dream, dream and dream to my heart's content," but it also exposed her to artists' unseemly requests, to which she responded with virginal confusion. Anaïs was newly conscious of her appearance, though, and she began the lifelong practice of denying herself food—which turned her slender figure into evidence of her own will in an otherwise passive existence, although she also used the excuse of helping her mother reduce expenses.

Nin read widely during this time, but she only made half-hearted efforts to complete her proper schooling: she took classes at Columbia— not in literature, but in "Composition, Grammar, French and Boys." She was known as a fashionable flirt at local dances, and in 1919 she began a romantic correspondence with her cousin Eduardo Sanchez, whose father, a wealthy cattle breeder in Cuba, disdained his poor niece and succeeded in keeping her from his son. But in 1921, at a party in Forest Hills, she met Hugo Guiler, who had graduated from Columbia University after a strict childhood in Scotland. By the time he met Nin, Guiler had been working in the National City Bank of New York for two years: he told himself that he was putting "firm ground" under his poetic ambitions, although he seems to have enjoyed his work with the bank, managing accounts and eventually recruiting clients. Guiler and Nin began a correspondence and exchanged poems, and Guiler was the first one to say that "some day the world will recognize Anaïs Nin Guiler as one of its great women of all times."

Like Sanchez, Guiler's parents tried to prevent a union. Guiler came from wealthy Scots, whose family had worked in the sugar industry in Puerto Rico, and young Guiler had been raised with a combination of progressive ideas about art and individualism and what he called "terrible religious and moral oppression." He was raised in Puerto Rico until he was ten, and then he was put in a school in Scotland. Throughout his school years, he did not see his parents except every other year during leave, but now his parents opposed his pursuit of Nin—because she was poor but also because she was Catholic—and sent Guiler away from New York, but Guiler and Nin persisted and were engaged. In 1923, they were married in Cuba, in a ceremony attended by Nin's aunts but not by either of their parents. As a result, Guiler was cut off from his family—he would eventually be disinherited—but he also became the patriarch and provider for Nin and her struggling mother and brothers.

Nin and Guiler were both repressed and ignorant in sexual matters, and Nin wrote that they did not consummate the marriage immediately. She wrote in her journal that she believed that "Hugo controls and forces back much that is impulsive in him," but this may have been part of his appeal for her, for he promised not to assail her sexually. Nin herself was no more forward, though. She had been kept from a knowledge of sexual matters herself and recorded her mother's stern disapproval when she had asked about the wetness in her bathing suit that resulted from Guiler's caresses. Now that they were married, Nin called the marriage an "incestual brother-sister" relationship.

Nin and Guiler did not start a family of their own, so Guiler immersed himself in his banking job, and Anaïs kept herself occupied with running the household. When Rosa and Nin's brothers fled to Paris to escape from Rosa's creditors in 1924, Nin and Guiler followed them, and Guiler took a post in the bank's Paris office in 1925. The franc had been greatly devalued since the Great War, so they all lived together comfortably on his salary, but Nin was ambitious for artistic experiences, so she was constantly overextending herself with luxuries, and she frequently had to borrow from her mother's allowance or sometimes even from the maid's pay. She decorated their apartments with candles and rare furniture and decor to make the house an atmosphere for poetry, sensual and exotic. Miller's friend Alfred Perlès would later describe Guiler and Nin's house as "warm mahogany panellings, stained-glass windows as in Granada, Moorish lanterns, low couches with silk cushions, inlaid tables, mosaic patterns in stone and glass, Turkish coffee on hammered copper trays, bittersweet Spanish liqueurs. In a darkened corner, incense was burning." Nin's artistic designs paradoxically profited Guiler's career, since his clients appreciated his wife's refined tastes and thoughtfulness, but as his career took off, the bank kept Guiler from developing as an artist, and Nin ultimately complained in her journal that "our whole life is spoiled by his work in the bank."

Nin was cultivating her own arts in addition to decorating her house. During a visit from Guiler's college literature professor, John Erskine, Nin met Hélène Boussinescq, Sherwood Anderson's French translator, who was teaching American literature in a lycée, and Erskine and Boussie, as she was called, awakened Nin to modern literature. She began to read widely in Surrealist literature as well as in sensual French literature, trying to determine why sex was making her marriage so miserable. After the stock market crash of 1929, she economized by staying home, researching and writing a short volume of criticism focused on sex in D. H. Lawrence's novels. When it was eventually published, *D. H. Lawrence: An Unprofessional Study* so scandalized her mother and brother that they moved out of the house they had been sharing with her and Guiler.

Now that Nin was doing her research, she was more open to sexual experimentation, and she began to flirt widely. When she took dancing lessons, she aroused the passions of her instructor as well as one of the musicians, and as she was trying to publish her manuscript, she allowed a publisher's assistant, Lawrence Drake, to rub himself to climax between her legs. She began to test the uses of betrayal as well, and after some inconclusive gropings with Erskine—her husband's revered professor, who was twenty years older than her—she made a breakthrough discovery in October of 1931, when she confessed the encounter to her husband: Guiler was devastated, but his jealousy stirred a passion that vaulted them over the delicate sensibilities that had inhibited them in the beginning. Nin had learned to use jealousy to incite men's passions—she was starting to learn, like June, to elevate lovers' passions by playing one lover against the other. She was still aloof, though, and—again like June—she refused to give herself completely to any one man, even her husband.

IV.

Nin may have played June against Miller and Miller against her husband to gain their erotic attention, but after Nin and Miller discovered each other through their writings, sex was no longer simply a physical need: now it was a form of rebellious intimacy, and sexual infidelity became an act by which she and Miller devoted themselves to each other's writing

and their careers. Inspired by Miller's uninhibited sex life, Nin was lib-
erating herself at a time when Freud's theories about sex and repression
made erotic freedom seem like the last frontier in a deadening, dehu-
manizing, mechanized world: the times were defined by the carnage of
the Great War, the explosion of industrialism, and the new ubiquity of
machines, so it was easy to see the emotional intimacy attained through
sex as the last human experience in a dying culture. Rebelling against the
mechanization of the world—as much as against the complacency and the
hypocrisy of the bourgeoisie—Miller and Nin saw marriage as an obsolete
and absurd commitment, which only distracted people from their true
obligation: to know and express themselves, and to live out their lives—
specifically their contradictory urges—in spite of society's restrictions.
United in this common purpose, Miller and Nin fell into something more
than love: they shared a subversive-sacred mission against the world.

Starting in April 1932, Miller and Nin embarked on their rebellion
with gusto. They were turning their love into literature and new life—
they were "fecundating" the world, as they put it, and Nin used her hus-
band's money to give Miller everything he needed to work on his writ-
ing. As she described it in her journal, she felt "the perfect, inhuman,
divine *objectivity*. Later I gave love: do what you will—use me. I love you. I
want to serve you, aliment you. Henry used my love well, beautifully. He
erected books with it." The tension of her several love affairs—first the
flirtation with June, then the more serious affair with Miller, and then
the renewed attention she gave to her husband, and then to other lov-
ers—made Nin's writing incandescent as well, and she translated her sex
life into an unprecedentedly frank confessional literature in her journal.

Nin recognized that she was defying all of society's laws, but she was
venturing into her own nature as a sexual creature, and she was discover-
ing for herself the laws that governed love and writing, sex and psychol-
ogy. She was finding the detachment of the writer, the self-reliance of the
poet, and a Nietzschean self-overcoming—all of which together allowed
her to endure even the most degrading experiences. She was discovering
that as long as she recorded the truth of her experiences, she was fulfill-
ing a higher obligation to her own self-fulfillment. When she shared her
writing with Miller, he saw faithfulness to literature behind her infidelity
to her husband—and even behind her infidelity to him—and he encour-
aged her to revenge herself against the life that had limited her, injured
her, divorced her from herself in her years of repression.

When June came back to Paris in October 1932, Miller and Nin had been spending days and nights in literary conversation and lovemaking, and they were tasting a love that could be deeply supportive at the same time that they encouraged each other to rebel against convention: now they both had a healthy distrust of June's chaotic stories and doubtful promises. By this time, June's health had deteriorated—probably due to drug use—although now that Miller felt love for Nin, and now that he was enjoying Nin's financial support, he was more patient with June's manipulations, and he endured them without reacting the way he used to, with torments and jealousies. According to Nin, June finally appeared to him as "a pathological child—interesting as such, but stupid and empty."

Nin was exasperated by June this time as well, but now she was also threatened by June's effect on Miller, for Miller seemed to waver in spite of his new affection for Nin. To win Miller back, Nin showed him her "June" journal, offering him her feminine insights into June's power, allying herself with him against June. June sensed their alliance, and one night after some hard drinking, Nin's "beautiful voyage ended" when she saw June "inert on the floor, rolling in her vomit." June left Paris in January of 1933 after repudiating all of Nin's gifts. She left them in a bundle, bound by a love letter Nin had written her, along with a final note for Henry: "please get a divorce immediately."

June's departure left Miller and Nin alone together in a rapture. Nin wrote in her journal,

> Last night Henry and I got married. By that I mean a particular ceremony which binds two persons until they get a divorce! I let him read most of my journal (even half of what relates to June's kisses, etc.). It was an earthquake to both. He revealed the most gentle, warm tolerance, he *exonerated* me of all things.

Married more by sharing their confessions than by their "deft, acute core-reaching fucking," they were bound by what Nin called "the evolution . . . the new needs" that had brought them together. They were living at what Nin called "white heat," eating and drinking and fucking together, helping each other turn their lives and their love affair into a new kind of literature, a living art that forgave every guilt so long as experience could be clarified into writing.

In their letters and conversations, they surrounded their affair with all the significance of high literature and they traced out a broad array of literary associations, so they were aware of a large audience in their bedrooms. If they knew that Rabelais, Emerson, Nietzsche, Proust, Freud, Unamuno, and Lawrence would appreciate the liberty and vivacity of what they were doing, though, they were constantly afraid that Guiler would discover them and bring the affair and her marriage to an end. Nin courted the catastrophe nevertheless, and when Guiler told her that "his instinct assures him there is nothing between Henry and me," she slept with a passionate letter from Henry beneath her pillow. Guiler did not find the letter, but Nin acknowledged in her journal that "this diary proves a tremendous, all-engulfing craving for truth, since to write it I risk destroying all the edifices of my illusions, all the gifts I made, all that I created, Hugo's life, Henry's life; everyone whom I saved from truth, I here destroy."

Guiler never did catch them, but there is evidence that he knew about the affair nonetheless. After one close call, he began to tell Nin the exact time when he would come home. Nin still made efforts to protect herself—and Guiler—from the smash-up: she lied to him when he read her open journal, and he seemed to buy her stories about a separate journal for fictional experiences—and he accepted her lies as well when he confronted her about bills that had not been paid, when the money had gone to Miller.

Protected by Nin's lies and Guiler's blindness—or complicity—Miller and Nin spent 1932 and 1933 in a comfortable routine of writing and editing, lovemaking and long conversations. Their crime against Guiler only made them feel justified in following the laws of their inhuman, writerly natures into their writing. "There is in our relationship both humanness and monstrosity," Nin wrote.

> Our work, our literary imagination, is monstrous. Our love is human. I sense when he is cold, I am anxious about his eyesight. I get him glasses, a special lamp, blankets. But when we talk and write, a wonderful deformation takes place, whereby we heighten, exaggerate, color, distend. There are satanic joys known to writers only. His muscular style and my enameled one wrestle and copulate independently. But when I touch him, the human miracle is accomplished. He is the man I would scrub floors for.

In spite of the fact that she refused to leave her marriage, Nin was faithful to Miller as a patron. She drew as much as she could from her household finances, and she skimped on her own needs to give him everything he needed—wine, cigarettes, paper, books, phonographs, and then an apartment—and now he relaxed into the comfortable position of the writer with rich material to work on, and time and security to write.

While Nin worked on her journals, as well as a novel about June, Miller finished *Tropic of Cancer* in the summer of 1932, and then he began a similarly outrageous, semiautobiographical sequel, *Tropic of Capricorn*, as well as a book of biographical reflections called *Black Spring*. When a publisher suggested that he write something literary, to distinguish himself from the pornographers, Miller threw himself into researching and then writing a book about D. H. Lawrence as well. By April of 1933, after a year of Nin's love, support, editing, and encouragement, Miller had "enough work in preparation, in hand, that is, to last me three full years at least. I am working simultaneously on four books—because a vein has opened in me and I must exhaust it."

V.

Miller enjoyed his new peaceful and productive lifestyle so well that by the end of 1933, he began to dream about living with Nin as something like husband and wife, without Hugo and the bank in the background. But Nin could not imagine that future so easily. She began to suspect that she might always need sexual experiences beyond any one lover. "I love the groove in which my love for Henry has been running," she wrote in her journal. "Yet I am driven by diabolical forces outside of all grooves." Now that Miller had released her from her repression, she began to take other lovers. Her cousin Eduardo Sanchez came back into her life, and even though he had acknowledged his homosexuality, she took him as a lover, and when he convinced her to enter psychoanalysis, it was not long before she seduced her therapist, René Allendy, and then she tried to seduce the homosexual French writer Antonin Artaud, half to punish the other men in her life, with the intimacy, half out of sympathy for his sensitive artistic vision. In her journal she wrote that she was "always *between* two desires, always in conflict," and throughout 1932 and into 1933, she juggled love affairs. "To each one," she wrote in her journal, "I say, 'You are the favorite.'"

This juggling act began to take its toll on Nin's peace of mind, though, and she wrote in her journal that she "had counted on the ease with which I would distribute my body. But it is not true. It was never true. When I rushed towards Henry, it was all Henry . . . I should break up my whole life, and I cannot do it." When Miller talked about actually getting married, though, she wrote that "this talk about our marriage was incredible to me. At this point my imagination stops. I do not want to face the problem," but the financial problem—namely that Guiler was providing a level of financial support that Miller could not provide—"was only half the problem, I have my *human* problem, an insolvable one which Henry understands . . . I cannot abandon Hugh . . . like [Miller], I wait for the other to do something."

In almost all of their letters, Nin said that she could not leave Guiler because Miller did not have any money, and could not support her, but when we consider Guiler's willingness to ignore her affairs, we have to wonder whether Nin really only intuited that Miller would not have let her have the same freedom. But if Nin was juggling lovers, she nonetheless imposed a strict morality on her actions in order to protect Guiler: she refused to make him suffer. She had been burdened by the memory of him sobbing uncontrollably at his father's funeral in 1928—when he found out that his father had in fact disinherited him—and she did not have the courage to hurt him again: "I am afraid of my freedom," she confided to her journal.

> Hugo is the man I owe my life to. I owe him everything beautiful I have had; his devotion has been my stepping stone to *all* I have today . . . he has been my one true bountiful god. I am eternally indebted to him—to his touching and magnificent faithfulness. I could only be liberated if he were cruel, hard, mean—but now I have no justification whatsoever. He is the greatest man in the world, the man alone capable of *love* and *generosity*. *Il est facile pour les autres à donner.*

In spite of secondary or tertiary affairs, Nin oscillated primarily between Guiler and Miller. She acknowledged in her journal that she was "happy . . . to have found Henry, a genius to serve, to worship. Someone big enough to *use* my strength, to subject it to his complements. God, God, *marriage*-marriage, a *fecund* marriage. There is no fecundity in my marriage with Hugo. We *create* nothing." But when Henry proposed confessing their affair to Hugo, Nin recalls having told him: "one more word on this subject and I will walk out and you will never see me again."

When Nin realized that she did not have the courage to break up her marriage—even though she admitted that Miller fulfilled her in ways her husband could not—she turned her disloyalty to her own feelings against herself and then against life, and she wrote in disgust that "reality deserves to be described in the vilest terms." She kept an audacious account of her betrayals:

> I am playing tricks not on men but on life, which does not answer what I have demanded of it, and so I accept this juggling and my treacherous handling of life—it is life I bear a grudge against, for its absence of perfection, of completeness, of absolution. I will live my lies bravely and ironically, and dually, triply. In that way alone can I exhaust the love I contain.

By writing out the truth of her several affairs, she used writing as a way to "wound the world which has wounded both of us [herself and Miller]." While Miller was happily turning his conflict with the world into outrageous writing that was critical of society, Nin had kept her self-criticisms private in her journal, where the contradictions that surrounded her rebellious affairs would remain intact: "God, I hate myself," she wrote— but in the next sentence, "And yet I am happy, healthy."

While Nin was privately tormenting herself over her infidelities, Miller still saw her as a supportive patron, a brave lover, and a daring writer, and by 1934, he was beginning to love her in earnest, beyond his rebelliousness and the outrageousness of their affairs. Some loyalty to her person was beginning to eclipse his loyalty to the idea of her sexual freedom, and he started to imagine a time when their affairs would end and they could be together full-time. They had always spoken of their relationship in terms of a diabolical marriage, but now Miller started to want to make an honest marriage with Nin, and he urged her to make a clean break. "Listen, Anaïs," he told her. "If things go smash, let them go smash. Don't try to patch them up. Don't worry about me . . . we'll manage somehow."

Nin had always refused to break with Guiler, but she left Miller a sliver of hope nonetheless: she had refused to consider a future with Miller for as long as he still relied on handouts from Guiler's salary—but now she allowed him to believe that if he published his books and made some money, they might have a future without Guiler. Having finished *Tropic of Cancer* in July of 1932, Miller threw himself into his other manuscripts, believing that he was making real strides toward his future marriage.

As early as the end of 1932, others beyond Nin began to see Miller's genius. He was picked up by literary agent William Bradley—whom author Janet Flanner called the "leading agent and prophet . . . on trans-atlantic affairs"—and when Bradley passed *Tropic of Cancer* to Obelisk Press, publisher Jack Kahane found it "the most terrible, the most sordid, the most magnificent manuscript that had ever fallen into my hands; nothing I had yet received was comparable to it for the splendour of its writing, the fathomless depth of its despair, the savour of its portraiture, the boisterousness of its humor." There were problems with publishing *Tropic of Cancer*, though: the mid-1930s were not a good time for pub-lishing controversial literature, since Europe was suffering through the Great Depression and there was already talk of a new war with Ger-many. When Kahane—who published primarily erotica and books that had been banned for obscenity—asked Miller to write the "brochure" on D. H. Lawrence, the Lawrence book began to swell beyond control almost from the beginning, and even though Miller was working harder and more productively than ever, the future with Nin remained out of reach.

As Nin bought Miller writing time with her allowance and household monies, as Miller threw himself into the Lawrence brochure, and as he did his part to get recognized and published, Nin wrote that the prospect of normalizing her relationship with Miller was a great and dreaded test: "to follow Henry would mean exposure to the *greatest pain* and my great-est *fear!* Every time I think of this I shake with terror, in the most abject cowardice." She wrote in her journal that she "lacked the courage" to tell even Allendy, the least important of her lovers, that their relationship was over. When she met Allendy at a hotel to break with him, he did not suspect that anything was amiss—he himself had shown up with a whip to humiliate Nin sexually, and instead of saying anything when he brandished it, she allowed him to use the whip in their lovemaking: she could not help "remembering that he exposed himself, his secrets, his flesh, his doubts, his fears, to me, and I cannot hurt him."

"Your only defect," Miller told her later, "is your incapacity for cruelty." Nin could not tell her lovers the truth, so she invented lies to protect herself—and her lovers—trying to give them each what they needed. As her affairs continued, she could only conclude in her journal that she must be "wreaking a kind of revenge upon men . . . I am impelled by a satanic force to win and abandon them . . . Life, or my own ingenuity, provides me with beautiful justifications." But Miller was still cultivating his own satanic forces in his writing—and using the language of satanic forces to describe their affair—so Nin was not only free but encouraged in perpetuating her numerous relationships.

VI.

Having flirted with June, and having then seduced Miller, Sanchez, Allendy, and Artaud—having failed to create a future in any of these relationships, Nin turned away from all of her affairs and sought out her father in the spring of 1933. She had been estranged from him ever since he abandoned the family in 1914, when she was eleven, but now she told some musicians he knew that she might like to see him again. Joaquín had married Maruca Rodriguez and continued to give concerts that were well received, and he was still as outwardly "wonderfully courteous"—and skilled at using a woman's attention to his advantage—so he sent what Anaïs called a "beautiful, tender" letter. She told him in response that

> when your letter came, it seemed to me that suddenly I was rewarded for all the art and the ingenuity that I have put into loving all my life long. It is sweet to receive . . . something that comes with so much subtlety, so much tenderness, with a thoughtfulness that enfolds one so skillfully, a quality uniquely yours.

Buoyed by the diabolical freedom and self-confidence Miller had inspired in her, she accepted her father's invitation to meet in May 1933, and then to vacation with him in Chamonix in June.

Anaïs was thirty when they reunited—her father was fifty-four years old—and she wrote that he appeared "looking fresh, immaculate, dressed with an ultimate, subtle elegance." Having followed her father's orders— having become sensitive and sensual, exotic, refined, and mysterious, she had become his ideal woman, and when he lavished his attention on her, she felt that she had been finally repaid for all the attention she had given Miller and her other lovers. Almost as soon as she arrived in Chamonix, she and her father seduced each other, and made love again and again, in spite of her father's lumbago.

Immediately after the visit, she wrote in her journal, "I say, let us fuck our parents and thereby rid ourselves of them. Fucking shadows of them accomplishes nothing." Miller encouraged her as well: "*love*—and keep your shirt on! Let your father devour you. It will give him dyspepsia." She wrote in her journal that she "had wanted at least my incestuous love to remain unwritten. I had promised Father utter secrecy," but she could not resist betraying him in the journal, by writing down long, explicit accounts of their lovemaking, including the requests her father made of her, her movements when she fulfilled them, the laughter they shared in their delicious complicity, and even the abundance of his sperm.

After her time with her father, Nin vacationed with Miller in Avignon, but Joaquín's attentive seductions made her see her relationship with Miller in a harsher light. After her father's refined seductions, she wanted "the love I deserve. Nothing less," and she was "weary to death of giving, emptying myself." She was critical of Miller's self-contentment, and she complained in her journal, "He is always wanting me because I make him happy, wanting me because of what I give—not what I am." But now she lamented,

I'm hellishly lonely. What I need is someone who could give me what I give Henry: this constant attentiveness. I read every page he writes, I follow up his reading . . . I am ready at any moment to give up anybody for him, I follow his thoughts, enter into his plans—passionate, maternal, intellectual watchfulness.

He. He cannot do this. Nobody can. Nobody knows *how*. It's an art, a gift . . . I get lonely, and I have to turn to my journal to give myself the kind of response I need. I have to nourish myself. I get love, but love is not enough. People don't know *how* to love.

When Miller heard Nin say that she felt lonely, he offered to break things up and live with her, but she still refused to entrust herself to him. Using the excuse that he was selfish and that he could not support her, she distanced herself, although she did not break with him, and she did not interrupt the flow of money and support.

VII.

Nin met her father again in August of 1933 in the south of France, and in November, he came to Paris with his wife. In her home, she recognized her father's weak, fussy, and angry personality for what it was, and she began to see that her writing and her lovers had given her a richer world than she had originally lost. Never having been able to break with any of her lovers, she broke cleanly with her father. "Father . . . is not whole enough to suffer," she wrote in her journal—and she claimed to be free from any consequences of violating the incest taboo: she wrote in her journal, "if I am perverse, monstrous in certain eyes, *tant pis*. All I care about is my own judgment. I am what I am."

A certain guilt was pressing inside her, nonetheless, and in July of 1933, she said that she wanted "to go to Rank and get absolution for my passion for my Father." Otto Rank was a psychoanalyst she and Guiler had met through Allendy—he had been trained by Freud before he and Freud parted ways in 1926, but Rank was one of the few psychoanalysts who saw creativity as something more than a product of childhood sexual trauma. "Unlike the other psychoanalysts," Miller wrote to his friend Emil Schnellock, "[Rank] is almost entirely interested in the 'artist.'" Nin was particularly drawn to Rank's book *Don Juan and His Double*, which articulated a theory of "incestuous" love, in which one essentially seeks himself in the other. Nin and Miller had both enthused about his *Art and Artist*, which reinforced their sense that artists were alone at the forefront of society, expressing the dreams and fears for their people.

When they first met, Rank saw that Nin's journal was a "defense against analysis," and he took it from her, but then he asked her to take the additional step of breaking from her routine by living alone in a hotel for as long as they were working together on her analysis. Nin handed over her journal, but she began to write on fugitive scraps of paper almost immediately, and when she moved into the hotel, she booked an extra room for Miller, who worked beside her there for the months she spent working with Rank.

As the pressure to publish Miller's work and live with him openly got heavier—and as the guilty aftermath of her affair with her father weighed on her conscience—Nin ultimately seduced even Rank. Rank told Nin that he had "'denied myself life before, or it was denied me—first by my parents, then Freud, then my wife.' His entrance into life," Nin wrote, "is a beautiful spectacle." Soon Nin's new "intellectual giant" was speechless as he was swept away in their gigantic embraces: "all our joy is in lying body to body," she wrote in her journal. "We don't want letters, talks, ideas. We have nothing to create together. His creation is accomplished. He wants to live." Head over heels in love with her, Rank began, she wrote, "destroying his own creation (undermining psychoanalysis, from which he lives)." She attended his lectures, and she wrote that he "talks in the school for me, not for the others, and this talk is disruptive and baffling to the others." Bound so closely with her analyst, Nin began to work toward certification in psychoanalysis—which justified her spending more and more time with Rank—but she was still averse to coursework, and she dropped out of his course at the Cité Universitaire without completing the six-week program.

The affair with Rank did not help Nin clarify her other affairs. He had become, she said, "a stirring lover," although she did make the "mysterious expression of faithfulness [to Miller], to withhold the orgasm, as the whores do." Nin had been growing more distant from Miller, but she was determined not to hurt him. "I must get Henry's book published," she wrote in her journal. "I must do that for him. I must enthrone him securely before I abandon him." But if Jack Kahane was still confident of book's value, he was still also realistic about its prospects: *Tropic of Cancer* was almost certain to be banned, and in the whirlwind of Miller's reading and note-taking, the brochure on Lawrence was threatening to spiral out of control into a huge, four-volume criticism of modern literature. Kahane refused to publish *Tropic of Cancer* unless Nin paid the printing costs—and Nin said that Guiler would not pay for his "enemy's" work to be published—so Nin borrowed the first 5,000 francs from Rank and paid Kahane to publish *Tropic of Cancer*.

Nin's abandonment of Miller was complicated, in April of 1934, when she became pregnant with what she believed was Miller's child. Miller urged her to have the child and break up her marriage to live with him—in poverty if necessary, but in love—but Nin visited a *sage-femme* to procure an abortion. She wrote in her journal, "I killed the child . . . Not to be abandoned . . . I love man as lover and creator. Man as father I do not trust . . . With [man the lover and creator] I feel an alliance. In man the father I feel an enemy, a danger." The potions the midwife gave her were ineffective, though, and she carried the child until November, when it could only be aborted by inducing labor.

In the hospital, Nin was visited by Miller, Rank, and Guiler in turn, and by the time Nin was recovering, *Tropic of Cancer* was just coming back from the printer. When Miller brought her a bound copy of the book, she wrote in her journal, "Here is a birth which is of greater interest to me." Nin and Miller had collaborated on the preface, but it ran above her name, so that the book would announce her as well. "Here is a book," it read, which, if such a thing were possible, might restore our appetite for the fundamental realities. The predominant note will seem one of bitterness, and bitterness there is, to the full. But there is also a wild extravagance, a mad gaiety, a verve, a gusto, at times almost a delirium. A continual oscillation between extremes, with bare expanses that taste like brass and leave the full flavor of emptiness. It is beyond optimism or pessimism. The author has given us the last *frisson*. Pain has no more secret recesses.

Response to the book was positive—enough to soften the book's being immediately banned in Britain and America. French writer Blaise Cendrars announced the book in an article titled "An American Writer Is Born to Us," and Miller was recognized by established writers—T. S. Eliot, Ezra Pound, Jean Cocteau, and Aldous Huxley, among others—but because of the ban, the book did not sell enough copies to change his financial situation: he was still broke, still dependent on handouts from Nin and whatever other patrons he could find.

While *Tropic of Cancer* had been getting closer to publication—and even in spite of her affairs with Rank and with her father, and in spite of her determination to abandon Miller—Nin had still been making plans for a life with Miller. In August of 1934, after the publication timeline had been drawn up, but before the abortion, Nin had started to pay the rent for a studio at 18 Villa Seurat, where Miller could work and where he expected her to join him after the book came out. Miller and Nin had delighted in furnishing it as if it would be their home, but when it was clear that the book would not make him any real money, the breakup never came, and she never moved in with him.

Nevertheless, Nin would continue to pay the rent for Miller until he left Europe in 1939. At Villa Seurat, Miller was surrounded by a group whom Perlès described as "cranks, nuts, drunks, writers, artists, bums, Montparnasse derelicts, vagabonds, psychopaths." Nin devoted herself to making a comfortable place in the studio, but she was not settling down. Now, in addition to Rank and Miller, she took new lovers—one named Harry Harvey and another named Louis Andard, in addition to one of Guiler's colleagues, George Turner, whom she "fuck[ed] in the elevator." Her lies were getting deeper, and jealousies were rising between Miller, Rank, and Guiler. With no escape, Nin wrote angry outbursts to Miller:

This morning Hugo gave me 200 frs. to get underwear and stock-
ings. I bring them to you. Meanwhile you give Lowenfels the checks
you get, the first checks you got. Never occurred to you to think
of me. No. Never thought you might get me something—that you
might do something with it for me. I'm very *tired*. If I go to N.Y.
it's with a desperate idea of doing *anything*, anything to get out of
my ever narrowing financial life. I beg you not to have that book
bound—that's a luxury. There are other things I really need, like a
coat. You have done this a hundred times. Will always do it. Always.
I'm so tired of your lack of everything thoughtful, wise about you.
You act like a child, a child that just asks and asks and asks and
never thinks and sucks one to death, and I'm sitting here crying
because it's so hopeless to ever expect you to be otherwise. Don't
bind a book for me. Don't make empty gestures. I want plain things,
warm things.

Instead of sympathizing or extending himself toward her—he still felt
that Nin had given him money to foster his personal freedom—Miller
only defended himself against her accusations:

If it's to be a choice between doing work one doesn't believe in and
sleeping on people's floors, I choose the latter. I wouldn't mind
doing menial work, not connected with writing, if I were obliged to,
but after all the struggle to preserve integrity—not only on my part,
but on yours—I would consider myself a traitor to act otherwise.

If Nin held Miller's prolonged poverty against him, she did not break
with him. She remained in her marriage, she continued her affairs, and
she continued to document her affairs in her journal. In what time she
had left, she read Miller's work, and she struggled to turn her journal
into novels that could be published without revealing too much of her
own life and affairs—and without embarrassing Guiler. But the novels
were never convincing—her language was highly irregular on account of
her unconventional education—and Nin remained unpublished even as
Miller's career began to take off. Now Nin was the one who was waiting
to start a new life after her books were finally published.

VIII.

While Miller was beginning to get noticed at the end of 1934, Nin was beginning to feel more and more trapped by the stories she had been telling in order to make time for each of her lovers, and as her lies began to close in on her, she started to look for a way to escape from Paris. When Rank accepted a new position in New York, she accepted his invitation to work as his secretary and assistant.

When she sailed with Rank in December of 1934, though, she told Miller that she was going with her husband, not Rank, and when Miller finally realized that she had lied to him, he was torn apart with a jealousy none of her other affairs had inspired. With a long delay between letters, he panicked, and in his panic, he declared his love with a new urgency. "Your body burns in me," he wrote,

> and I want it uniquely, for myself alone. That is the mistake I made— to share you. That made the woman less, I fear. Now it's got to be you altogether, seven days in the week, and voyages included . . . If you think I've become a Puritan, think so. I don't care. I won't share you! You're mine and I'm going to keep you. I have become fiercely possessive.

Miller sent Nin a torrent of tortured, reflective letters, and when he saw that he had already become a bigger person—more loving, more trusting, and less willing to endure the torments of jealousy—when he found that he was willing to credit his human existence and feelings—he attributed the change to Nin, and he wrote long, impassioned letters that repudiated the sexual bravado they had encouraged in each other.

With the distance between them, Nin was never more than cryptic in her responses, but by the time Miller raised the fare and sailed to New York in January—at almost the same time as Guiler—there was no real change from how things had been in Paris: she installed him in one hotel, and Guiler in another, and carried on her affairs, with promises but no new commitments. If anything changed, it was only that Nin showed a new recklessness, and biographer Deirdre Bair describes Nin's affairs with "half a dozen men" who were business clients of Hugo's. Rank had given her patients to work with, and biographer Deirdre Bair adds that Nin even took one of her patients on the couch with Rank in the next room: "pulling down everything sacred, desecrating, cheapening," she wrote in her journal.

By the spring of 1935, her passion for Rank had subsided, and Nin returned to Paris—with Guiler and Miller both in tow—and resumed the role of wife to both men. Nothing had changed, though, and even though Miller was being celebrated as a promising new writer, he was still up against the same eternal problem: his book was banned, and his career was still effectively unbegun. He had intended the book to be so offensive that he should at least be lynched, and he was disappointed when he had to keep confronting the problem of making a living that left time for writing. He had met e. e. cummings, William Carlos Williams, William Saroyan, and Nathanael West in New York, but a few American booksellers served time in jail for having sold the books, and Miller's name was still only traded in literary circles: the books had not made the conflagration he had hoped for.

With his masterpiece banned for obscenity, and with two other obscene books under way—*Black Spring* and *Tropic of Capricorn* would both be banned as well—Miller turned forty-four years old in 1935, feeling both that he had done his life's work and that he had done nothing. After all the efforts Nin had made publishing and publicizing Miller's work, his lack of success strained their relationship. In her journal, Nin still frequently acknowledged Miller as her true husband, and she continued to support him, but she still refused to leave Guiler until they had made some money as writers. Miller suggested subtly that "you must admit that there have been other reasons besides the financial one for your hesitancy," but the financial reason was reason enough, and they continued as illicit lovers with dreams of a shared literary future.

In the present, Miller and his friends at Villa Seurat hatched one idea after another for getting published, but like his schemes with June, his projects bogged down in disorganized details, and never came to anything. The projects all involved writing, though, and these produced some small pieces that Miller eventually collected and published as *Max and the White Phagocytes*. One such piece was a portrait of Nin, "Un Etre Etoilique," or "A Starry Being," which Miller published in an attempt to publicize her writing. Instead of the diabolical artist, though, whose work exposed the decay of her society, Miller described her work as the integration of art and life. He wrote that she had almost completely effaced herself in the effort to arrive at a true understanding of life. It is in this sense again that the human document rivals the work of art, or in times such as these, *replaces* the work of art. For, in a profound sense, this *is* the work of art which never gets written—because the artist whose task it is to create it never gets born. We have here, instead of the consciously or technically finished work (which today seems to us more than ever empty and illusory), the unfinished symphony which achieves consummation because each line is pregnant with a soul struggle.

Nin's work had only been collecting rejections—her language was unconventional and strained, and her imagery was dreamy and hard to follow—but Miller defended her by saying that "her language . . . is a violation of language that corresponds with the violation of thought and feeling. It could not have been written in an English which every capable writer can employ." In spite of Miller's editorial assistance and support, though, Nin continued to be rejected by publishers, and she herself remained sensitive to criticism, and her writing would always be marked by what she herself identified as "bad craft, spelling, foreign locutions, grammatical unevenness, extremes." With nothing but rejections from publishers, Nin resolved to publish her work herself, and she and Miller, along with Perlès and Frankel, began the Siana Press (named for Anaïs, whose money they used), to publish each other's work in the absence of commercial interest.

If Nin had determined to abandon Miller during her affair with her father and then with Rank, she nonetheless settled into another productive routine with him through 1935. They traveled to New York together in January 1936, for a one-month visit that turned into a three-month stay, and they both worked as analysts. Miller even began to have some success with patients, whom he treated with "a little of the juice of St. Augustine and a little of Emerson," but when Nin returned to Paris in April, he went with her, drawn along on the eternal promise that she would break up her marriage and live with him—and of course he was still carried on the stream of the financial support she continued to divert from Guiler's salary.

Nin never ceased to pay the rent at Villa Seurat, but in April 1936, she rented a houseboat on the Seine for herself as well, and in July, she started an affair with Gonzalo Moré, a tall, handsome Scottish-Peruvian

Communist in exile in Paris, who had trouble with alcohol and drugs, but he serenaded Nin on his guitar, and told her romantic stories of Peru. Miller and Moré knew about each other, and Moré's wife Helba knew about the affair as well: when she learned that Nin dreaded her husband's ever learning about her affairs, Helba began to milk her for money, for doctors' bills and medicines as well as for clothing, expenses, and even holidays. Nin bought a printing press, ostensibly for the purpose of publishing Moré's revolutionary tracts and posters for the American Communist Party, but as soon as she was proficient at typesetting, she and Moré worked together at printing her own books. In the absence of a press' publicity, though, the books rarely covered the cost of printing, but now Nin was getting herself into print nonetheless.

Even with a book out and new books in the works, Miller was still struggling to support himself. He would not take regular work while he was writing, and in addition to a vast correspondence, which he still believed might be published profitably, he wrote and distributed his first begging letter, *What Are You Going to Do About Alf?* (Alf being Alfred Per-lès). Miller would write a number of these letters over the next twenty years—although they too rarely brought in enough to cover the cost of printing and postage—but he had always tried to turn literature into a personal affair—not an art in its own right, but a form of communica-tion and trust between like-minded fellows—and these begging letters were still better than impersonal work in the marketplace. Patrons came through with enough support to keep him writing, and by the late 1930s, his horizons were finally beginning to expand. In September 1935, *Tropic of Cancer* entered its second printing, with blurbs by Ezra Pound, William Carlos Williams, and Aldous Huxley. Miller's fame failed to bring in any money, but it did continue to introduce him to other artists and writers, and he was compensated with the infamy of having written a banned book, which made him a cause and continued to bring him patrons.

In March of 1937, Miller met Lawrence Durrell, a British expatriate, living in Greece, who had written a perceptive letter to Miller, and Miller called him the "first anybody who's hit the nail on the head." Durrell recognized Nin's value as well: he said that "what she says is biologi-cally true—from the very navel string." The three became fast friends when Durrell came to Paris—they would refer to themselves as the Three Musketeers—and over the next years, they would try to publish each other's work through the Siana imprint, which Nin funded, and then through the Villa Seurat series, with funding from Durrell's wife. Neither series attracted any critical notice, but by 1938, journals in England and America were increasingly willing to publish Miller's shorter pieces, as well as some of Nin's. Miller convinced Kahane to publish Nin's *The House of Incest*—which had developed out of half the June novel—and the book had come out in 1936, but Nin's reviews were not as enthusiastic as Miller's. She had made strenuous efforts to publish excerpts from the journals, but publishers could never see a way to "shape the material into book form that could be published," in the words of one rejection letter. Nin's novels never enjoyed a wide circulation, and when she tried to publish her journal, the forward, naked nature of the material—as well as the threat of lawsuits from people whose names she had mentioned—prevented the unexpurgated journal from being published until after her death. Nevertheless, Nin continued to fill her journal with details of her three marriages—to Guiler, Miller, and Moré—as well as her passing encounters, and she was only more free to conduct them after Guiler was posted to London in 1937. Nin remained in Paris, with the weekdays to herself—Guiler would come on the weekends—splitting her time between Miller and Villa Seurat and her houseboat and Moré.

At the first sign of Germany's saber-rattling over the Sudetenland, Miller had bought a ticket to America, and while the crisis passed in 1936, in 1939, when war was imminent, he was quick to leave Europe for America, refusing to be drawn into any fighting, for any cause. He stored his belongings in Paris, gave up the Villa Seurat studio, and he wrote a will that left everything to Nin, before he traveled to Greece, to visit Durrell in Corfu. When Nin met him in Aix on his way to Greece, it was the last time they would see each other as lovers. When France and England declared war in September 1939, Nin flew to London, but now it was Gonzalo she pined for. "This is a dying love," she wrote about Miller. "The most alive thing in me today is the passion I have for Gonzalo so I must follow it."

IX.

In 1940, Miller left Greece when Americans were all ordered out of the country because of the war. When he returned to America, though, he was not looking for a new lover: he was still waiting for Nin to make a life with him. Riding around on a wave of hospitality, Miller made visits in New York, Virginia, and Washington, D.C., but when Nin and Guiler landed in New York in 1940, Nin did not seek him out. She established her own circuit between Provincetown, Woodstock, and New York City, where she was taken up by Dorothy Norman and others who introduced her around and tried to help her publish her work. Every press she contacted insisted that she bear the costs of printing herself, though, and when she met young writers and painters who were starting new literary journals, she offered them encouragement and financial support: her husband was still working at the bank, and he was still letting her use their money for any cause that might result in her being published.

Now that they were back in America—at age forty-nine and thirty-seven, respectively, Miller and Nin had both already done most of the work that would define them. They had already made the innovations that would define their styles, but they were willing to try new things if they could make money. Determined to write something that would not be censored, Miller drove across the country in August of 1940 to gather material for *The Air-Conditioned Nightmare* with a $500* advance from Doubleday. In 1941, Miller concluded the trip in Hollywood, California, where artists, actors, and directors greeted him as an important writer, but the book that came out of his trip had to be delayed: with the country girding for war, Miller's acidic insights about the emptiness and meaninglessness of American industry were not particularly welcome, and the book was not published until 1945. Nin turned away from the market as well, and she wrote pornography for a private collector, Barnet Ruder. Until he was drafted in 1946, Ruder paid a dollar a page—about ten dollars a page in today's dollars—provided the pages were graphic, not sentimental, and that she and his other writers supply at least a hundred pages a month.

As they struggled to make money, Miller wrote to Nin continually, asking her to leave Guiler and live with him, but Nin's letters chided him for his "obvious reluctance" to live with her, even though his letters show him pleading with her to acknowledge their tie:

> Any time you are ready to make a break, I am. Is that clear? I won't push you into doing something which will make you miserable. If

---

* Roughly $7,500 in 2011 dollars.

we are ever to have a real life together it will probably be much more difficult than what we've known. But that's as it should be. We're paying dearly for our protection—*you* most of all. I see it all clearly and I tell you again that it's up to you. I have no problems any more—I'm free.

Nin always demurred, though. She continued to claim Miller's poverty as an excuse, even though by 1941, he was finally making enough to just get by, and as early as July 1941, when he arrived in Hollywood, he wrote to Nin to say that "I find more and more that I'm talked about everywhere—and so are you. We're almost legendary." Miller was getting, he wrote, "invitations from people (including critics and professors) from all over the country. I could just mosey along from place to place. But I don't really want to ... I repeat, I always did hope and believe you would join me somewhere." But even the first stirrings of widespread fame did not help them return to each other. Miller was still not in a position to support Nin, and it is not at all clear that he would have given her the freedom Guiler gave her, to conduct her affairs, so they continued on opposite coasts, writing back and forth, sending each other suggestions for reading, contacts for friends, and leads for possible support and publication.

X.

As Nin began to feel herself getting older—she would turn forty in 1943—as she became concerned about remaining young, she took casual lovers whose affection would give her evidence of her attractiveness. But her numerous affairs and encounters do not seem to have satisfied her: she described in her journal "the act of self-murder which takes place after my being with someone. A sense of shame for the most trivial defect, lack, slip, error, for every statement made or for my silence, for not being earthy enough, or for being too passionate, for not being free or being too impulsive, for not being myself, or being too much so." Now that she had given up the idea of a life with Miller—now that she had relinquished the brave future she and Miller had anticipated—now that she was essentially reconciled to a life as a banker's wife, Nin no longer kept detailed notes in her journal, and many of her affairs were relegated to silences or else to cryptic notes, and the affairs only became visible through her biographers, who conducted interviews or triangulated to see the lovers' presences.

When she did reflect on her affairs, she did not describe them with the same brave tone she had used with Miller or even her father. She wrote in her journal, "I am in truth a very very sick person, who needs a love like Hugo's to keep her from insanity and death." Later she acknowledged that "there is something very wrong with me. I need proof of love constantly and that is wrong and cruel for others." Finally she had a breakdown in September of 1942: she had too many lovers—and too many people were turning to her for encouragement and financial support: she was wearing herself down trying to take care of them all, when she herself still had not had any success or support for her own work. After a brief hospitalization, she worked with a female Jungian therapist who convinced her to start to take care of herself, to try to put on weight, and to admit that she was limited in her ability to provide for her lovers and the young homosexual artists whose journals and publications she was funding.

In California through the war, Miller was still taking money from Nin, but he was also enjoying his reputation as a writer of banned books, and he continued to try different schemes for making money. After trying to write for film in Hollywood, he settled in a shack in Big Sur in 1944, where he wrote begging letters and worked on *The Rosy Crucifixion*, a trilogy of novels about his marriage to June. He had promised Nin that he would never write about his relationship with her, so he had to return to his second marriage—relegating his relationship with Nin to his correspondence. He also began to paint watercolors, and in subsequent years, he made more money selling paintings than his writing. After years of poverty, Miller was becoming more spiritual, more willing than ever to trust himself to fate. He wrote to Nin in 1943, "As I always say—there is no real security, certainly not in this material realm. There's only *inner* security—and that I have . . . I believe so much in liberty that I would risk all on it. Whatever you do with your whole heart and soul is right. Try to believe the same of me." Soon he told Nin that he was even in a position to "give you what is needed to get [the printing of her journal] started." But Nin could not accept Miller's money—she could only see his generosity, toward herself and others, as wastefulness, and when he got money from an anonymous patron, she complained that she "always knew that the day you obtained what you wanted (a year of peace from the money problems, time to write) you would throw it away." As always, she saw her own generosity as martyrdom, without recognizing his independence, and she complained that she was "about to give 100 pages of the Diary to the linotypist and refrained, because you will need."

In 1944, Nin finally had some success in getting her work noticed, although this did not change the basis of her relationship with Miller, or her marriage. At her own expense, she had printed *Under a Glass Bell*, a collection of the stories that had been published in little magazines before the war. The collection gave her pieces a continuity they had not had individually, and it was well received, where individual pieces had passed from publisher to publisher. Edmund Wilson, a critic at *The New Yorker*, gave her a review in April of 1944 that established her reputation: "the main thing to say is that Miss Nin is a very good artist, as perhaps none of the literary surrealists is." Nin's reputation was also boosted by her friendship with Gore Vidal, whom she met in November of 1945. She and Vidal essentially used each other for publicity, but in spite of the malicious swipes they took at each other in private, Vidal helped negotiate a contract at his press for Nin to publish her novel *This Hunger*. Nin could still only publish her novels, though, because she could not find a publisher willing to brave the potential lawsuits to publish the journals. Nor could anyone see a way to abridge the journal without destroying its meaning—so she returned to her love affairs and her journal as her primary work.

By the end of the war, Nin began to be asked to speak at colleges, where she said that she was "giving the vision of the neurotic directly." At one such talk in the 1940s, she met writer James Herlihy, who would become a close friend for the rest of her life. When she said that she wanted "to give the world one perfect life," by "living the dream," Herlihy was inspired: he described an atmosphere of "youngsters who were just developing after the drab grayness of wartime, and who saw this sparkling, tinkling creature as perfection itself . . . When she told us that we, too, could live out our dreams, well—we were converted, to say the least."

Miller's and Nin's successes only began to gather real momentum after the war, when the French courts banned Miller's books. Prominent French writers, philosophers, and intellectuals—Jean-Paul Sartre among others—rallied to Miller's defense, and in 1946 they overturned the ruling on appeal. L'Affair Miller made Miller famous in France, and now his royalties were worth more than $30,000,* although he had difficulty

---

* Roughly $330,000 in 2011 dollars.

getting the money out of France because of restrictions on moving currency in France's postwar economy. Miller made about U.S.$7,500 in 1946, and by 1948, he would draw $500 a month*—when just four years earlier he had been scratching by each month on $50. The European sales of Miller's books liberated him, and he could finally send Nin money to help her print and distribute her own books.

If Miller and Nin were still trying to help each other into print, the relationship between them was no longer anything but nostalgic friendship. Nin moved in a circle of homosexuals and young artists in New York and Provincetown, and Miller established himself in Big Sur, and their lives no longer overlapped except in letters. Nin did continue to send Miller whatever money she could, but in 1944, Miller married a philosophy student from Yale, Janina Martha Lepska—who gave birth to a baby girl in October of 1945—and this finally put an end to Nin's support. Miller and Nin did see each other again in 1947, when Nin traveled to California for a speaking engagement, and they continued to correspond, but it was only their books that still had anything to do with each other, now.

XI.

After Miller's marriage to Lepska, Nin began a new major relationship herself. In 1947, she met Rupert Pole, a divorced twenty-eight-year-old actor, who was now a forestry student in California. Pole was the son of a prominent actor and grandson of Frank Lloyd Wright, and as he was leaving New York for a cross-country trip back to school, he invited her along. Scathing reviews and vicious gossip were making it difficult for Nin to endure literary rejections and manage her multiple affairs, so she reprised her escape from Paris with Rank and left town with Pole, starting a relationship on the way. Nin found Pole's youth invigorating: she said that he was the best lover she had ever known, and she began to split her time between her life with Guiler in New York and life with Pole at the forestry stations, where she would attend to housework her maid would perform in New York. Nin had told Pole that she and Guiler were in the process of divorcing, and she drew out this story for years, even though she and Guiler had never discussed divorce.

---

* Roughly $5,600 today.

In order to justify traveling back and forth from New York to California, Nin invented a web of health problems and European magazine assignments. These "jobs" allowed her to disguise her regular allowance from Hugo as income, and she told Rupert that her divorce from Hugo was moving slowly owing to complications in Cuba, New York, and Paris. When a job in New York fell through, she neglected to tell Pole, but she continued to use the job as a reason to return east. Eventually she needed to employ certain friends as collaborators in her lies, to help her preserve appearances, but she successfully kept her relationships from colliding. Both Guiler and Pole believed that she did not have a phone, although she had to invent some stories on the spot when friends innocently gave out one or the other of her numbers. But in spite of a few late-night phone calls from Pole to Nin at Guiler's apartment, she preserved appearances in both relationships.

Nin kept Pole from talking about marriage for years, but on a road trip in 1955, they drove past a sign for the Arizona justice of the peace, and Nin wrote that she could not "kill his joy" without feeling like a "murderer," so they stopped and were married, regardless of her marriage to Guiler. She managed to keep her bicoastal marriages separate, but in planning for her estate, she entrusted her journals to her agent and her analyst, not to either husband. As she juggled her two marriages, the pace of her affairs slowed down, and now she kept a locked "lie box," with index cards to record her stories, and she no longer kept a bound journal, but file folders into which she threw carbons from her letters, as well as whatever pieces of paper she made her notes on as she flew back and forth between husbands.

According to Deirdre Bair, neither Guiler nor Pole were faithful to her in turn, but when Hugo finally seemed happy with someone else, Nin tried to tell him that she had a lover as well. Bair writes that Guiler would not hear it, though, that he refused to accept the possibility that they might each be happier with other lovers. Friends and acquaintances have all tried to explain Guiler's complicity in Nin's affairs, but Guiler himself never wrote anything about it, and we only have secondhand accounts of his refusal to acknowledge them. But we cannot believe that he was completely ignorant: when one of Nin's friends, Robert Duncan, acidly recited a litany of Nin's infidelities to Guiler over lunch, Bair writes that Guiler "calmly paid the bill and left without responding."

Nin was no more monogamous in her literary relationships than she was in love, for she repeatedly negotiated deals without consulting her agents, who were almost always infuriated when it came out that she had signed her own contracts, and her lecturing agency let her go because she was always making arrangements without consulting them. After she made a name for herself in the 1940s, her books were greeted with less and less critical approval, but younger artists found her and kept up an underground following. She still could not publish the journal without hurting the people closest to her, so she continued to fictionalize it in books that were so surreal and so full of unexplained and symbolic significances that they are still only read in niches, even now. "I am living in the future," she said, when critics failed to comprehend her.

XII.

Miller and Nin remained bound by their reputations as personalities, though, as much as by their writing and the time they had spent together in Paris, when they were both working on their masterpieces. After the war, though, the *Tropics* books finally began to sell—soldiers were bringing them home from France—and as Americans idealized the rebellious sexual freedom Miller had come to stand for, there was more and more interest in Miller, and then, by association, in Nin. By the 1950s, as students and young artists found their work—as young people started to experiment with drugs, surreal experiences, and nontraditional lifestyles—Nin finally attracted an audience, and she wrote to Miller, "I believe the young America has chosen you and me to follow."

Having been estranged during and after the war, Miller and Nin discovered each other again in the early 1960s, when Barney Rosset of Grove Press fought to lift the ban on Miller's books. Rosset had just fought to revoke the ban on *Lady Chatterley's Lover*, and now he saw a market for Miller's work as well, so he assumed full responsibility for legal costs and pressed the case. When the *Tropics* books cleared the censor's office in 1961 (the U.S. Supreme Court would not clear the books of obscenity until 1964), Miller and Nin were seventy and fifty-eight, and finally the flow of funds was reversed for good, and Miller sent Nin money in significant quantities. Nin herself had been offered $50,000 for the diaries, but this was the sum Miller had received from Grove Press for *Tropic of Cancer* alone, and pride prevented her from accepting that sum for all of her diaries. She set her price at $100,000* and resigned herself to the

---

* Roughly $360,000 today.

reality that the diaries would not be published until after her death. Nin's works had only begun to make money after they were organized under one press in 1960, when Alan Swallow published her novellas and her short stories, each in their own volumes, as well as her five novels in a series. It was the first time that Nin would be published without paying printing costs herself, although her first royalties were only $32.56.

It was still only when American readers discovered Miller's work—the early *Tropics* books as well as the more recent, and still blatantly sexual *Rosy Crucifixion* trilogy—it was only as Miller burst full-grown on the literary scene in America, and the public became fascinated with all things Miller that there was any real demand for Nin's work. Capitalizing on this interest, Miller published his thoroughly expurgated *Letters to Anaïs Nin* in 1965, and when he gave her all of his royalties, he repaid her in one gesture for all of the money she had ever given him. The book only raised questions about Nin's relationship with Miller, though—as well as other questions about her marriage and her affairs—and in order to put the period in perspective, Harcourt Brace published the heavily edited first volume of her journal in 1965. 1966 brought Nin what she called "an avalanche!" of affection, as she finally became a personality on the national stage. As appreciative letters poured in from readers, she wrote to a friend that "all the love I gave has been returned." Her editor made it clear in his preface that "Miss Nin's truth, as we have seen, is psychological," but now the cryptic self-absorption for which she had always been faulted could finally be seen, in one critic's words, as a courageous "act of self-revelation."

Now that she was making money from her journal, though, Nin's income was being claimed in two households, and problems with the IRS forced her to confess to Pole that their marriage had not been valid: she told him that she had always been married to Guiler, and the marriage with Pole was formally annulled in June of 1966, shortly after her diaries were published. By this time, Miller had divorced and remarried as well. He and Lepska had split up in 1951, and then he had taken up with Eve McClure, a twenty-five-year-old painter who had just divorced her first sixty-year-old husband. Miller and McClure had married in 1953, after taking a trip to Europe together, where Miller was finally feted as a significant author, but they had divorced in 1960. Miller began to consider living in Europe, since he was getting tired of California—and also because he could not get money out of France easily. He had traveled around for a few years, looking for a place to settle down with a German girlfriend, but he returned to California, and in 1966, at age seventy-five, he married a twenty-eight-year-old Japanese nightclub singer, Hiroko Tokuda. Miller's friends suspected her of being a gold digger like June, for now that his books could be sold in America, Miller was making more money than he had ever made. In 1977, he and Tokuda divorced as well, after what Miller's biographers describe as an unsympathetic marriage.

After his letters to Nin were published, Miller felt free to recollect their time together, and in his *Book of Friends*—which was published in 1976, the year before Nin died—he described her "inveterate lying, her chicanery, her duplicity, and so on." He called her a "monstrous liar" who could not "accept reality," but "had to alter reality to suit her own view of the world." This was as much as he would say publicly, though: he still honored his promise not to write about their relationship.

After Nin died of cancer in 1977—after Miller died of old age in 1980 and Guiler in 1985—Nin's editor, Gunther Stuhlmann, published their correspondence as *A Literate Passion* in 1987. But it was only with the publication of Nin's unexpurgated diaries—in multiple volumes, as *Henry and June* in 1990, and *Incest* and *Fire* in 1992 and 1996 respectively—it was only after their letters and her journal were in print that Miller and Nin could be known as the daring and sacrilegious lovers they saw themselves as after June's departure from Paris left them alone in each other's company in January of 1931. Nin's writing was finally read by a wide audience—until then only her erotica, *Delta of Venus*, which had also been published posthumously, in 1977, had sold widely—but now her defiant journal, with its diabolical insights into love and emotions, psychology and art, could finally take its place as the counterpart to Miller's sacrilegious novels.

Epilogue

Love and Art at the Limits of Modern Culture

꧁ ❦ ꧂

The continual effort to raise himself above himself, to work a pitch above his last height, betrays itself in a man's relations. We thirst for approbation, yet cannot forgive the approver ... if I have a friend, I am tormented by my imperfections. The love of me accuses the other party ... A man's growth is seen in the successive choirs of his friends. For every friend whom he loses for truth, he gains a better.   RALPH WALDO EMERSON

More and more, as our era draws to a close, are we made aware of the tremendous significance of the human document. Our literature, unable any longer to express itself through dying forms, has become almost exclusively autobiographical. The artist is retreating behind the dead forms to rediscover in himself the eternal source of creation.   HENRY MILLER

Whenever sexual freedom is sought or achieved, sadomasochism will not be far behind.   CAMILLE PAGLIA

Taken side by side, these stories add up to more than the details of the artists' letters, their artwork, and their time together: they describe a particular response to modernity, a consistent experiment with its freedoms. These artists were exceptional and unique individuals—they were not aberrations, they were not, as a whole, pathological: they all started out as smart, upper-middle-class children who thought they could use their freedom and creativity to make their marriages more genuine—closer to human nature—than the marriages they saw. They were creative in love as in art, which is to say that they did not accept what they inherited—or even what they created for themselves—without a sense of irreverent, even amoral playfulness, which threw every form and term into question and rearranged them according to what they perceived as their own individual truths—or deeper truths, which they themselves would articulate

247

for the others. But they were not just using words, forms, and colors, to organize merely their personal experiences: they saw themselves as making a kind of contribution to modern culture in how they conducted their relationships as well. So these stories are not just the stories of certain lives: in our restless and confused times, they are examples of what can be done—deliberately, even conscientiously—in the name of the modern freedom of self-creation.

This collective story is also, however, the story of what the artists discovered after they vowed to invent their own marriages. If they were all surprised—or dismayed, at a certain point—by what their unique marriages required of them—or by what they elicited from them—they nevertheless used their creativity—in their work and in their decisions—to create a future in which they could still recognize themselves as themselves, and still have a certain freedom in their relationships. If their experiences led each of them to one crisis or another—and if, through their crises, they acquired a certain wisdom—if, in the end, they developed a certain self-awareness in regard to their desires, and a certain respect for the reality of other people's feelings—their art nonetheless remained part of their maturity, just as much as it had formed the core of their youthful rebellions, against marriage and even against their own feelings.

· · ·

The similarities between the artists' lives are stunning—but of course they must have had similar temperaments, to have used their relationships themselves as grounds for experimentation. They were not, after all, Rodins, Gertrude Steins, or Willa Cathers, with longtime nonartist companions—they weren't Faulkners, with nonartist wives and lovers, they weren't Hemingways or Picassos, with serial marriages, to beautiful women who were not also artists. Generally speaking, the artists presented here all followed Emerson, in taking their self-reliance seriously—or Nietzsche, in finding a certain genuineness in distancing themselves from their own lives. The prospect of self-reliance and self-trust gave them the artistic opportunity to do something unprecedented—simply by living their lives according to their own lights. What would that light illuminate in sex, in relationships, in jealousy, and the other irrational urges? No one had yet imagined or defined how free individuals could ultimately rely on their spouses or find what they needed in lovers, but the questions were in the air, and by the 1910s and '20s, as many of them were making their marriages, D. H. Lawrence, the prophet of anti-industrial sensuality, was writing the books that would lead generations to love and sex as the genuine avenues into the self. But the artists in these stories didn't yet live in an open, confessional culture—they would have to create the terms for that culture themselves. From where they stood at the turn of the twentieth century, love was a grounds for philosophical exploration and experimentation, and they all had their lives themselves to experiment with.

When you look at this collective temperament, there almost seems to be a formula for making a child creative in life and in love. To begin with, almost all of the artists were either first or only children—two were youngest, and O'Keeffe was the second child but eldest girl—and they all grew up between cultures, whether it was O'Keeffe's mother's aristocratic heritage and her father's lineage of poor Irish farmers, Beauvoir's aristocratic father and bourgeois mother, or Diego and Frida's European fathers and Mexican Catholic mothers. They all had the freedom to choose which culture they wanted to identify with—the nobility of the aristocrats or the passions and cruder vitality of the poor—and the role of the artist gave them the freedom to claim every identity.

With freedom to choose their cultures, they encountered themselves as unique individuals: they were the ones to whom freedom occurred as a set of choices between traditions and opportunities, and they savored their freedom so well that they held it in suspense. They would not choose—nor would they create—anything that would limit their freedom to create something new in the future. Wherever they could, they wanted it both ways: they wanted the dignity and the rebellion, the freedom and the culture, and they didn't have to commit to any one identity. They identified with themselves before anything else—even if they didn't have any evidence, yet, of the selves to which they committed themselves—and they invented powerful rationalizations for the things they couldn't control or compose.

By the time they came of age, and realized that they would like more than anything to make art for a living, they had to confront the questions of sex and marriage and what commitments they could really make. Having, for the most part, watched their parents humiliate themselves in extramarital affairs, they were all determined not to jeopardize their relationship with themselves by being hypocritical. They were going to be pure—at least in their own eyes—and if they practiced some hypocrisy in their relations with early lovers, they nevertheless continued to look for equals. When they found artists who felt the same way they did—who were willing to use creativity, as they did, in confronting the question of freedom and choice—they gave each other the freedom they felt they needed for themselves. It was their greatest gift, the fulfillment of their freedom, and the confirmation of their artistic philosophy, to let each other take lovers—to let themselves be bound by an open tie, stronger than any vow, of ongoing, shared creativity.

Open relationships—which, of course, preceded the artists' discovery of them—gave the artists a wider freedom of identifications, for now their creativity could be acknowledged. That was always the heart of the tie, but they could still also experience each of the different selves they became in the presence of other lovers. This freedom liberated them from their own feelings, for now they could decide—and the open relationship itself gave them a script for determining—which of their feelings to honor, and which to ignore. Their partners were bound to suffer, and they were bound to suffer, some, themselves, but there was a rationale for it all, and the sufferings were all justified—even dignified—by their artwork. In this sense, the open relationship—open as in "free" and also open as in "acknowledged"—was not just a bohemian aberration from middle-class conventions: it seemed to be a new, transcendent form of morality—or at the very least, it was an attempt to make something more legitimate than traditional marriage. It was the new modern form that would accommodate the realities of desire, even as it also gave the artists the transcendent bond of mutual trust beyond jealousy.

The artists' relationships were not only open to lovers: they were also open to the sex urge and jealousy, and all the chaotic emotions their parents had hoped they would free themselves from by making recognizable marriages. But with the power to make decisions about what to claim as their own, and what to renounce as merely the world's, or history's, or nature's, the artists' individualities themselves seemed to obligate them to make decisions, and create things, that would reveal their personalities. In their relationships with each other—the equals who shared their visions—they really entered into the most intimate relationships with themselves. In their relationships, they encouraged each other to become their own ideas of themselves; to relinquish or transform what was not theirs, and to invent the forms that would give them expression; to say the things, and be the selves no one had let them be anywhere else. Now their flaws and frustrations and lusts and rebellions and failures were just understandable, even forgivable human reactions, and all of it was just raw material for art: together they could forgive each other their human lives and failings—so long as they continued to create.

In the 1910s and '20s, these relationships were daring and appealing—the artists were known as much for their amours as for their art—so if lovers came, and offered themselves, or risked themselves in relationships that didn't have any future except in art, they themselves must have found that art and the complexity of open relationships were preferable to the other kinds of marriage they could make. Bohemian or artistic society itself seemed to require unconventional relationships, and the artists often acted like surrogate families, who were bound by common values: as outcasts, exiles, prophets, or celebrities, they all shared a certain resignation—a certain acceptance, which encompassed not only heartache and grief but all the repulsions that came with industrial modernity; they were bound as well by a certain despair, and a certain rhapsodic or creative stance toward that despair, and this shared understanding was the atmosphere within which they conducted all of their relationships. So long as the artists themselves were free, this counterculture seemed to say, no one should care how inhuman or violent or mechanized things had become. They could feel their own lives in their throats; they could feel each other's visions, as real as their own. They could let everything happen to them, beauty and terror, and they would still have art to justify, to testify to their unique individual lives.

.   .   .

Certainly, in each of these stories, there were moments when the artists' feelings *were* negligible, when their sufferings *were* justified by the beauty and integrity of the art, and people were willing to endure "a good deal of contradictory nonsense," to use Georgia O'Keeffe's terms, for the sake of the "clear and bright and wonderful" things they found in each other's artwork and creativities.

From the beginning, though, there was always an accumulating body of evidence that the open relationships were coming at a price—even that they might be just as expensive, emotionally, as traditional marriages might have been. There were always moments when the artists could almost not endure their emotions, but the pressure to create—and to earn each other's love by creating—was almost overwhelming. Nor could their art always justify or compensate for the very real feelings of loneliness, jealousy, and uncertainty, and the challenges associated with maintaining their relationships—with each other, with their lovers, and with themselves—seemed almost insurmountable. There were moments when the artists were no longer joyfully proclaiming themselves, in their open relationships, but the feelings they had refused to acknowledge returned to them in the shape of their lovers' hurt feelings, or their spouses'—or their own. They suffered breakdowns, or turned to drugs or alcohol or, more compulsively, to flings and joyless affairs, to escape from themselves and the relationships that couldn't, by definition, give them a simple, straightforward, and genuine pleasure and belonging. There came a point where the artists despaired that their relationships—their artistic identities themselves—would always be complicated by their hypersensitive aloofness and their numerous techniques they had developed for keeping themselves apart, and nurturing the uniqueness of their visions—not to mention the artistic bravado and amorous pride. There was always a point when they couldn't proceed in ignorance any longer, and they had to confront—they had to be ashamed by the lies or the cruelties or callous behavior that greased the wheels of their numerous relationships. Even as their art and their relationships proclaimed the complexity and contradictions of their unique individualities, something inside of them still wanted simple, unsophisticated love: their open relationships were not exactly giving them this.

In each of these cases, there was always this moment where the open relationships ultimately set the artists against themselves: they were going to have to tally the cost of their unique individualities—and the cost of their creativity—in terms of the sufferings they caused, in themselves or in others. There was always a moment when the decisions they had made in the name of artistic freedom affected them viscerally, in feelings their art could neither justify nor repay. The artistic lifestyle took its toll: all but one of the men in these stories abandoned women who'd borne them children, and three of five women aborted pregnancies. The artists' bodies were almost afterthoughts—many of the women were so underweight that they had to be urged to eat, and in many of the relationships, there was almost a hostility to the sensual life. When they found sensuality outside their relationships, they found that their trivial flings had acquired a painful urgency, which became torturous when they realized that their flings, or secondary relationships, could never turn into relationships in their own right.

None of this pain could ultimately be justified in art. The heartbreak the artists had evaded, since childhood, found them in spite of their creative evasions, and the affairs that once proved their freedom—and the art that once justified their affairs—the individuality itself, which sought art and love as its twinned vocabularies—all became torments in themselves, or failed to keep them safe from the sting of grief, from regret or self-knowledge, or self-loathing. They could make art that transcended morality, as it defined the laws of human life, of nature—but in their lives, their decisions had physiological consequences in pangs of conscience, of grief, of remorse, and now they couldn't feel free in themselves. Whether or not they loved each other in their daring way— whether or not they created their art, they had to pay the price of their relationships.

.   .   .

In this light, these stories all together seem to say that modern freedoms could not lift the artists above their own consciences, and if they had more freedom to fulfill themselves in their alternative marriages, they still had not transcended the age-old development, which applies to every human being: from innocence to arrogance to experience to wisdom. For in spite of their brave attempts to rise above human feelings—to be, themselves, eternal in their decisions and in their work—certain facts of the human heart still applied to them, and they had to accept that jealousy and anger, fear and desire, pride and self-loathing all took up time, and a definite amount of emotional energy. The artists all had to recognize, at some point, that they had entangled themselves in humiliating or agonizing dramas, and they found that they could only degrade or complicate their lives so far before they wanted to feel clean inside themselves.

The sense of degradation, they found, was not merely a product of modern culture—it was real in their hearts, and it also had very real remedies, as atonement, repentance, the sensation of having a clear conscience are all very real as well. Much of the open relationship's appeal had come from how it let the artists assert that they were different from the others, but it also came from channeling the guilt they felt, on account of their differences. Open relationships were appealing for how they gave desires what they wanted, but still preserved a certain image of honesty, even virtue, in the excesses they permitted. Open relationships exercised the artists' individuality but still immersed them in the transcendent life of art—they used the artists' whole lives—not just their inspirations—as raw material for art. Stripped of these contexts, though—considered, at last, solely on the grounds of human emotion, of raw, human states of need—their art and their relationships were not ultimately satisfying. Art could be part of the process of purifying the self, but it could not redeem everything, not when they had expressed themselves and their artistic visions in their very relationships.

No, to feel clean—to continue to live with themselves, the artists would have to redeem their own acts, or, if they could not actually redeem them, they would have to decide whether their sufferings—and the sufferings they caused—were really part of who they were, or whether they should have to distance themselves even from their own behavior, and give up their self-reliance to let some other reliance take its place—reliance on spouses, on publishers or dealers, on marriage, on families, on culture, on whatever transcendent thing would keep their individualities alive when they with their flaws and injuries and sufferings came to die. If the artists did not ask for absolution from each other—not all of them did—they asked it of their audiences, and their art became a kind of offering, to eternity and to culture, for the things they had not been able to compose within their lives.

.　.　.

Whether they absolved themselves to themselves, found absolution in others, or simply lived their lives without that grace, the artists used the open relationship as an invitation to a confrontation with the self, and when it combined with art, it was also an invitation to the widest self-recognition. Ultimately they all confronted, in one way or another, not only the artistic visions but the emotional chaos they came from—not only the delicious intimacy, but the ocean of sex and jealousy it came from—not only the experience of being alive as human individuals, but the experience of being one among the masses. In the same way that marriage subsumes individuals into families and kinship groups that transcend individual lives, so in their art had the artists died out of their individuality, for in rising above their own feelings, in looking down at their lives from the heavens—even as they lived them—the artists beheld the eternity in which their lives themselves would only be known by the forms they left behind them. From the perspective of that eternity, they knew that they would only be known—or loved—in other people. Certainly other artists used art and love to approach these mysteries from other avenues, and as cultural forms, open relationships still only provided one particular kind of transcendence—but at a certain point, the artists all had to decide what their legacies would be, not only their artistic legacies, but their human legacies as well, the stories other people would tell about their decisions.

What we recognize today as the literature of self-revelation began with these artists, as an attempt to define the record in their own terms, and we would not live in the open, permissive culture we live in without their examples. And of course we are remiss not to tell all the other stories in detail as well: the collective stories not just of the artists, but of the Hugo Guilers and Fred Andreases, who turned blind eyes to their wives' affairs; of June Mansfields and Simone Jollivets; of the Natalie Sorokines and Olga Kosakiewiczs; and of the other young artists and models who were drawn into artists' circles. We should tell the stories of Clara West-hoffs and Angelina Beloffs, who bound themselves to men who would desert them; of Malwida von Meysenbugs, or Elizabeth Nietzsches, or the Beauvoir family, who felt that the artists' relationships were corrosive to civilization. If we really want to know the stories of the artists, we would have to describe the thousands of little helps they got, from the people who encouraged them, the people who published, read, or collected them, and probably even from the people who resisted them, who fired their rebellions and galvanized their wills. We would, of course, ultimately have to tell the whole story of modern civilization, and then the artists' daring relationships would dwindle to tiny, individual instances of other, much larger trends, in marriage, religion, and art, in markets and new technologies, in industries and media and culture.

I would hardly presume to tell this broadest of stories. But if we look at the stories chronologically, they do seem to indicate a certain trajectory for the open relationship itself. From Andreas-Salomé and Rilke to Miller and Nin, it evolves from writers who downplayed or suppressed their infidelities—but elevated creativity into a form of religious devotion—to writers who celebrated their infidelities themselves as a kind of transcendent devotion to art. But when Miller and Nin left Paris at the end of the 1930s, they took two very different paths with regard to love and art: Anaïs Nin ended up lying compulsively to keep her two husbands from finding out about each other—and Henry Miller returned to a domestic routine with a wife and children in a ramshackle house in Big Sur. He may have divorced Lepska and remarried twice after her, but he was never the same after 1935, when he realized that Nin had lied to him, and he renounced their open relationship: "your body burns in me," he had written in his panic,

and I want it uniquely, for myself alone. That is the mistake I made—
to share you. That made the woman less, I fear. Now it's got to be
you altogether, seven days in the week, and voyages included . . .
If you think I've become a Puritan, think so. I don't care. I won't
share you! You're mine and I'm going to keep you. I have become
fiercely possessive.

These are two very different legacies: the willing return to marriage
and the willful insistence on the psychological truth, the temporary
morality that accommodates every contradictory desire. Of course the
open relationship itself has been evolving since the last of these artists
died in the 1970s and '80s, but the historical record hasn't had time, yet,
to digest more recent stories: for not only would the artists themselves
have to have died, but their lovers would have to have died, and their
papers would have to have been collected and published, before we could
say how people have used creativity, in art and in love, to make sense of
their lives in postmodern culture. So the field remains open, and as long
as young people are tempted to use their relationships to express their
individuality, this story will continue to evolve. With the sexual revolu-
tion, and now the gay rights movement, these questions will only be
answered—in print, deliberately—by more and more people. As much
as we seem to be watching each other's relationships in real-time, now,
though, it will still take years before full accounts can be made of con-
temporary lives, and people in the future will know where they are by
the hidden patterns they will be able to discern in our lives, loves, and
works.

As that future unfolds, these artists' lives keep us on the hooks of
certain questions, which are inseparable from our modern freedom and
self-reliance: are we living genuinely and deliberately, in what we create
as much as in how we love? Are we giving ourselves what we need, as we
create ourselves? How have we learned to handle that part of us that
demands its due in chaos, in deep, even self-destructive experiences? Are
we being completely honest about our urges? Are we getting the world
we want as the benefit of suppressing them? The artists' lives are only
rough examples of how these questions can be answered. As long as we
have the freedoms of modern individuality—as long as we believe that
our individuality can be fulfilled in our works and our loves, we have to
confront them ourselves, and let future generations tell the stories of
what kind of culture we made for them.

Notes and Bibliography

Introduction
ATTRIBUTIONS

PAGE:

ix   "I know now your eyes are wide open . . ." (Miller, Henry, and Anaïs Nin. *A Literate Passion. Letters of Anaïs Nin and Henry Miller, 1932-1953*. Gunther Stuhlmann, ed. New York: Harcourt Brace Jovanovich, 1987, 96).

xi   "What do we wish to know . . ." (Emerson, Ralph Waldo. *Essays*. New York: Thomas Nelson and Sons, 1905, 129).

"So far all that has given colour to existence . . ." (Nietzsche, Friedrich. *The Gay Science*. Bernard Williams, ed. Josephine Nauckhoff, trans. Cambridge: Cambridge University Press, 2001, 34).

"We are just now reaching the point . . ." (Rilke, Rainer Maria. *Letters to a Young Poet*. Joan Burnham, trans. Novato: New World Library, 2000, 62).

"The old ideals are dead as nails . . ." (Lawrence, D. H. *Women in Love*. New York, Penguin: 1950, 109).

Chapter One
The Great Triangulators: Lou Andreas-Salomé and Rainer Maria Rilke

ATTRIBUTIONS

3   "People who are not 'faithful' do not necessarily desert one . . ." (Andreas-Salomé, Lou. *The Freud Journal*. Stanley Leavy, trans. London: Quartet, 1964, 142).

"All companionship can consist . . ." (Rilke, Rainer Maria. *Letters of Rainer Maria Rilke*. Jane Bannard Greene and M. D. Herter Norton, trans. New York: W. W. Norton, 1945, 150).

"He was simply fixated . . ." (Andreas-Salomé, Lou. *Looking Back*. Ernst Pfeiffer ed.; Breon Mitchell, trans. New York: Paragon House, 1991, 131).

5   "Never forget that it would be a calamity . . ." (Binion, Rudolph. *Frau Lou: Nietzsche's Wayward Disciple*. Princeton: Princeton University Press, 1968, 79).

"I want to see no flower, no sky, no sun—except in you . . ." (Rilke, Rainer Maria. *Rilke and Andreas-Salomé: A Love Story in Letters*. Edward Snow and Michael Winkler, trans. New York: W. W. Norton & Co., 2008, 12).

6   "I hated you like something too great . . ." (Rilke, Rainer Maria. *Diaries of a Young Poet*. Edward Snow and Michael Winkler, trans. New York: W. W. Norton, 1997, 75).

7   "you alone know who I am," (*Love Story in Letters*, 46-47).

"allies in the difficult mysteries of living and dying . . ." (Ibid., 67).

8 "If I was your wife for years . . ." (*Looking Back*, 85).

"bound by small, secret demonstrations of tenderness . . ." (Ibid., 24).

"couldn't you drown just once?" (Ibid., 26).

"bitterly lonely among them all . . ." (*Frau Lou*, 9).

"my parents and their viewpoints . . ." (*Looking Back*, 2).

10 "who spoiled me mightily . . ." (Ibid., 2).

"Perhaps I knew too much . . ." (Ibid., 20).

"rarely . . . have had everything so much her own way as she had." (Ibid., 17).

"now all loneliness is at an end . . ." (Ibid., 156).

"capitulated completely," (Ibid., 157).

"stepped into God's place," (*Frau Lou*, 15).

11 "*want[ed]* to be responsible for this child" (*Looking Back*, 156, Lou's italics).

"when he misjudged me . . ." (*Looking Back*, 156).

"sleeplessness, loss of appetite, . . ." (*Frau Lou*, 19).

"excessive nervous irritation and mental strain . . ." (Ibid., 17).

"I have chosen you; I have called you by name, you are mine . . ." (Ibid., 19).

"To live for centuries, to think . . ." (*Looking Back*, 158).

"on Freud's account . . . that the pain be merely mental." (*Frau Lou*, 23).

12 "yours is a great task . . . we shall yet speak much of it." (Ibid., 39).

"a completely false tack, to my sorrow and rage . . ." (*Looking Back*, 45).

"to make him envision and understand . . ." (Ibid.).

"A simple dream convinced me of the feasibility of my plan . . ." (Ibid.).

13 "a new image and ideal of the free spirit" (*Frau Lou*, 70).

"forceful, unbelievably clever being . . ." (Ibid., 52).

"Greet the Russian girl for me . . ." (Ibid., 49).

"full of urgent desire for a new way of life . . ." (Ibid., 55).

"astoundingly well prepared . . ." (Ibid., 108).

"garden of Epicurus." (Ibid., 46).

"Mentally passionate nonmarital relationship . . ." (Ibid., 55).

14 "should consider myself duty-bound . . ." (Ibid., 53).

"Firmly as I am convinced of *your* neutrality . . ." (Ibid., 62).

"neither Mrs. Rée in Warmbrunn nor Miss von Meysenbug . . ." (Ibid., 63).

"I can't live according to some model . . ." (*Looking Back*, 45-46).

"you are the only person in the world whom I love." (*Frau Lou*, 57).

"not so wholly open and honest . . ." (Ibid., 59).

15 "Lou burst forth with a flood of invective against my brother . . ." (Ibid., 76).

"*Never* did I think that you should 'read aloud and write' for me . . ." (Ibid., 67).

"Snailie [Salomé] was her Housie's [Rée's] tenant . . ." (Ibid., 73).

16 "from the moment Lou was in Stibbe . . ." (Ibid., 71).

"I cannot deny it, [she is] my brother's philosophy *personified* . . ." (Ibid., 84).

"is and remains for me a being of the first rank . . ." (Ibid., 108).

"capable of enthusiasm for people without love for them ..." (Ibid., 98).
"This sort of person who lacks reverence must be avoided." (Ibid., 135).
"proposition by proposition, conclusion by conclusion," (Nietzsche, Friedrich. *On the Genealogy of Morals*, tr. Walter Kaufmann, New York: Vintage, 1969, 18).

17 "a relationship which may never exist again ..." (*Looking Back*, 51; 174).
"a woman may well enough form a friendship with a man ..." (*Frau Lou*, 91).
"the effect of hymns ..." (Livingstone, Angela. *Salomé, Her Life and Work*. Mt. Kisco, NY: Moyer Bell Ltd., 1984, 13.).
"at opposite ends" of Berlin "like children mad at each other" (*Frau Lou*, 132).

18 "was not that of a woman ..." (*Looking Back*, 125).
"My love for my husband began ... with an inner demand ..." (Ibid., 213).

19 "acceptance into our bond ... a condition of the marriage" (Ibid., 125).
"something we *have*, but something we *make*." (*Frau Lou*, 141).
"final gift to him, my final proof of love." (Ibid., 175).
"knives and tears" (Ibid., 175).

20 "I thought incessantly of the *knives beside the plates* ..." (Ibid., 176).
"the total freedom we each had to be ourselves ..." (*Looking Back*, 134).

21 "turning a bit female" and showing "the need to be desired" (*Frau Lou*, 191).
"certainly 'abused' Z. and the others ..." (Ibid., 204n.).
"natural love-life" which "is grounded in the principle of infidelity" (Ibid., 207).

22 "desolate counting house future" (Prater, Donald. *A Ringing Glass: The Life of Rainer Maria Rilke*. New York: Oxford University Press, 1986, 13).
"Yesterday was not the first twilight hour ..." (*Love Story in Letters*, 3).

23 "My father began the career of officer ..." (*Letters of Rainer Maria Rilke*, I, 98).

24 "for the greater part of the day ... to a serving-girl ..." (Ibid., I, 18).
"the woman whose first and most immediate care ..." (Ibid., I, 17-21).
"very good" to "excellent," "quiet and good-tempered" and "industrious" (*A Ringing Glass*, 8).
"more spiritually troubled than ill in body" (Ibid., 10).
"a truly brotherly affection based on mutual sympathy ..." (*Letters of Rainer Maria Rilke*, I, 21).
"I have taken off the Emperor's uniform ..." (*A Ringing Glass*, 10).

25 "stupid flirtation." (Ibid., 13).
"there is no one like me, there never has been" (Ibid., 408).
"all I do is cost more and more money ..." (Ibid., 34).

26 "[until] I met you, beloved and dearest Vally ..." (*Letters of Rainer Maria Rilke*, I, 21).

27 "At last I have a *home*" (*Love Story in Letters*, 8).
"split up into two beings ..." (*Frau Lou*, 216).
"whole tragic destiny is summed up in this tension ..." (*Looking Back*, 83).

28 "My joy will seem far-off and unfestive ..." (*Diaries of a Young Poet*, 6).

"Artists shall avoid each other. . . ." (Ibid., 21).
"couldn't muster any appreciation . . ." (*Love Story in Letters*, 364n).
"something *too great* . . ." (*Diaries of a Young Poet*, 75).
"Be always thus before me . . ." (Ibid., 77).

29   "I could say of myself that I (although no artist) . . ." (*Love Story in Letters*, 75).
"the spiritual life remains innocent and childlike . . ." (*Looking Back*, 36).
"vehemently warned us against participating . . ." (Andreas-Salomé, Lou.
You Alone Are Real to Me: Remembering Rainer Maria Rilke. Angela von der Lippe,
trans. Rochester: BOA Editions, 2003, 37).
"a far-off city; a word from you will be to me an island . . ." (*A Ringing Glass*,
57).
"can only come to one, or to a couple . . ." (Ibid., 57).
"perhaps his mother or his elder sister" (Ibid., 62).
"two are at one only when they stay two" (*Frau Lou*, 259).

30   "anxiety, almost states of terror" (*A Love Story in Letters*, xiii).
"almost depraved . . ." (Ibid., 31).
"everything seen must become a poem" (*Diaries of a Young Poet*, 218).
"to be awake and to be alive are deeds, not states . . ." (*A Love Story in Letters*, 35).

31   "If I can learn from people . . ." (*Diaries of a Young Poet*, 195).
"How much I learn in watching these two girls . . ." (Ibid., 174).

32   "Your home was for me, from the first moment . . ." (*Letters of Rainer Maria
Rilke*, I, 43-44).
"There is always only *one thing* in me . . ." (*Love Story in Letters*, 84).
"before you possessed me, / I didn't exist sometimes at home . . ." (Ibid., 39).

33   "To make Rainer go away, *go completely away* . . ." (Ibid., 39).
"*has* at all costs to find support, and an exclusive devotion . . ." (*A Ringing
Glass*, 75).
"Beginner of my joys! First one! Eternal!" (Ibid., 76).
"for all the caring fervour of our relationship . . ." (*Looking Back*, 146).
"Last Appeal . . ." (*Love Story in Letters*, 41-42).
"If one day much later you feel yourself in dire straits . . ." (Ibid., 41-42).
"obstreperously good . . ." (*Frau Lou*, 205).

34   "shattered" or fallen and "swallowed" in an abyss (*A Ringing Glass*, 76).
"linked in some way with God . . ." (Ibid., 83).
"it is an impossibility for two people . . ." (Ibid., 79).
"shed much of your old self and spread it out like a cloak . . ." (Leppmann,
Wolfgang. *Rilke: A Life*. New York: Fromm International, 1984, 139).

35   "dissolv[ing] our little household." (*Letters of Rainer Maria Rilke*, I, 74).
"I am my own circle," (*A Ringing Glass*, 86).
"each could live his life according to his own work and needs . . ." (Ibid., 86).
"of whose art, I expect the greatest things . . ." (*Letters of Rainer Maria Rilke*,
I, 74).

"With wonderful seriousness ... *il faut travailler, rien que...*" (Ibid., I, 84).

36 "as we have never worked before" (*A Ringing Glass*, 91).
"vast screaming prison" (Ibid., 97).
"just a single day ..." (*Love Story in Letters*, 44).
"stay with us any time, in difficult as in good hours ..." (Ibid.).
"I can't ask anyone for advice ..." (Ibid., 46-47).

37 "have you as their poet" (Ibid., 57).
"standing already where even in the best subsequent times ..." (Ibid., 58).
"write about how you feel and what's tormenting you ..." (Ibid., 48).
"I used to think it would be better ..." (*You Alone*, 45).
"no one can depend on me ..." (*Love Story in Letters*, 60).
"read them ... as you read these letters ..." (Ibid., 62).

38 "When your *Rodin* arrived ..." (Ibid., 65).
"had to turn their energy ..." (Ibid., 66).
"You have undergone such severe after-shocks ..." (Ibid.).
"you gave yourself to your opposite ..." (Ibid., 67).

39 "To love is good, for love is difficult ..." (Rilke, Rainer Maria. *Letters to a Young Poet*. Joan Burnham, trans. Novato: New World Library, 2000, 62).

40 "Clara and I ..." (*Letters of Rainer Maria* Rilke, I, 150).
"already seems a complicated little personality of her own ..." (*A Ringing Glass*, 115).
"I see for miles around no other thought ..." (*Love Story in Letters*, 123).

41 "odd people," (*Frau Lou*, 228).
"a reunion with you is the single bridge to my future ..." (*Love Story in Letters*, 144).
"for the first time the 'work' itself ..." (*Looking Back*, 91).

42 "this person, who plays such a big part ..." (*Letters of Rainer Maria Rilke*, I, 186).
"how can the circumstance refute me ..." (Ibid., I, 245).
"You overrate me. I am no support ... I'm only a voice." (*A Ringing Glass*, 153).
"I *implore* those who love me ..." (Ibid., 177).

43 "To be loved means to be consumed ..." (Ibid., 162).
"closer to this young girl than to any other woman." (Freedman, Ralph. *Life of a Poet: Rainer Maria Rilke*. NY: Farrar, Straus & Giroux, 1996, 311).

44 "There is no ill will between us ..." (*Love Story in Letters*, 190).

45 "how exceptionally life has favored you ..." (Ibid., 166).
"too fundamental a help for me ..." (Ibid., 177).
"Who, if I cried out, would hear me among the angels' hierarchies?" (Rilke, Rainer Maria. *Ahead of All Parting: The Selected Poetry and Prose of Rainer Maria Rilke*. Stephen Mitchell, trans. New York: Modern Library, 1995, 331).

46 "the joyful cry of the consummate artist ..." (*You Alone*, 58).
"when you feel longing, sing of women in love ..." (*Ahead of All Parting*, 333).
"an artificial psychic split ..." (*Frau Lou*, 336).

"we grasp a work of ours, something objectivized, as ourselves." (Ibid., 348).

47 "Even after we've talked about the most terrible things . . ." (*Looking Back*, 104).

"It should be possible for us . . ." (*Love Story in Letters*, 206).

"*must* suffer, and that it will always be so" (Ibid.).

"to be once more my own severest doctor: alone and quiet." (*A Ringing Glass*, 237).

"long walks in the woods, going barefoot . . ." (*Love Story in Letters*, 202).

48 "always standing before a telescope . . ." (Ibid., 225).

"I've never the experience which could help in a detached way . . ." (Prater, 223).

"What finally turned out so absolutely to my misery . . ." (*Love Story in Letters*, 238).

49 "terror, flight, retreat . . ." (Ibid., 270).

"what at most I can have in common . . ." (*A Ringing Glass*, 281).

"these three years past . . ." (*Frau Lou*, 438).

"I must always remind myself . . ." (*Love Story in Letters*, 306).

50 "work" of an "author" when he was trying to "create a universe." (*Life of a Poet*, 311).

"We are human beings, René," (*A Ringing Glass*, 320).

"For a spirit which finds fulfillment . . ." (Ibid., 334).

51 "now I know myself again" (*Love Story in Letters*, 332).

"sat and read and cried for joy . . ." (Ibid.).

"*I can never tell you*: how much this means to . . ." (Ibid., 338).

"that you are there, dear, dear Lou, to seal it . . ." (Ibid., 334).

52 "For two whole years I have been living . . ." (Ibid., 354).

"The tipping-over into the realm of the tormented . . ." (Ibid., 359).

"an inevitable mystery, which ought not to be analyzed too closely" (*A Ringing Glass*, 403).

"Lou must be told everything . . ." (Ibid.).

"asked him whether to write you again . . ." (*Frau Lou*, 455).

"Farewell, my love." (*Love Story in Letters*, 360).

53 "held aloof from them, antagonized them, offended against all civility . . ." (*Frau Lou*, 457).

"might look into your face for but ten minutes . . ." (Ibid., 377).

"even in that concerned and ardent closeness . . ." (*Looking Back*, 90).

Bibliography

Andreas-Salomé, Lou. *The Freud Journal*. Stanley Leavy, trans. London: Quartet, 1964.

———. *Looking Back*. Ernst Pfeiffer, ed.; Breon Mitchell, trans. New York: Paragon House, 1991.

———. *Nietzsche in His Work*. Siegfried Mandel, trans. Urbana and Chicago, University of Illinois Press, 1988.

———. *You Alone Are Real to Me: Remembering Rainer Maria Rilke*. Angela von der Lippe, trans. Rochester: BOA Editions, 2003.

Andreas-Salomé, Lou, and Rainer Maria Rilke. *Rainer Maria Rilke, Lou Andreas-Salomé: Briefweschel*. Ernst Pfeiffer, ed. Weisbaden: Insel Verlag, 1975.

Bernoulli, Carl. *Franz Overbeck und Friedrich Nietzsche. Eine Freundschaft*. Diederichs, Jena, 1908.

Binion, Rudolph. *Frau Lou: Nietzsche's Wayward Disciple*. Princeton: Princeton University Press, 1968.

Freedman, Ralph. *Life of a Poet: Rainer Maria Rilke*. NY: Farrar, Straus & Giroux, 1996.

Hendry, J. F. *The Sacred Threshold: A Life of Rainer Maria Rilke*. Manchester: Carcanet New Press, 1983.

Leppmann, Wolfgang. *Rilke: A Life*. New York: Fromm International, 1984.

Livingstone, Angela. *Salomé, Her Life and Work*. Mt. Kisco, NY: Moyer Bell Ltd., 1984.

Nietzsche, Friedrich. *On the Genealogy of Morals*. Walter Kaufmann, trans. New York: Vintage, 1969, p. 18.

Prater, Donald. *A Ringing Glass: The Life of Rainer Maria Rilke*. New York: Oxford University Press, 1986.

Prose, Francine. *The Lives of the Muses*. New York: HarperCollins, 2002.

Rilke, Rainer Maria. *Ahead of All Parting: The Selected Poetry and Prose of Rainer Maria Rilke*. Stephen Mitchell, trans. New York: Modern Library, 1995.

———. *Das Testament*, Frankfurt: Insel Verlag, 1975.

———. *Diaries of a Young Poet*. Edward Snow and Michael Winkler, trans. New York: W. W. Norton, 1997.

———. *Letters on Cézanne*. Joel Agee, trans. New York: Fromm International. 1952.

———. *Letters to a Young Poet*. Joan Burnham, trans. Novato: New World Library, 2000.

———. *Letters of Rainer Maria Rilke*. Jane Bannard Greene and M. D. Herter Norton, trans. New York: W. W. Norton, 1945.

———. *Rilke and Andreas-Salomé: A Love Story in Letters*. Edward Snow and Michael Winkler, trans. New York: W. W. Norton & Co., 2008.

———. *Rilke and Benvenuta: An Intimate Correspondence*. Joel Agee, trans. New York: Fromm International, 1987.

Torgersen, Eric. *Dear Friend: Rainer Maria Rilke and Paula Modersohn-Becker*. Evanston, IL: Northwestern University Press, 1998.

Vickers, Julia, *Lou von Salomé: A Biography of the Woman Who Inspired Freud, Nietzsche and Rilke*. Jefferson, NC: McFarland, 2008.

Chapter Two
Mutually Sustaining Visions: Alfred Stieglitz and Georgia O'Keeffe
ATTRIBUTIONS

55 "I believe it was the work . . ." (O'Keeffe, Georgia. *Georgia O'Keeffe: Art and Letters*. Sarah Greenough, ed. Boston: Little, Brown & Company, 1987, 200). "My biography will be a simple affair . . ." (McGrath, Roberta. "Rereading Edward Weston: Feminism, Photography and Psychoanalysis." *Illuminations: Women Writing on Photography from the 1850s to the Present*. Durham, Duke University Press, 1996, 265). "The relationship was really very good . . ." (Robinson, Roxanna. *Georgia O'Keeffe: A Life*. New York: Harper Perennial, 1990, 340).

57 "I dont love him—I don't pretend to . . ." (O'Keeffe, Georgia, and Anita Pollitzer. *Lovingly, Georgia: The Complete Correspondence of Georgia O'Keeffe & Anita Pollitzer*. Clive Giboire, ed. New York: Touchstone, 1990, 53). "nearer being in love . . ." (*Georgia O'Keeffe: A Life*, 119). "man I don't know what to do with . . ." (*Lovingly, Georgia*, 47).

58 "I would rather have Stieglitz like something . . ." (*Georgia O'Keeffe: Art & Letters*, 144). "looked . . . he thoroughly absorbed & got them . . ." (*Lovingly, Georgia*, xxii).

59 "spirit of 291—Not I." (Eisler, Benita. *O'Keeffe and Stieglitz: An American Romance*. New York: Penguin, 1991, 169).

60 "because what I was promised stirred . . ." (Norman, Dorothy. *Alfred Stieglitz: An American Seer*. New York: Random House, 1973, 13).

61 "straight, unmanipulated, devoid of all tricks . . ." (Stieglitz, Alfred. *Alfred Stieglitz on Photography*. New York: Aperture, 2000, 18). "In Stieglitz, there is no revolt . . ." (*O'Keeffe and Stieglitz*, 422). "when I make a picture I make love." (*Alfred Stieglitz: An American Seer*, 13).

62 "as clean as his mother." (*O'Keeffe and Stieglitz*, 45). "happiest and freest" (Ibid., 44) "from a sense of overpowering loneliness . . ." (*Alfred Stieglitz: An American Seer*, 35).

63 "during the entire period of five years . . ." (Ibid., 42). "Why do you always speak in that semi-abstract way?" (*O'Keeffe and Stieglitz*, 96). "You cannot think how bad it is for me . . ." (Fryd, Vivien Green. *Art and the Crisis of Marriage: Edward Hopper and Georgia O'Keeffe*. Chicago: University of Chicago Press, 2003, 32). "What good is the advancement of art . . ." (Ibid., 32). "I wish father would speak of things . . ." (*Alfred Stieglitz: An American Seer*, 225).

64 "in a room with paintings on the wall . . ." (*O'Keeffe and Stieglitz*, 289).

65 "Don't let anything I have said affect you . . ." (Stieglitz, Alfred. *Alfred Stieglitz*

Talking: Notes on Some of His Conversations, 1925-1931. Herbert J. Seligman, ed. New Haven: Yale University Press, 1966, 33).
"to call these rooms a gallery . . ." (*Alfred Stieglitz: An American Seer,* 115).
"Finally, a woman on paper" (*Lovingly, Georgia,* xxii).
"Between man and woman there is this reaching . . ." (*Alfred Stieglitz: An American Seer,* xi).

68 Regarding O'Keeffe's nickname and androgyny, cf. Eisler, 128.
"I am disgusted with myself . . ." (*Lovingly, Georgia,* 119).

69 "excited me so that I felt like a human being" (Ibid., 159).
"They do it to me too, or I wouldn't give a hang." (Ibid., 116).
"It is impossible for me to put into words" (*O'Keeffe and Stieglitz,* 81).
"I think letters with so much humanness in them . . ." (Ibid., 122).

70 "Both fell for him . . . almost lost my mind" (*Lovingly, Georgia,* 132).

71 "wanted to put my arms . . ." (*Georgia O'Keeffe: A Life,* 184).
"so many people had kissed me . . ." (Ibid., 185).
"I some way seem to feel . . ." (Ibid.).
"both cold women" (*O'Keeffe and Stieglitz,* 164).

72 Stieglitz "is probably more necessary to me than anyone . . ." (*Georgia O'Keeffe: A Life,* 196).
"She is the spirit of 291 . . ." (*O'Keeffe and Stieglitz,* 169).
"If I had some money . . ." (Ibid., 172).
"The best way I can tell you how things are . . ." (Ibid., 177).

73 "I'm sure she had made up her mind to come to New York . . ." (Ibid., 173).
"The coming or not coming is entirely in her hands . . ." (Ibid., 174).
"Why I can't believe she is at all . . ." (Ibid., 184).
"She is much more extraordinary than even I believed . . ." (Ibid., 184).

74 "I can never quite accustom myself . . ." (*Georgia O'Keeffe: A Life,* 206).
"[Emmy] slandered an innocent woman . . ." (*O'Keeffe and Stieglitz,* 193).
"Whenever she looks at the proofs . . ." (Ibid., 188).

75 "he loves her so." (Ibid., 236).
"If I could do anything I wanted . . ." (*Georgia O'Keeffe: A Life,* 207).

76 "His work is always a surprise to me . . ." (Lisle, Laurie. *Portrait of an Artist: A Biography of Georgia O'Keeffe.* New York: Washington Square Press, 1997, 128).
"A[lfred] gets on a prickly edge . . ." (*Georgia O'Keeffe: A Life,* 422).

77 "suffered while her paintings were being discussed" (*O'Keeffe and Stieglitz,* 213).
"as detached as though she had nothing to do with the paintings" (Ibid.).
"I think each painting very fine just after I've done it . . ." (*Georgia O'Keeffe: A Life,* 290).
"I get out my work and have a show for myself . . ." (O'Keeffe, Georgia. *Georgia O'Keeffe.* New York: Penguin, 1976, 31).

78 "The things they write sound so strange . . ." (*Georgia O'Keeffe: A Life*, 241).
"Whether you succeed . . ." (*Georgia O'Keeffe: Art and Letters*, 174).

79 "that, sir, is like suggesting that your daughter be a virgin . . ." (*Georgia O'Keeffe: A Life*, 265).
"I knew very well that you have communicated . . ." (*O'Keeffe and Stieglitz*, 264).

81 "If I had the power, I'd pull up by the roots . . ." (Ibid., 308).
"It seems we have been moving all winter . . ." (*Georgia O'Keeffe: Art and Letters*, 177).

82 "since the 291 exhibitions I haven't had anything . . ." (Ibid., 183).

83 "Stieglitz liked the idea of a group . . ." (*Georgia O'Keeffe: A Life*, 369).
"it has been very painful for him and the poor little thing is quite wore out" (Ibid., 296).

84 "'You will discover,' he remarked . . ." (*Alfred Stieglitz: An American Seer*, 10-11).
"The way he saw it, said it, spoke his life out loud . . ." (*O'Keeffe and Stieglitz*, 121).
"I go into the Room once more . . ." (*Encounters*, 56).
"As soon as Stieglitz spoke to you . . ." (*O'Keeffe and Stieglitz*, 121).

85 "Either one worked with Stieglitz in perfect trust or not at all . . ." (*Alfred Stieglitz: An American Seer*, 203).
"no one picture was his . . ." (*O'Keeffe and Stieglitz*, 285).
"was one of those people who adored Stieglitz . . ." (Ibid., 367).
"The city's very hard" (*Georgia O'Keeffe: A Life*, 317).
"mostly all dead to me" (*Georgia O'Keeffe: Art and Letters*, 195).
"I oftentimes—most times—feel like a criminal . . ." (*Georgia O'Keeffe: A Life*, 307).

86 "I wished you had seen my work . . ." (*Georgia O'Keeffe: Art and Letters*, 180).
"I am West again and it is as fine as I remembered it . . ." (*Georgia O'Keeffe: A Life*, 326).
"Right now as I come fresh from six days mostly spent . . ." (*O'Keeffe and Stieglitz*, 397).
"the cunt has no memory" (Miller, Donald. *Lewis Mumford: A Life*. Grove Press, 2002, 340).

87 "diapers of my children" and the "dreams of youth" (*O'Keeffe and Stieglitz*, 401).
"That's death riding high in the sky . . ." (*Georgia O'Keeffe: A Life*, 337).
"finally beyond all Hurt" (Ibid., 336).
"My photographs—the Equivalents—are what that Self is . . ." (*O'Keeffe and Stieglitz*, 399).
"I had a marvellous wire from Georgia . . ." (*Georgia O'Keeffe: A Life*, 337).
"It is wonderful to be here and be with my funny little Stieglitz . . ." (*Georgia O'Keeffe: Art and Letters*, 196).

"divided between my man and a life with him . . ." (Ibid., 207).
88 "I think of you and think of you . . ." (*O'Keeffe and Stieglitz*, 443).
89 "For the first ten days I was sort of in the house by myself . . ." (*Georgia O'Keeffe: A Life*, 396).
"What you give me makes me feel more able to stand up alone . . ." (Ibid., 401).
"more and more toward a kind of aloneness . . ." (*Georgia O'Keeffe: Art and Letters*, 219).
"The center of you seems to me to be . . ." (Ibid., 216).
90 "There were talks [with Stieglitz] that seemed almost to kill me . . ." (Ibid., 219).
91 "has such a clean untouched feeling . . ." (*Georgia O'Keeffe: A Life*, 448).
"the second of O'Keeffe's slaves . . ." (*O'Keeffe and Stieglitz*, 472).
92 "If I could just get down all Im thinking about . . ." (*Georgia O'Keeffe: Art and Letters*, 179).
"You sound a bit lonely up there on the hill . . ." (*O'Keeffe and Stieglitz*, 464).
"I greet you on your coming once more . . ." (Ibid., 477).
94 "It is a week or more and I do not write you . . ." (*Georgia O'Keeffe: Art and Letters*, 264).
95 "You have written your dream picture of me," (*Lovingly, Georgia*, 320).
96 "If it is real," marriage "must be based on a wish . . ." (*Art and the Crisis of Marriage*, 42).
97 "You must not let the things you cannot help destroy you" (*Georgia O'Keeffe: Art and Letters*, 200).

BIBLIOGRAPHY

Eisler, Benita. *O'Keeffe and Stieglitz: An American Romance*. New York: Penguin, 1991.

Fryd, Vivien Green. *Art and the Crisis of Marriage: Edward Hopper and Georgia O'Keeffe*. Chicago: University of Chicago Press, 2003.

Hapgood, Hutchins. *A Victorian in the Modern World*. Seattle: University of Washington Press, 1967.

Lisle, Laurie. *Portrait of an Artist: A Biography of Georgia O'Keeffe*. New York: Washington Square Press, 1997.

Miller, Donald. *Lewis Mumford: A Life*. Grove Press, 2002.

Norman, Dorothy. *Alfred Stieglitz: An American Seer*. New York: Random House, 1973.

———. *Encounters: A Memoir*. New York: Harcourt, 1987.

O'Keeffe, Georgia. *Georgia O'Keeffe: Art and Letters*. Sarah Greenough, ed. Boston: Little, Brown & Company, 1987.

———. *Georgia O'Keeffe*. New York: Penguin, 1976.

———. O'Keeffe, Georgia and Anita Pollitzer. *Lovingly, Georgia: The Complete Correspondence of Georgia O'Keeffe & Anita Pollitzer*. New York: Touchstone, 1990.

Pollitzer, Anita. *A Woman on Paper: Georgia O'Keeffe*. New York: Simon & Schuster, 1988.

Robinson, Roxanna. *Georgia O'Keeffe: A Life*. New York: Harper Perennial, 1990.

Rudnick, Lois. *Mabel Dodge Luhan: New Woman, New Worlds*. Albuquerque: University of New Mexico Press, 1984.

Stieglitz, Alfred. *Alfred Stieglitz Talking: Notes on Some of His Conversations, 1925-1931*. Herbert J. Seligman, ed. New Haven: Yale University Press, 1966.

Stieglitz, Alfred. *Alfred Stieglitz: With an Essay by Dorothy Norman*. New York: Aperture Foundation, 1997

———. *Alfred Stieglitz on Photography*. New York: Aperture, 2000.

———. *Dear Stieglitz, Dear Dove*. Ann Lee Morgan, ed. Newark: University of Delaware Press, 1988.

———. *Stieglitz, Alfred*. New York: Aperture, 1976.

Whelan, Richard. *Alfred Stieglitz: A Biography*. Boston: Little, Brown, 1995.

ChapterThree
Intellectuals in Love: Jean-Paul Sartre and Simone de Beauvoir
ATTRIBUTIONS

99   "I'm a genius because I'm alive . . ." (Hayman, Ronald. *Sartre: A Life*. New York: Simon & Schuster. 1987, 64).

"The only sort of person . . ." (Beauvoir, Simone de. *Prime of Life*. Peter Green, trans. New York: Paragon House, 1992, 69).

"With Sartre, too, I have a physical relationship . . ." (Rowley, Hazel. *Tête-à-Tête*. New York: HarperCollins, 2005, 91).

"a world that was without God . . ." (*Prime of Life*, 151).

100   "had all explored much more fundamentally . . ." (Beauvoir, Simone de. *Memoirs of a Dutiful Daughter*. James Kirkup, trans. New York: Harper Perennial, 1958, 344).

101   "Man was to be remolded . . ." (*Prime of Life*, 18).

"about all kinds of things, but especially . . ." (*Memoirs of a Dutiful Daughter*, 340).

"There were no scruples, no feelings of respect . . ." (*Prime of Life*, 19).

102   "not an overwhelming passion . . . but it's happiness . . ." (*Tête-à-Tête*, 23).

"demolished . . . pluralist philosophy . . ." (*Memoirs of a Dutiful Daughter*, 344).

"many of my opinions . . ." (Ibid.).

103   "not inclined to be monogamous . . ." (*Prime of Life*, 23).

"sign a two-year lease . . . for a longer or shorter period . . ." (Ibid., 24).

"not only would we never lie . . ." (Ibid.).

104   "Anne Marie, chilled with gratitude" (Sartre, Jean-Paul. *The Words*. Bernard Frechtman, trans. New York: Fosset Crest, 1964, 17).

"under surveillance, who is obedient to everyone" (Ibid., 13).

"my mother and I were the same age . . ." (Ibid., 136).

105 "my failure had not affected me . . ." (Ibid., 49).
"whether the adults listen to my babbling . . ." (Ibid., 25).
106 "Since nobody laid claim to me seriously . . ." (Ibid., 69).
"too loved to have doubts" (Ibid., 136-146).
"physicist's temperament, pessimism, underhandedness . . ." (Sartre, Jean-
Paul. *Witness to My Life: The Letters of Jean-Paul Sartre to Simone de Beauvoir, 1926-*
1939, Simone de Beauvoir, ed. Lee Fahnestock and Norman MacAfee, trans.
New York: Scribners, 1992, 381).
"odd tone and role . . . among groups of men . . ." (Ibid., 399).
"what had changed profoundly since my arrival in Paris . . ." (Sartre, Jean-
Paul, *War Diaries*. Quintin Hoare, trans. New York: Pantheon Books, 1984,
270-1).
107 "I became a traitor and have remained one . . ." (*Words*, 149).
"Though I throw myself heart and soul into what I undertake" (Ibid.).
108 "You might as well tell it to the League of Nations . . ." (*Witness to My Life*,
17).
"Why should you have less ability to see than I?" (Ibid., 20).
"Who has made you what you are? . . ." (Ibid., 9).
109 "appreciated elegant gestures . . ." (*Memoirs of a Dutiful Daughter*, 33).
"contemptuous of successes . . ." (Ibid.).
"the more serious virtues esteemed by the bourgeoisie." (Ibid.).
"first memories of her are of a laughing" (Ibid., 37).
"the ability to pass over in silence . . ." (Ibid., 17).
"in our universe, the flesh had no right to exist." (Ibid., 58).
"world free from all irregularities" (Ibid., 66).
"forbidden to play with strange little girls . . ." (Ibid., 47).
"alter ego, my double; we could not do without . . ." (Ibid., 42).
"even when I was just doing transfers . . ." (Ibid., 43).
110 "If I was describing in words an episode in my life . . ." (Ibid., 70).
"the trade bored him . . ." (Ibid., 98).
"My mother dressed me badly . . ." (Ibid., 182).
111 "live dangerously. Refuse nothing." (Ibid., 273).
"Apart from . . . rare exceptions . . ." (Ibid.,187).
112 "the august high-priestesses of Knowledge . . ." (Ibid., 122).
"thought their lives out," (Ibid., 223).
"in everything she did . . ." (Ibid., 93).
"did not entirely correspond . . ." (Ibid., 118).
113 "a solution and not as a point of departure," (Ibid., 218).
"not possible to reconcile . . ." (Ibid., 212).
"hunting for extraordinary experiences," (Ibid., 282).
"comfort in the warmth of a strange hand . . ." (Ibid., 273).
"I didn't know what to do or say . . ." (Ibid.,161).

"There was talk of sending me abroad . . ." (Ibid., 192).
"the only people who, without cheating . . ." (Ibid., 230).
"had given their lives to combating . . ." (Ibid., 160).
"nothing better than a licensed brothel," (Ibid., 175).
"to train for a profession was a sign of defeat" (Ibid., 175).
"life of debauchery" (Ibid., 293).

114 "revolting fate that had lain ahead of us" (Ibid., 360).
"succeed in laying bare reality . . ." (Ibid., 114).
"one single aim fired us . . ." (*Prime of Life*, 26).
"perfect agreement" (Ibid., 27).
"never amount to more than a Worm's whore." (Bair, Deirdre. *Simone de Beauvoir: A Biography*. New York: Summit Books, 1990, 197).

115 "sadden me . . ." (*Witness to My Life*, 129).
"and all the smaller jewelry . . ." (*Prime of Life*, 42).
"heroines of Meredith's . . ." (Ibid., 54).
"the opening chapters held up pretty well . . ." (Ibid., 179).

116 "felt I had played a practical joke on someone" (Ibid., 16).
"I discharged the duties of a philosophy teacher . . ." (Ibid., 275).
"the advantages of a double post . . ." (Ibid., 66).
"to the common customs and observations" (Ibid., 67).
"I felt such absence of affinity . . ." (Ibid.).
"to show, without complacency . . ." (*Words*, 158).

117 "had all the advantages of a shared life . . ." (*Tête-à-Tête*, 72).
"illegitimate relationship was regarded . . ." (*Prime of Life*, 288).
Regarding Beauvoir's encounter with Pierre Guille in 1931, see *Tête-à-Tête*, 42.
"neither took me by surprise . . ." (*Prime of Life*, 149).

118 "agreed there could be no future in this relationship," (Ibid.).
"Anything at all . . ." (Beauvoir, Simone de. *Adieux: A Farewell to Sartre*. Patrick O'Brian, trans. New York: Pantheon Books, 1984, 296).
"Most of the time a woman . . ." (Ibid., 298).

119 "set about turning them inside-out . . ." (*Prime of Life*, 104).
"Like every bourgeois . . ." (Ibid., 288).

120 "eager and indiscriminate appetite . . ." (Ibid., 186).
"fresh, childlike quality about her enthusiasms" (Ibid.).
"her impetuous, whole-hogging nature," (Ibid.).
"first filled her up with hatred . . ." (Ibid., 184).
"dream of becoming a ballet dancer," (Ibid.).
"admirably placed to come to her aid . . ." (Ibid.).
"promised [Olga] she would blaze her own trail into it." (Ibid.,185).
"the sense of private solidarity . . ." (Ibid.).
"chronic fantasy flourished" (Ibid., 225).

"I want you to know that there is not one . . ." (*Tête-à-Tête*, 54).
Deeply similar in their rebellions, Beauvoir and Olga may or may not have become lovers, (Ibid., 60—Bair insists otherwise).

121 "shrank from burdening a stranger . . ." (*Prime of Life*, 192).
"for the first time in my life . . ." (Hayman, Ronald. *Sartre: A Life*. New York: Simon & Schuster, 1987, 116).
"Music bores me; I only enjoy sounds" (*Prime of Life*, 192).
"Sartre now began to devote . . ." (Ibid.).
"became Rimbaud, Antigone . . ." (Ibid., 194).

122 "no one should mean as much to Olga as he did," (Ibid., 193).
"bring [his relationship with Olga] to a climax . . ." (Ibid., 192).
"any expression of reserve or indifference," (Ibid., 204).
"when I said 'We are one person' . . ." (Ibid., 209).
"whether the whole of my happiness . . ." (Ibid. 209).

123 "other people" (Ibid., 233).
"daughter before Lucifer" (Ibid., 204).
"no ambitions . . ." (Ibid., 197).
"satanic sense of humor," (Ibid., 199).

124 "Each conscience seeks the death of the other" (Beauvoir, Simone de. *She Came to Stay*. New York: W. W. Norton, 1999).
"by killing Olga on paper . . ." (*Prime of Life*, 270).

125 "I contemplated doing a brief preface . . ." (*Witness to My Life*, 180).
"I had two beautiful and tragic nights . . ." (Ibid., 156).
"You're very sweet to have told me . . ." (Beauvoir, Simone de. *Letters to Sartre*. Qiuntin Hoare, trans. New York: Arcade Publisher, 1992, 21).

126 "I have only *one* sensual life . . ." (*Tête-à-Tête*, 91).
"feels in a sharper, fuller way . . ." (Sartre, Jean-Paul. *Quiet Moments in a War: The Letters of Jean-Paul Sartre to Simone de Beauvoir, 1940-1963*. Simone de Beauvoir, ed. Lee Fahnestock and Norman MacAfee, trans. New York: Scribners, 1993, 38).
"it takes the violence of arguments . . ." (*Tête-à-Tête*, 92).
"I do miss you . . ." (*Witness to My Life*, 183).
"on the insipid side." (Ibid., 197).
"undertaken to gradually tear down . . ." (Ibid., 198-199).

127 "obvious beauty . . . brilliant, piercing, bold intelligence . . ." (Lamblin, Bianca. *A Disgraceful Affair*. Julie Plovnik, trans. Boston: Northeastern University Press, 1993, 17).
"I think ultimately . . ." (*Tête-à-Tête*, 90).
"we agreed that we should dissuade you . . ." (*Witness to My Life*, 204).

128 "I've never felt so intently . . ." (Ibid., 242).
"Write me everything in detail . . ." (Ibid., 252).
"It's a terrible bore . . ." (*Quiet Moments in a War*, 138).

"immediately renew the lease for ten years" (*Witness to My Life*, 280).
"less in my life and more in things," (*Letters to Sartre*, 72).
"a rootless being . . ." (Ibid., 63).
"My life's full but terribly barren . . ." (Ibid., 254).
129 "her life is me . . ." (*Witness to My Life*, 377).
"envisaged . . .[the trio] as an exact tripartite division . . ." (*Letters to Sartre*, 160).
"really could have reproached us . . .with not having made things clear," (Ibid.)
"hint of depravity . . ." (Ibid., 155).
"vague, lousy idea . . .that I should at least 'take advantage'" (Ibid.)
"My love, what barren nourishment . . ." (Ibid., 74).
"gives me what used to be precious . . ." (Ibid., 269).
130 "had regard for the brilliant students . . ." (*A Disgraceful Affair*, 19).
"I feel a bit like some clumsy seducer . . ." (*Letters to Sartre*, 107).
"I'll have to sleep with her . . ." (Ibid., 212).
"it interested her as an experience . . ." (Ibid., 243).
"a very keen taste for her body . . ." (Ibid., 255).
"harem of women," (*Witness to My Life*, 424).
"either [Sorokine] exacts promises . . ." (*Letters to Sartre*, 294).
131 "never ask a question . . ." (Ibid., 227).
"consciousness is such an absolute . . ." (*Prime of Life*, 7).
"conjugal days" (*Letters to Sartre*, 299).
"as far as possible to accept . . ." (*Letters to Sartre*, 156).
"theorize her life rather than us . . ." (Ibid., 161).
"blamed us—myself as much as you . . ." (Ibid., 285).
"Birnenschatz is strangely similar . . ." (*Disgraceful Affair*, 74).
132 "carte blanche . . ." (*Quiet Moments in a War*, 165).
"I never loved you . . ." (Ibid., 73).
"very profoundly disgusted with myself." (Ibid., 74).
"to play the neighborhood Don Juan? . . ." (Ibid.).
133 "Today I wrote: you well know . . ." (Ibid., 75-76).
"My feelings for [Wanda] . . ." (Ibid., 84).
134 "that shifty sort of generosity . . ." (Ibid.).
"severe letter" (Ibid., 88).
"I've never been this uneasy with myself . . ." (Ibid., 87-89).
"very disagreeable to know that she's panic stricken" (Ibid., 179).
"It's odd, she is becoming . . ." (Ibid., 180).
"slam the brakes on marriage," (Ibid., 183).
135 "suffering from an intense and dreadful attack . . ." (*Letters to Sartre*, 389).
"charming vermin." (Ibid., 231).
136 "The police interviewed everyone involved—but they had all coordinated and rehearsed their stories, so the case was dropped." (*Tête-à-Tête*, 131).

138 "according to his accounts . . ." (Beauvoir, Simone de. *Force of Circumstance.* Volume I. Richard Howard, trans. New York: Harper Colophon, 1964, I, 69).

139 "Dolores' love for me scares me . . ." (*Quiet Moments in a War*, 274).
"found her exactly as I'd imagined . . ." (*Letters to Sartre*, 415).

140 "his lust transfigured me . . ." (Beauvoir, Simone de. *The Mandarins.* Leonard M. Friedman, trans. South Bend, IN: Regnery/Gateway, 1979, 139).
"the only truly passionate love in my life" (*Simone de Beauvoir: A Biography*, 344).
"I love you too much . . ." (Beauvoir, Simone de. *A Transatlantic Love Affair: Letters to Nelson Algren.* Sylvie Le Bon Beauvoir, ed. Ellen Gordon Reeves, trans. New York: The New Press, 1998, 116).
"conjugal life" (Ibid., 479).
"I can't regret this affair being dead . . ." (*Letters to Sartre*, 460).
"extract yourself as best you can . . ." (Ibid.).

141 "apprenticeship in abandonment . . ." (Beauvoir, Simone de. *Second Sex.* H. M. Parshley, trans. New York: Knopf, 1953, 711).
"the free woman is just being born." (Ibid., 715).

142 "the big thing about sexual love . . ." (Madsen, Axel. *Hearts & Minds: The Common Journey of Simone de Beauvoir and Jean-Paul Sartre.* New York: Morrow Quill Paperbacks, 1977, 140).
"the pain and the pleasure of writing . . ." (*Force of Circumstance*, I, 128).

143 "not the slightest question of rivalry with Sartre" (Bair, 444).
"temporary moral code" (*Tête-à-Tête*, 246).
"could hardly understand" (Bair, 513).

145 "is as thoroughly interwoven in my life . . ." (Ibid., 507).
"the Beaver often used to tell me . . ." (*Tête-à-Tête*, 310).
"This did not keep Beauvoir from urging Le Bon to have an affair." (Ibid., 320).
"it is an absolute relationship . . ." (Bair, 509).

BIBLIOGRAPHY

Bair, Deirdre. *Simone de Beauvoir: A Biography.* New York: Summit Books, 1990.

Beauvoir, Simone de. *Adieux: A Farewell to Sartre.* Patrick O'Brian, trans. New York: Pantheon Books, 1984.

——. *Force of Circumstance.* Volume I. Richard Howard, trans. New York: Harper Colophon, 1964.

——. *Letters to Sartre.* Qiuntin Hoare, trans. New York: Arcade Pub, 1992.

——. *The Mandarins.* Leonard M. Friedman, trans. South Bend, IN: Regnery/Gateway, 1979.

——. *Memoirs of a Dutiful Daughter.* James Kirkup, trans. New York: Harper Perennial, 1958.

——. *Prime of Life.* Peter Green, trans. New York: Paragon House, 1992.

———. *Second Sex*. H. M. Parshley, trans. New York: Knopf, 1953.

———. *She Came to Stay*. New York: W. W. Norton, 1999.

———. *A Transatlantic Love Affair: Letters to Nelson Algren*. Sylvie Le Bon Beauvoir, ed. Ellen Gordon Reeves, trans. New York: The New Press, 1998.

Hayman, Ronald. *Sartre: A Life*. New York: Simon & Schuster. 1987.

Lamblin, Bianca. *A Disgraceful Affair*. Julie Plovnik, trans. Boston: Northeastern University Press, 1993.

Madsen, Axel. *Hearts & Minds: The Common Journey of Simone de Beauvoir and Jean-Paul Sartre*. New York: Morrow Quill Paperbacks, 1977.

Rowley, Hazel. *Tête-à-Tête*. New York: HarperCollins, 2005.

Sartre, Jean-Paul. *Quiet Moments in a War: The Letters of Jean-Paul Sartre to Simone de Beauvoir, 1940-1963*. Simone de Beauvoir, ed. Lee Fahnestock and Norman MacAfee, trans. New York: Scribners, 1993.

———. *Witness to My Life: The Letters of Jean-Paul Sartre to Simone de Beauvoir, 1926-1939*. Simone de Beauvoir, ed. Lee Fahnestock and Norman MacAfee, trans. New York: Scribners, 1992.

———. *War Diaries*. Quintin Hoare, trans. New York: Pantheon Books, 1984.

———. *The Words*. Bernard Frechtman, trans. New York: Fosset Crest, 1964.

Chapter Four
The Sacred Monsters: Diego Rivera and Frida Kahlo
ATTRIBUTIONS

147   "I am not merely an 'artist' but a man . . ." (Marnham, Patrick. *Dreaming with His Eyes Open: A Life of Diego Rivera*. New York: Knopf, 1998, 260).

"I will not speak of Diego as 'my husband,' . . ." (*Frida by Frida*, 310).

"The most joyous moments . . ." (Rivera, Diego. *My Art, My Life*. New York: Dover, 1991, 180).

"Whenever you feel like caressing her . . ." (Kahlo, Frida. *Frida by Frida*. Raquel Tibol, ed., Gregory Dechant, trans. Mexico: Editorial RM, 2003, 25).

149   "so fervently," (*Dreaming*, 69).

"prepared to become [Rivera's] fiancée." (*Dreaming*, 69).

"I was feeling more or less destroyed by my reaction . . ." (Ibid., 73).

151   "badly trained tigress" (Ibid., 123).

"'she-devil' . . .not only because of her wild beauty . . ." (*My Art, My Life*, 68).

"interested in launching [Vorobiev] as a painter" (*Dreaming*, 121).

"caught up in a dangerous game . . ." (Ibid.).

"a young woman who called herself a friend . . ." (Ibid.).

153   "for my part I wish to be with you . . ." (*Frida by Frida*, 24).

"Sometimes I'm very afraid at night . . ." (Ibid.).

For details of Kahlo's affairs in the summer of 1925, see Herrera, Hayden. *Frida: A Biography of Frida Kahlo*. New York: Perennial, 1984, 42-43.

"Concerning what you say about Anita Reyna . . ." (*Frida by Frida*, 26).

154 "such a bad reputation" (*Frida by Frida*, 58).
"said 'I love you' to many, and I have kissed . . ." (Ibid., 46).
155 "In your heart, you understand me, you know I adore you! . . ." (Ibid., 80).
"like a real mariachi" (Ibid., 100).
156 "Why, I asked her, didn't she trust my judgment? . . ." (*My Art, My Life*, 103).
"no matter how difficult it is for you, you must continue to paint," (Ibid.).
"if I showed my excitement she might not let me come at all." (Ibid., 104).
157 "dearly beloved but extremely ungrateful son . . ." (*Dreaming*, 132).
"images and ideas flow through his brain . . ." (*Frida by Frida*, 319).
158 "by no means negligible," (*Dreaming*, 101).
"was always one of my most prolific painters . . ." (Wolfe, Bertram. *The Fabulous Life of Diego Rivera*. New York: Stein and Day, 1963, 86).
For Maria Smvelowna-Zetlin, see Marnham, 125.
160 "look at those marvels, and we make such *trivia* and nonsense." (Ibid., 131).
161 "I foresaw a new society . . ." (*My Art, My Life*, 66).
162 "there was something hypnotic about him . . ." (*Dreaming*, 305).
"His alleged lying is in direct relation to his powerful imagination . . ." (*Frida by Frida*, 315)
"I have become terribly 'Mexicanized' . . ." (*The Fabulous Life*, 125).
164 "I often think, too, that perhaps the supposed difficulties . . ." (Ibid., 126).
"tall, proud of bearing, almost haughty . . ." (*Dreaming*, 164).
"a family of bourgeois respectability." (Ibid., 165).
"beautiful, spirited animal, but her jealousy and possessiveness . . ." (*My Art, My Life*, 83).
165 "rediscovered one of the ancient secrets of the Aztecs!" (*Dreaming*, 170).
"incorrigible philanderer," (*My Art, My Life*, 150).
"hot lunch" (*Dreaming*, 196).
"theatrical quality, a high eccentricity . . ." (*Frida: A Biography*, 234).
168 "beginning to grow accustomed to suffering," (Ibid., 51).
"I have no choice but to endure it." (*Frida by Frida*, 36).
"No one in my house believes that I am really sick . . ." (*Frida: A Biography*, 75).
169 "why do you study so much? . . ." (*Frida by Frida*, 47).
"From that time [of the accident] my obsession was to begin again . . ." (*Frida: A Biography*, 74).
170 "because I am so often alone, because I am the subject I know best," (Ibid.).
171 "*un demonio oculto*" (*Dreaming*, 224).
"Gentlemen, is it not true that we are play-acting?" (*My Art, My Life*, 104).
172 "I did not have a home, the Party having always been my home." (*Frida: A Biography*, 102).
"The Mexican women who do not wear it . . ." (Ibid., 111).
"I must have full skirts and long, now that my sick leg is so ugly." (Ibid., 234).

173 "his great gifts, great indulgence was in order," (Ibid., 108).
"couldn't care less," (Ibid., 107).
"Diego's very spinal column is painting, not politics." (Ibid., 128).
"feted at parties, dinners, receptions" (Ibid., 175).

174 "Henry Ford made the work of the socialist state possible." (*My Art, My Life*, 115).

175 "I don't think Diego is very interested in having a child . . ." (*Frida by Frida*, 100).
"I was so excited about having a little Dieguito . . ." (Ibid., 103).
"never before had a woman . . ." (*Frida: A Biography*, 124).
"reinflated and not disinflated again under any circumstances." (*Dreaming*, 263).

176 "he feels he must go back there for Frieda's sake . . ." (*Frida: A Biography*, 175).
"the people . . .always respond with obscenities . . ." (*Dreaming*, 259).

177 "Here in Mexico I have no one, I had only Diego . . ." (*Frida by Frida*, 130–131).

178 "Why must I be so stubborn and dense . . ." (Ibid., 136).

179 "I've painted. Which is something after all . . ." (Ibid., 162).
"loved her very much . . .[Frida] was a lovely person . . ." (*Frida: A Biography*, 200).

180 "the hidden springs of the social revolution" (*Dreaming*, 280).
"not simply a 'painting,' . . ." (*Frida: A Biography*, 209).

181 "They thought I was a surrealist . . ." (Ibid., 266).
"treats me with great affection and they are all very kind," (Ibid., 232).
"Like you I've been starved for true affection," (Ibid., 270).
"I have no words to tell you . . ." (*Frida by Frida*, 169).
"You can only kiss as much as you want Mam . . ." (Ibid., 176).

182 "of the three of us there was only two of you," (*Frida: A Biography*, 269).
"a milieu of understanding and sympathy . . ." (*Dreaming*, 293).
"We had been married now for thirteen years . . ." (*My Art, My Life*, 139).
"there is no change in the magnificent relations between us . . ." (*Frida: A Biography*, 273).
"I am already old and no longer have much to offer her." (Ibid., 274).
"he likes to be alone . . ." (Ibid., 275).

183 "dreaded a long, heart-wrenching discussion . . ." (*My Art, My Life*, 138).
(note) "by the end of 1939 . . . she was drinking . . ." (*Frida: A Biography*, 276).
"He took me to the hospital . . ." (Ibid., 300).
"I don't take a damn cent from Diego." (*Frida by Frida*, 187).
"that her life is of more value to me . . ." (*Dreaming*, 308).
"milieu of understanding . . ." (Ibid., 293).

184 "When I found out that you had in your possession . . ." (*Frida by Frida*, 207).

185 "wants me to [remarry] because he says he loves me . . ." (Ibid., 215).

"Diego loves you very much . . ." (*Frida: A Biography*, 298).

186 "the film actresses Dolores Del Rio and Paulette Goddard . . ." (*Dreaming*, 306).

"María Félix, Dolores Del Rio and Pita Amor . . ." (Ibid., 306).

"The re-marriage is working well . . ." (*Frida by Frida*, 230).

"Better than ever because there is mutual understanding . . ." (Ibid., 248).

187 "shooting pains." (*Frida: A Biography*, 353).

"The atoms of my body are yours . . ." (*Frida by Frida*, 270).

"I feel that we have been together . . ." (Ibid., 298).

188 "I entrust the big-child to you . . ." (*Frida: A Biography*, 303).

"Diego exists to one side of all personal, limited and precise relations . . ." (*Frida by Frida*, 312).

189 "the greatest proof of the renaissance of the art of Mexico" (*Frida: A Biography*, 362).

"You suffer a lot in this goddamned life . . ." (*Frida by Frida*, 275).

190 "following the loss of her leg . . ." (*My Art, My Life*, 178).

"many things in this life now bore me . . ." (*Frida: A Biography*, 396).

"something useful" (Ibid., 397).

"there was a party on in Frida's room every day," (Ibid., 390).

"They amputated my leg six months ago . . ." (Ibid., 420).

"I hope the exit is joyful—and I hope never to come back." (Ibid., 431).

For more on Rivera at Kahlo's funeral, see *Dreaming*, 311.

191 "Too late now I realized . . ." (*My Art, My Life*, 180).

BIBLIOGRAPHY

Herrera, Hayden. *Frida: A Biography of Frida Kahlo*. New York: Perennial, 1984.

Kahlo, Frida. *Frida by Frida*. Raquel Tibol, ed., Gregory Dechant, trans. Mexico: Editorial RM, 2003.

Levy, Julien. *Memoir of an Art Gallery*. New York: Putnam, 1977.

Marnham, Patrick. *Dreaming with His Eyes Open: A Life of Diego Rivera*. New York: Knopf, 1998.

McMeekin, Dorothy. *Diego Rivera: Science and Creativity in the Detroit Murals*. East Lansing, MI: Michigan State University Press, 1985.

Rivera, Diego. *My Art, My Life*. New York: Dover, 1991.

Wolfe, Bertram. *The Fabulous Life of Diego Rivera*. New York: Stein and Day, 1963.

Chapter Five
The Miracle Accomplished by Blood and Joy: Henry Miller and Anaïs Nin
ATTRIBUTIONS

195 "Henry has found himself. (Nin, Anaïs. *Incest*. New York: Harcourt Brace Jovanovich, 1992, 131).

"I am saying to myself here is the first woman . . ." (Miller, Henry, and Anaïs

Nin. *A Literate Passion. Letters of Anaïs Nin and Henry Miller, 1932-1953.* Gunther Stuhlmann, ed. New York: Harcourt Brace Jovanovich, 1987, 33). "The journal is a product of my disease . . ." (Nin, Anaïs. *Henry and June.* New York: Harcourt Brace Jovanovich, 1990, 207).

196   "parties, orgies," (*Henry and June*, 11).
     "fulfillment in other directions," (Ibid., 3).
     "I love my husband . . ." (Ibid., 1).

197   "I would never let Henry touch me . . ." (Ibid., 40).

198   "the only woman who ever answered" (Ibid., 16).
     "God, Henry, in you alone I have found . . ." (*A Literate Passion*, 36).
     "*éblouissants*, staggeringly beautiful." (*Henry and June*, 43).
     "Nobody has ever told us how and what women think" (*A Literate Passion*, 98).
     "nobody else is doing anything like this. Ecstatic. Wonderful" (*Incest*, 75).

199   "one literary fuck fest . . ." (*A Literate Passion*, 82).
     "going to open [her] very groins." (Ibid.).
     "You're food and drink to me . . ." (Ibid.).

200   "I really believe that if I were not a writer . . ." (*Henry and June*, 12).
     "This is a little drunken . . ." (*A Literate Passion*, 33).
     "What I have found in Henry is unique . . ." (*Henry and June*, 234).

201   "We are living something new," (Ibid., 67).
     "'The mountain of words has sundered . . ." (Ibid., 78).

203   "went crazy" and was "taken away," (Dearborn, Mary. *The Happiest Man Alive: A Biography of Henry Miller.* New York: Touchstone, 1991, 21).
     "*had* to be the autocrat to keep her sisters in line." (Ibid., 21).
     "[throwing] her hands up in despair . . ." (Ferguson, Robert. *Henry Miller: A Life.* New York: W. W. Norton, 1991, 6).
     "a sort of harmless monster, an angel . . ." (*Happiest Man Alive*, 27).
     "sober, industrious, frugal." (Ibid., 21).
     "It was all too easy for me. I felt like a trained monkey," (*A Literate Passion*, 215).

204   "never thought of fucking" (*Happiest Man Alive*, 39).
     "the unattainable one." (*Henry Miller: A Life*, 15).
     "his first sexual experience at sixteen in a whorehouse." (*Henry and June*, 263).
     "delicate, petite, beautifully proportioned . . ." (Miller, Henry. *Book of Friends.* San Bernardino, California: Borgo Press, 1990, 274).
     "Not only was Pauline my mistress . . ." (Ibid., 280).

205   "what good is all that reading going to do you?" (Ibid., 278).
     "a tremendous moral obligation towards her," (*Henry Miller: A Life*, 29).
     "the devil's own torments lately . . ." (Ibid., 38).

206   "like an oracle to me," (Ibid., 36).
     "felt so ashamed . . ." (*Book of Friends*, 283).
     "I got myself married overnight . . ." (Miller, Henry. *Tropic of Capricorn*, Paris: Obelisk Press, 1939, 284).

"the better the fuck, the worse she felt afterwards." (*Henry Miller: A Life*, 44).

208 "a gaily caparisoned cacique among cormorants . . ." (Miller, Henry. *Letters to Emil*. New York: New Directions, 1989, 5).

"It was a crushing defeat . . ." (*Tropic of Capricorn*, 32).

"knowing, mysterious, fugitive." (*Henry Miller: A Life*, 77).

"was always innocent and starry-eyed . . ." (Ibid., 84).

209 "the more lovers she garnered . . ." (*Happiest Man Alive*, 86).

"misery over June's golddigging, which constantly preys on my mind." (*Henry Miller: A Life*, 107).

"purposeful, literary buffoonery" (Ibid.).

210 "dopes and saps" (*Happiest Man Alive*, 103).

"Bed unmade all day . . ." (*Henry and June*, 46).

"my love for Val is only like . . ." (*Henry Miller: A Life*, 147).

212 "The sap is running," (*Letters to Emil*, 67).

"fuck everything" (Ibid., 60).

"will further alienate the reader . . ." (Ibid., 73).

213 "a little peace now, a little security . . ." (Ibid., 87).

"a world on which I have slammed the door . . ." (Ibid., 99).

"whom life made drunk" (*Henry and June*, 6).

215 "pampered by women . . ." (Nin, Anaïs. *Linotte: The Early Diary of Anaïs Nin*. New York: Harcourt Brace Jovanovich, 1978-1985, 326, 449).

"I believe this really happened . . ." (Bair, Deirdre. *Anaïs Nin: A Biography*. New York: Putnam's, 1995, 18).

For more information about Nin's childhood and her sexual relationship with her father, see *Anaïs: The Erotic Life*, pages 124, 128 and *Anaïs Nin: A Biography*, 555.

"he always wanted me naked. All admiration came by way of the camera." (Fitch, Noel Riley. *Anaïs: The Erotic Life of Anaïs Nin*. Boston: Little, Brown, 1993, 3).

"My father did not want a girl . . ." (*Henry and June*, 115).

216 "created a void between me and other people." (Ibid., 31).

"I learn things that I don't want to learn . . ." (*Anaïs Nin: A Biography*, 35-36).

217 "sit there hour after hour . . ." (Nin, Anaïs. *Early Diaries of Anaïs Nin*. New York, Harcourt Brace Jovanovich, 1978, 2, 367).

"Composition, Grammar, French and Boys." (Ibid., 2, 197).

"firm ground" (*Anaïs Nin: A Biography*, 56).

"some day the world will recognize Anaïs Nin Guiler . . ." (Ibid., 68).

"terrible religious and moral oppression" (Ibid., 56).

218 "Hugo controls and forces back . . ." (*Early Diaries*, 2: 266).

"incestal brother-sister" (*Anaïs Nin: A Biography*, 65).

"warm mahogany panellings, stained-glass windows . . ." (Perlès, Alfred. *My Friend Henry Miller*. London, Neville Spearman, 1955, 107).

219 "our whole life is spoiled by his work in the bank." (*Henry and June*, 46).

220 "the perfect, inhuman, divine *objectivity* . . ." (*Incest*, 34).

221 "a pathological child—interesting as such, but stupid and empty." (Ibid., 12).
"beautiful voyage ended . . ." (Ibid., 34).
"please get a divorce immediately." (Ibid., 43).
"Last night Henry and I got married . . ." (Ibid., 46).
"deft, acute core-reaching fucking," (*Henry and June*, 93).
"the evolution . . . the new needs" (*Incest*, 42).

222 "his instinct assures him there is nothing between Henry and me," (*Henry and June*, 162).
"This diary proves a tremendous, all-engulfing craving for truth . . ." (*Incest*, 232).
"There is in our relationship both humanness and monstrosity . . ." (*Henry and June*, 265).

223 "enough work in preparation, in hand . . ." (*Letters to Emil*, 117).
"I love the groove in which my love for Henry . . ." (*Henry and June*, 250).
"always *between* two desires, always in conflict," (*Incest*, 25).
"To each one I say, 'You are the favorite.'" (Ibid., 116).
"had counted on the ease with which I would distribute . . ." (*Henry and June*, 143).

224 "this talk about our marriage was incredible to me . . ." (*Incest*, 85).
"I am afraid of my freedom . . ." (Ibid., 29).
"My God, how happy I am to have found Henry . . ." (Ibid., 115).
"One more word on this subject . . ." (*Anaïs Nin: A Biography*, 165).

225 "reality deserves to be described in the vilest terms," (*Incest*, 148).
"I am playing tricks not on men but on life . . ." (Ibid., 100).
"wound the world which has wounded both of us." (*Anaïs Nin: A Biography*, 162).
"God, I hate myself. And yet I am happy, healthy." (*Incest*, 60).
"Listen, Anaïs, if things go smash, let them go smash . . ." (Ibid., 163).

226 "leading agent and prophet . . . on transatlantic affairs" (*Henry Miller: A Life*, 212).
"the most terrible, the most sordid, the most magnificent manuscript . . ." (*Happiest Man Alive*, 155).
"to follow Henry would mean exposure to the *greatest pain* . . ." (*Incest*, 128).
"lacked the courage . . . remembering that he exposed himself . . ." (Ibid., 154).
"Your only defect is your incapacity for cruelty." (Ibid., 154).
"wreaking a kind of revenge upon men . . ." (Ibid., 196).

227 "beautiful, tender" (Ibid., 131).
"when your letter came, it seemed to me . . ." (Ibid., 231).
"looking fresh, immaculate, dressed with an ultimate, subtle elegance." (Ibid., 205).

"I say, let us fuck our parents . . ." (*A Literate Passion*, 191).

"*Love*—and keep your shirt on! Let your father devour you . . ." (Ibid., 171).

228 "had wanted at least my incestuous love to remain unwritten . . ." (*Incest*, 216).

"the love I deserve. Nothing less . . ." (Ibid., 171).

"He is always wanting me because I make him happy . . ." (Ibid., 224).

"I'm hellishly lonely. What I need . . ." (Ibid., 272).

229 "Father . . . is not whole enough to suffer," (Ibid., 320).

"if I am perverse, monstrous in certain eyes, *tant pis* . . ." (Ibid., 235).

"to go to Rank and get absolution for my passion for my Father." (Ibid., 221).

"Unlike the other psychoanalysts . . ." (*Letters to Emil*, 143).

"defense against analysis," (*Henry Miller: A Life*, 231).

"'denied myself life before, or it was denied me . . ." (*Incest*, 370).

"All our joy is in lying body to body . . ." (Ibid., 367).

"destroying his own creation . . ." (Ibid., 357).

230 "a stirring lover . . . mysterious expression of faithfulness . . ." (Ibid., 355).

"I must get Henry's book published . . ." (Ibid., 229).

"I killed the child . . . Not to be abandoned, I killed the child . . ." (Ibid., 382).

"Here is a birth which is of greater interest to me." (Ibid., 383).

"Here is a book which, if such a thing were possible . . ." (Nin, Anaïs. *Anaïs Nin Reader*. Philip Jason, ed. Chicago: Swallow Press, 1972, 277).

231 "cranks, nuts, drunks, writers, artists . . ." (*Henry Miller: A Life*, 255-256).

"fuck[ed] in the elevator." (*Anaïs Nin: A Biography*, 224).

232 "This morning Hugo gave me 200 frs. . . ." (*A Literate Passion*, 232).

"If it's to be a choice between doing work . . ." (Ibid., 331).

233 "Your body burns in me . . . and I want it uniquely . . ." (Ibid., 269).

"half a dozen men" (*Anaïs Nin: A Biography*, 206).

234 "pulling down everything sacred, desecrating, cheapening." (Ibid., 206).

"you must admit that there have been other reasons . . ." (*A Literate Passion*, 340).

235 "almost completely effaced herself . . ." (Miller, Henry. *The Henry Miller Reader*. Lawrence Durrell, ed. New York: New Directions, 1959, 295).

"her language . . . is a violation of language . . ." (*Henry and June*, 265).

"bad craft, spelling, foreign locutions, grammatical unevenness, extremes." (*Anaïs Nin: A Biography*, 192).

"a little of the juice of St. Augustine and a little of Emerson" (*Happiest Man Alive*, 176).

236 "first anybody who's hit the nail on the head." (*Henry Miller: A Life*, 251).

"what she says is biologically true—from the very navel string." (*Anaïs Nin: A Biography*, 240).

237 "shape the material into book form that could be published" (Ibid., 235).

"This is a dying love," (Ibid., 252).

"The most alive thing in me today . . ." (Ibid., 253).

238 "obvious reluctance" (*A Literate Passion,* 336).
"any time you are ready to make a break, I am. Is that clear? . . ." (Ibid., 334).
239 "I find more and more that I'm talked about everywhere . . ." (Ibid., 335).
"invitations from people (including critics and professors) . . ." (Ibid., 338).
"the act of self-murder which takes place . . ." (*Anaïs Nin: A Biography,* 311).
240 "I am in truth a very very sick person . . ." (Ibid., 269).
"there is something very wrong with me . . ." (Ibid., 259).
"As I always say—there is no real security . . ." (*A Literate Passion,* 358).
"give you what is needed to get this particular work started." (Ibid., 360).
"always knew that the day you obtained what you wanted . . ." (*A Literate Passion,* 363).
241 "about to give 100 pages . . ." (Ibid.).
For more information on Miller's postwar finances, see Dearborn, 242.
"the main thing to say is that Miss Nin is a very good artist . . ." (*Anaïs Nin: A Biography,* 297).
"giving the vision of the neurotic directly" (Ibid., 312).
"to give the world one perfect life . . ." (Ibid., 330).
243 "kill his joy . . ." (Ibid., 374).
For more about Guiler and Pole's affairs, see *Anaïs Nin: A Biography,* 369.
"calmly paid the bill and left without responding," (Ibid., 272).
244 "I am living in the future," (*Anaïs: The Erotic Life,* 325).
"I believe the young America has chosen you and me to follow," (*A Literate Passion,* 367).
"all the love I gave has been returned," (*Anaïs Nin: A Biography,* 480).
245 "Miss Nin's truth, as we have seen, is psychological." (Nin, Anaïs. *The Diary of Anaïs Nin.* Gunther Stuhlmann, ed. New York: Swallow Press, 1966, Stuhlmann's intro, xi.).
246 "act of self-revelation." (*Anaïs: The Erotic Life,* 373).
"inveterate lying, her chicanery, her duplicity, and so on . . ." (*Book of Friends,* 265).

BIBLIOGRAPHY

Bair, Deirdre. *Anaïs Nin: A Biography.* New York: Putnam's, 1995.
Dearborn, Mary. *The Happiest Man Alive: A Biography of Henry Miller.* New York: Touchstone, 1991.
Faure, Elie. *History of Art.* Walter Pach, trans. Garden City, NY: Garden City Pub. Co. 1937.
Ferguson, Robert. *Henry Miller: A Life.* New York: W. W. Norton, 1991.
Fitch, Noel Riley. *Anaïs: The Erotic Life of Anaïs Nin.* Boston: Little, Brown, 1993.
Franklin V, Benjamin, ed. *Recollections of Anaïs Nin.* Athens: Ohio University Press, 1996.
Kahane, Jack. *Memoirs of a Booklegger.* London: Michael Joseph, 1939.

Miller, Henry. *Letters to Anaïs Nin*. New York: Paragon House, 1988.

———. *Art and Outrage*. New York: Dutton, 1961.

———. *Book of Friends*. San Bernardino, California: Borgo Press, 1990.

———. *The Books in My Life*. New York: New Directions, 1952.

———. *Letters to Emil*. New York: New Directions, 1989.

———. and Anaïs Nin. *A Literate Passion. Letters of Anaïs Nin and Henry Miller, 1932-1953*. Gunther Stuhlmann, ed. New York: Harcourt Brace Jovanovich, 1987.

———. *The Henry Miller Reader*. Lawrence Durrell, ed. New York: New Directions, 1959.

———. *Plexus (Book Two of The Rosy Crucifixion)*. Paris: Olympia Press, 1953.

———. *Sexus (Book One of The Rosy Crucifixion)*. Paris: Obelisk Press, 1949.

———. *Stand Still Like the Hummingbird*. New York: New Directions, 1962.

———. *Tropic of Cancer*. New York: Grove Press, 1961.

———. *Tropic of Capricorn*. Paris: Obelisk Press, 1939.

———. *The World of Sex*. Chicago: Ben Abramson, Argus Book Shop, 1940.

Nin, Anaïs. *Anaïs Nin Reader*. Philip Jason, ed. Chicago: Swallow Press, 1972.

———. *The Diary of Anaïs Nin*. Gunther Stuhlmann, ed. New York: Swallow Press, 1966.

———. *D. H. Lawrence: An Unprofessional Study*. New York: Swallow Press, 1964.

———. *Early Diaries of Anaïs Nin*. New York: Harcourt Brace Jovanovich, 1978.

———. *Henry & June*. New York: Harcourt Brace Jovanovich, 1990.

———. *Incest*. New York: Harcourt Brace Jovanovich, 1992.

———. *Linotte: The Early Diary of Anaïs Nin*. New York: Harcourt Brace Jovanovich, 1978-1985.

Perlès, Alfred. *My Friend Henry Miller*. London: Neville Spearman, 1955.

Epilogue

"The continual effort to raise himself . . ." Emerson, Ralph Waldo. "Circles" in *Essays*.

"More and more, as our era draws to a close . . ." (*Henry Miller Reader*, 288).

"Whenever sexual freedom is sought or achieved . . ." (Paglia, Camille. *Sexual Personae*. New York: Vintage, 1991, 3).

Note: currency equivalencies were calculated based on Robert Sahr's "Consumer Price Index (CPI) Conversion Factors 1800 to estimated 2014 to Convert to Dollars of 2004." ©2005. This document is available at: www.oregonstate.edu/cla/polisci/sahr/sahr.

Acknowledgments

Many of the facts of these artists' lives are matters of public record, but I would not have been able to write this book without the many biographers who researched and documented the artists' lives, the numerous editors and translators who published their works and letters, and the families who allowed the details of their relationships to be aired in print.

It's been an honor to work with my agent, Bob Lescher, and Jack Shoemaker and Julie Pinkerton at Counterpoint. Thanks too to Corinne Demas and the Cushman Café writers group, and to the many close friends who've read chapters and given feedback—I won't list them by name for fear of leaving someone out, but the book benefited by a number of thoughtful responses. I do need to thank Meaghan McDonnell in particular: her countless readings, penetrating insights, and considered feedback improved not only the manuscript but its author.

Finally, thanks to my family, and Dick Schappach and Terry D'Andrea, for their longstanding support and encouragement.

Permissions

The author would like to extend his thanks to the following publishers, organizations, and estates for permission to use material from the following works:

From *Diaries of a Young Poet* by Rainer Maria Rilke, edited by Ruth Sieber-Rilke & Carl Sieber, translated by Edward Snow & Michael Winkler. Copyright 1942 by Insel Verlag 1997 by Edward Snow & Michael Winkler. Used by permission of W. W. Norton & Company, Inc.

From *Frida by Frida*. Copyright 2006, Raquel Tibol, Gregory Dechant, trans. Translation used by permission of D.R. 2006 Editorial RM.

Excerpts from Frida Kahlo's letters and journals as printed in *Frida by Frida*. Copyright 2006, Raquel Tibol, Gregory Dechant, trans. Reproduction by permission of Banco de México as trustee for Frida Kahlo's estate.

From *Georgia O'Keeffe: Art and Letters*, Sarah Greenough, ed. Copyright 2011. Used by permission of the Georgia O'Keeffe Museum/Artists Rights Society (ARS), New York.

Excerpts from Georgia O'Keeffe's letters to Elizabeth Stieglitz Davidson, August 16, 1918 and October 16, 1923, and Georgia O'Keeffe's letter to Joe Obermeyer, October 31, 1918, reprinted by permission of Yale Collection of American Literature, Beinecke Library.

Excerpts from *Henry & June: From A Journal of Love*, from *The Unexpurgated Diary of Anaïs Nin*. Copyright 1986 by Rupert Pole as Trustee under the last will and testament of Anaïs Nin, reprinted by permission of Houghton Mifflin Harcourt Publishing Company.

Excerpts from *Incest: From A Journal of Love*. Copyright 1992 by Rupert Pole as Trustee under the last will and testament of Anaïs Nin, reprinted by permission of Houghton Mifflin Harcourt Publishing Company.

From *Letters of Rainer Maria Rilke: 1892-1910*, translated by Jane Bannard Greene and M. D. Herter Norton. Copyright 1945 by W. W. Norton & Company, Inc., renewed © 1972 by M. D. Herter Norton. Used by permission of W. W. Norton & Company, Inc.

From *Letters to a Young Poet*. Copyright © 2000 by Rainer Maria Rilke. Reprinted with permission of New World Library, Novato, CA. www.newworldlibrary.com.

Excerpts from *A Literate Passion: Letters of Anaïs Nin and Henry Miller, 1932-1953*. Copyright 1987 by Rupert Pole as Trustee under the last will and testament of Anaïs Nin, reprinted by permission of Houghton Mifflin Harcourt Publishing Company.

Excerpts from *Linotte, The Early Diaries of Anaïs Nin*. Copyright 1978 by Rupert

Index

B

Bartolí, José, 187

Beauvoir, Simone de: affairs and
intimacy with Sartre, 118–119;
agrégation exam and, 99, 101, 113, 115;
alcohol and drug use, 142; bourgeois
ideals and, 113–114; conjugal visits
to Sarte and Bost, 131; contingent
relationships and, 103, 104, 117, 118,
119, 125, 138; correspondence with
Sartre, 119, 127, 146; domination by
Sartre, 102; education, 100–101,
109–114; and existential literature,
142; family of, 101–102, 108–114,
109–111; finances of, 110–111, 113,
115, 116, 119, 130, 137, 139, 141, 143;
as French cultural asset, 137; health
of, 123; on homosexuality, 127, 130;
life of debauchery, 113; on marriage,
116; as mentor, 120, 122, 129–130,
145; and morganatic marriage, 103,
128, 146; on open relationships, 103;
philosophical development, 101,
111, 112, 113; relationships: with
Bianca Bienenfeld, 126–127, 129,
130, 131, 135, 145; with Claude
Lanzmann, 143; with Elizabeth
Le Coin (Zaza), 112, 114; with
Jacques-Laurent Bost, 123, 124, 125,
126, 127, 128, 131, 135, 136, 145; with
Nathalie Sorokine, 129, 130, 131,
135, 136; with Nelson Algren, 139,
140, 141, 142, 143, 145; with Olga
Kosakiewicz, 119–124, 126, 128,
129, 130, 131, 134, 143; with Pierre
Guille, 117; as Resistance intellec-
tual, 136–137; support for the
Family, 130; and Sylvie Le Bon, 145;
teaching career of, 115, 117, 118, 119;
travels: to Africa, 138; to New York,
139, 140, 141; and Trios, 121–124,
126, 128, 129, 131; and "two-year
lease," 103; and Vichy government,
136–137; works: *All Said and Done*,
145; *The Blood of Others*, 138; *The Force
of Circumstance*, 142; *Letters to Sartre*,
145; *The Mandarins*, 140; *Memoirs of a
Dutiful Daughter*, 142; *The Prime of Life*,
142; *The Second Sex*, 141; *She Came to
Stay*, 124, 138; *Useless Mouths*, 138; *The
Useless Mouths*, 136; *When Things of the
Spirit Come First*, 124; and World War
II, 127–128, 132, 135, 137; writing
and, 115, 118

Becker, Paula, 31, 34, 42

Beer-Hoffman, Richard, 21

Beloff, Angelina, 149–150, 151, 156,
159, 160, 163, 164, 165, 177, 178

Berggruen, Heinz, 183

Bienenfeld, Bianca, 126–127, 129,
130, 131, 135, 145

Binion, Rudolph, 11, 15, 18

Bjerre, Poul, 46

Blake, William, 170

Bloch, Lucienne, 176, 179

Bohemian culture, xiii, xiv, xv,
150–151, 155, 172, 197, 209, 212, 213,
250, 251. *See also* rebelliousness

Bohus, Irene, 185

Bosch, Hieronymus, 170

Bost, Jacques-Laurent, 123, 124, 125,
126, 127, 128, 131, 135, 136, 145

Botticelli, Sandro, 170

bourgeois culture, 104, 108, 109,
110–111, 113, 119, 130, 136–137, 144,
151, 152, 159, 161, 164, 172, 178, 200,
209, 213, 220, 249

Bradley, William, 226

Breton, André, 180, 181

Breton, Jacqueline, 181

Brooklyn Parks Department, 211

C

Cachuchas, 152

Camera Club of New York, 63

Camera Work, 57, 68, 69

Campo, Germán de, 170

Camus, Albert, 138

Carl-Ferdinand University (Prague),
25

Casa Azul, 171, 177, 180, 192, 1267

Cassati, Cristina, 173

Printed in the United States
by Baker & Taylor Publisher Services